The Deviant Prison

Early nineteenth-century American prisons followed one of two dominant models: the Auburn System, in which prisoners performed factory-
style labor by day and were placed in solitary confinement at night,
and the Pennsylvania System, where prisoners faced 24-hour solitary
confinement for the duration of their sentences. By the close of the
Civil War, the majority of prisons in the United States had adopted
the Auburn System – the only exception was Philadelphia's Eastern
State Penitentiary, making it the subject of much criticism and a fascinating outlier. Using the Eastern State Penitentiary as a case study,
The Deviant Prison brings to light anxieties and other challenges of
nineteenth-century prison administration that helped embed our prison
system as we know it today. Drawing on organizational theory and
providing a rich account of prison life, the institution, and key actors,
Ashley T. Rubin examines why Eastern's administrators clung to what
was increasingly viewed as an outdated and inhumane model of prison
– and what their commitment tells us about penal reform in an era when
prisons were still new and carefully scrutinized.

Ashley T. Rubin is Assistant Professor in the Department of Sociology at
the University of Hawai'i at Mānoa. Her work has been published in top
international journals for interdisciplinary studies of law, punishment,
and criminology and has appeared as a TEDx talk.

Cambridge Historical Studies in American Law and Society

Recognizing legal history's growing importance and influence, the goal of this series is to chart legal history's continuing development by publishing innovative scholarship across the discipline's broadening range of perspectives and subjects. It encourages empirically creative works that take legal history into unexplored subject areas, or that fundamentally revise our thinking about familiar topics; it also encourages methodologically innovative works that bring new disciplinary perspectives and techniques to the historical analysis of legal subjects.

Series Editor

Christopher Tomlins
University of California, Berkeley

The Deviant Prison: Philadelphia's Eastern State Penitentiary and the Origins of America's Modern Penal System, 1829–1913

ASHLEY T. RUBIN

University of Hawai'i at Mānoa

CAMBRIDGE
UNIVERSITY PRESS

Shaftesbury Road, Cambridge CB2 8EA, United Kingdom

One Liberty Plaza, 20th Floor, New York, NY 10006, USA

477 Williamstown Road, Port Melbourne, VIC 3207, Australia

314–321, 3rd Floor, Plot 3, Splendor Forum, Jasola District Centre, New Delhi – 110025, India

103 Penang Road, #05–06/07, Visioncrest Commercial, Singapore 238467

Cambridge University Press is part of Cambridge University Press & Assessment, a department of the University of Cambridge.

We share the University's mission to contribute to society through the pursuit of education, learning and research at the highest international levels of excellence.

www.cambridge.org
Information on this title: www.cambridge.org/9781108718882

DOI: 10.1017/9781108754095

First published 2021
First paperback edition 2022

A catalogue record for this publication is available from the British Library

Library of Congress Cataloging-in-Publication data
NAMES: Rubin, Ashley T., author. | State Penitentiary for the
Eastern District of Pennsylvania.
TITLE: The deviant prison : Philadelphia's Eastern State Penitentiary and
the origins of America's modern penal system, 1829–1913 / Ashley T. Rubin,
University of Hawai'i,Mānoa.
DESCRIPTION: Cambridge, United Kingdom ; New York, NY :
Cambridge University Press, 2021. | Series: Cambridge historical studies
in American law and society | Includes bibliographical references and index.
IDENTIFIERS: LCCN 2020020525 (print) | LCCN 2020020526 (ebook) |
ISBN 9781108484947 (hardback) | ISBN 9781108718882 (paperback) |
ISBN 9781108754095 (epub)
SUBJECTS: LCSH: Prisons–Pennsylvania–History–19th century. | Prison
administration–Pennsylvania–History–19th century. |
Corrections–Pennsylvania–History–19th century. | Corrections–United
States–History–19th century.
CLASSIFICATION: LCC HV9475.P42 E377 2021 (print) | LCC HV9475.P42 (ebook) |
DDC 365/.974811–dc23
LC record available at https://lccn.loc.gov/2020020525
LC ebook record available at https://lccn.loc.gov/2020020526

ISBN   978-1-108-48494-7   Hardback
ISBN   978-1-108-71888-2   Paperback

Contents

Figures

Tables

Acknowledgments

Most books are the product of many people's generosity to the author, and this book is no exception. Over the years, I have been extremely fortunate to receive great generosity from mentors, colleagues, and students – many of whom I also consider friends – who encouraged me, listened to my ideas and concerns, and read large chunks of this book project.

Some of the earliest (and longest lasting) thanks belong to my graduate school mentors at UC Berkeley: Lauren Edelman, Malcolm Feeley, Cybelle Fox, David Lieberman, Rob MacCoun, Justin McCrary, Charles McClain, Rebecca McLennan, Calvin Morrill, Kevin Quinn, and Jonathan Simon. I owe Rebecca and Jonathan an extra debt of gratitude for first introducing me to the study of punishment and then cementing my interest in the subject early in undergraduate school. They then continued to shape how I think about penal history throughout graduate school and beyond, including reading and commenting on parts of this project in my years since leaving Berkeley. I also need to thank Cal extensively for introducing me to organizational theory, despite my initial skepticism. He deserves further credit for helping me to think through Eastern's impact on the larger field and the development of prisons and innumerable other pieces of advice and support, particularly when I had doubts about the project or about how much it mattered. I owe the most to Malcolm for championing me throughout graduate school and for his continued support of my career (even seven years post-graduation).

During this time, I also benefited from the conviviality of fellow graduate students in Berkeley's Jurisprudence and Social Policy Program and other departments on campus: Hillary Berk, Chase Burton, Trevor Gartner, Daniel Kluttz, Johann Koehler, David Kwok, Nicole Lindahl,

Brent Nakamura, Keramet Reiter, Jamie Rowen, Stephen Smith Cody, Tobias Smith, Aaron Smyth, Christina Stevens, Sarah Tahamont, and (other) members of the Berkeley Empirical Legal Studies (BELS) seminar. Johann, Tobias, and Keramet in particular have continued to provide friendship and support over the years, including reading the *entire* manuscript and giving me extremely helpful feedback – thank you so much you guys!

Since my time at Berkeley, I have been fortunate to have many colleagues support this project in various ways. Parts of the manuscript were read by Michael Meranze, Michael Campbell, Heather Schoenfeld, Eric Baumer, Ted Chiricos, Deana Rohlinger, Alex Tepperman, Stephen Tillotson, Sida Liu, Ellen Berrey, Steve Hoffman, Kim Pernell-Gallagher, Randol Contreras, Hae Yeon Choo, Phil Goodman, Paula Maurutto, Gail Super, Jerry Flores, Lori Sexton, Santhi Leon, Hadar Aviram, Michelle Phelps, and Josh Page. I especially want to thank both Michaels (Meranze and Campbell), Phil, Hadar, and Josh for their enthusiasm about the project. Additionally, even though they were not subjected to reading my manuscript, I wish to thank Carter Hay, John Eason, Fergus McNeill, Katie Young, Jenny Carlson, Neda Maghbouleh, and Liz Chiarello for their support of the project.

The resulting manuscript has benefited from further comment from other members in the field at various talks. I have presented excerpts from my dissertation and later book manuscript at multiple annual meetings of the American Society of Criminology, the Law and Society Association, the Western Society of Criminology, and the American Society of Legal History, where I received valuable feedback. I also thank the members of the Centre for Criminology and Sociolegal Studies at the University of Toronto and the Department of Sociology at the University of Hawai'i at Mānoa for their comments when I gave my first two book talks. Additionally, I thank the rotating and permanent community of scholars at Berkeley's Jurisprudence and Social Policy Program and Center for the Study of Law and Society, where I have returned several times to present different parts of this project over the years.

In doing the nitty-gritty research through polishing various drafts of this manuscript, I was assisted by a veritable army of research assistants: At UC Berkeley, these were Katarina Blagojevic, Javier Garcia, Adam Garzoli, Young Ji Kim, Nora Lambrecht, Haley Lee, and Amir Salehzadeh, all through the Undergraduate Research Apprenticeship Program (URAP). At Florida State University, these were Audrey Hertzler, through the Undergraduate Research Opportunity Program (UROP), and my graduate research assistant, Miltonette Olivia Craig. At the University of Toronto – Mississauga, these were Rumsha Daimee and Simona Stallone (through the Research Opportunity Program (ROP)) and Shadi Laghai, Andrew Plummer, Jonowin Terrance, Joyce Ho, and Seema Shafei (through the University of Toronto Jackman Humanities Scholars-in-Residence (SiR) Program). Thank you all so much for the hours and hours of work you put into this project!

Additionally, my project has been funded by multiple organizations. From UC Berkeley, I received a Dean's Normative Time Grant, a BELS Fellowship, and a Jurisprudence and Social Policy Dissertation Improvement Grant. From Florida State University, I received a Faculty Research Library Materials Grant. From the American Philosophical Society, I received a Library Resident Research Fellowship and a Franklin Research Grant. I also wish to thank the staffs of the UC Berkeley Law Library, the American Philosophical Society's Library, the Pennsylvania State Archives, the Philadelphia Historical Society, and Eastern State Penitentiary, especially Valerie-Ann Lutz, Earle Spamer, Roy Goodman, Baryard Miller, Linda Musumeci, and Scott Ziegler.

Over the years, I have published several articles using the primary sources and some of the insights gleaned from this project. I am grateful to the editors, reviewers, and friendly readers of these earlier pieces. The two pieces that I draw on most directly both come from *Law & Social Inquiry*: "Professionalizing Prison: Primitive Professionalization and the Administrative Defense of Eastern State Penitentiary, 1829–1879" (2018, Vol. 43, Issue 1, pp. 182–211) and "The Consequences of Prisoners' Micro-resistance" (2016, Vol. 42, Issue 1, pp. 138–162).

About as early as I seriously began working to transform my dissertation into a book, I have received guidance and support from Chris Tomlins. I cannot express enough my gratitude for his belief in the project and his patient support over the years. Thank you so much for being my editor and accepting my project into the Historical Studies in Law and Society Series!

Finally, I wish to thank my family for their love and support over the years. Special thanks to my mom (Ginny), dad (Bob), and brother (Pete) for actually reading my "very academic" manuscript. The most gratitude goes to my husband, David, who more than anyone else has lived through the ups and downs of this project. He also read the manuscript very carefully. Thank you, Sweetie.

Abbreviations

APS   American Philosophical Society
HSP   Historical Society of Pennsylvania
PSA   Pennsylvania State Archives

REFORM SOCIETIES

BPDS   Boston Prison Discipline Society
NYPA   New York Prison Association
PSAMPP Philadelphia Society for Alleviating the Miseries
               of Public Prisons
SPPNY   Society for the Prevention of Pauperism in the
               City of New York

PERIODICALS

NAR   *North American Review*
JPDP   *Pennsylvania Journal of Prison Discipline and Philanthropy*

A Brief Timeline

Year	Event
1786–1794	Significant changes to Pennsylvania penal laws and practices underway, especially at the reconstructed Walnut Street Prison, which soon becomes the model for proto-prisons emerging around the country.
1787	Philadelphia Society for Alleviating the Miseries of Public Prisons (PSAMPP) is formed.
1810s	Multiple efforts to reform the penal laws and practice.
1818	Construction and planning for new Western State Penitentiary in Pennsylvania authorized under the principle of solitary confinement.
1821	Construction and planning for Eastern State Penitentiary is authorized under the principle of solitary confinement. A hybrid system is adopted in New York at Auburn State Prison.
1823	New York ends its reliance on long-term solitary confinement at Auburn State Prison in favor of the Auburn System.
1825	The Boston Prison Discipline Society (BPDS), a penal reform society and supporter of the Auburn System, is founded.
1826	Two publications call attention to insanity, illness, and death that resulted from long-term solitary confinement at Auburn State Prison and Maine State Prison. Western State Penitentiary opens and faces implementation difficulties from the beginning.
1828	Pennsylvania Commissioners Shaler, King, and Wharton endorse the Auburn System; the Eastern building commissioners endorse pure, continuous solitary confinement.
1829	Legislation authorizes the Pennsylvania System in its final form at both Eastern and Western. Eastern receives its first prisoner.
1833	New Jersey adopts the Pennsylvania System at its prison.
1834–1835	A legislative committee investigates various charges against Eastern's administrators, focusing on misuses of power, including fraud and torture.

1838	Rhode Island adopts the Pennsylvania System at its prison. Legislation authorizes hiring a paid Moral Instructor at Eastern.
1843	The staff physician at Eastern is required to be a resident physician at the prison.
1844	Rhode Island abandons the Pennsylvania System and joins in criticizing the Pennsylvania System.
1854	Long-time Pennsylvania System critic and BPDS founder Louis Dwight dies.
1858	Pennsylvania State Legislature authorizes a commission to alter the penal code (enacted March 31, 1860). New Jersey passes legislation that begins to depart from the Pennsylvania System at its prison after years of partial implementation. Pennsylvania is the last state to use the Pennsylvania System.
1860s–1870s	Eastern's administrators increasingly focus on their own status as professional penologists and begin to refer to the Pennsylvania System as the "Individual Treatment System."
1861	The so-called Commutation Law is passed at the behest of PSAMPP.
1862	The Pennsylvania Supreme Court strikes down the 1861 legislation in *The Commonwealth ex rel. Johnson* v. *Halloway*.
1866	Postwar crime increases bring overcrowding at Eastern and necessitates the double-celling of prisoners. Western's administrators publicly condemn the Pennsylvania System.
1869	New legislation reauthorizes the commutation law. Pennsylvania legislature creates Board of Public Charities, which is authorized to oversee the state's prisons and other "charitable" institutions. Pennsylvania legislature authorizes the congregation of prisoners at Western. Eastern officially becomes the last American prison to follow the Pennsylvania System.
1870s	Efforts to reduce overcrowding at Eastern do not keep pace with flood of prisoners; solitary confinement becomes an impossibility for most prisoners.
1911	Cellblock 11 opens at Eastern on the "big house" model.
1913	Legislation authorizes congregation at Eastern, officially ending the Pennsylvania System.

Important Actors

Introduction

[T]here are two systems of imprisonment in the United States,...those of the separate and congregate or silent systems.

The separate system exists nowhere in the United States out of Pennsylvania; indeed, it may be almost said nowhere in Pennsylvania, except in the Eastern penitentiary, at Philadelphia....

Everywhere, then, beyond the limits of Pennsylvania, the system of imprisonment in the United States is that which is called, indifferently, the Auburn, congregate, or silent system.

Enoch C. Wines and Theodore W. Dwight, (1867), *Report on the Prisons and Reformatories of the United States and Canada*[1]

AMERICA'S MODERN PRISONS AND EASTERN STATE PENITENTIARY

When the modern prison first emerged in the early nineteenth century, the question of how such facilities should be designed, organized, and managed – tellingly referred to as "prison discipline" – was of paramount importance. The success or failure of the prison as a new approach to punishment, reformers and statesmen[2] believed, depended on this question.

For much of the century, the vast majority of American prisons operated a mode of confinement innovated at New York's Auburn State Prison

---

[1] Enoch C. Wines, and Theodore W. Dwight, *Report on the Prisons and Reformatories of the United States and Canada Made to the Legislature of New York, January 1867*. Albany, NY: Van Benthuysen and Sons' Steam Printing House, 1867, pp. 50, 56.

[2] Throughout this work, I use gendered language. Although this practice may appear dated, it reflects male dominance in most areas relevant to prisons and punishment at the time.

between 1821 and 1823. Under the Auburn System, prisoners worked in large factorylike rooms performing assembly-line labor, retreating at day's end to cramped solitary cells. To prevent prisoners from communicating with each other, prisoners were required at all times to remain silent and to keep their eyes downcast. Auburn-style prisons were run under a kind of military order: prisoners wore striped uniforms, they marched in lockstep to and from their cells,[3] and misbehavior was punished at the end of a lash. Champions of the Auburn System argued that the rule of silence would prevent the types of conversations that allow prisoners' mutual "contamination" and render prisons "schools of vice." Hard labor would be reformative and instill discipline. Moreover, the Auburn System would be profitable for the state, which could sell prisoner-made goods to offset (at minimum) the costs of construction and maintenance, a particularly attractive feature for states with limited abilities to tax their citizens. The Auburn System was immediately copied by a dozen states within as many years, governing prisons in both the North and the South. Auburn's dominance was virtually complete by the Civil War while, a century after its creation, some version of the Auburn System continued to shape the experience of most prisoners.[4]

Pennsylvania followed a different model of prison discipline for most of that period. Under the Pennsylvania System, which was first implemented in 1829 at Eastern State Penitentiary in Philadelphia, prisoners were housed separately in cells large enough to work, sleep, pray, read, and exercise alone, without leaving except to walk in a small private yard attached to each cell. Prisoners were not permitted to talk, except with Eastern's administrators and staff and official visitors (local and visiting penal reformers, state-level politicians, other prisons' administrators, and occasional diplomats who were given special permission). Supporters argued that prisoners' silent existence, with solitary labor and time for prayer, would enable their reformation. Prisoners' physical separation, moreover, would more effectually prevent the kind of contamination Auburn sought to prevent with silence alone. Finally, prisoners

---

[3] The lockstep "was a curious combination of march and shuffle, the march aiming to impose discipline, the shuffle trying to make certain that the men did not become too prideful." Rebecca M. McLennan, *The Crisis of Imprisonment: Protest, Politics, and the Making of the American Penal State, 1776–1941*. New York: Cambridge University Press, 2008, p. 122.

[4] For descriptions of New York's prisons and the Auburn System, see McLennan, *The Crisis of Imprisonment*, and W. David Lewis, *From Newgate to Dannemora: The Rise of the Penitentiary in New York, 1796–1848*. Ithaca: Cornell University Press, 1965.

were known by numbers only and, during any egress from their cells, prisoners were hooded to protect their identities even from guards. According to supporters, the Pennsylvania System made it possible for prisoners to reenter society unrecognized and unimpeded by stigma.

The Pennsylvania System's answer to the prison discipline question was thus diametrically opposed to the Auburn System. Where the Auburn System relied on silence among congregated prisoners, the Pennsylvania System relied on full-time solitary confinement alleviated by intermittent contact with prison staff. Where the Auburn System worked prisoners together in large factories for more efficient production, the Pennsylvania System relied on less efficient workshop-style labor that offered prisoners vocational skills. Where the Auburn System used striped uniforms to mark its prisoners and paraded them around the prison in lockstep, the Pennsylvania System protected their prisoners' identities with hoods and numbers so they could reenter society unstigmatized. Where the Auburn System whipped its prisoners for talking or failing to work enough, the Pennsylvania System used solitary confinement to remove the temptation to speak and, if prisoners refused to work, relied on boredom by withholding their work until prisoners begged to work again. Contemporaries pithily summarized these differences by calling the Auburn System the "congregate" or "silent" system and the Pennsylvania System the "solitary" or "separate" system.

While the Pennsylvania System offered states an alternative approach to prison discipline, it never escaped Auburn's shadow. Reformers debated its merits against the Auburn System, and statesmen seriously considered it as an option when authorizing their new prisons, but the Pennsylvania System always remained the heterodox system. Outside of Pennsylvania, only Rhode Island and New Jersey adopted the Pennsylvania System for their state prisons before eventually abandoning it for the Auburn System. Other states' decision makers remained unconvinced of the Pennsylvania System's value, thanks in large part to reformers' arguments that the Pennsylvania System was vastly inferior to the Auburn System.

Even before Eastern received its first prisoner, the prison had been criticized by reformers who believed its Pennsylvania System would be cruel and inhumane, dangerous to prisoners' physical and mental health, too expensive and unprofitable, and simply impractical and ineffective. Once the prison opened, however, the criticism intensified as penal reformers flocked to Eastern to see the Pennsylvania System in practice and pored over Eastern's annual reports to the legislature, searching for evidence of its failures and repeating their prophecies.

Perhaps most famously, after visiting Eastern in 1842, Charles Dickens criticized the Pennsylvania System for (among other things) imposing on its prisoners "an anguish so acute and so tremendous, that all imagination of it must fall far short of the reality."[5] Convinced of such charges, administrators at the few other Pennsylvania System–style prisons requested permission from their state legislatures to convert their prisons to the Auburn System. Rhode Island abandoned the Pennsylvania System after a mere six years. New Jersey State Prison officially subscribed to the Pennsylvania System for a few decades but rarely followed it in practice, as its administrators admitted when they formally requested the change. A writer for the *North American Review*, a popular literary magazine, summarized the general perception by exclaiming in 1848, "we cannot believe that even Pennsylvania will any longer allow the prison at Philadelphia, with its annual train of horrors, to cast an opprobrium on the justice and humanity of the State."[6] For Theodore W. Dwight and Enoch C. Wines, two penal reformers from New York surveying the country's prisons after the Civil War, the Pennsylvania System was a resounding failure, its unpopularity a demonstration of its inferiority as a mode of confinement in state prisons.[7] By 1869, even administrators at Eastern's sister prison, the Western State Penitentiary in Pittsburgh, requested the legislature to allow them to congregate prisoners under the Auburn model.

The Pennsylvania System was officially abandoned at Eastern in 1913.

* * *

Eastern retained the Pennsylvania System longer than any other prison, even though it faced the largest share of the criticism for this retention. Even more surprising, when Eastern finally abandoned the Pennsylvania System, it did so after national support for the Auburn System itself had subsided. For these reasons alone, Eastern represents a fascinating prison whose curious history demands further explanation. More than an

---

[5] Charles Dickens, *American Notes for General Circulation.* ed. Patricia Ingham. London: Penguin Books, 2000 [1842], p. 121.

[6] "*Prison Discipline in America* by Francis C. Gray," *The North American Review* 66:138 (1848), pp. 145–190, p. 190.

[7] Wines and Dwight did believe the Pennsylvania System was a necessary mode for jails and as such was not entirely "worthless." Wines, and Dwight, *Report on the Prisons and Reformatories of North America and Canada*, pp. 50, 55,56

historical anomaly, however, Eastern's lengthy retention of the Pennsylvania System offers more general lessons – about this important period of prison development, about the causes and consequences of penal trends, and about the organizational dynamics of criminal punishment. With these interests in mind, this book examines why Eastern State Penitentiary alone retained its unique system of prison discipline.

EASTERN STATE PENITENTIARY IN THE GRAND SWEEP OF HISTORY

The Problem with Exceptions in Prison History

Traditional histories of the prison's emergence have examined how changes in American society – its economy, political structure, culture, gender and racial relations – have encouraged, each in their own way, the early development of the prison.[8] Eastern is frequently mentioned

---

[8] The early prisons, from the Early Modern Period in Europe to the Jacksonian Era in America, have been the subject of numerous books. See Edward L. Ayers, *Vengeance and Justice: Crime and Punishment in the 19th-Century American South*. New York: Oxford University Press, 1984; S. Bookspan, *A Germ of Goodness: The California State Prison System, 1851–1944*. Lincoln: University of Nebraska Press, 1991; Bernard E. Harcourt, *The Illusion of Free Markets: Punishment and the Myth of Natural Order*. Harvard University Press, 2012; Michael Hindus, *Prison and Plantation: Crime, Justice, and Authority in Massachusetts and South Carolina, 1767–1878*. Chapel Hill: University of North Carolina Press, 1980; Hirsch, *The Rise of the Penitentiary*. New Haven: Yale University Press, 1992; Mark E. Kann, *Punishment, Prisons, and Patriarchy: Liberty and Power in the Early American Republic*. New York University Press, 2005; Paul W. Keve, *Prisons and the American Conscience: A History of U.S. Federal Corrections*. Carbondale: Southern Illinois University Press, 1991; Orlando F. Lewis, *The Development of American Prisons and Prison Customs, 1776–1845: With Special Reference to Early Institutions in the State of New York*. Albany: Prison Association of New York, 1922; Lewis, *From Newgate to Dannemora*; Blake McKelvey, *American Prisons: A History of Good Intentions*. Montclair, NJ: Patterson Smith, 1977 [1936]; McLennan, *The Crisis of Imprisonment*; Michael Meranze, *Laboratories of Virtue: Punishment, Revolution, and Authority in Philadelphia, 1760–1835*. Chapel Hill: University of North Carolina Press, 1996; Janet Miron, *Prisons, Asylums, and the Public: Institutional Visiting in the Nineteenth Century*. University of Toronto Press, 2011; David Oshinsky, *Worse than Slavery: Parchman Farm and the Ordeal of Jim Crow Justice*. New York: Free Press, 1997; Robert Perkinson, *Texas Tough: The Rise of America's Prison Empire*. New York: Metropolitan Books/Henry Holt, 2008; Nicole Rafter, *Partial Justice: Women in State Prisons, 1800–1935*. Boston: Northeastern University Press, 1985; David J. Rothman, *The Discovery of the Asylum: Social Order and Disorder in the New Republic*. New York: AldineTransaction, 2002 [1971]; Jodi Schorb, *Reading Prisoners: Literature, Literacy, and the Transformation of American Punishment, 1700–1845*. New Brunswick, NJ: Rutgers University Press, 2014; Thornsten Sellin, *Slavery and the Penal System*. New York: Elsevier, 1976; Michele Lise Tarter and Richard Bell, eds.,

in these accounts for its status as the flagship and exemplar prison of the Pennsylvania System, and thus an important alternative approach to prison discipline. Such accounts typically explain why the Pennsylvania System failed to spread across the United States: Relative to the Auburn System, many contemporaries believed, it was too expensive and the association between solitary confinement and mental illness among prisoners was too stigmatizing.[9] But other than its status as a failed rival to the Auburn System, Eastern has featured little in these standard accounts.

For some such histories, Eastern is simply a variation on a general theme; as such, its unique features and its stubbornly persistent retention of the Pennsylvania System are unnecessary to explain. David J. Rothman's *Discovery of the Asylum* (1971), which ignited interest in America's early prisons as entities worth studying, is typical in this regard. For Rothman, Eastern and its Pennsylvania System represented a more extreme manifestation of Jacksonian Americans' desire to create ordered environments to counteract the criminogenic environment of their rapidly transforming society, which was becoming increasingly devoid of the powerful social controls provided by community, family, and church.

Buried Lives: Incarcerated in Early America. Athens: University of Georgia Press, 2012. For the broader Anglo-American and European context, see Georg Rusche and Otto Kirchheimer, *Punishment and Social Structure.* New York: Columbia University Press, 1939 [1968]; Michel Foucault, *Discipline and Punish: The Birth of the Prison.* New York: Vintage Books, 1977; Michael Ignatieff, *A Just Measure of Pain: The Penitentiary in the Industrial Revolution, 1750–1850.* New York: Pantheon Books, 1978; Dario Melossi and Massimo Pavarini, *The Prison and the Factory: Origins of the Penitentiary System.* Totowa, NJ: Barnes and Noble Books, 1981; Patricia O'Brien, *The Promise of Punishment: Prisons in Nineteenth-Century France.* Princeton University Press, 1982; Pieter Spierenburg, *The Prison Experience: Disciplinary Institutions and Their Inmates in Early Modern Europe.* New Brunswick, NJ: Rutgers University Press, 1991. For reviews of early prison history, see Ashley T. Rubin, "Early US Prison History beyond Rothman: Revisiting *The Discovery of the Asylum*," *Annual Review of Law and Social Science* 15:1 (2019), pp. 137–154; Michael Meranze, "Histories of the Modern Prison: Renewal, Regression, and Expansion," in *The Oxford Handbook of the History of Crime and Criminal Justice,* ed. Paul E. Knepper and Anja Johansen. New York: Oxford University Press, 2016, pp. 672–694; Mary Gibson, "Global Perspectives on the Birth of the Prison." *The American Historical Review* 116:4 (2011), pp. 1040–1063.
9 e.g., McLennan, *The Crisis of Imprisonment,* pp. 63–64; Rothman, *The Discovery of the Asylum,* pp. 85–97; Harry Elmer Barnes, *The Evolution of Penology in Pennsylvania.* Indianapolis: The Bobbs-Merrill Company, 1968 [1927], p. 172; Melossi and Pavarini, *The Prison and the Factory,* p. 61; see also Ashley T. Rubin, "A Neo-Institutional Account of Prison Diffusion," *Law & Society Review* 49:2 (2015), pp. 365–399. For an analysis of views on solitary confinement and its effects throughout history, see Ian O'Donnell, *Prisoners, Solitude, and Time.* Oxford University Press, 2014.

The magnitude of the ensuing debate between the two modes of confinement reflected how imperative reformers perceived their quest. Rothman suggests that support for both systems was so intense because of the very "high stakes." However, he does not explain why "[t]he Pennsylvania camp had no doubt of its superiority" beyond their convictions about the system's features, or why its administrators maintained this position despite the increasing consensus among reformers around the nation that it was inferior or deeply flawed. Overall, in Rothman's account, Pennsylvania simply represented a small variation in reformers' quest for perfectly ordered institutions to cure society's ills, rather than an important exception to American prisons' historical trajectory.[10]

For other histories, Eastern and its exceptional Pennsylvania System are irrelevant because they represent small exceptions to otherwise general trends. This is the case in arguably the most important recent contribution to prison history, Rebecca McLennan's *The Crisis of Imprisonment*, which explores the underexamined role of labor activities in structuring prison regimes from the Revolution to the Second World War.[11] McLennan describes the dominance of prisoner labor over every aspect of life in most prisons, which were primarily managed by contractors and run on the Auburn System for most of this period. By virtue of its exceptional reliance on the Pennsylvania System, Eastern alone was managed solely by prison administrators, not contractors. Consequently, Eastern (and Pennsylvania more generally) played a small role in her narrative, at least until the post–Pennsylvania System years. While Eastern's unique history neither contradicts nor corrects McLennan's masterful account, her account cannot explain Eastern. While labor was important in all prisons, it played a different role when structuring life at Eastern. Thus, we cannot look to labor's dominance and financial incentives to make sense of Eastern's retention of the Pennsylvania System. The greater control of administrators, not contractors, at Eastern is important for understanding its unique status, but administrative (or rather non-contractor) control alone does not explain why the Pennsylvania System remained the dominant model at Eastern for so long.

Eastern thus represents an important exception to traditional accounts of America's early prison history, an exception that demonstrates the

---

[10] Rothman, *The Discovery of the Asylum*, p. 85.
[11] McLennan, *The Crisis of Imprisonment*.

limits of generalist accounts.[12] To explain Eastern and its unique history, we cannot look to factors that explain the rise and persistence of prisons in other states. To the extent that macro-level economic, political, and cultural factors affected penal development in Pennsylvania, they apparently had a very different outcome than they had elsewhere. And yet Pennsylvania was not so different from other states that we should expect such factors to have this different an outcome.

An underlying point merits emphasis: whatever similarities we, a contemporary audience, see between these types of prisons, nineteenth-century penal actors took their differences seriously. Each system used solitary confinement, labor, and even corporal punishments despite its proclaimed enlightened and humane status. Nevertheless, differences in the types of solitary confinement, labor, and corporal punishments mattered greatly to supporters, opponents, and other observers at the time. Dominant explanations of the prison's development cannot explain why these elements took a different shape in Pennsylvania. Moreover, even if we treat these two systems as similar programs, these national-level explanations do not explain why Eastern alone continued to use a

---

[12] Recent interdisciplinary punishment scholars have been increasingly interested in mapping variation in penal trends, particularly at the local or state level, in opposition to earlier studies that indicated more widespread and comprehensive change. These newer studies have emphasized the influence of distinctive political structures, interest groups, individual personalities, and local history and culture. Lisa Miller, *The Perils of Federalism: Race, Poverty, and the Politics of Crime*. New York: Oxford University Press, 2008; Vanessa Barker, *The Politics of Imprisonment: How the Democratic Process Shapes the Way America Punishes Offenders*. New York: Oxford University Press, 2009; Perkinson, *Texas Tough*; Mona Lynch, *Sunbelt Justice: Arizona and the Transformation of American Punishment*. Stanford, CA: Stanford University Press, 2010; Heather A. Schoenfeld, *Building the Prison State: Race and the Politics of Mass Incarceration*. University of Chicago Press, 2018; Joshua Page, *The Toughest Beat: Politics, Punishment, and the Prison Officers Union in California*. New York: Oxford University Press, 2011; Michael C. Campbell, "Politics, Prisons, and Law Enforcement: An Examination of the Emergence of 'Law and Order' Politics in Texas," *Law & Society Review* 45:3 (2011), pp. 631–665; Michael C. Campbell, "Ornery Alligators and Soap on a Rope: Texas Prosecutors and Punishment Reform in the Lone Star State." *Theoretical Criminology* 16:3 (2012), pp. 289–311; Heather Schoenfeld, "Mass Incarceration and the Paradox of Prison Conditions Litigation," *Law & Society Review* 44:3–4 (2010), pp. 731–768; Liam Kennedy, "'Longtermer Blues': Penal Politics, Reform, and Carceral Experiences at Angola," *Punishment & Society* 15:3 (2013), pp. 304–322; Michael C. Campbell and Heather Schoenfeld, "The Transformation of America's Penal Order: A Historicized Political Sociology of Punishment," *American Journal of Sociology* 118:5 (2013), pp. 1375–1423; Philip Goodman, Joshua Page, and Michelle Phelps, *Breaking the Pendulum: The Long Struggle over Criminal Justice*. New York: Oxford University Press, 2017.

heavily criticized system. Indeed, if the two systems were interchangeable, Eastern's administrators and supporters would have been free to exchange the Pennsylvania System for the Auburn System and save a great deal of anxiety. Their refusal to do so, however, is not well explained by more traditional social change accounts.

The Problem with Easy Answers

If Eastern is often assigned a supporting but background role in surveys of American prison history, it has certainly not been ignored by prison historians generally.[13] While these scholars have not seriously considered why Eastern retained the Pennsylvania System, they have explored a variety of other questions about the Pennsylvania System. Scholars have been particularly interested in the *emergence* of the Pennsylvania System and its particular features at Eastern. Such analyses have focused on the Pennsylvania System's relationship to the historical development of the prison as punishment and the larger sets of social changes affecting the Atlantic world. In particular, scholars have located the Pennsylvania System's development in specific episodes within Pennsylvania's early colonial history and its later postcolonial period as well as significant cultural changes to which elite penal reformers and statesmen were

---

[13] For a range of treatments on Eastern's creation and history, see Barnes, *The Evolution of Penology*; Thomas Dumm, *Democracy and Punishment: Disciplinary Origins of the United States*. Madison: University of Wisconsin Press, 1987; Kenneth Finkel Norman Johnston and eds. Jeffrey A. Cohen, *Eastern State Penitentiary: Crucible of Good Intentions*. Philadelphia: University of Pennsylvania Press, 1994; Paul Takagi, "The Walnut Street Jail: A Penal Reform To Centralize the Powers of the State," *Federal Probation* 39 (1975), pp. 18–26; Thorsten Sellin, "Philadelphia Prisons of the Eighteenth Century," *Transactions of the American Philosophical Society* 43:1 (1953), pp. 326–331; Meranze, *Laboratories of Virtue*; Jen Manion, *Liberty's Prisoners: Carceral Culture in Early America*. Philadelphia: University of Pennsylvania Press, 2015; Negley K. Teeters, *They Were in Prison: A History of the Pennsylvania Prison Society, 1787–1937*. Philadelphia: The John C. Winston Company, 1937); Negley K. Teeters and John D. Shearer, *The Prison at Philadelphia, Cherry Hill: The Separate System of Penal Discipline, 1829–1913*. New York: Columbia University Press, 1957; Paul Kahan, *Eastern State Penitentiary: A History*. Charleston, SC: The History Press, 2008; Jennifer Lawrence Janofsky, "'There Is No Hope for Me': Eastern State Penitentiary, 1829–1856." PhD thesis, Temple University, Proquest Dissertation Publishing, 2004. 3128544; Erica Rhodes Hayden, "'Plunged into a Vortex of Iniquity': Female Criminality and Punishment in Pennsylvania, 1820–1860." PhD thesis, Vanderbilt University, ProQuest Dissertations Publishing, 2013. 3709888; Kristin O'Brassill-Kulfan, *Vagrants and Vagabonds: Poverty and Mobility in the Early American Republic*. New York University Press, 2019. This book differs from these studies by taking seriously the question why Eastern retained its Pennsylvania System.

exposed.[14] Some of these scholars have also emphasized Pennsylvania's Quaker heritage and the many members of the Society of Friends active in penal reform when the Pennsylvania System was formed.[15] Other treatments of Eastern State Penitentiary have offered detailed descriptions of its history, including some accounts focused on Eastern's unique architecture, but not the reason for the Pennsylvania System's persistence.[16]

That scholars have not seriously considered why the Pennsylvania System persisted at Eastern is less an oversight than a problem of assumptions about easy answers. Most commonly, scholars assume or intimate that the Pennsylvania System's longevity – as well as its initiation – at Eastern stemmed from religion. In an assumption that has taken on a mythlike quality, the Pennsylvania System is characterized as a niche approach to prison discipline that fit the unique social context of its innovator city and state. Indeed, Eastern is often called the "Quaker Prison" because of its location in Philadelphia, the "Quaker City," and the large role of the Society of Friends in local penal reform efforts throughout Pennsylvania's history.[17] This label is buoyed by the potential affinity between the contemplative style of Quaker Meetings and solitary confinement's supposed ability to promote reflection. (This myth can be traced to a statement made by William Penn a century and a half before Eastern opened.)[18] Additional support comes from the fact that each state that adopted the Pennsylvania System – Pennsylvania, Rhode Island, and New Jersey – were Quaker-stronghold states.

While the Society of Friends played a powerful role in penal reform during the Early Republic (and continue to be active penal reformers

[14] Dumm, *Democracy and Punishment*; Meranze, *Laboratories of Virtue*; Barnes, *The Evolution of Penology*; Janofsky, "There Is No Hope for Me."
[15] e.g., Dumm, *Democracy and Punishment*; Barnes, *The Evolution of Penology*; Kai T. Erikson, *Wayward Puritans: A Study in the Sociology of Deviance*. New York: John Wiley and Sons, 1966.
[16] e.g., Barnes, *The Evolution of Penology*; Johnston, Finkel, and Cohen, *Eastern State Penitentiary: Crucible of Good Intentions*; Norman Johnston, "The World's Most Influential Prison: Success or Failure?" *The Prison Journal* 84:4 (2004), pp. 20–40; Janofsky, "There Is No Hope for Me."; Kahan, *Eastern State Penitentiary: A History*.
[17] E.g., Dumm, *Democracy and Punishment*; Barnes, *The Evolution of Penology*; Erikson, *Wayward Puritans*; Michael Welch, *Escape to Prison*. Oakland: University of California Press, 2015.
[18] Based on this connection, some scholars even incorrectly attribute the Pennsylvania System to William Penn. While Penn was likely the first governing authority in North America to institute incarceration in place of capital and corporal punishments in 1682, he said nothing of solitary confinement, the hallmark of the Pennsylvania System.

today), they have received too much credit (or blame) for the early use of solitary confinement. Indeed, their greatest impacts came from supporting incarceration generally (rather than solitary confinement specifically) as an alternative to capital and corporal punishments.[19]

Importantly, however, Quaker support for solitary confinement does not fully account for the Pennsylvania System at Eastern. Quakers were active penal reformers in several states that shunned the Pennsylvania System, including New York, the innovator of the Auburn System, making Quaker support an insufficient explanation for the Pennsylvania System's adoption. More striking, each state that adopted the Pennsylvania System also abandoned it, and even the Pennsylvania legislature proved it was uncommitted, making Quaker support an insufficient explanation for the Pennsylvania System's retention. Finally, this myth of Quaker support overlooks the more numerous administrators, penal reformers, and statesmen who supported the Pennsylvania System but did not belong to the Society of Friends, as well as the nefarious or negligent actions of Quaker administrators and reformers that undermined the Pennsylvania System.

A second simplistic assumption is one of sunk costs. Eastern was one of the most expensive prisons built at the time. After spending so much money, perhaps officials felt they could not afford to change course. However, this assumption also overlooks the fact that other Pennsylvania-style prisons did successfully abandon the Pennsylvania System and adopt the Auburn System, even after expending large outlays to build or rebuild their prisons on the Pennsylvania System. Notably, converting a prison from the Pennsylvania System to the Auburn System typically necessitated only adding several large "workshops" for the prisoners to work in, which was far less expensive than demolishing and rebuilding. Moreover, the cost of maintaining Eastern over time escalated to millions of dollars, particularly as the physical plant aged; if contemporary estimates of the cost to build an Auburn-style prison were accurate, it would have been cheaper to demolish and rebuild. Even so, although legislators were tightfisted in their fiscal allocations, they were willing to allocate money when necessary for system (re)design: Pennsylvania's Western State Penitentiary was entirely demolished and rebuilt when its initial design was not conducive

---

[19] For useful treatments on the role of the Quaker religion and penal reform, see Dumm, *Democracy and Punishment*; Meranze, *Laboratories of Virtue*. For more on the role of religion in prisons in this period, see Jennifer Graber, *The Furnace of Affliction: Prisons and Religion in Antebellum America*. Chapel Hill: University of North Carolina Press, 2014.

to the Pennsylvania System.[20] Decades later, the legislature was willing to again redesign Western to fit the Auburn System. Only in the 1890s, when the Pennsylvania System had already been abandoned in practice for several decades, does the expense of abandoning *Eastern* appear to have made a difference. In 1895, Governor Daniel Hastings vetoed a bill to raze Eastern and establish a new prison (with a 2,000-prisoner capacity) on the principle of solitary confinement, as Eastern had been designed. The Governor explained the endeavor would be too expensive.[21] The new prison would have been about four times Eastern's capacity for much of the nineteenth century – a much more significant investment – but it would have followed the Pennsylvania System.

Finally, scholars sometimes posit person-level explanations such as the role of a charismatic leader, the death of an earlier generation of committed supporters, or Pennsylvanians' need to save face and avoid defeat in the great debate over prison discipline. These explanations come the closest to what I argue is the true answer, but they are generally insufficient. Harry Elmer Barnes, a historian of Pennsylvania penology and the only scholar (to my knowledge) to directly, if briefly, address the question of why Eastern retained the Pennsylvania System, has argued that one of Eastern's administrators, Inspector Richard Vaux, was the primary actor responsible for Eastern's lengthy retention of the Pennsylvania System. Vaux was certainly an active administrator at Eastern and a staunch supporter of the Pennsylvania System – indeed, he plays a recurring role in the narrative that follows. However, Vaux, who joined Eastern's Board of Inspectors in 1842 and became the Board's president in 1851, was not in a position of great influence until after Eastern's most embattled period (the 1830s and 1840s). Moreover, Vaux continued to serve as an inspector until his death in 1895, by which time the Pennsylvania System was a dead letter, suggesting Vaux's support was not enough to keep it alive. Additionally, Barnes does not explain Vaux's motivations for supporting the Pennsylvania System for as long as he did; instead, Barnes seems to

[20] Eugene E. Doll, "Trial and Error at Allegheny: The Western State Penitentiary, 1818–1838," *The Pennsylvania Magazine of History and Biography* 81:1 (1957), pp. 3–27.
[21] Daniel Hastings, "Veto of 'An Act Providing for the Removal of the Penitentiary for the Eastern District of Pennsylvania from Its Present Location, the Selection of a Site and Erection Thereon of a Building of Larger Capacity, and Making an Appropriation Therefor.' (July 6, 1895)," in *Pennsylvania Archives. Fourth Series. Papers of the Governors, Vol. XI. 1891–1897*, ed. George Edward Reed. Harrisburg: Wm. Stanley Ray, 1902 [1895], pp. 688–689.

imply that Vaux was simply a true believer. That explanation is not only unsatisfying, but it also has limited utility.[22]

The passing of an earlier generation is another explanation that comes close: the deaths in the 1890s and 1900s of Vaux, as well as several other important prison administrators and local penal reformers who had lived through the Pennsylvania System's golden days, very likely precipitated the series of events that led to the formal abolition of the Pennsylvania System in 1913, as Barnes and others have suggested.[23] But again, this explanation misses the fact that the Pennsylvania System actually died well before its avid supporters, and that even their support waned over time; it also fails to explain why they supported it.

One may suppose these supporters simply wanted to "save face" and not admit that they had been wrong to support a discredited system. However, this face-saving assumption can be dismissed by identifying the "counterfactuals" offered by the three other prisons that adopted the Pennsylvania System. Their administrators began as enthusiastic support-ers, but eventually condemned the system. This reversal occurred at West-ern, where administrators initially supported the Pennsylvania System as strongly as those at Eastern. Likewise, the Pennsylvania legislature had no qualms about abandoning the Pennsylvania System at either prison – first authorizing the Auburn System at Western and then slowly suffo-cating the Pennsylvania System at Eastern. Finally, periodic turnover in prison administration provided multiple opportunities to blame earlier generations for failure and were useful opportunities to reject the system while saving face. The fact that multiple generations of administrators avoided this option, even while blaming earlier generations of adminis-trators for other errors, suggests that fear of public shame for abandoning their prized system did not keep the Pennsylvania System alive.

Easy answers, from religious commitment to architectural predeter-mination to face saving, do not help us account for Eastern's ongoing retention of its unique Pennsylvania System.

---

[22] Barnes, *The Evolution of Penology*, p. 302. The role of a charismatic leader can be used to explain Western's retention of the Pennsylvania System. Historian Eugene Doll traces Western's retention of the Pennsylvania System to Armistead Beckham, Western's warden for two decades; soon after his death, the inspectors requested an end to the Pennsylvania System. Importantly, Doll, like Barnes, traces Beckham's commitment to ideology. Doll, *"Trial and Error at Allegheny," p. 27.*

[23] Barnes, *The Evolution of Penology*, p. 302; Teeters, *They Were in Prison*, pp. 202–211.

The Problem with Maintaining a Deviant Prison

What each of these explanations overlooks most substantially is the difficulty the state of Pennsylvania – the legislators, governors, penal reformers, and (more than anyone else) Eastern's administrators – faced by maintaining the Pennsylvania System. Pennsylvania, and ultimately Eastern, was alone in its reliance on what was essentially full-time solitary confinement: this isolation presented multiple challenges. Technical problems, prisoner and staff insubordination, resource constraints, and disagreements among officials (including administrators, legislators, and local reformers) constantly impeded implementation. When full implementation was impossible or difficult to achieve, administrators were frequently uncertain about how to proceed. Although Eastern was not alone in experiencing such technological challenges, its position as a unique, highly criticized prison exacerbated these difficulties.[24] With no external model to follow in a period full of anxiety about the prison as a new technology – and intense apprehension about the consequences to mind and body of long-term confinement, in solitary or not – administrators had to muddle through and make their own decisions about translating law into action, theory into practice. Criticism from prominent writers at home and abroad was another important consideration: the state as a whole, but especially Eastern's administrators, were explicitly accused of immoral or inefficient behavior for continuing to maintain what many believed was a cruel, expensive, and ineffective system. This criticism compounded the problems of uncertainty by planting seeds of doubt about the propriety of maintaining the Pennsylvania System and raising the stakes even for otherwise minor, everyday decisions. By contrast, administrators at other prisons could enact policies secure in the knowledge that as long as they copied what other administrators did, even if their policies failed, they would not be criticized as severely as Eastern's administrators were.[25]

---

[24] A major theme of institutional-level prison histories in this and other periods is the impossibility of making practice match theory. See, for example, Lewis, *From Newgate to Dannemora*; McLennan, *The Crisis of Imprisonment*; Meranze, *Laboratories of Virtue*. On the point that, despite its unique status, Eastern's general experience with these difficulties shared definite similarities with other prisons, see Janofsky, *"There Is No Hope for Me."* While it is important to emphasize the generality of these difficulties, it is equally important to recognize that these difficulties were exacerbated at Eastern because of its unique status.

[25] These insights manifested empirically, but they are also suggested by neo-institutional theory, described below. See, for example, John W. Meyer and Brian Rowan, "Institutionalized Organizations: Formal Structure as Myth and Ceremony," *American Journal of*

Eastern's retention of the Pennsylvania System cannot be understood without recognizing the consequences of that retention. An open and routine violation of increasingly solidified national norms about prison discipline, Eastern's reliance on the Pennsylvania System made it not only a unique prison, but also a heavily criticized prison. Stated otherwise, Eastern was *a deviant prison*.

Sociologists emphasize that deviance is behavior that society (or some social group) labels deviant; the behavior (such as various forms of nonreproductive copulation considered deviant in a previous era) is considered improper because it has been labeled as such, not because it is inherently immoral or harmful – although its critics may imply or claim that it is both. As Howard Becker has explained, deviance "is the product of a process which involves responses of other people to the behavior."[26] Because the central consideration is the deviant label, much criminal behavior is automatically considered deviant (where social norms agree with legal norms). However, deviance also includes legal behavior that violates strongly held social norms (such as displaying facial piercings, tattoos, unnatural hair color, and all-black attire in more traditional settings). Such deviant behavior need not be objectively more harmful or immoral than other behaviors that have not been labeled deviant (compare the regulation and judgment of drug and alcohol use). In sum, deviance is socially constructed and contingent on strongly held norms.

Deviance is generally ascribed to individual behavior, but it can also be applied to organizational behavior. Scholars most commonly use the term "organizational deviance" to describe criminal or unlawful organizational behavior, as in white-collar crime, abuses by social control agents, or civil rights violations.[27] Sociologist Diane Vaughan has promoted a

Sociology 83:2 (1977), pp. 340–363; Paul J. DiMaggio and Walter W. Powell, "The Iron Cage Revisited: Institutional Isomorphism and Collective Rationality in Organizational Fields," *American Sociological Review* 48:2 (1983), pp. 147–160; Paul J. DiMaggio and Walter W. Powell, "Introduction," in *The New Institutionalism in Organizational Analysis*, ed. Walter W. Powell and Paul J. DiMaggio. University of Chicago Press, 1991, pp. 1–40.

[26] Howard Becker, *Outsiders*. New York: Free Press, 1963, p. 14. Becker helped to launch the study of deviance in modern sociology, but his work builds greatly on Emile Durkheim, who noted, "we should not say that an action offends the common consciousness because it is criminal, but rather that it is criminal because it offends that consciousness. We do not condemn it because it is a crime, but it is a crime because we condemn it." Emile Durkheim, *The Division of Labor in Society*, Trans. by W. D. Halls, New York: The Free Press, 1984[1893], p. 40.

[27] John Braithwaite, *Corporate Crime in the Pharmaceutical Industry*. London: Routledge & Kegan Paul, 1984; Mike Owen Benediktsson, "The Deviant Organization and the Bad

broader definition that includes lawful organizational behavior that inadvertently results in negative consequences, as in technological disasters or school shootings.[28] Instead, I offer a third conception of organizational deviance grounded in *abnormal*, but not necessarily harmful, organizational behavior. I define organizational deviance as organizational behavior that is criticized for violating the norms, standards, or expectations about how organizations should operate. To understand the strength of norms about organizational behavior, and their contribution to conceptions of organizational deviance, I turn to neoinstitutional theory.

Organizational sociologists in the neoinstitutional tradition have theorized the strong influence of norms within an organizational field – the aggregate of all similar organizations and their affiliates, including regulators, resource-granting agencies, clients, and competitor organizations – and the costs to organizations who defy such norms.[29] As these neoinstitutional theorists point out, many organizational fields become increasingly, and seemingly inescapably, homogeneous: organizations within a particular field – such as those involved with medicine, education, or punishment – typically adopt similar policies and practices. Some organizations conform to these norms because it is the easiest option when faced with uncertainty – they can simply copy the policies or practices that other, seemingly successful, organizations are using. Some organizations conform because experts have recommended such policies or practices as particularly effective, efficient, or practicable. Other organizations are forced to adopt such policies or practices by laws

---

Apple CEO: Ideology and Accountability in Media Coverage of Corporate Scandals," *Social Forces* 88:5 (2010), pp. 2189–2216; Tom R. Tyler, Patrick E. Callahan, and Jeffrey Frost, "Armed, and Dangerous (?): Motivating Rule Adherence among Agents of Social Control," *Law & Society Review* 41:2 (2007), pp. 457–492; Susanne C. Monahan and Beth A. Quinn, "Beyond 'Bad Apples' and 'Weak Leaders': Toward a Neo-Institutional Explanation of Organizational Deviance," *Theoretical Criminology* 10 (2006), p. 361; Erin Kelly, "Failure to Update: An Institutional Perspective on Noncompliance with the Family and Medical Leave Act," *Law & Society Review* 44:1 (2010), pp. 33–66.

[28] Diane Vaughan, "The Dark Side of Organizations: Mistake, Misconduct, and Disaster," *Annual Review of Sociology* 25 (1999), pp. 271–305; Cybelle Fox and David J. Harding, "School Shootings as Organizational Deviance," *Sociology of Education* 78 (2005), pp. 69–97.

[29] Neoinstitutional theorists would emphasize that norms are only one of several powerful constraints on behavior; other significant constraints are cognitive frames and rules. Richard W. Scott, *Institutions and Organizations*. Thousand Oaks, CA: Sage, 1995, pp. 44–70. As it is difficult to distinguish these constraints' competing roles (norms often become rules, and both will reflect and shape cognitive frames), I simply retain the term *norms*, but in doing so, I do not intend to downplay the important role of formalized rules or the influence of cognition on expectations and evaluations.

and regulations. Regardless of the mechanism, these policies or practices take on normlike status. Importantly, those organizations that fail to adopt normalized policies or practices, neoinstitutionalists argue, lose legitimacy and become vulnerable; failing to conform may even harm an organization's ability to survive over time.[30] So strong is the theoretical expectation that rejecting such norms is fatal to an organization that, to date, scholars have not discussed the costs to an organization that continuously and publicly rejects the norms of its homogenous field.[31]

---

[30] Meyer and Rowan, *"Institutionalized Organizations"*; DiMaggio and Powell, "The Iron Cage Revisited"; Pamela S. Tolbert and Lynne G. Zucker, "Institutional Sources of Change in the Formal Structure of Organizations: The Diffusion of Civil Service Reform, 1880–1935," *Administrative Science Quarterly* 28:1 (1983), pp. 22–39; Mark C. Suchman, "Managing Legitimacy: Strategic and Institutional Approaches," *The Academy of Management Review* 20:3 (1995), pp. 571–610

[31] In recent decades, a new wave of neoinstitutional scholars have poked holes in the original theory, demonstrating exceptions to this otherwise powerful framework. For example, Matthew S. Kraatz and Edward J. Zajac, "Exploring the Limits of the New Institutionalism: The Causes and Consequences of Illegitimate Organizational Change," *American Sociological Review* 61:5 (1996), pp. 812–836; Jesper Strandgaard Pedersen and Frank Dobbin, "In Search of Identity and Legitimation: Bridging Organizational Culture and Neoinstitutionalism," *American Behavioral Scientist* 49:7 (2006), pp. 897–907; Candace Jones and Felipe G. Massa, "From Novel Practice to Consecrated Exemplar: Unity Temple as a Case of Institutional Evangelizing," *Organization Studies* 34:8 (2013), pp. 1099–1136; D. Michael Lindsay, "Organizational Liminality and Interstitial Creativity: The Fellowship of Power," *Social Forces* 89:1 (2010), pp. 163–184; Jeffrey J. Sallaz, "Politics of Organizational Adornment: Lessons from Las Vegas and Beyond," *American Sociological Review* 77:1 (2012), pp. 99–119; Linda Quirke, "Rogue Resistance: Sidestepping Isomorphic Pressures in a Patchy Institutional Field," *Organization Studies* 34:11 (2013), pp. 1675–1699; Michael A. Haedicke, "'Keeping Our Mission, Changing Our System': Translation and Organizational Change in Natural Foods Co-ops," *The Sociological Quarterly* 53 (2012), pp. 44–67; Donald C. Hambrick, Sydney Finkelstein, Theresa S. Cho, and Eric M. Jackson, "Rethinking Social Control," *Research in Organizational Behavior* 26 (2005), pp. 307–350. Additionally, several classic (or instant classic) works have examined examples of organizational exceptionalism of various kinds. Burton R. Clark, *The Distinctive College*. New Brunswick, NJ: Transaction Publishers, 1970, 2009; Herbert Kauffman, *The Forest Ranger: A Study in Administrative Behavior*. Washington, D.C.: Resources for the Future, 1960, 1967; Seymour Martin Lipset, Martin Trow, and James S. Coleman, *Union Democracy: The Internal Politics of the International Typographical Union*. New York: Free Press, 1956; David L. Sills, *The Volunteers: Means and Ends in a National Organization*. New York: Free Press, 1957; Victoria Johnson, *Backstage at the Revolution: How the Royal Paris Opera Survived the End of the Old Regime*. University of Chicago Press, 2008; Daniel N. Kluttz, "The Path of the Law Review: How Interfield Ties Contribute to Institutional Emergence and Buffer against Change," *Law & Society Review* 53:1 (2019), pp. 239–274. However, to my knowledge, scholars have not yet discussed the case of an organization that is strongly rooted in an otherwise homogenous field and overtly resists norms despite strong pressures to conform to those norms – that is, the case of a deviant organization.

Eastern is one example of such organizational deviance. By persistently relying on a unique system of prison discipline in an increasingly homogenous field, Eastern became the subject of intense criticism. Identifying Eastern as a deviant organization is only an initial step that helps illuminate Eastern's puzzling nature; it does not explain why or how Eastern was able to persist in its deviance. Becker's (and others') theories of deviance are theories of individuals; while some of these theories can be scaled up to organizations, we must proceed with care. Although neoinstitutional theory is an organizational theory, it excels at explaining conformity – not deviance – and field-level trends – not individual (especially aberrant) organizations. How – and why – does such an organization persist in its deviance?

ACCOUNTING FOR EASTERN'S DEVIANCE

In the narrative that follows, I demonstrate that Eastern's administrators were the driving force behind their prison's exceptional retention of the Pennsylvania System. Over the main period examined (1829–1879), Eastern was governed by a warden, a Board of Inspectors – five volunteers who set internal policy and advised the warden – a physician, and a moral instructor; I refer to these men collectively as Eastern's administrators. These administrators, more than any other group, determined what happened at Eastern, from its behind-the-scenes activities to its formal policies, including the Pennsylvania System itself.

The prison administrators' role in sustaining the Pennsylvania System becomes apparent when contrasting their control and actions with the state legislature and a group of local penal reformers, two groups that we should expect to have played more important roles in Eastern's history. The legislature had nominal authority over the prison; indeed, it was the governing body that formally authorized and later deauthorized the Pennsylvania System. In practice, however, the legislature frequently passed laws at others' request rather than on its own initiative. The prison administrators themselves frequently requested changes from the legislature, particularly when legislative lethargy impeded Eastern's operations. However, the administrators also rebuffed occasional legislative incursions into Eastern's operations that threatened to change the Pennsylvania System.

The legislature often acted following the lobbying efforts of an active group of penal reformers, members of the Philadelphia Society for Alleviating the Miseries of Public Prisons (PSAMPP). This group in particular was largely responsible for establishing the Pennsylvania System,[32] but it had little sway over Eastern's internal policies once the prison opened. Indeed, PSAMPP members visited prisoners on a semimonthly basis and would often complain to the prison administrators about the conditions in which the prisoners were held and other elements of daily practice at Eastern, but to little effect.

While PSAMPP was responsible for the Pennsylvania System's creation, and the legislature had authorized the Pennsylvania System at Eastern, both groups later tried to mitigate the Pennsylvania System's most controversial elements and sought to align the state with national trends. These efforts put the legislature and PSAMPP at odds with Eastern's administrators, who fiercely and uncompromisingly defended the Pennsylvania System throughout Eastern's period of deviance (1829 to the late 1870s), never publicly acknowledging problems with the Pennsylvania System, always fighting any effort for formal change.

Administrative commitment to the Pennsylvania System at Eastern can be contrasted with administrative behavior at the three other Pennsylvania System–style prisons. In each of these prisons (in Rhode Island, New Jersey, and western Pennsylvania), administrators openly criticized the Pennsylvania System before eventually requesting their state legislature to replace it with the Auburn System, requests that each state's legislature granted – further reifying Eastern's deviant status. At Eastern, the Pennsylvania System survived this period of extensive criticism without the administrators contributing to the criticism. Indeed, when the Pennsylvania System finally ended at Eastern in the 1870s, the administrators did not publicly acknowledge its demise. It was merely a formality when an entirely different generation of Eastern's administrators publicly requested an end to the Pennsylvania System in the early twentieth century.

Recognizing the unique role of administrative support for the Pennsylvania System at Eastern, the central question becomes why Eastern's administrators continued to embrace, defend, and protect the Pennsylvania System from attempts to force Eastern to join the several dozen prisons following the Auburn System. The administrators' stance is particularly puzzling given the pressure from their own state legislature, local penal reformers (many of whom were their personal friends and extended family), and the example of their administrative

---

[32] Meranze, *Laboratories of Virtue*; Teeters and Shearer, *The Prison at Philadelphia*.

counterparts in other states. It is also puzzling given the severe national and international criticism of Eastern's administrators for most of this period from penal reformers, prison administrators, diplomats, statesmen, and some celebrities. Ultimately, I argue that Eastern's administrators defended the Pennsylvania System (rather than giving in to pressures to conform to national trends) because the system offered them something – the means to claim a unique status – that was not available under the Auburn System.

The Institutional Theory of Philip Selznick

To understand the importance of status – how it arises and how it impacts policy – I draw on the work of mid-century organizational theorist, Philip Selznick. One of Selznick's central points was that an organization, once formed, takes on "a life of its own,"[33] generating its own momentum and motivations. Whatever the external forces facing an organization, the organization's internal momentum offers a counterforce. The primary source of this internal momentum comes from the people who populate the organization: they develop their own sets of goals for themselves in relation to the organization and for the organization itself – goals that often diverge from the original stated goals of the organization. One of the most powerful causes of these unexpected goals is what Selznick called *institutionalization*.

Before explaining Selznick's conceptualization of institutionalization, it will be useful to first explain the more common version of institutionalization developed by later scholars extending Selznick. For these neoinstitutional scholars writing since the 1970s, institutionalization is the process by which something becomes taken for granted – that is, cognitively or normatively normalized.[34] Under this neoinstitutional conception, things (organizations, policies, practices) can become institutionalized when they become sufficiently common that people grow used to them, expect to see them, and notice when they are absent. Alternatively, things can become institutionalized because people believe they are normatively or pragmatically preferable – the organization, policy, or practice is morally good or has some practical utility.[35] This

---

33 Philip Selznick, *TVA and the Grassroots*. Berkeley: University of California Press, 1949, p. 10.

34 See, e.g., Scott, *Institutions and Organizations*.

35 In practice, it is difficult to distinguish whether something gets taken for granted because it is common or because it is believed to be normatively or pragmatically

version of institutionalization is often used at a fairly broad unit of analysis such as an organizational field. By contrast, Selznick's earlier version of institutionalization, which operated at the organizational level, was much more personal. To distinguish between these two versions, I refer to Selznick's version as *personal institutionalization*.

For Selznick, a personally institutionalized entity had been "infuse[d] with value beyond the technical requirements of the task at hand."[36] Once personally institutionalized, the entity is no longer a mere "tool" for some technical goal; instead, it becomes "a valued source of personal satisfaction." Once it holds this greater nontechnical value, it is no longer "expendable" even when "a more efficient tool" is available.[37] Organizational actors may pursue small alterations to protect the personally institutionalized entity, but its special value motivates them to resist any attempts to change or abandon it. The personally institutionalized entity persists. That is, Selznick described personal institutionalization as a process independent from how widespread an entity becomes or general beliefs about the entity's pragmatic utility or normative appeal – in contrast to later versions of institutionalization. Personal institutionalization is thus a far more intimate, even self-interested, process for organizational actors.

Organizational actors can find nontechnical value or importance in organizational phenomena in a variety of ways. Value may stem from the status or prestige that comes with holding a particular position within the organization.[38] It may be a sense of meaning that infuses one's work,

---

preferable: Many things believed to be preferable become common and people come to believe that something that is common is also preferable. Indeed, both mechanisms of institutionalization may be occurring simultaneously (DiMaggio and Powell, "The Iron Cage Revisited").

[36] Philip Selznick, *Leadership in Administration: A Sociological Interpretation*. New York: Harper & Row, 1957, p. 17. Selznick actually wrote of organizations becoming personally institutionalized, but later neoinstitutional theorists expanded his definition beyond organizations to policies, practices, offices, etc.

[37] Ibid., pp. 10, 17.

[38] Ibid., p. 14. Selznick's theory was not entirely original; it is a more fully elaborated version – and one more attuned to contingent variation – of Robert Michels' "Iron Law of Oligarchy," about the nature of political parties, applied to all organizations. Responding to Marxist political history, Michels argued that anyone elected to power will always strive to remain in power, ultimately sacrificing the needs of the many for the needs of the few. Political parties, he argued, begin as "a means to secure an end. Having, however, become an end in itself, endowed with aims and interests of its own, it undergoes detachment, from the teleological point of view, from the class which it represents." Robert Michels, *Political Parties: A Sociological Study of the Oligarchical Tendencies of Modern Democracy*, Trans. by Eden and Cedar Paul. Kitchener, Ontario: Batoche Books,

giving it (and one's life) a larger purpose, thereby quenching some deeply rooted "psychological needs."[39] Both the status and meaning can be reinforced and elaborated upon when individuals repeat narratives about why they do what they do. These narratives accumulate and are reinforced over generations as new organizational actors are trained in the ways of their organization; through this repetition and accumulation, the narratives become truth.[40] This process generates a firm commitment on the part of organizational actors to the source of this status or meaning – the institutionalized entity.

Indeed, the personal institutionalization process can be highly personal. As Selznick explains, "Professionally, too, the personnel becomes identified with the agency, deriving prestige and disesteem from the fortunes of the organization itself."[41] Under such circumstances, criticism of the organization is a criticism of its participants. Consequently, "[t]o defend the organization is often to defend oneself." Importantly, this defense becomes a pathway for organizational actors to derive additional benefits from their organization. Selznick continues, "These defensive activities are aided when a set of beliefs is so fashioned as at once to fortify the special needs or interests of the organization and to provide an aura of disinterestedness under which formal discussion may be pursued." And this is the key: organizational defense creates opportunities for organizational actors to make claims about themselves they could not otherwise make because they are made in the service of the embattled organization.

As this last point indicates, personal institutionalization is more likely to occur under certain conditions than others. While Selznick noted that "no organization of any duration" is immune to the pressures of personal institutionalization,[42] he specified two organizational characteristics that were most conducive to personal institutionalization. First, Selznick argued that organizations with a large amount of discretion and

1915 (2001), p. 232. In an important break with Michels, Selznick questioned the extent to which this tendency was an "iron law." Instead, Selznick illustrated certain conditions under which this tendency was more likely to manifest, rather than assuming it always occurred with equal force. On Michels' influence on Selznick, see Martin Krygier, *Philip Selznick: Ideals in the World*. Stanford, UA: Stanford University Press, 2012, pp. 21–24, 53–55.
39 Selznick, *Leadership in Administration*, pp. 8–9; See also Neil Fligstein and Doug McAdam, *A Theory of Fields*. New York: Oxford University Press, 2012.
40 Selznick, *TVA and the Grassroots*, p. 252.   41 Ibid., p. 51.
42 Selznick, *Leadership in Administration*, p. 16.

ambiguity, and that lack either specialization or mechanical simplicity, are more prone to personal institutionalization. Specifically, individuals in such organizations have more room to think and act beyond the narrow constraints of technical work as well as more opportunities for the "interaction" that enables group commitment.[43] This interaction is fertile ground for the creation of narratives that can infuse organizational structures with value.

Second, Selznick argued, where organizational actors have a greater need for meaning, they are more likely to experience personal institutionalization. He explained,

> This quest for an ideology, for doctrinal nourishment, while general, is uneven. Organizations established in a stable context, with assured futures, do not feel the same urgencies as those born of turmoil and set down to fend for themselves in undefined ways among institutions fearful and resistant. As in individuals, insecurity summons ideological reinforcements.[44]

When an organization's position is not secure, it must "feel its way. This require[s] the formulation of a policy that would reassure external elements and would so educate its own ranks as to maximize the possibilities of social acceptance."[45] In these ways, contention and criticism can become a crucible for personal institutionalization.

Selznick's theory of personal institutionalization applies well to criminal justice organizations generally, particularly in periods immediately surrounding significant innovation. As sociologist John Sutton has noted, criminal justice organizations face extensive discretion, substantial ambiguity about their role, and they are often charged with competing, even contradictory imperatives, such as rehabilitating and deterring criminals with humane and cost-effective methods. These ambiguities are exacerbated in periods of innovation, when criminal justice administrators first attempt to reconcile these competing imperatives against a backdrop of uncertainty surrounding an untried technology. As criminal justice policy typically experiences intermittent periods of change, periods of uncertainty following innovation are fairly frequent.[46]

The period surrounding the early prisons represents a special case of heightened uncertainty specifically because the technology of the

---

[43] Philip Selznick, *Leadership in Administration: A Sociological Interpretation*. New York: Harper & Row, 1957, p. 16.

[44] Selznick, *TVA and the Grassroots*, p. 48.   [45] Ibid., p. 49.

[46] John R. Sutton, "Rethinking Social Control," *Law & Social Inquiry* 21:4 (1996), pp. 943–958.

prison was so novel. Rather than just another iteration of an underlying technology, modern prisons represented a significant shift in American criminal justice, as illustrated by the extensive debates that emerged over the right way to confine prisoners.[47] Consequently, we should expect to see heavier pressure toward personal institutionalization in this unstable period, particularly in the beginning when the uncertainty was the highest. However, the pressure toward personal institutionalization is primarily an organizational-level development and will vary across organizations within the same place or period.

Eastern experienced both of Selznick's conditions, which directly encouraged the personal institutionalization of – or value infusion into – the Pennsylvania System for its administrators. Personal institutionalization helps us explain why Eastern's administrators retained the Pennsylvania System despite the many personal and practical costs associated with it. This personal institutionalization was initiated by the founding conditions surrounding the Pennsylvania System's creation and authorization: the strife out of which it iteratively emerged, the many failures that surrounded the first two generations of American prisons, and the extensive internecine debate within Pennsylvania over how its prisons should be structured. Once Eastern was established, however, the constant need to defend the Pennsylvania System against criticism only strengthened the personal institutionalization process, as it repeatedly gave Eastern's administrators the chance to describe themselves in flattering terms, deriving status through their defense of the system. Behind the scenes, moreover, we see the way in which administrators valued the Pennsylvania System not for its technical appeal – they significantly, and often strategically, violated it in practice – but for the advantage of difference it bestowed. The personal institutionalization of the Pennsylvania System was thus simultaneously caused by, and offered a counterforce to the challenges of deviance.

More than a claim to fame, the very need to defend the prison – and themselves – from constant criticism gave Eastern's administrators the

---

[47] e.g., McLennan, *The Crisis of Imprisonment*. Certainly, one can overstate this shift – there were some continuities between the first generation of prisons and earlier ideas that were not enacted widely, nor was the shift particularly sudden, taking place over several decades. e.g., Ashley T. Rubin, "The Prehistory of Innovation: A Longer View of Penal Change," *Punishment & Society* 20:2 (2018), pp. 192–216. However, the modern prisons represented a qualitative and quantitative shift in the American reliance on incarceration. The magnitude of this change bred extensive anxiety.

opportunity to describe themselves as benevolent, humanitarian, progressive gentlemen running what they described as a superior prison. Rather than an unseemly display of self-promotion, these descriptions could be justified as defenses of their embattled prison and defenses against specific attacks on their own character. Criticizing their opponents also elevated Eastern's administrators. Their opponents, Eastern's administrators argued, were inhumane, driven by indecorous motivations of profit, and insufficiently versed in penological knowledge to evaluate the Pennsylvania System's functioning. Over time, Eastern's administrators also described themselves as experts in all matters related to crime and punishment, an expertise they alone enjoyed thanks to their unique ability to observe prisoners in a way administrators elsewhere (as well as reformers and legislators) could not. These statements helped to neutralize the sting of the calumny about the Pennsylvania System and the pains of deviance for Eastern's administrators. Moreover, their repeated defense and justification of the Pennsylvania System encouraged them to internalize their positive claims and overcome residual doubts. Should Eastern's administrators abandon the Pennsylvania System, they could no longer make such claims, nor would they receive the same level of attention from foreign dignitaries who often wished to visit Eastern along side other American landmarks. Maintaining and defending the Pennsylvania System offered Eastern's administrators attention, status, prestige, and a unique and vaunted identity as benevolent gentlemen managing the country's only humanitarian prison – in their minds, at least. Ultimately, Eastern's administrators resisted any effort to abandon or change the Pennsylvania System, even when other models seemed to be technologically superior, because it provided them with a unique status unobtainable under any other system of prison discipline. In this way, it was advantageous to be different.

Have I mistaken these administrators' genuine belief in the Pennsylvania System for something more selfish? Certainly, their public defense of the Pennsylvania System gave the impression of genuine belief in the Pennsylvania System's superiority. The administrators' public accounts presented the Pennsylvania System as a flawless model of confinement. When confronted with prisoner illness, insanity, or death, or deficits in their annual budget, administrators attributed the problematic outcome to conditions beyond their control. (Inability to secure sufficient funds to implement the Pennsylvania System fully, or the prisoners' poor health upon their arrival, for example, could account for these failures, thereby removing any blame from the Pennsylvania System.)

Their public accounts notwithstanding, these administrators were also pragmatic realists. In practice, Eastern's administrators manipulated the Pennsylvania System behind the scenes to minimize costs, achieve some measure of profitability, and preserve prisoner health and sanity. Though not common (before 1866), double-celling and out-of-cell labor were some of the most extreme strategies administrators consciously used to improve their prison's functioning.

Again, we can contrast the administrators' actions to the PSAMPP reformers, who tended to be more ideological and less managerial than Eastern's administrators. The reformers objected to these practices as inappropriate violations of the Pennsylvania System. Eastern's administrators, however, had a different set of motivations than the local reformers: privately and strategically manipulating the Pennsylvania System allowed administrators to mitigate controversial aspects of the program that would otherwise appear in their public annual reports – especially their budget and their health and mortality statistics – without openly admitting their prized system was flawed. Such alterations allowed administrators to continue to claim their prison's – and their own – superiority.

However, by the 1870s, the Pennsylvania System no longer offered the same benefits it had in the 1830s and 1840s. The Auburn–Pennsylvania debate subsided in the 1850s, especially after the most vociferous critic of the Pennsylvania System, the lead organizer of the Boston Prison Discipline Society, passed away in 1854 and national attention shifted away from penal reform in the years immediately prior to the Civil War. After the war, penological debate shifted to the value of adult reformatories and different kinds of early release programs anticipating parole. Although Eastern's administrators initially continued to defend the Pennsylvania System, in the absence of critique, continued defense of the Pennsylvania System – along with its administrators' accompanying claims to personal excellence – would have appeared unnecessary, excessive, and self-serving. By the 1870s, moreover, Eastern's administrators had fully embraced their identity as professional experts in the new field of penal science. By claiming a professional identity and positioning themselves against other new professionals in the field, they could derive an alternative status; they no longer needed the Pennsylvania System.

Other changes helped usher in the transition. Shortly after administrative status began decoupling from the Pennsylvania System, the system itself faced new technical challenges. In the years following the Civil War, overcrowding struck Eastern, and its administrators had to resort to widespread double-celling of their prisoners, in violation of their central principle. Although they demanded the legislature alleviate the situation, the administrators slowly gave up on the Pennsylvania System. Increasingly, they resolved the conflict between theory and reality by emphasizing their use of "individual treatment" rather than "separate confinement," their long-preferred description of the Pennsylvania System.

By 1880, Eastern's administrators, content with their alternative source of status in professionalization, had quietly abandoned the Pennsylvania System, letting it succumb to record levels of overcrowding. Without ever publicly rejecting the Pennsylvania System, they effectively replaced it with an entirely new regime. Over the next three decades, administrators almost never mentioned the Pennsylvania System or their own, and their predecessors', prior commitment to "solitary or separate confinement." When the state legislature finally authorized prisoner congregation at Eastern in 1913, the Pennsylvania System was a distant memory: Eastern's administrators did not acknowledge the legal change in their report for that year.

THE DEVIANT PRISON AND ITS LESSONS

Although Eastern is a "deviant case" in the sociomethodological sense[48] as well as a deviant prison in the way I have argued, Eastern's history parallels – variously leading, intersecting, and deviating from – U.S. prisons' early history. Despite its differences, Eastern's history throws into relief important developments that have previously been lost in studies that relate penal change to significant social change alone. In particular, Eastern's history under the Pennsylvania System highlights the role of factors internal to penal implementation and administration, including the way in which penal organizations and their actors ultimately shape penal trends. In making this argument, I extend the work of sociologist Lauren Edelman who developed the concept of legal endogeneity, the process by which organizations shape the very laws that seek to regulate organizational behavior.[49] Adapting legal endogeneity to the penal

---

[48] Jason Seawright and John Gerring, "Case Selection Techniques in Case Study Research: A Menu of Qualitative and Quantitative Options," *Political Research Quarterly* 61:2 (2008), pp. 294–308.

[49] Lauren B. Edelman, *Working Law: Courts, Corporations, and Symbolic Civil Rights.* University of Chicago Press, 2016.

context, I call these internal factors the endogenous causes of penal change. In doing so, I seek to contrast the endogenous factors to what might be termed exogenous factors – the significant, macro-level changes in civil society, whether political, economic, or cultural – that scholars commonly use to explain penal change.

One significant endogenous factor is the legacy of failure for penal change and future development. Eastern and the Pennsylvania System – as well as the Auburn System – emerged out of the failure of America's first generation of state prisons, the proto-prisons.[50] These failures both precipitated initial changes and created lasting reminders of past failures that would continue to shape the contours of penal change, influencing designs and goals for the new generation of prisons.[51] To discuss the rise of modern prisons and their systems of prison discipline without understanding the significant impact of penal failure is to miss one of the most significant and lasting causes of these developments. While large-scale (or macro) social changes contributed to these developments, there has been far less attention to this more internal or endogenous factor.[52]

A second endogenous factor is the strength of penal norms in shaping these developments. Penal norms, or shared conceptions about how punishment should look and function, can emerge not only from exogenous social changes but also from developments within the penal system, including uncertainty about penal technologies, the role of penal reformers' public statements, and the power of example (including past

[50] For other important accounts that highlight various kinds of failure in early penal history, see Meranze, *Laboratories of Virtue,* and McLennan, *The Crisis of Imprisonment.* In making this point, I draw heavily on their work on the early, post–American Revolution era in particular, but I extend it throughout the nineteenth century.

[51] What I refer to here as legacies some scholars have called "policy feedback" effects in more contemporary contexts. See David Dagan and Steven Teles, "Locked In? Conservative Reform and the Future of Mass Incarceration," *The Annals of the American Academy of Political and Social Science* 1 (2014), pp. 266–276; Heather Schoenfeld, "Mass Incarceration and the Paradox of Prison Conditions Litigation," *Law & Society Review* 44:3/4 (2010), pp. 731–767; Heather Schoenfeld, "A Research Agenda on Reform," *The ANNALS of the American Academy of Political and Social Science* 664:1 (2016), pp. 155–174; Schoenfeld, *Building the Prison State.*

[52] For a more general discussion on this point, see Ashley T. Rubin and Keramet Reiter, "Continuity in the Face of Penal Innovation: Revisiting the History of American Solitary Confinement," *Law & Social Inquiry* 43:4 (2018), pp. 1604–1632. Importantly, penal failure is often visible in prior accounts of prison history. In Meranze's account, the failed wheelbarrow law was a precipitating cause for reforming the old Walnut Street Jail, one of the first proto-prisons. Meranze, *Laboratories of Virtue.* Likewise, McLennan emphasizes the importance of proto-prisons' riots for precipitating the rise of modern prisons. McLennan, *The Crisis of Imprisonment.*

failures). Notably, penal norms can be strong enough, as they were in antebellum America, to overcome countervailing socioeconomic factors often thought to explain penal trends. Until the Civil War, the Auburn System was adopted in every state with a prison, except (ultimately) Pennsylvania. Even states in the South or on the frontier, which had little practical need for a prison and lacked the industrial strength of the coastal northeast, adopted the striped uniforms, rule of silence, and factory-style labor of the Auburn System. The anxiety of uncertainty, penal reformers' vitriol, and the legitimacy provided by simply conforming to norms provided powerful disincentives against adopting the Pennsylvania System or, even more dangerous, creating a different system altogether. Similarly, the fate of the Pennsylvania System in Rhode Island and New Jersey demonstrates the difficulty of maintaining a heterodox system once adopted. Scholars focusing on how macro-level social change shaped penal norms, however, have overlooked the power of these norms beyond the social contexts in which they were developed.[53] Instead, focusing on penal norms themselves shows the influence of factors other than macro-level social change on penal trends.

A final endogenous factor is the personal connection between penal policy and the people charged with meting it out. Like other scholars, I emphasize the importance of prison administrators who were frequently *de facto* policymakers. Both the Auburn System and Pennsylvania System were prison administrators' innovations – another illustration of the way in which penal policy emerged from within, not just beyond the prison walls, a trend that has continued in the twentieth and twenty-first centuries.[54] But by moving beyond simplistic characterizations of these men as solely driven by faith in their policies,[55] the convenience of administration,[56] or sadistic or greedy

[53] This is an argument I have developed more fully in Rubin, "A Neo-Institutional Account of Prison Diffusion."

[54] Lewis, *From Newgate to Dannemora*; Keramet Reiter, "Reclaiming the Power to Punish: Legislating and Administering the California Supermax, 1982–1989," *Law & Society Review* 50:2 (2016), pp. 484–518; Keramet Reiter, *23/7: Pelican Bay Prison and the Rise of Long-Term Solitary Confinement*. New Haven: Yale University Press, 2016.

[55] See, for example, Teeters, *They Were in Prison*; Teeters and Shearer, *The Prison at Philadelphia*, Barnes, *The Evolution of Penology*; Johnston, "The World's Most Influential Prison."

[56] See, for example, David J. Rothman, *Conscience and Convenience: The Asylum and Its Alternatives in Progressive America*. Hawthorne, NY: Aldine de Gruyter, 1980; James B. Jacobs, *Stateville: The Penitentiary in Mass Society*. University of Chicago Press, 1977.

desires,[57] this book reveals additional, and more complex, motivations that shape prison practice and policy.[58] It suggests that other personal or psychic benefits and costs exist and – more than local values, history, and personalities – can shape administrators' willingness to continue such policies. At Eastern, major social change provided important context for the Pennsylvania System's decline, but the administrators' decision to finally stop fighting to save it must be understood in relation to their own status needs.

In pointing out the limitations of traditional accounts grounded in significant social change, I do not mean to discount the important role of social context that has been amply demonstrated by previous histories of this and other periods, but rather to add something new to the discussion. Indeed, generations of punishment scholars have taken pains to demonstrate that punishment is not simply a function of crime rates but rather stems from cultural, economic, and political factors that seem to have little connection to crime and society's technical need for punishment.[59] It would be inaccurate to argue that these factors are irrelevant. Instead, I argue that they are not enough to account for Eastern's unique history, the modern prison's rise to penal dominance more generally, or even penal trends in other times and places.

A METHODOLOGICAL NOTE ON SOURCES

As this book is a work of history and social science, it reflects the epistemological influence of both approaches. A healthy skepticism of sources is necessary for historians and social scientists alike. This necessity is particularly salient when examining a highly criticized organization like Eastern, where supporters – whether administrators or penal reformers – would be prone to displaying their prison in the best possible light

---

57 For recent examples of such accounts, see Manion, *Liberty's Prisoners*; Heather Ann Thompson, *Blood in the Water: The Attica Uprising of 1971 and its Legacy*. New York: Pantheon Books, 2016.

58 For a longer discussion of how scholars have relied on each of these three presentations to describe penal actors throughout history, see Ashley T. Rubin, "True Believers, Rational Managers, and Bad Actors: Reconsidering *The Prison and the Factory* in Light of Recent Penal Historiography," *Punishment & Society*, forthcoming (2020), available at: https://doi.org/10.1177/1462474520918813.

59 Durkheim, *The Division of Labor in Society*; Rusche and Kirchheimer, *Punishment and Social Structure*; Foucault, *Discipline and Punish*; David Garland, *Punishment and Welfare*. Brookfield, VT: Gower, 1985; David Garland, *Punishment and Modern Society: A Study in Social Theory*. University of Chicago Press, 1990.

while their opponents would have the opposite tendency. Indeed, a common theme in the relevant primary documents from this period is the accusation that someone (an opponent) is lying or misinformed – and decidedly wrong. It is also possible to witness contemporaries' efforts to rewrite history, claiming that they (or their colleagues or predecessors) had never done or said things that they clearly had done a few years or decades before. As a check against the limitations imposed by untrustworthy sources, I have employed three strategies: the first two involve triangulating sources and the third is a matter of interpretation.

First, I have strategically mobilized both public and private writings. Public documents included Eastern's annual reports; pamphlets, treatises, travel logs, and letters written and published by penal reformers and prison administrators around the United States and some from around the Atlantic world; newspaper and other periodical articles; Pennsylvania governors' speeches and remarks upon vetoing bills; legislation from multiple states and the Pennsylvania House and Senate journals; and Pennsylvania Supreme Court cases. Private documents from Eastern included the warden's daily log, the inspectors' meeting minutes, records of prisoner labor, and some prisoners' letters. Other private documents included Philadelphia reformers' meeting minutes and a reformer's diary detailing his prison visits. These public and private documents offer a range of experiences and perspectives, which is useful in itself. The private documents in particular form a check on potentially misleading public documents. In general, I put more stock in private documents because they were, most of the time, not intended for public consumption and were, consequently, more forthcoming.

The warden's log is a useful example of private documents' special utility. Wardens mostly used the log to record information for recollection – such as receiving, releasing, or punishing prisoners; hiring, firing, or reprimanding staff; and noteworthy visits – some of which were later summarized in the warden's monthly reports to the inspectors and annual reports to the legislature. Officially, this log was not a private document: The 1829 law that authorized the Pennsylvania System at Eastern required the warden to maintain this "journal";[60] after each warden's tenure, the log was handed over to his successor and now resides in the state archives. Nevertheless, the wardens treated the

---

[60] Pennsylvania, "No. 204: A Further Supplement to an Act, Entitled 'An Act to Reform the Penal Laws of This Commonwealth'," in *Laws of the General Assembly of the State of Pennsylvania.* Harrisburg: Office of the Reporter, 1829, pp. 341–354, p. 348.

log as a private document – and for good reason. The log was only twice requested for review by external sources. An 1863 court case read "extracts from the warden's journal." Although the case was not antithetical to prison administration,[61] the extracts were "read under exception."[62] The warden's log was also subpoenaed for a major investigation into the prison in 1834–1835. Even after the investigation, in which administrators were warned to stop using certain extreme punishments, the warden so warned continued to record the use of such punishments in the log, apparently undeterred. Additionally, each warden recorded not only quotidian ephemera of official prison business but also personal reflections, including, sometimes, cutting descriptions of other power holders. The rarity with which the log was actually read by others thus gave wardens a (generally accurate) sense of security, enough to record their honest assessments. These unguarded reflections were like miniature treasure troves revealing insights into an otherwise carefully curated record. Undoubtedly, their writing was not a perfect account of their full range of thoughts, but wardens recorded events and opinions they likely would not have wanted others to read at the time. Most importantly, these private documents often contradicted their public documents; many such contradictions feature in this book.

Second, as others have noted, a prison is a highly contested environment in which tensions exist within and across prisoners, guards, prison administrators, penal reformers, and state government officials;[63]

---

[61] The case was a rather interesting one. Two years into a five-year sentence for forgery, J. Buchanan Crosse was pardoned in June 1862 in order to participate in a secret mission for the Secretary of War. Apparently, Crosse had "peculiar talents" that the war department considered "valuable." The mission was so secret, that neither the prison administrators nor Crosse himself were to be informed of the reason for his pardon, "knowledge of which … would be fatal to him and defeat the purposes of his mission." In fact, the letter from the Secretary of War requesting the pardon was a forgery, and one noticed soon after the prisoner's release into a U.S. Marshal's custody; "the forgery was detected by the frank being on a different side of the envelope from that on which it was customary to write it." The prisoner was returned the following day. Months later, the prisoner presented a habeas corpus petition demanding to be released from prison on the basis that his pardon was still valid, regardless of the false pretenses that inspired it (*The Commonwealth ex rel. James Buchanan Crosse v. John S. Halloway*, 44 Pa. 2010 1863).

[62] Ibid.

[63] Alyson Brown and Emma Clare, "A History of Experience: Exploring Prisoners' Accounts of Incarceration," in *The Persistent Prison: Problems, Images and Alternatives*, ed. Clive Emsley. London: Francis Boutle, 2005, pp. 49–73; Philip Goodman, "'It's Just Black, White, or Hispanic': An Observational Study of Racializing Moves in California's Segregated Prison Reception Centers," *Law & Society Review* 42:4 (2008), pp. 735–770; McLennan, *The Crisis of Imprisonment*, Janofsky, *"There Is No Hope for Me."*

Eastern was no exception. Even among supporters – PSAMPP and Eastern's administrators – there were personality conflicts, ideological disagreements, and animosities. This contestation not only became a focus of my research, but also proved to be an invaluable resource for helping to illuminate (typically) hidden phenomena. PSAMPP at times had motivation to record the prison administrators' wrongdoings, including offering accounts of behind-the-scenes behavior that were not otherwise recorded in administrators' (and other public) reports of the prison. Likewise, disagreements among the administrators often caused the administrators to record behavior that would not otherwise have been discoverable. There is, however, the risk of too naïvely believing every reported bad act. For example, after they had been fired, disgruntled prison guards sometimes reported administrative misbehavior; their motivations for doing so obviously cast doubt on the veracity of their claims. Likewise, sometimes PSAMPP members or prison administrators were so convinced of their own rectitude and others' failures that they incorrectly stated the facts (e.g., by misremembering earlier events) or offered stark interpretations not shared by others who were similarly situated. In my usage, where the source of information was someone whose motivations may have encouraged them to exaggerate or fabricate, I have included their information only where I had additional evidence, either of the specifics of a given case or similar stories that suggest a particular case was part of a larger trend, that strengthened the probability of its veracity.

Third, much of this book is concerned with the public depiction of Eastern and the Pennsylvania System. Thus, a major data source was Eastern's annual reports. These documents were explicitly written for a public audience and their content was contrived with that audience in mind. Although I believe the administrators stopped short of outright fabrication,[64] I do not treat these documents as anything resembling

---

[64] As an example, the administrators kept detailed records about the number of prisoners, their criminal histories, and other demographics; with the exception of transcription errors, their reports match their private records. A similar check is difficult to perform for their profit and loss records, but the administrators were at times selective about which expenses they included in their calculations. Thus, while they did not fabricate the records, they took license in how some of the more controversial material was represented. As another example, administrators sometimes included letters they claimed former prisoners had sent them. These frequently obsequious letters were written with excellent vocabulary and grammar that does not match the writing quality of unpublished prisoner letters. I suspect these letters were originally written by prisoners, but were "improved" before inclusion in the annual reports.

perfect representations of Eastern's history. Indeed, a host of private documents confirm they certainly are not. Instead, I treat these and other public documents as documents that have been strategically written for an audience in mind. Because I am interested in how the administrators presented and defended their prison, the reports' strategic nature is useful: It does not matter (for my purposes) whether these documents are true representations of reality at Eastern. Thus, to understand what occurred behind the scenes, I turn to private documents; to understand how the administrators presented their prison, I turn to their public documents.

Terminology Note

In the following narrative, I use the term "administrators" when collectively referring to the officials at Eastern – the inspectors, wardens, physicians, and moral instructors. The administrators were not a homogenous cluster of like-thinking men, and they often disagreed with one another. Some administrators were quieter than others, pursued their duties less vigorously than the average administrator, or left the prison after only a short period of service; other administrators were extremely vocal, went above and beyond all expectations, or continued to work at the prison for decades or even until their death. The latter certainly dominate my discussions, as they tended to produce more records or were disproportionately present for important developments.

Despite these differences, the administrators as a group had much in common, behaved similarly, articulated similar goals, and offered similar justifications for their work at Eastern. Their writings and actions reveal a kind of *Gemeinschaft* at the prison. When important exceptions to the "party line" existed, I make note. When certain arguments are only issued by a particular set of administrators (e.g., the inspectors or the warden) or by particular men with colorful personalities (e.g., Inspector Thomas Bradford, Inspector Richard Vaux, Physician William Darrach, Physician Robert Given), I identify these actors as well. Quotations from particular sources (e.g., Warden's Log, Inspectors' Meeting Minutes) reflect the title of their author and, when applicable, the author (e.g., Warden Wood's Annual Report). But where trends emerged without clear exceptions, I use "administrators" instead of tediously listing the full set of actors involved. In the end, this account offers both a general account of several generations of administrators as a group and a deep account of particularly noteworthy administrators that, taken together, present a coherent picture of why they (collectively) maintained the Pennsylvania System for so long.

PART I

BECOMING THE DEVIANT PRISON

*Establishing the Conditions for Personal
Institutionalization*

A

THE CONTEXT OF CREATION

Organizations established in a stable context, with assured futures, do not feel the same urgencies as those born of turmoil and set down to fend for themselves in undefined ways among institutions fearful and resistant.

Philip Selznick[1]

[1] Selznick, *TVA and the Grassroots*, p. 48

I

Faith and Failure

Experimenting with Solitary Confinement in America's Early State Prisons

Wherever solitary confinement has been tried, it has produced the most powerful consequences. In the state prison of Philadelphia, offenders of the most hardened and obdurate description – men who entered the cells assigned them with every oath and imprecation that the fertility of the English language affords – beings who scoffed at every idea of repentance and humility – have in a few weeks, been reduced by solitary confinement and low diet to a state of the deepest penitence. This may be set down as a general result of this kind of punishment in that prison.

Society for the Prevention of Pauperism in the City of New York (1822), *Report on the Penitentiary System of the United States*[1]

AUBURN'S FATAL EXPERIMENT

On Christmas Day 1821, New York's bold experiment with solitary confinement began.[2] Prison administrators at Auburn State Prison sent eighty of their "oldest and most heinous offenders" to the new, mostly complete solitary cellblock. There, prisoners would remain alone, sleeping and eating in cells nearly four feet wide, with no work, communication, or other distractions except a Bible; they were further prohibited "from laying

[1] Society for the Prevention of Pauperism in the City of New York (SPPNY), *Report on the Penitentiary System in the United States*. New York: Manlon Day, 1822, pp. 51–52.
[2] Orlando F. Lewis, *The Development of American Prisons and Prison Customs, 1776–1845: With Special Reference to Early Institutions in the State of New York*. Albany: Prison Association of New York, 1922, p. 81.

5

down in the day time."[3] The first experiment with long-term solitary confinement would be severe and extreme.

Its results were disastrous. The solitary cells were too narrow to allow prisoners sufficient exercise, causing muscle atrophy and disease;[4] insanity and suicide were also common. Auburn's agent, Gershom Powers, reported, "one [prisoner] was so desperate that he sprang from his cell, when the door was opened, and threw himself from the gallery upon the pavement.... Another beat and mangled his head against the walls of his cell until he destroyed one of his eyes."[5] The surviving prisoners – whose "health and constitutions ... had become alarmingly impaired" – received pardons, and the experiment was officially concluded in 1823.[6] Adding insult to these injuries, the experience had apparently not deterred the prisoners: twelve were reconvicted within several years and one other man "committed a burglary ... the very first night after being released from a long confinement."[7]

* * *

Failures like this one with solitary confinement had a significant impact on the development of the modern prison – especially Eastern State Penitentiary, still under construction during Auburn's fatal experiment. America's early prisons – first the proto-prisons built after the American Revolution and then the modern prisons built in the 1820s and later – failed repeatedly and dramatically. These failures, and the debates they precipitated, gave modern prisons a perennial air of uncertainty. Would they solve the problems endemic to the proto-prisons – and serve the prison's original purpose? Moreover, news of penal failures like Auburn often had sudden and unpredictable impacts on the penal imagination and what commentators believed to be acceptable design choices for the new prisons. In the resulting atmosphere, deviations from the norm seemed even more risky and penal actors routinely sought assurance that they were on the right path. Thus, it is only by understanding this tumultuous, unstable beginning – when reformers repeatedly experimented with

---

[3] Gershom Powers, *A Brief Account of the Constitution, Management, & Discipline &c. &c. of the New-York State Prison at Auburn.* Auburn, NY: U. F. Doubleday, 1826, p. 32. See also W. David Lewis, *From Newgate to Dannemora: The Rise of the Penitentiary in New York, 1796–1848.* Ithaca: Cornell University Press, 1965.

[4] Harry Elmer Barnes, "The Historical Origin of the Prison System in America," *Journal of the American Institute of Criminal Law and Criminology* 12:1 (1921), pp. 35–60, p. 53.

[5] Powers, *A Brief Account*, p. 36.   [6] Ibid.   [7] Ibid.

variations of prison and failed – that we can begin to understand how Eastern became a deviant prison, and how the Pennsylvania System could become personally institutionalized at Eastern in the decades to follow.

The American Revolution had ushered in a new era of penal reform in the former colonies.[8] New state constitutions included provisions requiring legal reforms that would reduce states' reliance on corporal and capital punishment. In the 1780s, states began writing new penal codes, many of which replaced traditional corporal punishments with calls for incarceration. County or city-run jails (often called prisons), however, were ill-equipped for this influx of prisoners who would spend lengthier periods in confinement. Penal reformers, building on sentiment around the Atlantic world and especially England, focused their attentions on reforming their local jails and experimenting with other punishments like public labor.

In the 1780s and early 1790s, a handful of states – Massachusetts, Connecticut, and Pennsylvania – began authorizing the first-ever state prisons in the United States. These "proto-prisons" were significant for their time: they were the first facilities designed to confine convicted criminals for long-term incarceration as punishment. But they also had much in common with the jails reformers hoped they would replace. The prison at Massachusetts was housed on an island military fort and the

---

[8] There is some contention among penal historians about the significance of the American Revolution. Adam Hirsch argues that the Revolution stalled reform that was underway, while other historians like Michael Meranze and Louis Masur have illustrated how Republican ideology helped propel the shift toward incarceration and the move away from capital punishment. I have also argued that the Revolution provided an opportunity for reform. Rothman, *The Discovery of the Asylum: Social Order and Disorder in the New Republic*. New York: AldineTransaction, 2002 [1971]; Adam J. Hirsch, *The Rise of the Penitentiary: Prisons and Punishment in Early America*. New Haven: Yale University Press, 1992; Michael Meranze, *Laboratories of Virtue: Punishment, Revolution, and Authority in Philadelphia, 1760–1835*. Chapel Hill: University of North Carolina Press, 1996; Louis P. Masur, *Rites of Execution: Capital Punishment and the Transformation of American Culture, 1776–1865*. New York: Oxford University Press, 1989; Ashley T. Rubin, "Penal Change as Penal Layering: A Case Study of Proto-prison Adoption and Capital Punishment Reduction, 1785–1822," *Punishment & Society* 18:4 (2016), pp. 420–441. Ashley T. Rubin, "Early US Prison History beyond Rothman: Revisiting *The Discovery of the Asylum*," *Annual Review of Law and Social Science* 15:1 (2019), pp. 137–154.

prison at Connecticut was built atop a coal mine.[9] Of these early prisons, Philadelphia's Walnut Street Prison was the most advanced.

Walnut Street Prison

Walnut Street's design – perfected through a series of reforms between 1789 and 1794 – promised to solve all of the problems reformers had identified with jails. Jails in colonial America, England, and elsewhere were little more than overcrowded holding tanks for society's refuse – accused criminals awaiting trial, convicted criminals awaiting their (corporal or capital) punishment, witnesses held over for trial, vagrants, debtors, and sometimes their families as well. They were all housed together in large rooms with little to do except socialize, drink, sleep, or prey on each other.[10] Of particular concern to reformers was the way in which seasoned criminals could tell impressionable youngsters of their exploits and thereby recruit new members into the criminal underworld. Another concern, however, was the jailer or "keeper" himself, who made his living off the room and board (and bribe) payments from the jailed. A keeper had few responsibilities and even less oversight, often enabling violence, disease, and other poor conditions to develop.

These poor conditions did not go unnoticed, especially in Philadelphia – the nation's one-time political, if not cultural, capital. The Philadelphia Society for Alleviating the Miseries of Public Prisons (PSAMPP) was formed in 1787 by "thirty-seven leading citizens of Philadelphia."[11] Driven by "benevolence," "humanity," "compassion," and "Christianity," they sought to end prisoners' suffering "the miseries which penury, hunger, cold, unnecessary severity, unwholesome apartments, and guilt (the usual attendants of prisons) involve." They would also pursue "such degrees and modes of punishment ... as may,

---

[9] For more, see Hirsch, *The Rise of the Penitentiary*; Ashley T. Rubin, "The Prehistory of Innovation: A Longer View of Penal Change," *Punishment & Society* 20:2 (2018), pp. 192–216.

[10] John Langbein, "The Criminal Trial Before Lawyers," *The University of Chicago Law Review* 45:2 (1978), pp. 263–316; Adam J. Hirsch, "From Pillory to Penitentiary: The Rise of Criminal Incarceration in Early Massachusetts," *Michigan Law Review* 80:6 (1982), pp. 1179–1269; Hirsch, *The Rise of the Penitentiary*; Rothman, *The Discovery of the Asylum*, Michael Ignatieff, *A Just Measure of Pain: The Penitentiary in the Industrial Revolution, 1750–1850*. New York: Pantheon Books; Rubin, "The Prehistory of Innovation."

[11] Negley K. Teeters, "The Pennsylvania Prison Society. A Century and a Half of Penal Reform." *Journal of Criminal Law and Criminology* 28:3 (1937), pp. 374–379, p. 374.

instead of continuing habits of vice, become the means of restoring our fellow creatures to virtue and happiness."[12] Membership grew quickly and added such notables as Founding Father Benjamin Franklin.[13] The members paid an annual subscription – varying at different times from ten shillings to one dollar – to support the society (e.g., publishing its pamphlets, providing necessities to prisoners), supplemented with larger donations.[14]

As charged, PSAMPP members visited their local jails to provide aid and comfort to the prisoners. They also policed prisoners' treatment at the hands of the keeper and actively agitated for reform. Following a series of "memorials" sent to the legislature,[15] PSAMPP secured a series of statutes designed to reform Walnut Street Jail into a new vision of punishment.[16] These laws helped to gradually transform Walnut Street from a typical colonial jail into a model state prison. First, the keeper became an employee of the state, answerable to local authorities and salaried – no longer permitted to accept bribes or sell alcohol to the prisoners. Additionally, a group of local elites – many of whom were PSAMPP members – were appointed as a Board of Inspectors to supervise the keeper and ensure the laws were obeyed. Second, prisoners would become increasingly separated from each other, first by gender and then by the reason for their confinement: importantly, convicted criminals would be held separately from other types of prisoners, including debtors and

---

[12] Ibid., p. 374 (PSAMPP Constitution Preamble).
[13] Peter P. Jonitis and Elizabeth W. Jonitis, *Members of the Prison Society: Biographical Vignettes, 1776–1830, of the Managers of the Philadelphia Society for Assisting Distressed Prisoners and the Members of the Philadelphia Society for Alleviating the Miseries of Public Prisons 1787–1830.* Haverford College Library, Collection No. 975 A. ND.
[14] Roberts Vaux, *Notices of the Original, and Successive Efforts to Improve the Discipline of the Prison at Philadelphia and to Reform the Criminal Code of Pennsylvania.* Philadelphia: Kimber and Sharpless, 1826.
[15] Ibid., p. 23 (Memorial of January 29, 1788); Ibid., pp. 26–30 (Memorial of December 15, 1788).
[16] Pennsylvania, "An Act to amend an Act entitled 'An Act for Amending the Penal Laws of this State'," in *The Statutes at Large of Pennsylvania, 1682 to 1801, Vol. XIII 1787–1790.* Harrisburg: Harrisburg Publishing Co., 1908 [1789], pp. 243–251; Pennsylvania, "An Act to Reform the Penal Laws of the State," in *The Statutes at Large of Pennsylvania, 1682 to 1801, Vol. XIII 1787–1790.* Harrisburg: Harrisburg Publishing Co., 1908 [1790], pp. 511–528; Pennsylvania, "An Act for the Better Preventing of Crime, and for Abolishing the Punishment of Death in Certain Cases," in *The Statutes at Large of Pennsylvania, 1682 to 1801, Vol. XV 1794–1797*, ed. James T. Mitchell and Henry Flanders, Commissioners. Harrisburg: C. E. Aughinbaugh, 1911 [1794], pp. 174–181.

those awaiting their trial. Third, prisoners were given labor assignments intended both to reform them – and their perceived lazy tendencies – or train them to enter the workforce. Importantly, their labor was also expected to offset the costs of the prison – including the keepers' salary. Fourth, the prisoner population was expanded and the prison's penal character extended. In 1790 and 1794, Walnut Street was opened up as a receptacle for the state's population of convicted criminals sentenced to one year or more. These laws also changed the penalties in the penal code, slowly shifting the punishment for serious offenses – except first-degree murder – from death to long-term incarceration. Finally, for offenses previously deemed capital, these laws gradually introduced solitary confinement for at least some portion of an offender's prison sentence as a punishment.[17]

By 1794, Walnut Street Prison was the most advanced state prison in the country – a reputation its Board of Inspectors and other PSAMPP members made sure to advertise. According to Walnut Street Inspector and PSAMPP member Caleb Lownes, writing in 1793, Walnut Street had accomplished the impossible. The previously overcrowded, disease-ridden, violent, and disorderly jail was now a clean, orderly facility with virtually no disease. Prisoners labored productively and profitably, offsetting the prison's expenses. Moreover, he saw other proofs of the prison's deterrent and rehabilitative effects, most especially in the fact that crime rates had decreased substantially.[18]

With this initial report from Lownes, reformers, statesmen, and other interested parties toured Walnut Street to see for themselves. These

---

[17] For a more detailed history of these changes, see Thorsten Sellin, "Philadelphia Prisons of the Eighteenth Century," *Transactions of the American Philosophical Society* 43:1 (1953), pp. 326–331; Paul Takagi, "The Walnut Street Jail: A Penal Reform To Centralize the Powers of the State," *Federal Probation* 39 (1975), pp. 18–26; Thomas Dumm, *Democracy and Punishment: Disciplinary Origins of the United States.* Madison: University of Wisconsin Press, 1987; Teeters, "The Pennsylvania Prison Society," Negley K. Teeters, *The Cradle of the Penitentiary: The Walnut Street Jail at Philadelphia, 1773–1835.* Philadelphia: Temple University Press, 1955. The best critical overview remains Meranze, *Laboratories of Virtue.* For a more recent synthetic account, see Jen Manion, *Liberty's Prisoners: Carceral Culture in Early America.* Philadelphia: University of Pennsylvania Press, 2015. See also Ashley T. Rubin, "Innovation and Diffusion: Theorizing Penal Change before and after the Ideal Type." *Unpublished manuscript* (ND); Rubin, "The Prehistory of Innovation."

[18] Caleb Lownes, *An Account of the Alteration and Present State of the Penal Laws of Pennsylvania, Containing Also, an Account of the Gaol and Penitentiary House of Philadelphia – and the Interior Management Thereof.* Boston: Young & Minns, 1799 [1793].

visitors – including French social reformer François Alexandre Frédéric, Duc de la Rochefoucauld-Liancourt (in exile from the French Revolution), and Robert J. Turnbull, a politician and reformer from South Carolina – became proselytizers spreading word of Walnut Street's potential and initial success.[19] Soon, Walnut Street became the template for all other proto-prisons built in the United States. Between 1796 and 1822, a total of seventeen (out of twenty-four) states authorized their own proto-prisons. Many of these prisons were near-replicas of Walnut Street, borrowing everything from its architecture to its rules. From all appearances, Walnut Street was a total success, not only in achieving its desired goals but also in providing a replicable model that was well received across the country. But U.S. reformers had set their hopes too high on a small amount of evidence indicating the proto-prison's early success. Over time, the template at Walnut Street quickly deteriorated and the limitations of its design became apparent.

Although a conceptually significant innovation, Walnut Street constantly failed to function as intended. As historian Rebecca McLennan explains, "a deep fissure divided the workaday reality of the penitentiary and the abstract theory of penitential penology."[20] Despite the vaunted descriptions of Walnut Street's success, the experiment never fully conformed to the plan. The "unremitted solitude" officials had imagined was never a primary feature of prison management. The prison ultimately had only sixteen solitary cells,[21] while most prisoners remained in large rooms, albeit segregated by sex and criminality. Although partly a failure of architecture and motivation, the rare use of solitary was also the product of judicial sentencing: Only a small fraction of prisoners (4 of 117 in 1795; 7 of 139 in 1796) sent to Walnut Street were sentenced to spend any part of their term in solitary confinement.[22] Ultimately,

---

[19] Francois Alexandre Duc de la Rochefoucauld-Liancourt, *On the Prisons of Philadelphia: By an European*. Philadelphia: Moreau de Saint-Mery, 1796; Robert J. Turnbull, *A Visit to the Philadelphia Prison*. Philadelphia: Printed. London: Reprinted by James Phillips &c Son, 1797.

[20] Rebecca M. McLennan, *The Crisis of Imprisonment: Protest, Politics, and the Making of the American Penal State, 1776–1941*. New York: Cambridge University Press, 2008, p. 49.

[21] Teeters, *The Cradle of the Penitentiary*, p. 19.

[22] Sellin, "Philadelphia Prisons of the Eighteenth Century," p. 329. A later pamphlet explained that the statute had authorized thirty solitary cells, although neither the 1790 nor the 1794 statutes seem to confirm this claim. George Washington Smith, *A View and Description of the Eastern State Penitentiary of Pennsylvania*. Philadelphia: Philadelphia Society for Alleviating the Miseries of Public Prisons and C. G. Childs, 1830, p. 2.

only those criminals who misbehaved while incarcerated were sent to solitary cells and forced to remain silent, alone, without work or other distractions – for a few days – but even that was rare: Solitary was "the last, not the first, resort of discipline." More commonly for rule violators, "Contact with and pressure from prison officers was the immediate response."[23] As historian Michael Meranze explains, "Although solitary confinement had an important role in support of prison authority, it was not the linchpin of the prison order."[24]

New problems emerged in the prison's early history, such that Walnut Street's storied success was soon eroded by circumstance.[25] When Walnut Street was declared a state prison in 1794, overcrowding struck the young prison and its internal order began to fray. In June of 1798, despite efforts at fireproofing, arson destroyed one of the prison's workshops. A few months later, a yellow fever epidemic broke out in Philadelphia, flooding the prison with more charges.[26] Occurring so closely together, these episodes "shattered the internal structure of the prison," according to Meranze.[27] In addition to prisoners' constant disobedience and rule violations, the prison's guards were complicit in aiding or overlooking prisoners' schemes; the number of successful and attempted escapes increased.[28] Meanwhile, rapid population growth in the city and state (and thus more criminal convictions) continued to expand the population inside Walnut Street. Without any alterations to expand the prison's capacity, this population growth quickly yielded too many prisoners for the numbers of cells and precluded any degree of separation. Overcrowding also interfered with the ability to put prisoners to work, particularly after losing workshop space to fire.[29]

By the early 1800s, the public depiction of Walnut Street was already shifting. These chronic problems, which destroyed the prison's early success, generally manifested after the initial glowing reviews by Lownes in 1793, Rochefoucauld-Liancourt in 1796, and Turnbull in 1797. After a decade of innovations celebrated as improvements, old concerns returned.

A pamphlet produced half a century after the Walnut Street experiment had taken place likewise claimed that there were "thirty cells" and "an average of one hundred convicts." PSAMPP, *Sketch of the Principal Transactions of the "Philadelphia Society for Alleviating the Miseries of Public Prisons," from Its Origin to the Present Time.* Philadelphia: Merrihew & Thompson, Printers, 1859, p. 8.

[23] Meranze, *Laboratories of Virtue*, p. 196.   [24] Ibid.
[25] For a full account of Walnut Street's multiple failures, see Meranze, *Laboratories of Virtue.*
[26] Meranze, op. cit., pp. 193, 211.   [27] Ibid., p. 211.   [28] Ibid., pp. 220–223.
[29] Ibid., pp. 220, 223.

According to PSAMPP, now that prisoners were once again "crowded together" (with little order and no regular work), "they are likely to come out intimately acquainted with the arts of villany [sic], and combined with an extensive association of persons of similar character to make depredations on the public."[30]

Predictably, the situation worsened in the 1810s as the country faced continued population growth, war, and economic depressions. As one commentator later explained, "The embargo deprived many reckless persons of employment, and above all, the termination of the war of 1812, 13, 14, and 15, inundated our community with hordes of corrupt, lawless, idle desperadoes."[31] Many citizens interpreted the increase in convictions as a crime wave. Overcrowding in the now-aging, inadequately sized prison was further exacerbated by an increase in convictions following the end of the War of 1812 (see Figure 1.1). A grand jury described "the present very crowded state of the penitentiary" as "an evil of considerable magnitude," noting that "thirty to forty" people were "lodged in rooms of eighteen feet square."[32]

By 1817, commentators circulated descriptions of Walnut Street that could have been written in the 1780s. In that year, PSAMPP reported,

So many are thus crowded together in so small a space, and so much intermixed, the innocent with the guilty, the young offender, and often the disobedient servant or apprentice, with the most experienced and hardened culprit; that the institution already begins to assume, especially as respects untried prisoners, the character of a European prison, and a seminary for every vice, in which the unfortunate being, who commits a first offence, and knows none of the arts of methodised villainy, can scarcely avoid the contamination, which leads to extreme depravity, and with which from the insufficiency of the room to form separate accommodations, he must be associated in his confinement.[33]

As historian Harry Elmer Barnes has noted, "by 1816 the Walnut Street Jail had returned to about the same level of disciplinary and administrative demoralization that had characterized it before 1790."[34]

---

[30] PSAMPP Memorial of 1803/4, cited in Vaux, *Notices*, p. 38.

[31] George W. Smith, *A Defence of the System of Solitary Confinement of Prisoners Adopted by the State of Pennsylvania*. Philadelphia: G. Dorsey, Printer, 1833 [1829], p. 17.

[32] Quoted in PSAMPP, *A Statistical View of the Operation of the Penal Code of Pennsylvania. To Which Is Added a View of the Present State of the Penitentiary and Prison in the City of Philadelphia*. Philadelphia: Philadelphia Society for Alleviating the Miseries of Public Prisons, 1817, p. 5.

[33] Ibid., pp. 5–6.

[34] Harry Elmer Barnes, *The Evolution of Penology in Pennsylvania*. Indianapolis: The Bobbs-Merrill Company, 1968 [1927], p. 154.

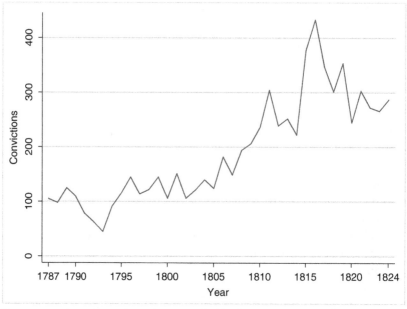

FIGURE I.I Annual number of convicted offenders brought to Walnut Street,
1787–1824

Source: Roberts Vaux, *Notices of the Original, and Successive Efforts to Improve the Discipline of the Prison at Philadelphia and to Reform the Criminal Code of Pennsylvania*. Philadelphia: Kimber and Sharpless, 1826, pp. 65–75

Widespread knowledge of the prison's internal disorder, combined with the apparent crime wave, increased dissatisfaction with the prison. Commentators and private citizens alike feared that the now-disordered prison was *causing* the increase in crime.[35] By late in the decade, the situation at Walnut Street appeared untenable as "four large-scale prison riots broke out again between 1817 and 1821."[36] One of these riots, in 1820, "came dangerously close to resulting in the escape of the entire convict population."[37]

A National Crisis

The country's model prison was not alone in experiencing these problems. Similar governance failures, design flaws, and disorder were common

[35] Meranze, *Laboratories of Virtue*.   [36] McLennan, *The Crisis of Imprisonment*, p. 44.
[37] Barnes, *The Evolution of Penology*, p. 155.

throughout the country, as were the apparent increase in crime and popular fears that the prisons were to blame. As at Walnut Street, a large gap existed between the theory and practice of America's proto-prisons. Although solitary confinement had been adopted widely, its actual use was limited. Maryland's use of solitary confinement mirrored Pennsylvania's: "Because single cells were more expensive to build than congregate cells, only twenty-two existed at the Maryland Penitentiary, not nearly enough to carry out one of the original aims of the penitentiary system...." Like Walnut Street, Maryland's solitary cells were reserved for punishing refractory prisoners.[38] Similarly, at the new Massachusetts State Prison, solitary confinement was only used for the first few days or weeks of a prisoner's sentence; the solitary cellblock itself "was far too small to be put to any more extensive use."[39]

Other gaps between theory and practice proved more scandalous. At Virginia's new proto-prison, "there was virtually no perimeter security ... Once a prisoner got out of his cell, there was nothing further to delay his departure. Another problem was that it was most difficult to prevent outsiders from approaching the building at night and passing contraband through the windows."[40] Georgia's proto-prison "became the object of severe criticism after only one year of operation" because of prisoners' disrespectful and unreformed behavior.[41] As early as 1799, in New York, Newgate Prison's "guards were forced to open fire when fifty or sixty men revolted and seized their keepers ... In 1800, the assistance of the military was necessary to break up a riot."[42] The prison soon became a forum for partisan squabbles and competition over patronage, leading Thomas Eddy (who had first lobbied for and then managed the prison) to resign in disgust in 1804, leaving behind an overcrowded and badly governed prison.[43] One commentator summarized the following years thus: "In 1804, there occurs a destructive fire; in 1805, the prisoners cost more and earned less; in 1806, the propensity to vice is much increased

---

[38] Wallace Shugg, *A Monument to Good Intentions: The Story of the Maryland Penitentiary, 1804–1995*. Baltimore, MD: Maryland Historical Society, 2000, p. 20.

[39] Hirsch, "From Pillory to Penitentiary," p. 1258.

[40] Paul W. Keve, *The History of Corrections in Virginia*. Charlottesville: University Press of Virginia, 1986, p. 26.

[41] James C. Bonner, "The Georgia Penitentiary at Milledgeville 1817–1874," English. *The Georgia Historical Quarterly* 55:3 (1971), pp. 303–328, p. 308.

[42] Lewis, *From Newgate to Dannemora*, p. 33.   [43] Ibid., p. 34.

by indiscriminate confinement, *lessons of infamy* are inculcated, and little reformation is seen."[44]

Indeed, Walnut Street's promoters had set expectations too high regarding not only the prison's perfectly orderly environment, but also its economy. Around the country, in addition to facing problems of disorder and recidivism, penal reformers and prison administrators were disappointed to find that prisoner labor did not repay all the costs of their confinement. The prison at New York "not only failed" to provide the expected profits, but its costs were "too oppressive to be continued" according to an 1817 report.[45] The Massachusetts legislature commissioned a report on the proto-prisons in Connecticut, New York, New Jersey, Pennsylvania, and Maryland, as well as the prisons in their own state. Although the commission still believed the proto-prison was worth its costs, the commission concluded, "It is not to be expected that a penitentiary will support itself." They recommended lengthening prison sentences because, they calculated, the prison would offset its costs if prisoners were retained for at least three years.[46]

By the 1810s, the country's proto-prisons were in crisis, with the oldest facilities suffering most spectacularly. Overcrowding had reached record levels. In New York, "in 1818, the governor was *compelled* to pardon and send out about 280 [prisoners], in order to make room for new comers," and the situation was repeated in 1821. Over the years, "1,200 more" had been "prematurely discharged by pardon for want of room."[47] Finally, "[p]risoners at Newgate staged serious insurrections in 1818, 1819, 1821, and 1822." Similar upheavals were repeated to varying degrees in Massachusetts, Maryland, and Virginia, in addition to those already discussed in Pennsylvania.[48] American states' first sustained experiments with long-term confinement as punishment for convicted offenders, drawing on Pennsylvania's example, had failed – visibly and spectacularly.

---

[44] William Roscoe, *Additional Observations on Penal Jurisprudence, and the Reformation of Criminals*. London: T. Cadell, in the Strand; John, and Arthur Arch, Cornhill, 1823, p. 53.

[45] Cited in William Roscoe, *Observations on Penal Jurisprudence and the Reformation of Criminals; With an Appendix, Containing the Latest Reports of the State Prisons or Penitentiaries of Philadelphia, New York, and Massachusetts, and Other Documents*. London: T. Cadell and W. Davies, 1819, p. 97.

[46] Ibid., appendix, 92, 99–100 (Massachusetts Report in 1817).　　[47] Ibid., p. 56.

[48] McLennan, *The Crisis of Imprisonment*; For an analysis on the importance of these insurrections, as well as later riots, see McLennan, *The Crisis of Imprisonment*.

SOLITARY CONFINEMENT AS THE SOLUTION

In the late 1810s, American penal reform had stalled and its prospects were bleak. Penal reformers and state legislators around the country were searching for new solutions to their inability to reform criminals or generally stop the large-scale riots, fires, mass escapes, general chaos within the facilities, and a perceived crime wave.[49] Some reformers' ideas about punishment had taken on a more punitive tone. A few commentators suggested abandoning the whole prison project.[50] The Massachusetts Senate criticized the attempt to reform criminals through incarceration as "vain and illusory."[51] Frustrated by the proto-prisons' failure, many penal reformers were anxious to institute harsher punishments. Despite a long-term decrease in the number of capital offenses remaining in states' penal codes in this period, some states began to reauthorize capital punishment. The New York legislature made prison arson a capital offense in 1817 after one of the large riots at Newgate Prison.[52] In 1821, Connecticut authorized a new penal code that expanded its range of capital crimes.[53] Corporal punishments also started to make a comeback: in 1819, New York authorized whipping disruptive prisoners.[54] While some commentators advocated a return to capital and corporal punishments, however, other commentators remained committed to the prison. Nowhere was this commitment stronger than in Philadelphia.

Philadelphia's Continued Commitment to Solitary Confinement

At the root of the problem, as many saw it, was that the original plan of the prison had never been implemented. Walnut Street had never conformed to the original plan – solitary confinement was only a marginal component as authorized by the 1790 and 1794 laws and, given the limited number of cells, in practice as well. Constructing new penitentiaries

---

[49] Meranze, *Laboratories of Virtue.*
[50] McLennan, *The Crisis of Imprisonment*, p. 51; Rothman, *The Discovery of the Asylum*, p. 93.
[51] Hirsch, "From Pillory to Penitentiary," p. 1255.
[52] Stuart Banner, *The Death Penalty: An American History.* Cambridge, MA: Harvard University Press, 2002, p. 131.
[53] Connecticut, "An Act concerning Crimes and Punishments," in *Statute Laws of the State of Connecticut, as Revised and Enacted by the General Assembly.* Hartford: S. G. Goodrich, & Huntington & Hopkins, 1821, pp. 151–177; Rubin, "Penal Change as Penal Layering," p. 12.
[54] Roscoe, *Additional Observations on Penal Jurisprudence*, p. 53.

designed to contain all prisoners in solitary confinement, with no distractions from their personal introspection, was simply to be true to the original goals of the reform movement that had begun decades earlier. Moreover, under this design, the problems of the 1800s and 1810s would be prevented: Confined to solitary cells, prisoners could not conspire with one another to embark on mass escapes, or fight, or talk and thereby pollute each other further into criminality or distract themselves from wholesome reflection. Disease would not spread as easily. Order would be restored.

This image of what a prison should look like had been a long-term goal in Pennsylvania. Even before problems at Walnut Street had reached crisis proportions, PSAMPP members were pointing out the gap between the theory of "penitentiary" punishment and the practice at Walnut Street. As early as 1801, PSAMPP was adamant a "fair experiment" of their system had not yet been tried.[55] Their tone contrasted with the early celebratory reports PSAMPP member and Walnut Street Inspector Caleb Lownes had offered nearly a decade earlier.[56] True, they were cautious to avoid criticizing the fruits of their reforms too harshly: Even though the "experiment" was initially "imperfectly made," it nevertheless "has not only increased our internal security, but has been so far approved of as to be adopted in several of our sister states." But the reforms had not gone far enough, they argued. PSAMPP's members wanted to make a "fair experiment of solitude and labour," but "in the present state of the Prison, such an attempt, however desirable, is impracticable."[57] Increasingly, they emphasized that it was the prison's architecture (not the system's impracticality) that was to blame for their mounting woes. The only solution was for the legislature to authorize a new prison. Indeed, by 1803, PSAMPP was ready to abandon the Walnut Street facility in order to build a better, stronger, larger prison that would be more amenable to "solitary confinement at hard labour," as they explained in another memorial in 1803.[58] In response to this memorial, the legislature authorized another, albeit old-style jail to be built on Arch Street in Philadelphia to alleviate the overcrowding at Walnut Street. However, it would be more than a decade before the new facility would open.[59] Consequently, Arch

---

[55] PSAMPP Memorial of December 14, 1801, reprinted in Vaux, *Notices*, p. 37.
[56] See especially Lownes, *An Account.*   [57] Reprinted in Vaux, *Notices.*
[58] PSAMPP Memorial of 1803, reprinted in Vaux, *Notices*, p. 37.
[59] Barnes, *The Evolution of Penology in Pennsylvania*, p. 97.

Street's authorization did not stem the tide of overcrowding, and Walnut Street's conditions deteriorated.

By the late 1810s – in the midst of the "crime wave," riots, and record overcrowding at Walnut Street – PSAMPP reformers and Walnut Street's inspectors were even more convinced that overcrowding lay at the heart of their prison's failures. Their "penitentiary system" was flawless – it was their inability to implement it that prevented their prison from flourishing. In 1818, PSAMPP responded to an inquiry from the British Parliament and the London Society for the Improvement of Prison Discipline about the efficacy of their system. Mortified by the growing level of chaos at Walnut Street, PSAMPP President William White explained, "the penitentiary system ... has not, from divers causes, been so effectually carried into operation as to produce all the results which reason and benevolence had fondly anticipated." He went on to clarify that failure was not the fault of "the system itself, but to the difficulties which have occurred in reducing it to practice," especially "the impractability of confining the convicts to solitary labour."[60]

As the conditions at Walnut Street deteriorated, the reformers' perennially hoped-for solution – a larger prison (to prevent problems of overcrowding) and faithfulness to the original design with its emphasis on solitary confinement (for the reformation of prisoners as well as their control) – had become an urgent necessity. In 1817, the new Arch Street Prison opened, fourteen years after authorization. Unfortunately for Walnut Street's supporters, Arch Street only absorbed the city's debtors, thus having little impact on Walnut Street's overcrowding.[61] In 1818, cognizant that their long-desired solution had failed, Walnut Street's inspectors sent a memorial to the legislature asking them to build yet another prison because Walnut Street "at times is so crowded to a degree alarming to the health of the prisoners, and the space occupied to be altogether insufficient to class them according to their merits, and to admit solitary confinement."[62]

A grand jury echoed these sentiments in December 1818. They began respectfully, with Walnut Street's inspectors in mind, noting "the greatest order and decorum" at Walnut Street, despite its well-known poor conditions and disorder. They continued, the "institution reflects the highest

---

[60] Cited in Vaux, *Notices*, p. 42.
[61] The ultimately disappointing Arch Street Prison would close in 1823 (Barnes, *The Evolution of Penology*, p. 97).
[62] Ibid., p. 156.

honour on the *inspectors*, and the keepers of the prison." With these necessary accolades out of the way, the grand jury placed the blame for the prison's shortcomings on its insufficient physical plant. The grand jury called for the construction of "a place more extensive, and more remote from the populous part of the city ... constructed on a more enlarged plan, better proportioned to the growing population" in the state.[63]

While a better, stronger, larger prison was apparently necessary, the prospect of a single state prison for a state as large as Pennsylvania seemed inefficient and dangerous. Western counties had long complained about the expense of sending their prisoners to Walnut Street.[64] PSAMPP had also grown critical of the practice of concentrating prisoners from all over the state in one prison: as the reformers explained it, once released into the city, friendless and with few resources to make the expensive journey home, former prisoners predictably turned to crime, disproportionately preying on Philadelphians' homes and businesses, rather than those in the criminals' hometowns.[65] In its 1818 memorial, PSAMPP requested the legislature to build not one prison, but several "penitentiaries in suitable parts of the state."[66] By suitable parts, they meant another prison in Philadelphia and one in the western half of the state, although there was also talk of building a prison in the middle of the state.[67] Larger, sturdier prisons, designed to uphold the penitentiary's original principles faithfully, and in more convenient locations, was the answer to their problems.

Shortly after receiving these new requests for action – in the midst of repeated riots at Walnut Street – the state legislature finally complied. In 1818, the legislature authorized funds and a five-man commission to build a "State Penitentiary" in Allegheny (near Pittsburgh). The new penitentiary, later called Western State Penitentiary, would follow "the principle of solitary confinement of convicts," or more specifically "on the plan exhibited to the legislature by the [Walnut Street] inspectors."[68]

---

[63] Reproduced in Roscoe, *Observations on Penal Jurisprudence*, appendix, p. 143. This formulaic approach was not atypical. For similar grand jury investigations in Canada, see Peter Oliver, *"Terror to Evil-Doers": Prisons and Punishments in Nineteenth-Century Ontario*. University of Toronto Press, 1998.

[64] e.g., Eugene E. Doll, "Trial and Error at Allegheny: The Western State Penitentiary, 1818–1838," *The Pennsylvania Magazine of History and Biography* 81:1 (1957), pp. 3–27, p. 5.

[65] Vaux, *Notices*, pp. 42–43 (PSAMPP 1818 response to British Inquiry).

[66] Ibid., 41 (PSAMPP Memorial of 1818).

[67] Ibid., p. 55.

[68] Pennsylvania, "No. 74: An Act to provide for the erection of a State Penitentiary on the public land adjoining the town of Allegheny opposite Pittsburg, in the county of

The earlier requests for the construction of a second new prison – specifically, one in Philadelphia to replace Walnut Street – were answered more slowly. The 1818 law that authorized Western also authorized Walnut Street's inspectors to sell the prison and disperse its prisoners to another prison facility in Philadelphia on Mulberry Street until a new "penitentiary" could be built in Philadelphia that would also follow the principle of solitary confinement.[69] However, nothing came of this effort for several years.

The Initial Authorization

In the winter of 1820–1821, growing frustrated with the lack of progress, several commentators renewed their calls to construct another state prison in Philadelphia with great effect. In December 1820, Governor William Findley included a reminder in his Annual Message to the legislature that "part of the law has not been carried into effect," and suggested the legislature proceed with authorizing a state prison in Philadelphia.[70] In response to the governor's message, the Senate formed a committee.

When that committee reported on January 27, 1821, they echoed the governor's sentiments and recommended that the legislature authorize appropriations to construct a state prison in Philadelphia. The committee explained, "these measures are absolutely necessary, to be adopted, *during the present session of the legislature.*"[71] After briefly recounting the history of Pennsylvania's penal reform efforts – which illustrated, they argued, the legislature's preference for "temporary expedients" over long-term planning[72] – the committee noted the inadequacy of the current facility on Arch Street, the most recent attempt at reducing Walnut Street's overcrowding. Western State Penitentiary, moreover, would not be a sufficient solution because sending prisoners from Eastern Pennsylvania to the Western Penitentiary once it opened would be too expensive: "in

Allegheny, and for other purposes," in *Acts of the General Assembly of the Commonwealth of Pennsylvania*. Harrisburg: C. Gleim, 1818, pp. 138–140, pp. 138, 139.

[69] Ibid., pp. 139–140.

[70] William Findley, "Annual Message to the Assembly–1820," in *Pennsylvania Archives. Fourth Series. Papers of the Governors, Vol. V. 1817–1832*, ed. George Edward Reed. Harrisburg: Wm. Stanley Ray, 1901 [1820], pp. 224–233, pp. 227–228.

[71] Pennsylvania, *Journal of the Senate of the Commonwealth of Pennsylvania*. Harrisburg: William F. Buyers, 1821, p. 331.

[72] Ibid., p. 333.

some cases" it might cost the same amount as "the whole expense of supporting a convict for two or three years" in prison.[73] This expense led them to argue that a prison must be built in Philadelphia, and soon. Walnut Street's "actual condition … is such a nature, as to demand the immediate attention of the legislature, and to excite the regret of all who are actuated by a regard for the temporal as well as eternal welfare of those who are immured within its walls." The committee punctuated this point by describing the "insurrection" in early 1820,

> which threatened the destruction of the lives of the jailors and the escape of all who were confined, and was only quelled by the efforts of a large body of armed citizens, who assembled at the ringing of the alarm bell, after the discharge of a number of muskets, by which one man was killed, and several were wounded.[74]

Their "once celebrated penitentiary" now offered a "distressing portrait."[75]

To buoy their case, the committee included a letter, dated January 8, submitted by the inspectors of the Walnut Street Prison. Walnut Street's inspectors did not mince their words: their prison "was intended to be a school of reformation, but it is now a school of vice."[76] Overcrowding, they wrote, had made separation impossible; now, "the petty thief becomes the pupil of the highway robber; the beardless boy listens with delight to the well-told tale of daring exploits and hair-breadth escapes of hoary headed villainy, and from the experience of age derives instruction which fits him to be a pest and terror to society."[77] Walnut Street, they reminded the legislature, was once well-regarded: "Pennsylvania obtained a name among her sister states as well as in Europe for her mild penal code and her well regulated Penitentiary. But this fame was short lived."[78] They bemoaned an increase in crime – and a worse "character" of prisoners – combined with the growing use of mechanization in the local economy that frustrated their ability to continue prisoner labor at cost. But, ultimately, it was the lack of solitary confinement they most despised. "The great penitentiary system of Pennsylvania is not now in operation, and cannot be, without the erection of a new prison in this part of the state."[79] Solitary confinement promised to be the solution to all their problems.[80] They closed by requesting a new penitentiary with

[73] Ibid., pp. 333–334.　[74] Ibid., p. 334.　[75] Ibid., p. 334.　[76] Ibid., p. 334.
[77] Ibid., p. 335.　[78] Ibid., p. 336.　[79] Ibid., p. 336.　[80] Ibid., pp. 336–337.

the capacity to hold "two hundred and fifty prisoners on the principle of solitary confinement" built in Philadelphia.[81]

The legislative committee went on to describe how the state should replace its current system, "now fully proved to be inadequate to the end proposed."[82] Specifically, they argued, the state should replace "imprisonment at *hard labour*" with "*solitary confinement*," or "an entire seclusion of convicts from society and from one another." As the committee imagined it, "no one shall see or hear, or be seen or heard by any human being except the jailor, the inspectors, or such other persons, as for highly urgent reasons may be permitted to enter the walls of the prison." One of the "most beneficial effects" of this new punishment would be that prisoners could reenter society unimpeded – they will be free from mutual recognition because they "will never be able after their discharge to recognize each other"; they will be free from stigma because no one will "have witnessed their degradation."[83] The new punishment would make gubernatorial pardons less necessary and bring certainty back to the law.[84] The punishment would be more efficient, moreover, because it would require less time and expense: "*one* year of solitary confinement will be more efficacious than *three* years at labor in the society of others." They also noted that the inspectors would "serve without any compensation, as those of Philadelphia do," referring to the voluntary capacity of Walnut Street's inspectors. They concluded, "[regarding] the *economy* of this measure, there can be no diversity of opinion."[85]

Importantly, the committee emphasized that solitary confinement would be a replacement of the old system, which relied on prisoner labor. Contradicting the glowing reports of Walnut Street in the 1790s, the committee explained, "The revenue derived from the labor of convicts has never, even during the most prosperous times, been adequate to their support."[86] Moreover, labor "diminishes in a very great degree the tediousness of confinement."[87] Instead, they suggested that labor should be "abandoned altogether" and employed only "as an *indulgence* to penitent convicts, and as a relaxation from the *much more painful task of being compelled to be idle*."[88] The new system, then, was to privilege solitary confinement above all else.

---

[81] Ibid., 337. They also referenced, but did not quote, pamphlets forwarded by Dr. James Mease to support their claims (Ibid., p. 338).

[82] Ibid., p. 338.   [83] Ibid., p. 339.   [84] Ibid., p. 340.   [85] Ibid., p. 339.

[86] Ibid., p. 339.   [87] Ibid., pp. 339–340.   [88] Ibid., p. 340.

In the end, the committee's report was tabled, although copies of the report were ordered to be printed,[89] and the Senate moved on to other business. Over the next two months, progress moved slowly. Senator Condy Raguet, one of the committee members, twice introduced bills to effect the requested changes, but with little success.[90] After still no progress had been made, PSAMPP sent another memorial to the legislature. They praised the efforts to construct the Pittsburgh penitentiary, but requested "the establishment of a similar one in the eastern part of the state ... in which the benefits of solitude and hard labour may be fairly and effectively proved."[91] Their "petition" was "read and laid on the table" on February 5, 1821.[92] On February 10, 1821, the Senate as a whole reviewed Raguet's earlier proposed bill to create a new state penitentiary in Philadelphia.[93] Several weeks later (February 28), Raguet introduced a resolution to determine "the number of convicts and the expense of their transportation to the penitentiary of Philadelphia for the last ten years."[94] Once a report fulfilling this resolution was presented on March 6, the Senate, and then the House, moved relatively quickly discussing, amending, and passing a bill to erect a state penitentiary in Philadelphia. By March 20, the bill was submitted to the governor for his signature, and it was signed the same day.[95]

The law authorized a group of eleven men, primarily PSAMPP members and inspectors from Walnut Street,[96] to select a site and supervise the construction of a "state penitentiary capable of holding two hundred and fifty prisoners, on the principle of solitary confinement of the convicts ... for the eastern district" of the state.[97] The commission ultimately

[89] Ibid., p. 340.   [90] Ibid., pp. 370, 379.   [91] Cited in Vaux, *Notices*, pp. 43–45.

[92] Pennsylvania, *Journal of the Senate*, p. 384.

[93] Ibid., p. 423. Moved by PSAMPP's latest memorial, the legislature also appointed PSAMPP's Vice President, Dr. William Rogers, and member Samuel R. Wood, as a committee to provide more information (Vaux, *Notices*, p. 46). However, this is not mentioned in the *Journal*. Thomas Bradford, a PSAMPP member and WSJ inspector, is also said to have "drafted the penitentiary bill, which was passed with only 'a slight amendment.' " Doll, "Trial and Error at Allegheny," p. 6. See also PSAMPP, Committee for Eastern, *Minute Books. Vol. 1–3*; Pennsylvania Prison Society Records (Collection 1946), Series I, Vol. 27–29. Historical Society of Pennsylvania, and Teeters, *The Cradle of the Penitentiary*, pp. 110–111.

[94] Pennsylvania, *Journal of the Senate*, p. 525.   [95] Ibid., pp. 655, 675.

[96] Barnes, *The Evolution of Penology*, p. 100; Richard Vaux, *Brief Sketch of the Origin and History of the State Penitentiary for the Eastern District of Pennsylvania at Philadelphia*. Philadelphia: McLaughlin Brothers, Printers, 1872, p. 56.

[97] Pennsylvania, "No. 64: An Act to Provide for the Creation of a State Penitentiary within the City and County of Philadelphia," in *Acts of the General Assembly of the Commonwealth of Pennsylvania*. Harrisburg: C. Gleim, 1821, pp. 94–97, p. 94.

consisted of Roberts Vaux, Coleman Sellers, Peter Mierecken, John Bacon, George A. Baker, Samuel R. Wood, Daniel H. Miller, James Thackera, Caleb Carmault, Thomas Sparks, and Thomas Bradford, Jr.[98] In something of a geographic reversal of power, the legislature ordered that the new penitentiary should copy Western's design, "subject to such alterations and improvements as the commissioners or a majority of them ... with the approbation of the Governor, approve and direct. *Provided always*, That the principle of the solitary confinement of the prisoners be preserved and maintained."[99] Planning for the prison and its construction proceeded soon thereafter. Even so, it would be a full eight years before Eastern, still incomplete, received its first prisoner.

Solitary's Widespread Appeal

The sentiment in Pennsylvania between 1817 and 1821 – favoring solitary confinement within better, stronger, larger prisons – was paralleled elsewhere. Despite some opposition, most commentators believed, like the Philadelphia reformers, the prison was a wonderful development that had done much good, but it had failed to achieve its objectives thus far. The leading problem, again echoing Philadelphians, was that proto-prisons – those first iterations of prison – had not adhered to the original plan, largely because of overcrowding. The superintendent of Virginia's prison noted a significant decline in capital crimes between 1800 (when the prison opened) and 1815, which he (like many others) attributed to "the certainty of punishment, because of its mildness." Even so, he noted, "The penitentiary system has measurably failed to answer the ends of its institution" for many of the reasons enumerated by others, including that "too many are lodged in a room – the confinement not sufficiently solitary."[100] As in Pennsylvania, the perceived solution was not to jettison the prison but to improve it.[101] A British jurist and reformer, William Roscoe, surveying American opinions, concluded

that although a general sentiment prevails in the different states of America, that the penitentiaries have not fully answered the intended purpose, or fulfilled the expectations of their promoters, yet that the causes of their failure are so evident, and so capable of being removed, that the expediency of supporting them is almost unanimously recommended and insisted on.[102]

---

[98] Vaux, *Brief Sketch*, pp. 53–55.
[99] Pennsylvania, "An Act to Provide for the Creation of a State Penitentiary," p. 95.
[100] Cited in SPPNY, *Report on the Penitentiary System*, appendix, p. 70.
[101] Ibid., appendix, p. 71.
[102] Roscoe, *Additional Observations on Penal Jurisprudence*, p. 106.

It was overcrowding, he found, that was "the chief, if not the sole and entire occasion, of all the inconveniences and disappointments complained of, and that almost *all other disadvantages are resolvable into this cause.*"[103] Somewhat mistakenly, Roscoe noted that PSAMPP alone had explicitly recognized overcrowding as the root cause. He argued that the general failure to realize the easy solution at hand (reduce overcrowding) was leading many states "to resort to measures of so severe and repulsive a nature as cannot fail to terrify the most hardened offender from the perpetration of crimes," including solitary confinement.[104]

Although Roscoe was somewhat mistaken on the contours of American sentiment, he was correct that solitary confinement had gained widespread appeal by the early 1820s. Around the country, penal reformers had come to the conclusion that solitary confinement – not just alleviating overcrowding, but forbidding crowding of any kind – would solve their many problems. For some commentators, solitary confinement would restore the deterrent power that prison had lost. A Massachusetts legislative committee reported in early 1818 "that it is become necessary to render the state prison, in future, a place of terror and punishment" and called for "a more strict and severe system of discipline."[105] A follow-up report called for punishing all crimes with solitary confinement and hard labor, but in local jails to save money.[106]

Indeed, the vision emerging from some commentators was quite punitive, with solitary confinement representing a uniquely effective punishment. One commentator from Maryland recommended a detailed plan for a stratified system. For petty larcenists, and the like, he recommended "rebuild[ing] the whipping post and the pillory." For the "incorrigible offenders, for whose reformation there is no hope," he recommended a continuation of the present system, what he called a "perpetual workhouse," where they would stay for the duration of their lives.[107] But for a middle class of criminals – those "violators of public trust, housebreakers, cheats, swindlers, counterfeiters, horse-thieves, &c." who "have some regard to character, and are susceptible to punishment by disgrace," the penitentiary was the answer, but

a penitentiary in the true sense of the word; not a workshop, but a real penitentiary. In it the cheerful sound of the hammer of industry should never be heard.

---

[103] Ibid., p. 106.   [104] Ibid., p. 107.   [105] Ibid., appendix, pp. 61, 63.
[106] Ibid., appendix, pp. 59, 64.
[107] Cited in SPPNY, *Report on the Penitentiary System*, appendix, pp. 48–49.

The tenants of it should remain in perfect idleness and solitude. They should see no human being but their keeper; unless indeed it might be well occasionally to expose them to public view for the purpose of humiliation. They should be clothed in the garments of humiliation and disgrace. They should wear chains, not only for their safety, but as a badge of their character. It would be well to keep them in darkness as much as possible....[108]

There would be some limitations on this draconian punishment. He continued,

I am told a man cannot endure total darkness more than about twenty days at a time before he becomes deranged, &c. Confinement in this penitentiary should never be long enough to destroy those habits which are necessary to enable a man to procure a livelihood by his own industry; nor long enough for him to acquire other habits incompatible with his freedom and voluntary industry. I would therefore never have a person confined in this penitentiary more than six months, and in most cases not so long.[109]

Pennsylvania was thus not alone in imagining in solitary confinement an adequate punishment, nor was its vision the most extreme. But around the country, Pennsylvania was viewed as the exemplar for reform.

In 1820, the Society for the Prevention of Pauperism in the City of New York (SPPNY), investigating methods for penal reform and solitary confinement in particular, wrote to PSAMPP for advice. Roberts Vaux, one of PSAMPP's more active members and member of the commission to build Eastern, responded by supporting New York's inclination to institute strict solitary confinement. Although Vaux endorsed labor as an important part of the "Penitentiary System of the United States," he believed solitary confinement was the crucial component. Conveniently forgetting that solitary confinement was only a small part of Walnut Street's practice, Vaux concluded his brief letter, "solitary confinement appears to be the only rational, and efficient mode of punishment – its beneficial influence was strikingly illustrated in the prison of this city, some years ago."[110] When the SPPNY published their report reviewing the penitentiary system throughout the country in 1822, they concluded that a "radical and fundamental" change was needed: "They are fully persuaded that nothing less than solitary confinement will ever enable us to give [the penitentiary system] a fair and full trial in the United States."[111]

---

[108] Ibid., appendix, p. 48.   [109] Ibid.   [110] Ibid., appendix, pp. 22, 23.
[111] Ibid., p. 51.

Indeed, by this time, the early years at Walnut Street – and its use of solitary confinement – had taken on mythic status. Nearly every report circulated mentioned the well-known statistics that only one convict had returned within the first year and four within a few years – and solitary confinement was deemed the main reason for this success.[112] The SPPNY noted,

Wherever solitary confinement has been tried, it has produced the most powerful consequences. In the state prison of Philadelphia, offenders of the most hardened and obdurate description – men who entered the cells assigned them with every oath and imprecation that the fertility of the English language affords – beings who scoffed at every idea of repentance and humility – have in a few weeks, been reduced by solitary confinement and low diet to a state of the deepest penitence. This may be set down as a general result of this kind of punishment in that prison.[113]

The report concluded "[t]hat solitary confinement by night and day, combined with other regulations suggested in this report, will remedy all existing evils."[114]

More and more reformers were echoing and extending the sentiments found in Pennsylvania by supporting the use of continuous solitary confinement without labor. Ultimately, the SPPNY endorsed a system of solitary confinement with labor as the modal approach for average criminals, while the most hardened offenders would be so confined without labor, which could be provided as a reward if the prisoner earned it.[115] In fact, this was the direction New York had already enacted, albeit quietly, at its new Auburn State Prison.

THE FAILURE OF EARLY EXPERIMENTS WITH SOLITARY CONFINEMENT

Driven by the failure of Newgate, its proto-prison located in New York City, the New York legislature had authorized a new prison in the upstate town of Auburn in 1816. As Newgate erupted near the end of the decade, however, reformers and the legislature sought additional modifications that would enhance control and prevent similar disruptions at their new facility. In 1819, anxious that the new Auburn State Prison – which had recently started receiving prisoners – would suffer upheavals similar to

---

[112] e.g., Roscoe, *Observations on Penal Jurisprudence*, p. 89.
[113] SPPNY, *Report on the Penitentiary System*, pp. 51–52.   [114] Ibid., p. 96.
[115] Ibid., p. 52.

those at Newgate, the New York legislature authorized the prison's agent (a kind of contractor in charge rather than a state-employed warden) to construct a cellblock for solitary cells. Further strengthening New Yorkers' resolve, prisoners set fire to the new cellblock, which was "pretty much destroyed" in the conflagration and the block had to be rebuilt.[116] By 1821, the legislature "had become so dissatisfied and discouraged with the existing mode and effects of penitentiary punishments."[117] They were apparently convinced that a "severer system" was necessary or else they must restore "the old sanguinary criminal code."[118] To this end, the legislature authorized a new, hybrid system of prison discipline at Auburn.[119] All prisoners would be kept in solitary cells at night, as soon as there was sufficient capacity.[120] Some prisoners would be kept in solitary cells around the clock.[121] With this system, Auburn would become the first prison to rely on long-term solitary confinement for some portion of its prisoner population.

As we have seen, the New York experiment proved dangerous almost immediately. Even after the first signs of problems, however, Auburn's administrators did not give up on their experiment. As Auburn's agent later reflected, "For a considerable time, we had the most entire confidence in the success of this experiment."[122] An early report from Auburn's inspectors – echoing the optimism of Walnut Street's inspectors in the early 1790s – noted that the prisoners in solitary "are yet as healthy as the laboring class" and that "experience thus far fully confirms" the utility of solitary confinement.[123] Their report the following year again confirmed their confidence in the system.[124] Indeed, a separate report presented by a Select Committee to the New York Senate in 1822 called for extending the use and severity of solitary confinement at Auburn and elsewhere, diminishing the use of the pardon power, the complete removal of labor from Auburn, and a firm prohibition on visitors to Auburn. In place of labor, the report argued, the state should institute "severe but short confinement in cells, with solitude, silence, darkness, and stinted food of coarse quality."[125] The legislative committee prefaced

---

[116] Powers, *A Brief Account*, p. 30.   [117] Ibid., p. 32.   [118] Ibid., p. 32.
[119] New York, "An Act Concerning State Prisons, Passed April 2, 1821," in *Laws of the State of New-York*. Albany: Cantine and Leake, 1821, pp. 215–218.
[120] Ibid., p. 217.   [121] Ibid., p. 216.   [122] Powers, *A Brief Account*, p. 32.
[123] Ibid., p. 33.   [124] Ibid., pp. 34–35.
[125] Report laid before the New York Senate, cited in Roscoe, *Additional Observations on Penal Jurisprudence*, p. 41.

their recommendations by explaining that, for punishment to deter, "there must be *suffering ... such suffering* as will excite feelings of terror."[126] As we have seen, the SPPNY made similar recommendations the following year.[127] As far as most penal reformers knew, the experiment was going well.

In 1823, however, the prison came under local scrutiny. The prison's staff physician reported a sufficiently high number of deaths, particularly among the solitary prisoners, and other physical problems like difficulty breathing and chest pains. The physician located these problems in the "sedentary life" which brings on "melancholy, grief, &c.," while "confinement" generally "operates upon the existing germ of diseases, and hastens the progress of all those that must have otherwise terminated in death."[128] Following another report from the inspectors, the Governor "visited the prison, personally, examined the solitary convicts, and ... determined to pardon them all."[129] Although a law passed around the same time still "authorised Courts, at their discretion" to sentence repeat offenders to solitary, by 1826 the prison's agent could claim that "there is not a convict now in the Prison thus sentenced."[130] All prisoners now spent only part of their days in solitary confinement (at night) and worked together, silently, in factorylike rooms. Even still, prisoners who had previously spent time in solitary continued to crowd the Physician's report of death and disease, illustrating the long-term effects of the earlier experiment.[131]

While New York was altering its mode of confinement to a partial reliance on solitary, its earlier experience was repeated elsewhere. Other states, responding to the chaos in their own proto-prisons, embraced solitary confinement as the answer to their problems of disorder and chaos. Copying New York's early example, Maine instituted a hybrid system at its new state prison in 1823. Some prisoners worked during the day and spent the night in solitary, while others were held continuously in solitary confinement with similar results. As at Auburn, Maine's cells were wholly inadequate. They resembled "pits" rather than cells: they were dark, cold, and partially subterranean – prisoners "entered *from the top* through an aperture two feet square, secured by an iron grating" and then descended by a removable ladder.[132] Prisoners sentenced to two

---

[126] Ibid., 48; italics in original.
[127] SPPNY, *Report on the Penitentiary System.*   [128] Powers, *A Brief Account*, p. 35.
[129] Ibid., p. 35.   [130] Ibid., p. 36.   [131] Ibid., p. 36.
[132] Lewis, *The Development of American Prisons and Prison Customs*, p. 147.

or two and a half months of continuous solitary confinement committed suicide days after beginning their confinement. "Many prisoners had to be repeatedly taken from solitary confinement to the hospital in order to be restored to a condition that would permit them again to be returned to the same torture!" Maine finally abandoned the system in 1827.[133]

Just as Maine was about to end its use of solitary confinement, opinion at the national level began to shift as well. Two events allowed stories of New York's – and soon, Maine's – disaster to circulate widely, prompting a staunch condemnation of solitary confinement. The first was the founding in 1825 of a penal reform society in Boston, which would document and extend the case against solitary confinement (see Chapter 4). The second was the publication in 1826 of a report recollecting Auburn's brief history written by its agent, Gershom Powers. Although the most shocking results of solitary confinement had occurred years earlier, these two developments publicized their occurrence, with great effect on public opinion.

Ultimately, the early experiments with solitary confinement convinced reformers and administrators that solitary confinement was wholly inappropriate for a civilized society. As Powers noted, proponents of continuous solitary confinement without labor experienced "an entire change of opinion."[134] Powers himself sought "frankly to acknowledge and fully expose a dangerous error ... in carrying the doctrine of solitary confinement entirely too far" and urged his audience to avoid endorsing "exclusive solitary confinement without labor, on the ground of *health, expense, reformation and unnecessary severity.*"[135] The experience with solitary confinement at Auburn left a lingering impression that sowed the seeds of opposition against the Pennsylvania System even before it was born.

Western's Architectural Challenges

In the same year that penal reformers around the Atlantic world learned of the deadly experiments with solitary at Auburn and Maine, Pennsylvania's Western State Penitentiary received its first prisoners. The law mandated that they be kept in solitary confinement. Instead, Western – with its construction finally nearing completion eight years after authorization – was plagued with architectural problems, its novel design preventing its planned reliance on solitary confinement.

---

[133] Ibid., pp. 147–148.   [134] Powers, *A Brief Account*, p. 37.   [135] Ibid., p. 38.

Unlike almost every American prison to follow, Western was loosely modeled on Brit Jeremy Bentham's Panopticon, an unrealized plan for a model prison that could also be used for a school, hospital, or any other setting that required supervision, but could be run more efficiently with limited personnel. The Panopticon consisted of an outer, ringlike building with cells facing a central observation tower. Through a strategic use of light, glass, and mirrors, a single guard could occupy the central tower and observe, unseen, the prisoners of the surrounding cells; as they would never know when they were being watched, they must always behave.[136] Bentham had limited impact on prison design in England and Europe, and many commentators dismissed him as something of an entrepreneurial crackpot. Nevertheless, Bentham's plan influenced Western's design; however, its implementation fell short.[137]

In practice, Western was no Panopticon. It contained the "single large ring-shaped cell building" but it "consisted of a double row of cells, back to back, each cell fronting on an open vestibule in such a way that the adjacent vestibules formed a continuous covered passageway around both the inner and outer sides of the ring."[138] The original plan for Western had also specified a central observation tower, which was not built, nor would the prisoners' cells be visible from a central location: the plan prevented adequate light from entering the cells and view of the cells was blocked by thick doors.[139] As the prison's warden later complained, "the keeper cannot inspect the convicts without being himself inspected."[140] In the end, the prison bore only "a general resemblance to Bentham's plan."[141] Indeed, although some commentators would lavish praise on the prison, calling it "a beautiful specimen of architecture" and "the finest piece of masonry in the United States," significant design flaws would plague Western's early years.[142]

These and other design flaws routinely frustrated administrators' attempts to preserve the principle of solitary confinement. The cells had inadequate plumbing, heating, and ventilation; they were "too dark

[136] Jeremy Bentham, *Panopticon: Or the Inspection House*. Dublin: Thomas Byrne, 1791; Michel Foucault, *Discipline and Punish: The Birth of the Prison*. New York: Vintage Books, 1977.
[137] Barnes, *The Evolution of Penology*, p. 139; Doll, "Trial and Error at Allegheny," p. 8.
[138] Doll, "Trial and Error at Allegheny," p. 8.
[139] Ibid., pp. 9–10; Barnes, *The Evolution of Penology*, p. 139.
[140] Cited in Doll, "Trial and Error at Allegheny," p. 19.
[141] Barnes, *The Evolution of Penology*, p. 139.
[142] Cited in Doll, "Trial and Error at Allegheny," p. 11.

and unhealthy" for long-term solitary confinement.[143] Prisoners needed exercise and fresh air, which they could not get while inside their cells. The legislature, however, refused the administrators' requests to build exercise yards for each cell to allow prisoners exercise while respecting the principle of solitary confinement. Consequently, administrators released prisoners together into the common yard.[144] However, letting prisoners walk about the prison, especially while construction workers were laboring on the still-incomplete structure, also proved problematic. Not a full year into Western's operation, a prisoner escaped; by January 1828, another five had escaped. These escapes were frequently blamed on the presence of work tools and workmen, which enabled prisoners to walk out the front gate.[145]

Complicating the situation was the question of putting prisoners to hard labor. Both the 1818 and 1821 statutes had authorized the construction of Pennsylvania's state penitentiaries on the principle of solitary confinement, but they had said nothing of hard labor. Thus, Western was constructed with only the principle of solitary confinement in mind. However, the penal code, written decades earlier and coinciding with the reforms at Walnut Street, still specified sentences to confinement at hard labor.[146] When Western opened, its cells (seven feet by nine) were too small for prisoner labor.[147] Western's Board of Inspectors lobbied the legislature for permission to institute something more similar to the practices at Walnut Street (solitary confinement only as necessary – i.e., to punish rule-breakers – and congregate labor in workshops for the rest) or to the current (post-disaster) regime at Auburn State Prison in New York (solitary confinement only at night and congregate labor in workshops during the day).[148] Limited by a tightfisted legislature, the prison's administrators also complained frequently of their lack of funds – another problem that, they believed, would be resolved by instituting

[143] Barnes, *The Evolution of Penology*, p. 140; Doll, "Trial and Error at Allegheny," pp. 12–14.
[144] Barnes, *The Evolution of Penology*, p. 157; Doll, "Trial and Error at Allegheny," pp. 14, 19.
[145] Doll, "Trial and Error at Allegheny," p. 14.
[146] Attempts to revise the penal code in the early 1820s, concomitant with the efforts to authorize new state prisons, were unsuccessful. "In 1821, a [legislative] committee on the penitentiary system had brought in a strong recommendation for punishment by solitary confinement without labor, but the resultant bills had failed of passage. Again, in 1822 and in 1823, other attempts to bring the penal code into line with the plan for solitary confinement died on the floor of the House." Ibid., p. 12.
[147] Ibid., p. 8.
[148] Ibid., p. 13.

prisoner labor. It would be years before the legislature answered these requests, forcing Western's administrators to muddle through their legal contradiction with less-than-ideal architectural conditions.

* * *

The path to the modern prison of the 1820s – nowhere more than in Philadelphia – was riddled with false starts, stumbling blocks, and circuitous detours. In one sense, penal reform was exceedingly fragile, as so many failures could have ended the reform effort. In another sense, however, penal reform was exceedingly robust. Reformers and statesmen were guided by a strange faith that the prison would eventually work, despite all of its previous failures. Part of this strange faith was an ongoing belief that solitary confinement of some kind – just not the totalizing, fatal kind used initially at Auburn – was a necessary ingredient for American prisons. In the coming decades, the biggest battle would be held over just what kind of solitary confinement was desirable. This question would be of central importance at Eastern State Penitentiary: Eastern's design, as well as its entire history, would be shaped by the debate over what type of solitary confinement was best. This debate itself would be endlessly haunted by the legacy of failure cast by the proto-prisons and the early experiments with solitary confinement in the new modern prisons. Indeed, penal reformers, prison administrators, and statesmen would work to prevent further failures, constantly tweaking the new prisons until they got it right. Even then, however, the memory of repeated, spectacular failures of the past lingered, making penal innovation a difficult, risky endeavor riddled with uncertainty and anxiety. In this context, the Pennsylvania System was the riskiest of all.

2

Born of Conflict

The Struggle to Authorize the Pennsylvania System

Pennsylvania has enjoyed the envied fame, the peculiar merit of first leading the way in the great experiment of Penitentiary Reform. The palm had long since been awarded to her by unanimous acclamation, and we regret that it was reserved for some of her own citizens to be the first to attempt the ungracious task of diminishing her reputation, by a strange and ignorant denial of the success, and even the existence, of that noble system, of which, until that moment, she had been the admitted founder.

George Washington Smith (1833), *A Defence of the System of Solitary Confinement of Prisoners Adopted by the State of Pennsylvania*[1]

STARTING ON THE DEFENSIVE

Writing in the winter of 1828–1829, a full decade after Walnut Street had imploded reformers' early hopes, Philadelphia penal reformer George Washington Smith began a campaign to convince the state legislature to adopt a new approach to imprisonment, the Pennsylvania System.[2] At its core, the Pennsylvania System would keep prisoners in long-term solitary confinement. Unfortunately for Smith, after the proto-prisons failed so dramatically, several states – including Pennsylvania – had already begun experimenting with solitary confinement with disastrous results. Urged on by his fellow members of the Philadelphia Society for Alleviating the Miseries of Public Prisons (PSAMPP), Smith wrote "A Defence" of the

[1] George Washington Smith, *A Defence of the System of Solitary Confinement of Prisoners Adopted by the State of Pennsylvania*. Philadelphia: G. Dorsey, Printer, 1833 [1829], p. 16.
[2] Ibid., p. 4.

type of solitary confinement proposed under the Pennsylvania System. His campaign thus served as a kind of damage control.

Smith emphasized that this new system was different from those early experiments with solitary confinement that had caused insanity and death. Although he continued to use the term, he also explained that the Pennsylvania System of "*solitary* confinement...is perhaps erroneously styled."[3] He, like his fellow reformers, thought that adding additional attributes would clarify the matter: "solitary confinement, or rather the confinement of prisoners *separate and apart from each other*, united with a system of *labour and instruction*."[4] Additionally, he sought to emphasize his own distaste for a regime built entirely on solitary confinement. He explained,

solitary confinement has been *occasionally* practised as one of the most dreadful means of vindictive punishment—a confinement unmitigated, absolute, and inhuman; a confinement at the mere mention of which the philanthropist shudders with horror, and the philosophic reformer turns aside with disgust and reprobation.[5]

By emphasizing his critique of such outdated punishments, Smith sought to establish that the Pennsylvania System was different. Such strategies were necessary for the in-state debate over prison design, but they would also be necessary throughout the Pennsylvania System's tenure at Eastern State Penitentiary.

* * *

The necessity of defending the Pennsylvania System – an omnipresent reality at Eastern State Penitentiary throughout the nineteenth century and a major cause of its personal institutionalization – was present from the very beginning. Indeed, if the early 1820s were challenging for Philadelphia's penal reformers, they paled in comparison to the late 1820s. By this point, Eastern had been authorized, but now several groups of Pennsylvanians would furiously debate what that prison's regime should look like. This debate would be shaped not only by the legacy of past failures, but also by mounting criticism of pure solitary confinement (continuous solitary without distractions) as well as other developments beyond Pennsylvania. The Pennsylvania System that was ultimately authorized at Eastern resulted from this contentious period.

---

[3] Ibid., p. 7.   [4] Ibid., p. 1.   [5] Ibid., p. 8.

Forged in conflict, it was designed to achieve the original goals of the first prisons, but it was also designed reactively to avoid repeating the failures previously experienced at Walnut Street Prison, Auburn State Prison, and Western State Penitentiary. Importantly, that this period would end with Pennsylvania deviating from the rest of the country was far from a foregone conclusion. For a while, it seemed that Pennsylvania might abandon its reformers' preference for continuous solitary confinement and copy New York's new approach to incarceration.

THE AUBURN SYSTEM

New York's fatal experiment with solitary confinement at Auburn State Prison in 1821 had shaken reformers, politicians, and prison administrators' faith in the new prisons: the experiment taught them that the prison could indeed be deadly and enact more torture than the gruesome punishments from which many American reformers sought to distance themselves. The Auburn experiment did not, however, warn off reformers and administrators from solitary confinement entirely. New York's prison administrators and reformers alike still saw the necessity of solitary confinement of some kind. As Auburn's Agent Gershom Powers explained, *pure* solitary confinement – continuous solitary confinement without labor – was an abomination, but "experience thus far fully confirms the conclusion, that solitude and silence are an indispensable part of a well regulated penitentiary system."[6]

Indeed, after the experiment with pure solitary confinement was called off in 1823, Auburn's administrators continued to implement solitary confinement. The 1821 statute that had authorized pure solitary confinement had also authorized two other modes of confinement at Auburn: while the "oldest and most heinous offenders" were kept in solitary cells continuously, the "less heinous" would spend three days a week in solitary cells and three days working, and "younger offenders," would "be permitted" to work each day, and everyone would spend their nights in solitary cells.[7] The hybrid approach given to young offenders was extended, in 1823, to the whole prisoner population.

---

6 Gershom Powers, *A Brief Account of the Constitution, Management, & Discipline &c. &c. of the New-York State Prison at Auburn.* Auburn, NY: U. F. Doubleday, 1826, p. 33.
7 New York, "An Act concerning State Prisons, Passed April 2, 1821," in *Laws of the State of New-York.* Albany: Cantine and Leake, 1821, pp. 216–217.

Under this new system, prisoners would sleep in solitary cells at night, but during the day, they worked together "in congregate" in factorylike workshops within the prison. To prevent potential mutual contamination during their congregation, prisoners were forbidden from looking at or speaking with each other – prisoners did not sit face to face at work or meals; instead, they kept their backs to each other.[8] Further, prisoners were ordered to march in lockstep – "silently marching ... at precise times, moving in separate corps, in single file, with a slow lock-step, erect posture, keeping exact time, with their faces inclined towards their Keepers" – to increase discipline and make conversation easy to detect. This manoeuvre was also said to provide an air of seriousness, invoking "somewhat similar feelings to those excited by a military funeral."[9] Prisoners' heads were shaven and they wore striped uniforms, which would become the visible symbol of prisoner status for the next century or more. Misconduct would be punished by lash. A series of bells rung throughout the day would signal the times for work, meals, marching, and other tasks. Through this quasi-military discipline, according to the plan's supporters, the risk of riot and other misconduct would all but disappear, while daytime silence and nightly solitude would prevent prisoners from plotting or further steeping in criminality. This new approach would be known as the Silent System, the Congregate System, or the Auburn System.

The Auburn System was a revolutionary approach to incarceration. As historian Rebecca McLennan has noted, Auburn was the first prison to have the vast majority of its population confined in cells for a large portion of the day – a goal that had never been attained under the Walnut Street model and that Pennsylvanians were still hoping Western State Penitentiary would fulfill once it opened.[10] Under this new regime, moreover, the prison was redesigned to realize the dream of total discipline – every minute of a prisoner's day was intricately planned. For example, at meals, prisoners who had extra food would "raise their right hand," signaling, at the appointed time, one of the "convict waiters" to collect the food and give it to a prisoner with his left hand raised "to signify that they want more."[11] Gone were the days of prisoners milling about large

---

[8] Powers, *A Brief Account*, pp. 5, 15.   [9] Ibid., p. 4.
[10] On Auburn's significance, see Rebecca M. McLennan, *The Crisis of Imprisonment: Protest, Politics, and the Making of the American Penal State, 1776–1941*. New York: Cambridge University Press, 2008.
[11] Powers, *A Brief Account*, p. 5.

rooms, talking, playing, fighting, and occasionally working. Auburn's cell blocks were "almost as still as the house of death" at night.[12] By contrast, Pennsylvania's two new state prisons were still under construction in the early 1820s. New York had surpassed the original center of penal reform.

Auburn's Diffusion and Pennsylvania's Isolation

By the early 1820s, New York thus stood at the forefront of penal innovation and it attracted attention accordingly. The Auburn System was actively publicized by a new PSAMPP-like organization, the Boston Prison Discipline Society (BPDS), founded in 1825 under the leadership of the Reverend Louis Dwight. In the BPDS's first annual report, Dwight gushed of Auburn, "It is not possible to describe the pleasure which we feel in contemplating this noble institution, after wading through the fraud, and material and moral filth of many Prisons. We regard it as a model worthy of the world's imitation. ... [T]he institution is immensely elevated above the old Penitentiaries."[13]

Dwight described Auburn's daily operations at length, often implicitly distinguishing it from the old proto-prisons, emphasizing Auburn's success precisely at the points where the older prisons failed. Unlike its diseased and odiferous predecessors, "The whole establishment from the gate to the sewer, is a specimen of neatness." In contrast to the ancient schools of vice, Auburn was characterized by order: "[At meals,] Not even a whisper is heard; though the silence is such that a whisper might be heard through the whole apartment. ...[In the workshops,] it is the testimony of many witnesses, that they have passed more than three hundred convicts without seeing one leave his work, or turn his head to gaze at them." In the spirit of the earlier prisons' original design as "penitentiaries," Dwight reported, at night, prisoners who "choose, read the scriptures undisturbed, and then reflect in silence on the errors of their lives." In contrast to the old-style "city Prison" (jail) still in use, where visitors recently observed "an unsubdued and audacious spirit in the culprits; this is never seen at Auburn." Instead, Dwight claimed, "the entire subordination and subdued feeling of the convicts, has probably no parallel among an equal number of criminals." These "generally subdued feelings"

---

[12] Ibid., p. 7.
[13] BPDS, *First Annual Report of the Board of Managers of the Boston Prison Discipline Society*, Fifth edition. Boston: T. R. Marvin, 1827 [1826], p. 36.

were likewise evident "to their religious teacher, as he passes from one cell to another."[14] More than creating a bigger and stronger prison, New York had constructed a regime that promised everything reformers had originally desired but had previously failed to achieve.

The Auburn System soon became tremendously popular, forming the new template for prisons across the North and the South, from the east coast to the expanding frontier.[15] State governors, legislators, and prison commissioners – men assigned to do the research necessary to plan and ultimately supervise the construction of a new state prison – visited Auburn to tour the facility. As Powers exclaimed in 1826, "Many distinguished individuals, from various parts of the United States as well as from Europe, are almost daily calling, to examine personally, [Auburn's] management and the peculiarities of its construction and discipline." Visitors and others, he reported, also "solicit prison reports or pamphlets, from which they can learn, at leisure and in detail, the whole concerns of an institution which strikes them so favorably on a general examination."[16] When officials could not visit, they wrote to request information.

These visitors and corresponders then adopted the model back home. By 1829, the Auburn System could be found in Maine, Kentucky, Connecticut, Virginia, Maryland, Massachusetts, the District of Columbia, as well as two prisons in New York; within a few years, it would spread to Illinois, Tennessee, Vermont, New Hampshire, and Georgia. By the time Western had fully implemented the Pennsylvania System, the Auburn System could also be found in Ohio, Louisiana, and Missouri.[17]

---

[14] Ibid., pp. 36–37.

[15] Ashley T. Rubin, "A Neo-Institutional Account of Prison Diffusion," *Law & Society Review* 49:2 (2015), pp. 365–399; Edward L. Ayers, *Vengeance and Justice: Crime and Punishment in the 19th-Century American South*. New York: Oxford University Press, 1984; McLennan, *The Crisis of Imprisonment*.

[16] Powers, *A Brief Account*, p. i.

[17] Rubin, *"A Neo-Institutional Account"*; See also Gustave de Beaumont and Alexis de Tocqueville, *On the Penitentiary System in the United States and Its Application in France*, Trans. by Francis Lieber. Philadelphia: Carey, Lea, and Blanchard, 1833, p. 20; BPDS, *Seventh Annual Report of the Board of Managers of the Boston Prison Discipline Society*. Boston: Perkins and Marvin, 1832, pp. 72–73; "Art. III [Review of Nine Works]." *The North American Review* 103:213 (1866), pp. 383–412, pp. 397, 398; Orlando Faulkland Lewis, *The Development of American Prisons and Prison Customs, 1776–1845: With Special Reference to Early Institutions in the State of New York*. Albany: Prison Association of New York/J. B. Lyon Company, 1922; Enoch C. Wines and Theodore W. Dwight, *Report on the Prisons and Reformatories of the United States and Canada Made to the Legislature of New York, January 1867*. Albany, NY: Van Benthuysen and Sons' Steam Printing House, 1867.

Rather than doing the difficult work of creating their own approaches to incarceration – and risk further failures – these states simply copied the dominant approach.[18]

PENNSYLVANIA'S INTERNECINE DEBATE

Pennsylvania was not immune to the Auburn System's attractions, but many Philadelphia-based reformers remained committed to a different vision of incarceration. As one commentator later explained, "The friends of the separate system had not only to educate the public mind in Pennsylvania as to its real merits, but also to combat opposition in England, New England, New York, and among various gentlemen who had some general opinions on penal jurisprudence."[19] Rather than sharing one mind, Pennsylvanians in the late 1820s were split on how to proceed with their ongoing penal reform efforts. Based on their own experience, Western's administrators were increasingly opposed to solitary confinement. They were particularly drawn to the promise that (congregate) prisoner labor offered: delivery from dependence on a lackluster legislature. By contrast, PSAMPP, Walnut Street's inspectors, and some other Pennsylvania reformers remained committed to solitary confinement. But even among this congenial group of men, there was dissension.

Most reformers in Pennsylvania continued to favor holding prisoners in solitary confinement for the duration of their sentence; they differed on whether prisoners should also be required to perform labor within their solitary cells. Some reformers favored pure solitary confinement – continuous solitary confinement without labor (what Auburn and Maine had initially tried and Western had unsuccessfully attempted). They

---

[18] Those few states that significantly modified the original – including Kentucky and Maryland – were simply recognized as variations on the Auburn System, never becoming models in their own right. Commentators were aware of these and other variations, and differences in practice, but they dismissed them. Writing in 1867, Wines and Dwight explained, for example, that the Auburn System's alternative label, the "silent system," "has become, in some prisons, quite inapplicable. Some do not even claim to conduct their discipline upon the strictly silent system; in others, where the claim is made, the rule of silence has but a partial enforcement; while, in comparatively few is the rigidity of the old discipline of absolute non-intercourse maintained in full force." Wines, and Dwight, *Report*, p. 56. They further explained, "With certain modifications on minor points, the rules and regulations relating to the deportment of convicts are substantially the same in all the prisons on the congregate plan, that is, in all the prisons of the United States, outside of Pennsylvania." Ibid., p. 134.

[19] Richard Vaux, *Brief Sketch of the Origin and History of the State Penitentiary for the Eastern District of Pennsylvania at Philadelphia*. Philadelphia: McLaughlin Brothers, Printers, 1872, p. 88.

opposed labor under the belief that it would distract from prisoners' reflection. Other reformers preferred solitary confinement with labor, believing that labor would limit the mental and physical damage of long-term solitary confinement and help reform prisoners.

This disagreement over the inclusion of labor was found even among the men who would soon be responsible for designing and then implementing the Pennsylvania System. Thomas Bradford, one of the PSAMPP members who would help write the relevant statutes and convince the legislature to pass them, was initially an advocate of continuous solitary confinement without labor. His colleague, Roberts Vaux, supported continuous solitary confinement with labor and moral instruction. A third colleague, Samuel Wood, supported labor but was initially equivocal over the type of confinement.[20]

A division thus emerged within Pennsylvania over how prisons should be designed – Eastern was still under construction and Western could be altered – and what regime should guide them. In particular, the debate surrounded the inclusion of prisoner labor and the appropriate level of solitary confinement: continuous solitary confinement without labor, continuous solitary confinement with labor, or solitary confinement only at night and congregate labor by day. As Historian Harry Elmer Barnes notes, "It was only out of the struggles of 1826 to 1829 that the Pennsylvania system was finally established."[21]

The Commission to Revise the Penal Code

The debate in Pennsylvania centered on formal efforts to revise the penal code, particularly the portion that described prison discipline in the two state prisons. Indeed, the ongoing need to revise the penal code took on mounting importance when Western opened. As we have seen, while the statutes authorizing Western and describing its prison discipline called for solitary confinement, the old penal statutes still specified the punishment for various crimes as sentences to confinement at hard labor. Holding prisoners in solitary confinement without labor thus technically violated the law.

---

[20] Ibid., p. 87; Smith, *A Defence of the System*, p. 18. Note that Bradford, an Episcopalian, was the lone non-Quaker in this triad and yet he was the most committed to pure solitary confinement. Membership in the Society of Friends was neither necessary nor sufficient for supporting solitary confinement.

[21] Harry Elmer Barnes, *The Evolution of Penology in Pennsylvania*. Indianapolis: The Bobbs-Merrill Company, 1968 [1927], p. 121.

Aware of the coming challenge as early as 1824 (two years before Western opened), Governor John Andrew Shulze had asked the legislature "whether a revision of the penal code will not be absolutely necessary," in light of the "alteration in the mode and degree of punishment" the two new state penitentiaries would present.[22] The following year, he sought "again respectfully, yet very earnestly, [to] press upon you a thorough revision of our whole criminal code."[23] However, Governor Shulze was not committed to any particular strategy of prison discipline and he was open to suggestions. He noted that

some of the penitentiaries of our sister states, are so economically and judiciously conducted that the labor of the convicts yield a profit to the state. It would be well, diligently, to inquire into the principles, discipline, and manner in which those prisons are governed that we might adopt in Pennsylvania, whatever is good, and embody it in our laws before our new state penitentiaries shall be finally organized and in complete operation.[24]

Pennsylvania could, he thus implied, copy the Auburn System as other states were doing.

With the possibility that solitary confinement would be curtailed, and a penal revision on the horizon, Philadelphia's reformers took action: it was crucial (from their perspective) that they lead the charge and ensure the correct course of events. Little more than a month after the Governor's message to the assembly, Roberts Vaux published his "Notices of the Original, and Successive Efforts, to Improve the Discipline of the Prison at Philadelphia and to Reform the Criminal Code of Pennsylvania." After describing the illustrious history of Walnut Street, and its subsequent decline due to reasons beyond the excellence of the underlying plan (as he described it), Vaux closed by recommending future steps. "A thorough revision of the criminal laws is indispensably necessary, to adapt them to that kind of imprisonment to which the new buildings are appropriate."[25] Vaux "respectfully suggested" that "a commission of three or five individuals" should be appointed to write "an essay of a system of penal laws and regulations for the government of the

[22] John Andrew Shulze, "Annual Message to the Assembly – 1824," in *Pennsylvania Archives. Fourth Series. Papers of the Governors, Vol. V. 1817–1832*, ed. George Edward Reed. Harrisburg: Wm. Stanley Ray, 1901 [1824], pp. 545–554, p. 551.

[23] John Andrew Shulze, "Annual Message to the Assembly – 1825," in *Pennsylvania Archives. Fourth Series. Papers of the Governors, Vol. V. 1817–1832*, ed. George Edward Reed. Harrisburg: Wm. Stanley Ray, 1901 [1825], pp. 588–599, p. 597.

[24] Ibid., pp. 597–598.   [25] Vaux, *Notices*, pp. 55–56.

new penitentiaries."[26] Undoubtedly, Vaux was hoping that he or his colleagues from Walnut Street's Board of Inspectors or from PSAMPP would be selected. Indeed, he spent the last eight pages of his pamphlet laying out what he saw as the serious considerations that should shape such a commission's work. Vaux's hopes would be disappointed.

In March 1826, the legislature passed a resolution requiring the governor to authorize a three-man commission to revise the penal code.[27] Specifically, this commission was charged with drafting a bill recommending a penal code and prison regime "modelled on the principle of labor and solitary confinement."[28] This requirement was a boon to the Philadelphia reformers. However, the Governor appointed to the commission Charles Shaler, a judge from Western Pennsylvania; Edward King, a Philadelphia judge; and Thomas J. Wharton, a Philadelphia-area lawyer. The absence of anyone connected with Walnut Street, Eastern's Building Commissioners, or PSAMPP was a snub to the reformers and boded poorly.

The results of the commission were both delinquent and quite different from what was expected. Although the commission had been required to report at the very next session of the legislature, they requested extra time and finally reported nearly two years later. Moreover, while they were expected to write a penal code based on Pennsylvania's by-now unique commitment to a system of continuous solitary confinement and hard labor, their 1828 report delivered a different document.

The cause for both the delay and difference was the extent of the research the committee had undertaken. They had toured several prisons in their own and nearby states, written to the administrators of others, and reviewed the growing penal reform literature – much of which opposed Pennsylvania's initial plans to rely on continuous solitary confinement.[29] Their research had convinced the three men to suggest abandoning Pennsylvania's commitment to solitary confinement in favor of the emerging Auburn System. The commission had been persuaded of the Auburn System's superiority by Boston's Louis Dwight.[30]

---

[26] Ibid., p. 56.
[27] Pennsylvania, "Resolution Relative to a Revision of the Penal Code," in *Acts of the General Assembly of the Commonwealth of Pennsylvania*. Harrisburg: Cameron and Krause, 1826, p. 413.
[28] Ibid.
[29] Charles Shaler, Edward King, and T. I. Wharton, *Report of the Commissioners on the Penal Code*. Harrisburg: S. C. Stambaugh, 1828, p. 6.
[30] Barnes, *The Evolution of Penology*, p. 101.

In a sense, the commission had been hijacked: rather than producing a new penal code appropriate to Pennsylvania's already relatively unique mode of punishment, the authors produced a penal code appropriate for a completely different mode of punishment. Apparently cognizant of the magnitude of this change in direction, the commission supported their recommendation with an extensive report defending their preference for the Auburn System. The report reviewed the various options for how to design and manage a prison, examining various permutations of labor (congregate labor, solitary labor, no labor) and solitary (continuous solitary, some solitary, no solitary). However, the commission seriously considered only three approaches: continuous solitary confinement without labor (currently authorized), continuous solitary confinement with labor (PSAMPP's official choice and the legislature's recommendation), and solitary confinement at night only with congregate labor during the day (the Auburn System). In the case of the first two options, the commission reviewed the alleged advantages before arguing that these advantages were misconceptions or else outweighed by disadvantages – typically in explicit comparison to the Auburn System.

As a starting point, the commission decided that solitary confinement was sufficiently severe that it should be used no more than necessary. They argued that the chief necessity for solitary confinement was to separate prisoners at night – when prisoners were better able to communicate among themselves or, even worse (to the commissioners), engage in another kind of intercourse. During the day, when prisoners would be better supervised, solitary confinement was unnecessary.[31] The commission then outlined the various ways in which solitary confinement would be ineffective as a reformative punishment. They argued that prisoners – as "persons of coarse, brutal temperament, of stupid ignorance, and low cunning, or of sufficient intellectual capacity, and some cultivation, but an entire aversion to the inconvenient restraints of the law, and a spirit to obtain a living in any other way, than by the pursuit of labour" – could not be reasoned with except by way of "bodily suffering," which apparently excluded solitary confinement.[32] The commission chided those commentators who criticized whipping, describing them as "worthy and respectable men, whose sympathy for criminals seems to increase in exact proportion with the growth or heinousness of their offence" – a

---

[31] Shaler, King, and Wharton, *Report of the Commissioners*, pp. 23–26, 29.
[32] Ibid., p. 27.

nineteenth-century way of calling PSAMPP reformers "soft on crime" or even "bleeding-heart liberals."[33] Somewhat contradictorily, however, the commission believed that this group of degenerate criminals who could not be reasoned with could be made into and, further, be swayed by, "the spectacle of an orderly, industrious, and submissive community" through the Auburn System.[34] The commission further argued that, while solitary would be an ineffective punishment against the hardened criminal, it would "torture the mind" to the point that "bodily pain would undoubtedly be preferable."[35] Without a hint of irony, they also argued that solitude would be ineffective as a punishment because prisoners would get used to the monotony: "the mind adapts itself with wonderful ease to its situation, and becomes almost reconciled to its new position." Others would hold out hope for a pardon, which would likewise "reduce the quantum of suffering," or plan their escape; either way, they would not reform.[36]

Shaler and colleagues also repeated earlier arguments against solitary that would continue to serve as critiques going forward. Solitary confinement was too expensive.[37] Its expense was unacceptable because, they stated matter-of-factly, "the system of punishment ought to be one, in which the least expense is incurred to arrive at a good result. The honest part of the community being already too heavily taxed by the depredation of offenders, it ought not to be additionally burthened by great annual expense in maintaining them."[38] Solitary confinement, they argued, would also be bad for prisoners' health and welfare: "the air of the narrow and close cell, in which the convict must be confined, will in all likelihood be unwholesome," while prisoners "will be deprived of the advantage of exercise, or at all events exceedingly limited in the use of it." Adding another cause, they noted, "wherever the mind or spirits of the convict become affected by his confinement, the body will suffer in proportion."[39]

---

33 Ibid., p. 28.   34 Ibid., p. 29.   35 Ibid., p. 31.   36 Ibid., p. 32.
37 Ibid., p. 42.   38 Ibid., p. 38.
39 Ibid., p. 43; They also spent several paragraphs arguing against maintaining prisoners undergoing solitary confinement on a "diet of bread and water" even though they acknowledged that the supporters of solitary had never actually said this would be the case. Ibid., p. 42; It seems they included this discussion because it had been the practice at Auburn during its fatal experiment with long-term, continuous solitary confinement without labor and for those Walnut Street prisoners maintained in short-term solitary confinement.

Having spent thirty pages criticizing continuous solitary confinement without labor, they allocated only eight pages to criticizing continuous solitary confinement with labor. Accounting for the difference, they argued that the critiques of solitary confinement without labor were essentially the same as those against solitary confinement with labor, although the commission agreed that solitary with labor was "beyond all comparison superior" to solitary without labor even though both were unsound.[40] They thus proceeded with the critiques introduced by adding labor to solitary confinement: The need to place labor within a prisoner's cell, the commission argued, restricted the possible tasks that they could perform.[41] Indeed, confining labor to a prisoner's cell, and forcing the prisoner to work alone, precluded the "most lucrative occupations," further condemning the prison to "comparatively small" profits.[42] Shoemaking and tailoring, the most likely occupations for solitary labor, "would soon break down the health of the convict, and compel his removal to the hospital," further cutting down on profits.[43] If prisoners were instead removed to attached yards to work outside, not only would the weather interfere, but it would be difficult to "prevent evil communication while the prisoners were in the exercising yards."[44] Moreover, it would be difficult to enforce discipline within the prison and get the prisoners to work, which would help neither their reformation nor the prison's profitability.[45] With these arguments provided, they again pointed to their other arguments against solitary without labor, and moved on to the Auburn System of solitary confinement at night and labor during the day.[46]

The Auburn System, the commission ultimately concluded, was the superior system. The benefits of employing solitary confinement at night were "so great, so obvious ... that we shall not trouble the legislature with any [further] comment upon it," but of course comment they did.[47] The Auburn System's use of "joint labor" rather than "solitary labor" was not only important for maintaining the prisoners' health and minds, but also "lighten[ed] the public burdens" on the state to support the prison, first by providing any kind of labor and second by ensuring the

---

[40] Ibid., p. 51.   [41] Ibid., p. 52.   [42] Ibid., pp. 52, 57.   [43] Ibid., p. 53.
[44] Ibid., pp. 54, 55.   [45] Ibid., pp. 57–58.
[46] They also argued that moral instruction would be rendered ineffective or wholly inconvenient by the separation of prisoners, or at least would necessitate combining them. This argument was, like several others, borrowed from the highly religious Boston reformers.
[47] Shaler, King, and Wharton, *Report of the Commissioners*, p. 71.

most profitable kinds of labor. Its economy was further supported by the comparatively cheaper cost of building an Auburn-style prison.[48] They argued that the Auburn System, with its use of a Sunday school, would enable prisoners' "mental and moral improvement."[49] Congregation was, in fact, necessary for achieving this end: "Religious worship, in a common assembly, is known to derive some of its impressive effects upon worshippers, from the principle of association, and the union of the individuals in the common purpose."[50] Thus, both solitary by night and congregation by day had their advantages over full-time solitary, with or without labor.

The commission did address possible criticisms of the Auburn System, including its reliance on corporal punishment, namely whipping. Noting that "the early legislators of Pennsylvania were not sensible of any thing unchristian, inhuman, or inexpedient, in the infliction of corporal punishment upon such as had violated the laws of the land" and that "our own navy" uses whipping, "we think that there is no great reason to be shocked at a proposal of administering it to felons who have first violated the laws of the land, and then violated the laws of the prison in which they are placed."[51] Apparently uncomfortable with their own statement, however, they buttressed their claims by noting the good health of prisoners in the Auburn System, the likelihood that other forms of discipline will make whipping infrequent, and that no system is perfect.[52]

By endorsing the Auburn System, Shaler and his colleagues apparently knew they had taken a stance that would be controversial in Pennsylvania. They explained that they did not "lightly" make their recommendation to abandon a "system which may be thought peculiarly the offspring of Pennsylvania." They also noted the difficulty of abandoning "the present buildings upon which so much of the public money has been expended" and the need to investigate whether the Auburn System could be implemented therein.[53] They concluded that while it would probably be possible to convert Western to their purposes, it would be cheaper to build a new cellblock on the Auburn plan at Eastern than to continue to build the remaining cellblocks on its original design. With these concerns out of the way, they submitted a new penal code specifying sentences to "punishment of hard labor in common workshops by day, and solitary imprisonment by night."[54]

---

[48] Ibid., p. 71.   [49] Ibid., p. 72.   [50] Ibid., p. 73.   [51] Ibid., pp. 75–76.
[52] Ibid., p. 77.   [53] Ibid., p. 78.   [54] Ibid., p. 81.

PSAMPP's Response

The Shaler, King, and Wharton report was indeed controversial. It was viewed by some – particularly PSAMPP – as an act of treason against Pennsylvania. As George Washington Smith reflected a few years later,

Pennsylvania has enjoyed the envied fame, the peculiar merit of first leading the way in the great experiment of Penitentiary Reform. The palm had long since been awarded to her by unanimous acclamation, and we regret that it was reserved for some of her own citizens to be the first to attempt the ungracious task of diminishing her reputation, by a strange and ignorant denial of the success, and even the existence, of that noble system, of which, until that moment, she had been the admitted founder.[55]

To men like Smith, the commission's report was entirely out of step with what he felt was the dominant feeling in Pennsylvania.

While the report's extreme views may have limited its appeal, its delinquency perhaps did more to tamper its effect. After waiting a year for the Commission to Revise the Penal Code to report their findings, and with the construction of Eastern nearing completion, the legislature invited the Commissioners for the Erection of the Eastern Penitentiary to suggest what mode of confinement they would recommend. Taking only several months to prepare, the "Building Commissioners" presented their report in early January 1828, just four days after the Shaler report had been finally presented.

The Building Commissioners offered a wholehearted endorsement of solitary confinement *without* labor. The only occupation a prisoner should have, they proposed, would be "the study of the Scriptures, connected with affectionate religious instruction." Reciting a common argument, they believed that labor would be a distraction; without labor, the punishment would be more efficient "because less time will be requisite to produce a beneficial result on the mind."[56] Notably, theirs was a minority view among Philadelphia reformers: even though the Building Commission included several PSAMPP members, most PSAMPP members (or at least those setting the agenda) favored solitary confinement *with labor*. More importantly, however, the Building Commission's conclusion was also the polar opposite of the report written by Shaler, King, and Wharton.

---

55 Smith, *A Defence of the System*, p. 16.
56 "Art. I–Brief History of the Penal Legislation of Pennsylvania." *Pennsylvania Journal of Prison Discipline and Philanthropy* 1:1 (1845), pp. 1–14, p. 10.

With two extreme and contradictory reports before them, legislative opinion was thoroughly divided. The House and Senate remained deadlocked for more than a year. As Barnes notes, "By taking advantage of this deadlock among the public authorities, the Philadelphia Society for Alleviating the Miseries of the Prisons was able to induce the legislature to enact into law its fundamental program in penal administration."[57] Indeed, the legislature's final decision was ultimately the result of PSAMPP's efforts.

In the wake of the Shaler report, PSAMPP member George Washington Smith began his campaign to defend their preferred system of solitary confinement with labor. At PSAMPP's behest, he wrote a series of essays in the *Philadelphia Gazette* "to counteract the effect of erroneous theories and statements on the minds of our Representatives."[58] On another front, PSAMPP sent Samuel Wood – a fellow member, Walnut Street inspector, and Building Commissioner – "to labor with the chairman of the judiciary committee of the legislature."[59] Finally, in April 1829, the legislature, convinced by PSAMPP's efforts, passed a statute authorizing a new mode of confinement for the state.

The 1829 act outlined what was increasingly known as the Pennsylvania System. Under the Pennsylvania System, prisoners would "suffer punishment by separate or solitary confinement at labour."[60] The law applied to those who had been convicted of a range of serious offenses – "murder in the second degree, manslaughter, high treason, arson, rape, sodomy or buggery, burglary, forgery, passing counterfeit money, robbery, kidnapping, mayhem, horse stealing and perjury."[61] The warden would interview the prisoners, record their personal information, store their personal effects, bathe them, and assign them a number "by which he or she shall thereafter be known during his or her confinement."[62] Prisoners would be fed and clothed decently enough, and they would spend their days at labor, although the type of work was left unspecified.[63] While they remained in the prison, prisoners would have no contact with the outside world, not with friends or family members, nor through letters and newspapers. Their only contact would come through

---

[57] Barnes, *The Evolution of Penology*, p. 121.   [58] Smith, *A Defence of the System*, p. 4.

[59] Barnes, *The Evolution of Penology*, p. 101.

[60] Pennsylvania, "No. 204: A Further Supplement to an Act, Entitled 'An Act to Reform the Penal Laws of This Commonwealth'," in *Laws of the General Assembly of the State of Pennsylvania*. Harrisburg: Office of the Reporter, 1829, pp. 341–354.

[61] Ibid., p. 341.   [62] Ibid., p. 351.

[63] Unlike earlier statutes, this one did not specify "hard labor."

official visits from the prison personnel, PSAMPP members, and anyone else who had the written permission of the prison's administrators.[64] Prisoners would also receive weekly "moral and religious instruction ... in such manner as to make their confinement as far as possible the means of their reformation, so that when restored to their liberty, they may prove honest, industrious and useful members of society."[65] Prisoners who misbehaved could be punished, but their punishment was left to the administrators to determine.[66] This system, the statute specified, would be instituted at both the Western and Eastern State Penitentiaries.

Western's Second Failure

After decades of effort, the Pennsylvania System had finally been authorized. Despite mounting criticism from outside the state, and despite several attempts to institute other systems of prison discipline, PSAMPP had won the day, securing their favored system at the state's two prisons, both of which could finally receive prisoners. Unfortunately (from the reformers, administrators, and legislators' point of view), it was almost impossible to implement this system at Western State Penitentiary, now three years into operations.

Following the new law, little changed in Western's daily routines. The physical plant continued as a hindrance, and the legislature refused to provide the necessary funds to mitigate these problems. Western's inspectors reported, "the cells ... [are] too small and dark ever to be used as working rooms, and ... [there are] no work shops or other conveniences for the introduction and prosecution of productive labour. ... There is no solitary confinement here."[67] As the inspectors noted, "It was unfortunate that the building was first put up and the system of punishment afterwards prescribed."[68] Lacking funds, the administrators continued to

[64] Pennsylvania, "No. 204: A Further Supplement" pp. 341–42, 351–352.

[65] Ibid., p. 353.   [66] Ibid., p. 348.

[67] Eugene E. Doll, "Trial and Error at Allegheny: The Western State Penitentiary, 1818–1838," *The Pennsylvania Magazine of History and Biography* 81:1 (1957), pp. 3–27, p. 19.

[68] Cited in Barnes, *The Evolution of Penology*, p. 140. Likewise, historian Eugene Doll has noted, the 1829 Act "rendered hopelessly obsolete the two-year-old $185,000 penitentiary on the hills above the Allegheny. It was manifestly impossible to set the prisoners at any sort of labor in the tiny, poorly ventilated cells practically devoid of light." Doll, "Trial and Error," p. 17. See also Barnes, *The Evolution of Penology*, p. 157.

employ prisoners around the prison.[69] As there was not enough labor to go around, idle prisoners were released into "the yard fifty or more at a time ... at least an hour a day" to preserve their health.[70]

Facing intractable problems, and a tightfisted legislature, Western would continue to limp along until, in 1833, at the warden's request, the legislature authorized the prison's complete reconstruction.[71] During the renovations, prisoners were employed in the effort and then, because of the lack of cells and growing prison population, double- or triple-celled at night.[72] In 1835, the inspectors complained that the construction was so shoddy that the prisoners communicated with one another through the privy pipes when they were empty. The Pennsylvania System was not fully implemented at Western until about 1837.[73] Even though Western had been authorized, constructed, and opened first, one consequence of its failure was that Eastern would become the flagship prison of the Pennsylvania System.

THE PENNSYLVANIA SYSTEM AT EASTERN STATE PENITENTIARY

When Eastern State Penitentiary opened in 1829, it was located beyond the two square miles to which Philadelphia was then limited.[74] Near the outskirts of the hilly district north of Philadelphia called Spring Garden, which consisted primarily of farmland, the new prison was built on a former cherry orchard atop a slightly elevated plot of land (see Figure 2.1). For many commentators, Eastern would be known simply as "Cherry Hill." Despite the cheerfulness of this more colloquial moniker, and Eastern's bucolic setting, the isolated castlelike edifice looming in the distance had the potential to terrify passersby. As Smith reported proudly the year after Eastern opened, "The design and execution impart a grave, severe, and awful character to the external aspect of this building. The effect which it produces on the imagination of every passing spectator, is peculiarly impressive, solemn, and instructive."[75] Certainly, for many of the thousands of people about to experience the Pennsylvania System as punishment, the sight of Eastern would have been terrifying. Let us imagine for a moment how the Pennsylvania System would have been

---

[69] Doll, "Trial and Error," p. 15.

[70] Ibid., p. 19.   [71] Ibid., p. 20.   [72] Ibid., p. 22.   [73] Ibid., p. 20.

[74] Although urbanization was beginning to stretch north, the new prison was for all intents and purposes outside of the city.

[75] George Washington Smith, *A View and Description of the Eastern State Penitentiary of Pennsylvania*. Philadelphia: Philadelphia Society for Alleviating the Miseries of Public Prisons and C. G. Childs, 1830, p. 3.

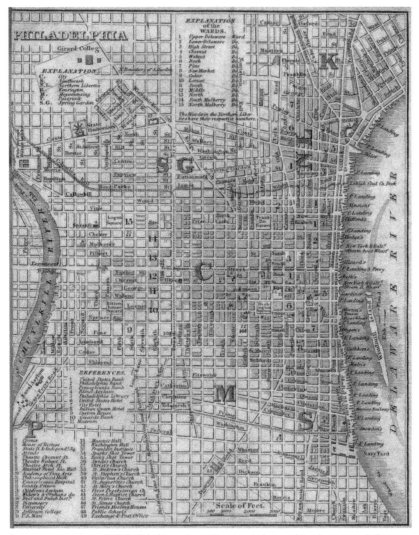

FIGURE 2.1 Map of Philadelphia, 1842. Eastern is located in the upper left quadrant.

Source: H. S. Tanner, The *American Traveller; or Guide Through the United States*. New York: T. R. Tanner, 1842. Scanned by University of Texas Libraries (Perry-Castañeda Library Map Collection). Available at https://legacy.lib.utexas.edu/maps/historical/philadelphia_1842.jpg (last accessed December 1, 2019)

FIGURE 2.2 The facade of Eastern State Penitentiary in the 1870s.

Source: Richard Vaux, *Brief Sketch of the Origin and History of the State Penitentiary for the Eastern District of Pennsylvania at Philadelphia*. Philadelphia: McLaughlin Brothers, Printers, 1872, n.p. Scanned by Google. Available at books.google.com (last accessed December 1, 2018)

experienced – as it was related by administrators and visitors to the prison during its first decades.[76]

Riding in a carriage, escorted by a county sheriff, the prisoner sees Eastern from a distance, situated on a modest hill surrounded by empty lots and open fields. The watered-down liquor he had drunk at the jail is quickly wearing off. Eastern is clearly visible now and distinct from the few buildings visible in the surrounding environs. It is an enormous structure. Surrounded on four sides by walls 670 feet long, 30 feet high, and 12 feet wide at their base, the prison encloses an area of slightly more than 10 acres.[77] Like other prisons of its generation, Eastern resembles a medieval castle or fortress (see Figure 2.2). Commentators often likened it to "those magnificent and picturesque castles of the middle ages, which contribute so eminently to embellish the scenery of Europe."[78] Arrow slits decorate the walls and crenellated turrets punctuate each of the four corners. At the center of the front wall stands a fortified front entry,

---

[76] This description is a creative interpretation of the process, but one that relies heavily on official accounts from the prison's administrators as well as those of visitors to the prison.

[77] Negley K. Teeters and John D. Shearer, *The Prison at Philadelphia, Cherry Hill: The Separate System of Penal Discipline, 1829–1913*. New York: Columbia University Press, 1957, p. 63; Smith, *View and Description*, p. 4. Early historian Orlando Lewis reports it was "approximately twelve acres." Lewis, *The Development of American Prisons and Prison Customs*, p. 124.

[78] Smith, *View and Description*, p. 3.

a barbican containing "a massive wrought iron portcullis, and double oaken gates studded with projecting iron rivets."[79] Like the turrets, the barbican is crowned with battlements. This fortress appears ready for war; escape seems unlikely.

The prisoner and his escort enter through the portcullis: the outer gate opens, the carriage moves forward, the gate closes, and another interior gate opens, allowing them to proceed. He is then taken to a reception room within the prison, where a physician inspects him before he is stripped, bathed, and given new clothes. With several overseers present, the warden interviews the man for relevant information and records his physical features.[80] His name is recorded in two places only; he will henceforth be referred to by his unique prisoner number. Before leaving the room, he is blindfolded or a hood is placed over his head.[81] This odd device would, supporters explained, protect his identity, and that of his fellow prisoners, so all could leave the prison free from the stigma of their criminal record.

The prisoner is silently escorted outside. Although he will not see the layout, the prison resembles a giant wagon wheel. Seven long corridors or "blocks," as well as a path to the front building he had first entered, are each connected to a round building in the middle of the prison's grounds, the center building, which serves as the hub (see Figure 2.3). From that center building, one can see into each of the seven blocks. On a quiet day, one can also hear any talking or even whispering from the cells.[82]

---

[79] Ibid., p. 4.

[80] The presence of the overseers was required by law. Pennsylvania, "No. 204: A Further Supplement," p. 351. However, there were no references to this practice in the prison's records.

[81] This practice of blindfolding was not frequently discussed in the primary documents. Sources referencing a blindfold: Smith, *View and Description*, p. 5; Eastern State Penitentiary, *Warden's Daily Journal*, Volumes 1–2. Eastern State Penitentiary Collection, Record Group 15 (#15.50). Pennsylvania State Archives, 1829–1877, November 21, 1829, October 26, 1833. Sources referencing a hood: Ibid., January 2, 1835, October 5, 1835; Charles Dickens, *American Notes for General Circulation*. ed. Patricia Ingham. London: Penguin Books, 2000 [1842], p. 112; Vaux, *Brief Sketch*, p. 69. By 1855, a new instruction from the inspectors required the use of "hood-caps, with eye holes." Eastern State Penitentiary, *Warden's Daily Journal*, September 3, 1855.

[82] Eastern's internal arrangements borrowed from contemporary designs developed, but not yet widely used, for British and European prisons. Norman Johnston, "The World's Most Influential Prison: Success or Failure?," *The Prison Journal* 84:4 (2004), pp. 20–40, p. 32. Indeed, while Eastern's external features were similar to other modern prisons of its generation (Auburn also had a castlelike appearance), its internal design – the cell blocks – remained distinct from the American norm. English-born architect John Haviland designed Eastern's cell blocks on a "radial" architectural plan popular in

FIGURE 2.3 Eastern State Penitentiary in the 1870s. The attached yards are visible in the foreground on either side of the main walkway. The cell blocks to the right were part of the original design; the double-story blocks to the left were added, after the prison opened, to accommodate a larger portion of prisoners.

Source: Richard Vaux, *Brief Sketch of the Origin and History of the State Penitentiary for the Eastern District of Pennsylvania at Philadelphia*. Philadelphia: McLaughlin Brothers, Printers, 1872, p. 64. Scanned by Google. Available at books.google.com (last accessed December 1, 2018)

England: within the square perimeter, the cells composing the prison were housed in seven long corridors (blocks) emanating from a central building like spokes in a wheel: three to the east, one to the north, and three to the west; where the eighth corridor would have lain, a walkway connected the center building to the front entrance and administrative building. This plan, however, immediately proved limited. In 1829, only 3 single-story blocks were complete, built on an initial plan that would allow for 200 cells in 7 blocks. It quickly became apparent that more cells would be needed. Form gave way to function: in the prison's initial 200-cell design, the blocks' edges would form a circle; when it became clear more cells would be needed, the blocks were extended farther toward the exterior walls and the new cellblocks were built to be two stories tall. In the end, each block contained between 36 and 100 prisoners depending on if it was one of the first or last blocks built. See also Norman Johnston, Kenneth Finkel, and Jeffrey A. Cohen, eds., *Eastern State Penitentiary: Crucible of Good Intentions*. Philadelphia: University of Pennsylvania Press, 1994. For the first several decades of the prison's existence, construction was ongoing. By the end of 1834, the prison had enough cells for 311 prisoners, by 1836, it would have 450; eventually, the prison would have space for 500 prisoners in 7 blocks.

FIGURE 2.4 Inside a cell block at Eastern State Penitentiary in the 1870s.
Source: Richard Vaux, *Brief Sketch of the Origin and History of the State Penitentiary for the Eastern District of Pennsylvania at Philadelphia*. Philadelphia: McLaughlin Brothers, Printers, 1872, p. 68. Scanned by Google. Available at books.google.com (last accessed December 1, 2018)

Even so, guards walk up and down the corridors, wearing socks to muffle the sound of their feet (see Figure 2.4). On either side of the corridor are small squares of wood covering holes that are opened only to provide each prisoner with his meal or to check on the prisoner "without attracting [the prisoner's] attention."[83] On top of each square is a number signifying the prisoner's identity. But no one enters through the corridor; instead, they enter through a small private yard attached to each cell.

Blindfolded, but breathing in the fresh, cooler outside air, the prisoner walks with his escort from the front building around another building and down its side. They stop as the guard unlocks a thick door that leads into a small yard, and then unlocks another set of double doors that lead, finally, into a cell. The hood is removed, the escort leaves, and the pair of doors to his cell – he can now see a metal grate and a heavy wooden door – close behind them. It is strangely silent, especially after the din of the city in the morning and the heavy doors closing. As one commentator described, "Occasionally, there is a drowsy sound from some lone weaver's shuttle, or shoemaker's last, but it is stifled by the thick walls and heavy dungeon-door, and only serves to make the general stillness more

---

[83] Smith, *View and Description*, p. 5. In practice, guards often communicated with the prisoner rather than just looking in on them.

profound."[84] The prisoner believes there are other men like him in the cells surrounding his own, but he cannot hear them and now he is unsure of their presence.

Alone inside his cell, the prisoner looks around his new home. It is large enough for him to remain healthful and productive without leaving his cell in the years to come – approximately eight feet wide by fifteen feet long and eleven feet high. The cell is roomy for a prison – he has heard of New York's prisoners who spent their nights in coffinlike cells little more than three feet wide and seven feet long. And it is bigger than his previous living quarters. Even so, to its new occupant, the cell is exceedingly claustrophobic.[85]

He examines the room's few contents: In addition to the bed, there is a "clothes rail, seat, shelf, tin cup, wash basin, victuals pan, looking glass, combs, scrubbing brush and sweeping brush ..." (see Figure 2.5).[86] To his surprise, there is also a flushable toilet and a flue that vents warm air – no one has told him that these are new, "cutting edge technolog[ies]" unavailable even in the White House or the U.S. Capitol building.[87] The bedstead on which he will sleep tonight is vertical and affixed to the wall, out of the way for the day; at night, he will unfold it to lie on the straw mattress with its "one sheet, one blanket and one coverlet."[88] He can see

---

[84] Dickens, *American Notes*, p. 112. Several visitors commented on the tomblike quiet of the prison. However, the prison's private records suggest talking, whispering, yelling, tapping, and other forms of communication were common. It was worse at night when there were fewer guards on duty and prison administrators were in their own beds.

[85] The dimensions of any given cell varied depending on when it was constructed, but most were between 7.5 and 8 feet wide, 12 to 16 feet long, and 11 to 14 feet high. Cells built as part of the original construction were often 7.5 × 15 × 11 feet, while the newer cells were slightly larger. Vaux, *Brief Sketch*, pp. 69–70. See also Smith, *View and Description*. Eastern's cells "were unusually large by contemporary and even today's standards." Norman Johnston, "Noble Ideas Collide with Reality," in *Eastern State Penitentiary: Crucible of Good Intentions*, ed. Norman Johnston, Kenneth Finkel, and Jeffrey A. Cohen. Philadelphia: University of Pennsylvania Press, 1994, pp. 47–68, p. 49. As early commentators noted as well, Eastern's cells "contain[ed] more cubic feet of air, or space, than a great number of the apartments occupied by industrious mechanics in our city" in which they too "work and sleep in the same chamber." Smith, *View and Description*.

[86] T. B. McElwee, *A Concise History of the Eastern Penitentiary of Pennsylvania Together with a Detailed Statement of Proceedings of the Committee Appointed by the Legislature (Vol. 1)*. Philadelphia: Neall & Massey, 1835, p. 8.

[87] Johnston, "The World's Most Influential Prison: Success or Failure?" p. 25. Eastern's central heating apparatus consisted of "flues [which] conduct heated air from large cockle stoves to the cells" – this was considered "[a] novel and ingenious contrivance." Smith, *View and Description*, p. 5.

[88] McElwee, *A Concise History of the Eastern Penitentiary of Pennsylvania*, p. 8.

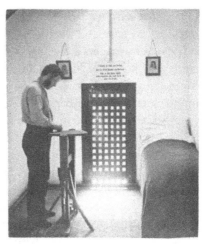

FIGURE 2.5 A cell at Eastern State Penitentiary in the 1870s.

Source: Richard Vaux, *Brief Sketch of the Origin and History of the State Penitentiary for the Eastern District of Pennsylvania at Philadelphia*. Philadelphia: McLaughlin Brothers, Printers, 1872, p. 98. Scanned by Google. Available at books.google.com (last accessed December 1, 2018)

a sliver of sky through a rectangular skylight in the center of the ceiling. He stares at it as the panic begins to set in.

After what seems like days, the prisoner hears a latch moving; it is not on the side with the door, but the wall opposite – the wall between his cell and the corridor. He approaches, opens a small square wooden door and retrieves his meal, but he cannot see out, nor can he see the person who delivers the meal. It is some broth and mutton, perhaps some okra as well, or some other fresh vegetable from the garden he does not know grows between the cellblocks or within the newly erected greenhouse he cannot see.[89] After another eternity, the light fades. It is deathly silent as he lies in his bed, dreading the years to come.

In the morning, he retrieves bread and coffee from the meal slot.[90] A new day. After several more hours, a guard comes and leads him outside through the double doors he had entered the day before. Outside his cell,

---

[89] Eastern State Penitentiary, Physician's Report, *Sixteenth Annual Report of the Inspectors of the Eastern State Penitentiary of Pennsylvania*. Philadelphia: Ed. Barrington and Geo. D. Haswell, 1845, p. 35. A greenhouse was erected in 1843 on the southeastern side of cellblock 3.

[90] Ibid., p. 35.

he can now see a walled-in yard, mirroring the dimensions of his cell. He is told to exercise and breathe in the fresh air; he has an hour. Outside, the prisoner whispers a message against the wall, but no one answers. He can hear others shuffling around in their yards, but they are far away – not in the yards on either side of his.[91] The hour passes far too quickly and the guard returns. Escorting the prisoner back inside, the guard tells the prisoner that in the future, he can grow various plants to supplement his rations, if he wishes.[92] This time when the guard leaves, he again locks the metal grate but leaves the outside wooden door open for ventilation. From this angle, the prisoner can see a bit of blue sky. More time passes and the evening meal arrives. The days repeat like this.

After a few days, mercifully, the prisoner is provided with work, a welcome reprieve from the boredom and melancholy that has set in. Now his room contains a "loom, or bench, or wheel" and even work tools; during the day, he folds his bed up against the wall so he has more room to work. He is also allowed "a Bible, and a slate and pencil," but so far these items remain untouched. [93] On Sunday, the prisoner opens a latch in his door and listens attentively to the minister preaching down the corridor; perhaps he does not believe the words, but it is better than the silence, so he listens.

He is not alone all the time. Most frequently, he interacts with an overseer who trains him in the craft he has been assigned and brings him new raw materials for the shoes, cabinets, or cloth he is making. Once a week, the physician inquires after his health and what he needs. On another day or two, the prison's minister, or "moral instructor" as he seems to be called, discusses morality and religion. Once a week – though possibly more often – the warden comes by to speak with him to see that his overseer is treating him well and that the other prison staff

---

[91] As Warden Halloway explained, "the prisoner is permitted to exercise [in the yard] for the space of one hour each morning in the Summer, and for a somewhat diminished period in the winter – the weather being suitable." Eastern State Penitentiary, Warden's Report, *Thirty-Third Annual Report of the Inspectors of the State Penitentiary for the Eastern District of Pennsylvania*. Philadelphia: McLaughlin Brothers, 1862, p. 46. Prisoners on the second story of newer blocks (blocks 4–7), who lacked an attached yard because of their elevation, were given "double cells" ($17 \times 12 \times 12$ feet) Vaux, *Brief Sketch*, pp. 69–70.

[92] Smith, *A Defence of the System*, p. 23. One commentator explained in the late 1840s, "many of them [the prisoners] cultivate a little garden, and raise both flowers and fruits." "Alleviation of the Miseries of Public Prisons," *Pennsylvania Journal of Prison Discipline and Philanthropy* 3:4 (1848), p. 210, p. 216.

[93] Dickens, *American Notes*, p. 113.

are catering to his needs. Other visitors also enter his cells. One day a week (most often Tuesday or Saturday), a local penal reformer who has been "assigned" to his block speaks with him for an hour or so, although their visits are less consistent. In addition, most frequently on Tuesdays or Saturdays but sometimes on other days, another prison administrator, called an "Inspector" also comes to his cell to see that he is being treated fairly by the warden and other staff; all of these visitors tell him how he should spend his time and what he should do when he is finally released.

Occasionally, someone important or famous comes to visit the prison and enters his cell to ask him questions about his experience. The prisoner now understands that foreign visitors and dignitaries see Eastern as a tourist destination representing the capacity of American progress and democracy, an improvement over previous barbaric punishments. As these visitors leave his cell, he hears them speaking with the warden or an inspector; one of the visitors exclaims, "we have never seen a building so admirably adapted to the purposes of security, seclusion, health and convenience, as this Penitentiary," despite having toured the prisons of "Europe and this country."[94] Sometimes there are questions about how much it cost to build such a magnificent prison, but the administrators seem to obfuscate, saying things like the price does not matter or it is difficult to calculate exactly.[95]

As the days and weeks pass, he becomes more efficient at his tasks, producing more shoes or woven cloth than he had when he first entered. He learns to look forward to the opportunity to leave his cell for his little yard. At first, he had hoped to hear from a neighboring prisoner, but he does not; neighboring prisoners are never allowed in their yards at the same time. Perhaps he will plant some vegetables in his yard when the weather improves. He also grows fond of the regular visits from the warden, the inspectors, the physician, even the moral instructor and the do-gooder volunteers from that penal reform society. Having improved in

---

94 Smith, *View and Description.*

95 In 1830, Smith claimed Eastern would have cost $432,000 by the time it was completed. Ibid., p. 3. This figure was repeated in a widely circulated report on the American penitentiary system by French visitors, Gustave de Beaumont and Alexis de Tocqueville, who noted this figure "makes the price of each cell 1624 dollars," or ten times the cost of those at Wethersfield State Prison (de Beaumont and de Tocqueville, *On the Penitentiary System*, p. 75). Another observer noted, "The cost of the building cannot be accurately ascertained ...." However, he recorded several legislative appropriations between 1821 and 1835 totaling $772,600.69. McElwee, *A Concise History*, p. 10; also cited in Vaux, *Brief Sketch*, p. 63.

his ability to read, he has started to read his bible before bed – the warden has permitted him a lamp for the purpose. He has even grown thankful for the solitude: he realizes that, having reformed, he can leave the prison unrecognized and untarnished by his punishment. The weeks continue like this. He thinks to himself, "It will be over one day," but he is also glad he has not had to face the public infliction of corporal punishment or spend any more time in an overcrowded, filthy jail. He is ultimately grateful to have this experience.

* * *

This romanticized experience was the aspiration. Through solitude, cut off from immoral distractions or influences, the prisoner is forced to learn the benefits of labor and take solace in religious ministrations; perhaps he even learns how to read. He becomes self-disciplined and leaves the prison a better man, or at the very least, the same as when he entered, unmarred by the contamination of other, more experienced criminals and unrecognized by compatriots who may seek to pull him back into the criminal underworld. Instead, he can resume his life and, sobered by the memory of his confinement, avoid crime. This was the Pennsylvania System as its supporters imagined it when it was first put into effect in 1829 – following years of debate and decades of failure. It was not, however, how the Pennsylvania System would function. For decades to come, Pennsylvania System supporters would repeatedly put forth this image, regardless of how different the reality might be. Ultimately, that reality, although structured by this image, would be determined not by statutes or reformers, but by the prison's administrators.

B

THE MEN IN CHARGE

Professionally, too, the personnel becomes identified with the agency, deriving prestige and disesteem from the fortunes of the organization itself.

Philip Selznick[1]

---

[1] Selznick, *TVA and the Grassroots*, p. 51.

3

Uncertainty and Discretion

The Contours of Control at Eastern State Penitentiary

There are in America as well as in Europe, estimable men whose minds feed upon philosophical reveries, and whose extreme sensibility feels the want of some illusion. These men, for whom philanthropy has become a matter of necessity, find in the penitentiary system a nourishment for this generous passion. Starting from abstractions which deviate more or less from reality, they consider man, however far advanced in crime, as still susceptible of being brought back to virtue. They think that the most infamous being may yet recover the sentiment of honour; and pursuing consistently this opinion, they hope for an epoch when all criminals may be radically reformed, the prisons be entirely empty, and justice find no crimes to punish.

Others, perhaps without so profound a conviction, pursue nevertheless the same course; they occupy themselves continually with prisons; it is the subject to which all the labours of their life bear reference. Philanthropy has become for them a kind of profession; and they have caught the *monomanie* of the penitentiary system, which to them seems the remedy for all the evils of society.

Gustave de Beaumont and Alexis de Tocqueville (1833), *On the penitentiary system in the United States and its application in France*[1]

PRE-BUREAUCRATIC CRIMINAL JUSTICE

American cities' and states' criminal justice systems modernized in the nineteenth century. Policing slowly transformed through the middle of the

---

[1] Gustave de Beaumont and Alexis de Tocqueville, *On the Penitentiary System in the United States and Its Application in France*, Trans. by Francis Lieber. Philadelphia: Carey, Lea, and Blanchard, 1833, p. 48.

century from a system of voluntary night watchmen responding to the hue and cry to a formal, trained, paid police force. Philadelphia experienced this transition rather early: growing Nativist tensions peaked in 1844 with a series of major riots, leading to the formation of a police department in Philadelphia in 1845, the same year as New York and a few years after Boston.[2] The nation's courts also transformed in this period. Like other large cities, Philadelphia began to replace its system of citizen-led criminal complaints by employing prosecutors, electing its first District Attorney in 1850. Around the country, lay judges, paid through a fee system, were slowly replaced by formally trained, officially employed judges. Here, Philadelphia was behind the curve, fully revising its system of lay judges under the state's Constitution of 1874.[3]

Prisons around the country were even slower to modernize, although they were not particularly far behind in this process. Most prisons were managed by untrained, inexperienced men with little oversight. The highest level of management was a board of supervisors, directors, or inspectors – functionally equivalent small groups of upper-class men, usually with interests in social reform or politics and careers in business or law. Outside of Pennsylvania, daily prison administration was given over to an agent, an entrepreneurial contractor. The agent made business decisions as well as internal management decisions about prisoners' food and punishment as well as hiring, firing, and otherwise managing the guards and overseers; in some cases, the agent had virtually sole control over the prison. Notably, these men were often businessmen who had little or no experience with prisons or criminal justice more generally. Prisons also employed (or hosted volunteer) ministers, teachers, and doctors to tend to the prisoners' spiritual, social, or physical needs. A few prisons employed matrons to supervise the handful of women incarcerated within their walls. Only rarely would personnel have experience working in another prison; instead, most personnel simply plied their trade in the prison setting with minimal training for the different context.[4]

---

[2] The Philadelphia police force was reformed in 1854.

[3] See Samuel Walker, *A Critical History of Police Reform: The Emergence of Professionalism.* Lexington, MA: Lexington Books, 1977; Roger Lane, *Policing the City: Boston, 1822–1885.* Cambridge, MA: Harvard University Press, 1967; Allen Steinberg, *The Transformation of Criminal Justice: Philadelphia, 1800–1880.* Chapel Hill: University of North Carolina Press, 1989.

[4] In many cases, this situation – in which prison wardens had no experience with prisons before their appointments – persisted into the twentieth century. At most, prison wardens may have had experience with law enforcement, such as working as a sheriff. e.g.,

Beyond this small cadre of administrators, staff, and volunteers, few others had any authority or direct influence over the prison. States lacked a supervising agency along the lines of contemporary departments of corrections; predecessors to such bureaucracies emerged after the Civil War, but for most of the nineteenth century, prisons were worlds unto themselves. Penal reformers, newspapers, grand juries, and legislatures made occasional investigations (of varying levels of formality) into the prisons, but rarely with any significant impact. Indeed, penal reformers (mostly confined to large cities) were the most vigilant in this regard, but, while they could sometimes influence state legislatures to make changes to the law, reformers had no authority over prisons. Inspired by reformers, authorized by their state legislatures, prisons around the country were run by prison administrators who had near-total control over their prisons.

*　*　*

Eastern was far from exceptional in the level of prison administrators' autonomy and inexperience, but two factors distinguished the administration at Eastern from that at other prisons. First, Pennsylvania did not employ contractors to run their prisons; consequently, the men in charge at Eastern saw themselves as trusted caretakers of the prison rather than men motivated by the promise of profit. Second, as some commentators recognized, Eastern's administrators were particularly active.[5] More than mere figureheads, they had greater control than at other prisons – and they took advantage of this greater control. It was, in effect, *their* prison, a feeling of ownership and responsibility that will become clear in the following chapters. This chapter introduces the administrative and legal framework that provided a group of largely untrained and inexperienced men with tremendous control over Eastern and especially the difficult, and sometimes evasive, task of translating the Pennsylvania System into practice. It was this group of men for whom the Pennsylvania System became personally institutionalized and who would fight to maintain it at Eastern.

James B. Jacobs, *Stateville: The Penitentiary in Mass Society.* Chicago: University of Chicago Press, 1977; Mona Lynch, *Sunbelt Justice: Arizona and the Transformation of American Punishment.* Stanford, CA: Stanford University Press, 2010.

[5] e.g., Enoch C. Wines, and Theodore W. Dwight, *Report on the Prisons and Reformatories of the United States and Canada Made to the Legislature of New York, January 1867.* Albany, NY: Van Benthuysen and Sons' Steam Printing House, 1867, p. 70.

ADMINISTRATION

Eastern's opening in 1829 divided Pennsylvania System supporters into two separate, and increasingly distinct, spheres: penal reformers, especially PSAMPP members but also unaffiliated reformers, who lent their rhetorical support and occasionally visited the prison, on the one hand, and prison administrators who managed Eastern, on the other.[6] Although PSAMPP was primarily responsible for initiating the Pennsylvania System, Eastern's administrators were responsible for interpreting and implementing the Pennsylvania System.

In practice, then, for most of its nineteenth-century history, Eastern State Penitentiary was managed by a relatively small group of men with tremendous power over their charges (see Table 3.1).[7] Officially, the prison was overseen by a five-man Board of Inspectors, each of whom was selected by the Pennsylvania Supreme Court (until 1874; thereafter by the governor) for a two-year term. They received no salary for their duties.[8] The inspectors established the prison's rules and policies, fleshing out the authorizing statute's minimal requirements. They were also responsible for discretionary judgments such as approving the warden's decision to punish refractory prisoners. Two inspectors were selected each month to visit the prison twice a week to speak with the prisoners. These "visiting inspectors" were available to the warden to approve punishment decisions or make short-term decisions until the full Board could convene. The Board held monthly meetings (at the prison or at the home or office of an inspector) to discuss internal prison policy, meeting more frequently

---

[6] At Walnut Street, PSAMPP reformers had never fully taken control of the prison – they enjoyed immense control over Walnut Street as appointed inspectors, but daily operation still fell to a keeper, whom they sought to control as well. Moreover, Walnut Street's inspectors never fully shed their identity as reformers. At Eastern, however, the prison administrators, including former PSAMPP members, enjoyed substantial autonomy.

[7] The authorizing 1829 statute specified certain responsibilities for each office. Pennsylvania, "No. 204: A Further Supplement To an Act, Entitled 'An Act to Reform the Penal Laws of This Commonwealth'," in *Laws of the General Assembly of the State of Pennsylvania*. Harrisburg: Office of the Reporter, 1829, pp. 341–354. Other responsibilities were described in the minute books of the Board of Inspectors and the warden's daily journal. See *Minute Books of the Board of Inspectors and Board of Trustees of the Eastern State Penitentiary*. Volumes 1–4. Eastern State Penitentiary Collection, Record Group 15 (#15.44). Pennsylvania State Archives. 1829–1885. Eastern State Penitentiary, *Warden's Daily Journal*, Volumes 1–2. Eastern State Penitentiary Collection, Record Group 15 (#15.50). Pennsylvania State Archives. 1829–1877.

[8] An exception emerged in later years when the inspector who served as the treasurer did receive a salary reflecting a significant increase in his duties.

TABLE 3.1 *Eastern's administrative positions*

Title	Term Length	Appointed By	Number	Residence	Contact with Prisoners
Inspector	2 years	Supreme Court (later: Governor)	5	Off-site	Biweekly visits by 2 inspectors
Warden	6 months	Board of Inspectors	1	On-site	Daily visits
Physician	6 months	Board of Inspectors	1*	Off-site (later: on-site)	Biweekly visits
Moral Instructor	6 months	Board of Inspectors	1	Off-site	Unspecified (later: weekly)

*For a short period, the prison maintained two physicians. Other named officers were the clerk, matron, and school teacher, but they did not write reports, although the clerk frequently assembled the tables compiled in the annual reports, as did the school teacher later in the prison's history. Moreover, the matron and school teacher were roughly equivalent, or less, to the overseers.

when necessary. Every six months, the Board appointed (or reappointed) the prison's warden, physician, moral instructor, and clerk.

The warden oversaw the prison's day-to-day operations. Wardens lived on the prison grounds and received an annual salary. The warden was required to visit all of the prisoners every day, a duty that became increasingly untenable when the prison contained 200 or more prisoners. The warden also supervised the prison's quotidian matters, including managing the guards, variously known as "overseers" or "keepers,"[9] and punishing recalcitrant prisoners, as well as the prison's business matters, including buying food, supplies, and raw materials and selling prisoner-made goods to offset the prison's costs. As the inspectors superseded the warden's authority, he often sought their permission or guidance and they occasionally instructed him to reverse certain policies or actions, or reminded him to comply with certain forgotten policies. Wardens sometimes quarreled with the inspectors and, more frequently, the prison's staff physician.

From the beginning, Eastern maintained a staff physician, but his duties and relationship to the prison changed over time. The physician was required to visit all prisoners twice a week and treat their ailments.

[9] In theory, overseers (a term, taken from workplace settings, equivalent to factory fore-man) referred to guards who were also charged with supervising prisoner labor and instructing prisoners in a trade. Keeper (an old term for jailer, short for prison keeper) referred to the custodial staff or "turnkeys," whose job was to ensure prisoners stayed put. In practice, these terms are used interchangeably.

Initially, this requirement allowed the physician to maintain a separate (private) practice "in the city" (Philadelphia). By the early 1840s, however, with the growing prison population – and after growing frustration with the physician's absence during medical emergencies – the Board hired a "Resident Physician" who would, like the warden, live on the prison grounds in order to respond to emergencies in a timely fashion and to devote his full time to the prisoners and their needs (see Chapter 8). The physician's place in the prison hierarchy was somewhat ambiguous: he could overrule the warden's decisions about punishment, labor, or any other area of prison life where a prisoner's health was concerned; this could, and did, create tensions between the men holding these two positions.

Among the named prison officers, the lowest-ranked official was the moral instructor. For the prison's first nine years, the position remained unfilled because, under the 1829 statute, the moral instructor would not be paid.[10] During these early years, a few inspectors, several members of the local clergy, and PSAMPP members filled the void by giving sermons on the sabbath and meeting with prisoners individually. After the administrators' repeated imploring, the legislature authorized a salary and the administrators immediately hired a minister. The moral instructor, administrators and reformers repeatedly emphasized, would not violate the prisoners' religious freedom – if a prisoner requested a minister of a different religion, someone from the community would be provided. Indeed, clergy members (and some lay persons) of multiple denominations visited the prison to speak on the sabbath, some on their own accord and others by administrative invitation.[11] The moral instructor did not have a specific, statutory requirement to visit the prisoners on a weekly basis, as did the other administrators, but he would typically make his rounds, speaking individually to prisoners in one or two blocks each week, getting

---

[10] The inspectors were also unpaid workers but, unlike ministers, they were generally quite wealthy and their duties were not as time consuming as the moral instructor's duties.

[11] e.g., Eastern State Penitentiary, Inspectors' Report, *Thirteenth Annual Report of the Inspectors of the Eastern State Penitentiary of Pennsylvania*. Philadelphia: Mifflin & Parry, 1842, p. 6; Eastern State Penitentiary, Inspectors' Report, *Fifth Annual Report of the Inspectors of the Eastern State Penitentiary of Pennsylvania*. Harrisburg: Welsh & Patterson, 1834, p. 4; Eastern State Penitentiary, Inspectors' Report, *Seventeenth Annual Report of the Inspectors of the Eastern State Penitentiary of Pennsylvania*. Philadelphia: Ed. Barrington and Geo. D. Haswell, 1846, p. 7.

to each prisoner at least once a month.[12] He would also provide sermons to the prisoners, but even when joined by other religiously inspired men (including some of the inspectors and PSAMPP members), it was several decades before every block of prisoners would routinely receive a weekly sermon. By the 1850s, the Board of Inspectors insisted that the moral instructor be present for most of the day, each weekday, and to visit all prisoners on a weekly basis.

These four sets of men – the inspectors, the warden, the physician, and the moral instructor – together determined what the Pennsylvania System would mean in practice and how prisoners should be treated. Although their contact with prisoners was surpassed by the more numerous guards, these administrators were not like managers today who set policy without knowing the people who are affected. Instead, running their prison in a hands-on fashion, they were simultaneously managers and frontline workers. The rest of this chapter identifies what sorts of prior experiences and structural challenges affected their administration.

Gentlemen Reformers

For much of the nineteenth century (and even into the twentieth century for some positions), the characteristics of Eastern's administrators were fairly constant. They were elites of Philadelphia society, selected as much for their assumed moral uprightness (as part of the "better sort") as for their interest in penal reform. With few exceptions, they were gentlemen reformers – middle- and upper-class men involved in a variety of charitable and civic endeavors, of which the prison was one. Indeed, prison work, for many of these men, was an extension of their charitable work. Consequently, while they may have been better versed in their understanding of benevolence (i.e., helping the less fortunate), they did not have the same level of experience in managing a penal institution.

[12] In 1850, for example, Moral Instructor Thomas Larcombe reported his "regular or stated visits" for the previous year "amounted to three thousand three hundred and seventy," not counting "many additional visits, of a general character." Eastern State Penitentiary, Moral Instructor Report, *The Twenty-First Annual Report of the Inspectors of the Eastern State Penitentiary of Pennsylvania.* Philadelphia: Edmond Barrington and George D. Haswell, 1850, p. 37. In 1849, 121 prisoners were discharged and 128 received, "[t]he whole number of prisoners in confinement during the year was 420," and the final number of prisoners in residence on January 1, 1850, was 299. Eastern State Penitentiary, Inspectors' Report, *The Twenty-First Annual Report of the Inspectors of the Eastern State Penitentiary of Pennsylvania.* Philadelphia: Edmond Barrington and George D. Haswell, 1850, p. 3.

For many administrators, their work at Eastern was not a full-time job, and it was distinct from their primary career. According to one inventory of the twenty-five men appointed as inspectors between 1829 and 1872, fifteen worked as businessmen, eight were lawyers, one a doctor, and one a wealthy philanthropist (a retired merchant).[13] Twelve of the businessmen and lawyers were also politicians. In their lifetimes, four of Eastern's inspectors had been mayors of Philadelphia,[14] three had been state senators,[15] and two had been members of the U.S. House of Representatives.[16] Three inspectors were appointed judges, including one state supreme court judge.[17] Despite their part-time commitment, one-third of Eastern's inspectors retained their position until their death or until their health prevented them from continuing (see Appendix A).

Only a handful of inspectors had direct experience with criminal justice: in addition to the three judges, several inspectors who had served as Philadelphia's mayor would have heard certain criminal cases.[18] One inspector, William A. Porter, was a High Sheriff of Philadelphia County (appointed by his father, Governor David Rittenhouse Porter); after his time as an inspector, he went on to a position on the state supreme court.[19] From the other vantage point, Singleton A. Mercer brought with him firsthand experience of spending a month and half in a New Jersey jail awaiting his first-degree murder trial (at which he was acquitted in a much-celebrated verdict resulting from jury nullification).[20] Among inspectors with any background in criminal justice, however, most of their experience was limited to promoting penal reform. More than a third

[13] Richard Vaux, *Brief Sketch of the Origin and History of the State Penitentiary for the Eastern District of Pennsylvania at Philadelphia.* Philadelphia: McLaughlin Brothers, Printers, 1872.

[14] These men were Inspectors Benjamin H. Richards (1829, 1830–1831), John Swift (1839–1841, 1845–1849), Richard Vaux (1856–1858), and Alexander Henry (1858–1866).

[15] Inspectors Daniel H. Miller (1823–1825, 1825–1829, 1831–1833), Charles Brown (1838–1841), and William Goodwin (1853–1855).

[16] Inspectors Charles Brown (1841–1843, 1847–1849) and Richard Vaux (1890–1891).

[17] Inspector William A. Porter was a Supreme Court of Pennsylvania judge. Inspector Charles Sidney Coxe was a District Court of Philadelphia judge. Inspector Thomas Bradford, Jr., was a judge of the U.S. District Court for the Eastern District of Pennsylvania.

[18] Steinberg, *The Transformation of Criminal Justice.*

[19] Vaux, *Brief Sketch*, p. 84; John H. Campbell, *History of the Friendly Sons of St. Patrick and of the Hibernian Society for the Relief of Emigrants from Ireland.* Philadelphia: The Hibernian Society, 1892, p. 503.

[20] Elizabeth Dale, "Popular Sovereignty: A Case Study from the Antebellum Era," in *Constitutional Mythologies: New Perspectives on Controlling the State*, ed. Alain Marciano. Springer, 2011, pp. 81–106.

of the inspectors appointed before 1840 were PSAMPP members – and, in this capacity, had visited Walnut Street Jail and other local carceral facilities in addition to devouring and discussing the available penal reform literature – but this association exhausted their prior experience.[21] More atypically, Inspector George Harrison – the last inspector appointed before 1880 – had served in the Board of State Charities (a predecessor to later Departments of Corrections, created in 1869), acting as its president at one point, and had visited Eastern several times in connection with that work.[22]

Only two inspectors had a measure more experience than was typical, and both were appointed early in the prison's history. First, Roberts Vaux, a member of PSAMPP since 1808, worked extensively on Eastern's legislation, construction, and early defense (as we saw in Chapter 2) before

---

[21] PSAMPP membership after 1830 is surprisingly difficult to establish. Prior to 1830, member signatures were recorded and have been compiled, with their dates of membership, by Peter P. Jonitis and Elizabeth W. Jonitis, *Members of the Prison Society: Biographical Vignettes, 1776–1830, of the Managers of the Philadelphia Society for Assisting Distressed Prisoners and the Members of the Philadelphia Society for Alleviating the Miseries of Public Prisons 1787–1830*. Haverford College Library, Collection No. 975 A. ND. Negley Teeters also offers a list of those who signed PSAMPP's Constitution; while many names are recorded, he notes that not all members signed. The last signature was added in 1848. Negley K. Teeters, *They Were in Prison: A History of the Pennsylvania Prison Society, 1787–1937*. Philadelphia: The John C. Winston Company, 1937, pp. 507–509. For members joining after 1830, I culled through the meeting minutes of PSAMPP and its Acting Committee. Around the middle of the century, however, PSAMPP dramatically increased the number of people it *nominated* to the Society, often without first eliciting the nominees' interest. Based on these nominations, PSAMPP publicly issued lists of its membership – for example, in the 1854, 1862, and 1887 issues of the *Pennsylvania Journal of Prison Discipline (PJPD)* – but these lists are incomplete, missing some men who had been admitted to the Society, and sometimes overreaching, including those who had been nominated but did not join, or listing as deceased those who had earlier resigned (including those who had immediately resigned after receiving their nomination). With the help of a research assistant, I produced a list of administrators with and without PSAMPP membership (see Appendix A). PSAMPP also seems to have directly targeted prison administrators in these membership drives, sometimes quite aggressively. For example, Richard Vaux was nominated PSAMPP's President in absentia: he apparently had never attended a meeting, nor did he ever preside over PSAMPP meetings during his term. To avoid confusing PSAMPP invitations with actual PSAMPP involvement, I count only the membership of those administrators who were nominated to join PSAMPP prior to their affiliation with the prison. Unlike the earlier generation of inspectors involved with PSAMPP, however, the only two men in this later period who were members of PSAMPP prior to their appointments as inspectors, Henry and Maris, were apparently not active members. (From the earlier generation, only Coxe was an inspector before joining PSAMPP.)

[22] Eastern State Penitentiary, *Warden's Daily Journal*, December 18, 1869; December 15, 1870; April 30, 1872; December 10, 1872; June 18, 1873.

becoming an inspector in 1829.[23] According to his son Richard, who likewise became an inspector, Roberts Vaux "was in no active business; he devoted his time to public institutions for education and benevolence. His labors on behalf of the separate system of prison discipline and public education are a part of the history of his time."[24] Second, Thomas Bradford, Jr., a lawyer, wrote several statutes introducing important penal reforms, including the 1829 statute establishing the Pennsylvania System at Eastern, before becoming an inspector the same year.[25] Bradford was a member of PSAMPP (since 1805) and served as an inspector at Walnut Street Jail, Eastern's predecessor facility.[26] However, these two men were the exception rather than the rule even though, by the time Eastern opened, state prisons had existed for about forty years. As time went on, the men appointed as inspectors continued to share this lack of experience despite the proliferation of state prisons.[27]

The six men who served as warden during this period came from backgrounds similar to those of the inspectors. Most were merchants, and several continued running their businesses while warden, creating some conflicts of interest when wardens had to purchase raw materials and food for the prisoners or sell prisoner-made goods to support the prison, occasionally buying from or selling to their own business at favorable rates.[28] A few men did change occupations for their wardenship, at least

[23] e.g., Roberts Vaux, *Notices of the Original, and Successive Efforts to Improve the Discipline of the Prison at Philadelphia and to Reform the Criminal Code of Pennsylvania.* Philadelphia: Kimber and Sharpless, 1826; Roberts Vaux, *Letter on the Penitentiary System of Pennsylvania Addressed to William Roscoe.* Philadelphia: Jesper Harding, 1827; Jonitis and Jonitis, *Members of the prison society.*

[24] Vaux, *Brief Sketch*, p. 83.

[25] Thomas B. McElwee, *A Concise History of the Eastern Penitentiary of Pennsylvania together with a Detailed Statement of Proceedings of the Committee Appointed by the Legislature (Vol. 1).* Philadelphia: Neall & Massey, 1835; George W. Smith, *A Defence of the System of Solitary Confinement of Prisoners Adopted by the State of Pennsylvania.* Philadelphia: G. Dorsey, Printer, 1833 [1829], p. 17.

[26] Jonitis and Jonitis, *Members of the prison society.*

[27] This pattern only began to change in the late 1870s and 1880s. We have already seen Inspector Harrison's prior work with the State Board of Charities. As another example, Dr. J. William White became an inspector in 1885 after serving as the prison's physician from 1874 to 1877. But other inspectors continued the earlier trend: Caleb J. Milne was an active member of PSAMPP before becoming an inspector in 1888. Very gradually, then, men with prior experience with prison work joined the Board of Inspectors, but many, including those with prior experience, continued to fit the profile of earlier gentlemen reformers.

[28] As we shall see (Chapter 8), Warden Samuel Wood (1829–1840) was accused of embezzling money from the prison and diverting contracts to his family business. Pennsylvania,

temporarily: Nimrod Strickland (1854–1856) was a judge in Chester County before he became warden, and he later became a newspaper editor. Dr. Edward Townsend (1870–1881) began his career as a druggist and then studied dentistry, which he abandoned for his wardenship, his last occupation.[29]

Like the inspectors, few of Eastern's wardens had any experience with prisons, including Eastern itself (even after it had been in operation for decades). In fact, some wardens had little or no experience with Eastern before their appointment. Wardens who began as PSAMPP members had occasionally visited the prison as members of PSAMPP's Visiting Committee.[30] The future Warden Thomas Scattergood (1845–1850) sporadically visited Eastern in this way for two years before becoming warden, while the future Warden Edward Townsend (1870–1881) did so for decades before his appointment.[31] Non-PSAMPP members who became warden had even less prior experience. After he had been elected to his position as warden, but before taking office, the future Warden George Thompson (1840–1845) visited the prison several times, but these were apparently his first visits.[32] Likewise, the future Warden Nimrod Strickland (1854–1856) was invited to visit the prison while working as a judge, as many Pennsylvania judges were invited to do, and visited once;[33] like Thompson, once Strickland was elected warden, he spent a few days at the prison before taking on his duties.[34] Wardens' experience

---

Report of the Joint Committee of the Legislature of Pennsylvania Relative to the Eastern State Penitentiary at Philadelphia (Mar. 26, 1835). Harrisburg: Welsh and Patterson, 1835; McElwee, *A Concise History* (Vol. 1). Although he was cleared of the embezzling charges, he later incurred a significant debt to the prison, eventually prompting the inspectors to prohibit wardens from contracting with their own businesses. Eastern State Penitentiary, *Minute Books of the Board of Inspectors and Board of Trustees*, July 13, 1842; October 15, 1845; December 27, 1851.

[29] *JPDP*, "In Memoriam." *Pennsylvania Journal of Prison Discipline and Philanthropy* 35/36 (1896), pp. 30–32.

[30] When assigned to Eastern, they were required to visit the prison at least once a month and some attended on a weekly basis. But some members were assigned to visit the county prison, and membership on the two visiting committees varied.

[31] Eastern State Penitentiary, *Warden's Daily Journal*, e.g., Scattergood: October 14, 1843; November 18, 1843; April 10, 1844; Townsend: September 4, 1843; August 6, 1854; June 29, 1859. See also PSAMPP, *Acting Committee Minute Books*, Series I, Vol. 2–6, Pennsylvania Prison Society Records (Collection 1946) Series I, Vol. 6–10. Historical Society of Pennsylvania. 1798–1883. Scattergood appears in 1843–1845 and Townsend in 1846 to 1870.

[32] Eastern State Penitentiary, *Warden's Daily Journal*, June 23–27, 1840.

[33] Ibid., e.g., April 26, 1854.   [34] Ibid., e.g., June 22, 27, 1854.

with other prisons was similarly minimal. In the end, only two of the six wardens in this period had any experience managing a prison before becoming warden.

Eastern's first warden, Samuel R. Wood, held the most prior experience in penal matters. Wood had served (without compensation) as an inspector of Walnut Street and been a member of PSAMPP since 1816.[35] To better understand the nature of incarceration and penal reform, he toured European jails in the early 1820s (and he continued to tour the prisons of the United States after his appointment as warden at Eastern), which cemented his reputation as "the great apostle of Penitentiary reform."[36] Around the same period, Wood became a member of the Building Committee in charge of overseeing the design and construction of Eastern. When Eastern opened in 1829, he was "[s]trongly solicited to accept the appointment" as warden of the new penitentiary,[37] a position he held for more than ten years (1829–1840).

Decades later, John Halloway also began his position as warden with extensive prior experience. He was the son of one of the "principal keepers" at Walnut Street.[38] As a young man, he began a long employment as Eastern's clerk – in addition to his secretarial work, he often supervised the prison when wardens left on business trips or vacation. He ultimately served an unprecedented two nonconsecutive terms as warden (1850–1854, 1856–1869), serving for nearly two decades in total. Like England's famous penal reformer John Howard, Halloway died (while warden) of "typhoid pneumonia, contracted in the zealous discharge of official duty, in the 65th year of his age."[39] No other administrator could offer such a resume.

Moreover, while their average tenures at Eastern lasted for nearly ten years, the men who served as warden did not see their connection with the prison as a career, as illustrated by several wardens' desire to maintain their private business enterprises while working at Eastern. Thomas Scattergood (1845–1850) accepted his nomination to warden on the

---

35 Thomas B. McElwee, *A Concise History of the Eastern Penitentiary of Pennsylvania together with a Detailed Statement of Proceedings of the Committee Appointed by the Legislature (Vol. 2)*. Philadelphia: Neall & Massey, 1835, 15 (Yarnell testimony); Jonitis and Jonitis, *Members of the Prison Society*.
36 McElwee, *A Concise History*, p. 17 (Fry testimony).
37 Ibid., p. 14 (Barclay testimony).
38 Teeters and Shearer, *The Prison at Philadelphia*, p. 90.
39 Eastern State Penitentiary, *Warden's Daily Journal*, March 9, 1870 (Dr. Klapp).

condition that he need not give up his business.[40] When George Thompson was reelected warden in late 1850, he turned down their offer;[41] according to PSAMPP member, William Foulke, Thompson declined because the inspectors had insisted (following previous wardens' misconduct) that he not continue his business and Thompson had refused.[42] Moreover, when wardens left Eastern, they ended their involvement with prisons. Despite his lengthy commitment to penal reform, Wood's wardenship at Eastern was apparently his last sustained involvement with the cause, eventually becoming "first Master" at the Northumberland Post Office after his merchant business failed.[43] Only one warden, John S. Halloway (1850–1854, 1856–1870), spent his entire lifetime in prison work. For the most part, these men were not specialists.

Far from focusing their energies on criminal justice, Eastern's administrators were quite active in reform circles beyond the criminal justice system. As Historian Ronald Walters has noted, the antebellum period experienced one of "the most fervent and diverse outburst[s] of reform energy in American history … it was a rare person who was engaged in only one" reform activity.[44] Eastern's administrators were no exception, and their enthusiasm for volunteerism persisted even after the Civil War, when other reformers' energies waned.[45]

In addition to their quasi-volunteer work at Eastern, many of Eastern's administrators were involved with at least one charity, civic society, or other voluntary work in their lifetime, though not always during their tenure at Eastern. Roberts Vaux, one of the founders of the Pennsylvania System and one of Eastern's first inspectors (although he only served several months in 1829), was an extreme case: He was involved with the Old Man's Home of Philadelphia, the Pennsylvania Institution for the Blind, the Pennsylvania Institution for the Deaf and Dumb, the Association of Friends for the Instruction of Poor Children, the Academy of Natural Sciences, the Athenaeum, the Historical Society of Pennsylvania,

---

[40] Eastern State Penitentiary, Minute Books of the Board of Inspectors and Board of Trustees of the Eastern State Penitentiary, September 19, 1845.

[41] Ibid., September 21, 1850.

[42] William Foulke, *Notebooks Concerning Prisons and Prisoners*, Box 7, William Parker Foulke Papers. American Philosophical Society, Philadelphia, 1846–1852, October 17, 1850. He may have also had personal reasons for abstaining; see Chapter 8.

[43] Ibid., October 15, 1849.

[44] Roger G. Walters, *American Reformers, 1815–1860*. New York: Hill and Wang, 1978 [1997], p. xiii.

[45] Ibid.

the Pennsylvania Hospital, the House of Refuge, the Pennsylvania Abolition Society, the Bible Association of Friends, the Adelphi Society, and PSAMPP.[46] His son, Richard Vaux, who was the longest-serving inspector at Eastern, likewise had myriad pursuits: he was a member of the American Philosophical Society, a director of Girard College, and a long-time Freemason (at one point, their Grand Master), in addition to holding several local-level political offices and his career as a lawyer.[47]

Most administrators, however, were typically involved with only one or two other endeavors – another institution, a church, a bank, the University of Pennsylvania, or short-term planning committees for one-time events (such as the Centennial Exhibition).[48] Warden Townsend, for example, worked "as a manager of the Wills Eye Hospital, and for most of that time one of the managers of the Pennsylvania Institution for the Instruction of the Blind, and for many years its President."[49] Warden Halloway had long served as clerk at Eastern and had worked at the Philadelphia House of Refuge before becoming warden. The common thread in their varied interests was, superficially at least, the desire to improve society, especially its disadvantaged members. These were men, according to Gustave de Beaumont and Alexis de Tocqueville, "for whom philanthropy has become a matter of necessity, [who] find in the penitentiary system a nourishment for this generous passion."[50]

But de Beaumont and de Tocqueville overstated the case somewhat when describing "the *monomanie* of the penitentiary system." Some men, according to de Beaumont and de Tocqueville, "occupy themselves continually with prisons; it is the subject to which all the labours of their life bear reference. Philanthropy has become for them a kind of profession."[51] In some ways, this description characterizes well some of Eastern's administrators, like Warden Wood, Inspector Bradford, and the two Inspectors Vaux. But however disproportionately these men pursued penal reform,

[46] John Thomas Scharf and Thompson Westcott, *History of Philadelphia, 1609–1884.* (Three volumes) Philadelphia: L. H. Everts & Co., 1884, pp. 1201, 1207, 1459, 1462, 1475, 1541–1542; Patricia D'Antonio, *Founding Friends: Families, Staff, and Patients at the Friends Asylum in Early Nineteenth-Century Philadelphia.* Bethlehem: Lehigh University Press, 2006, p. 186.
[47] Scharf and Westcott, *History of Philadelphia*, pp. 1543–1544.
[48] See also Walters, *American Reformers*; D'Antonio, *Founding Friends*.
[49] *JPDP*, "In Memoriam," p. 32.
[50] de Beaumont and de Tocqueville, *On the Penitentiary System in the United States and Its Application in France*, p. 48.
[51] Ibid., p. 48.

they always had other philanthropic and civic commitments. Where de Beaumont and de Tocqueville are especially accurate is the way in which this all-encompassing commitment to penal reform was a sudden evolution – men *"caught* the *monomanie* of the penitentiary system" – it *"bec[a]me* for them a kind of profession," but it did not begin that way. Most administrators entered their positions with more enthusiasm than knowledge, experience, or training.

LEGAL AMBIGUITY

While administrators had little in the way of training or experience with criminal justice, they also had few positive sources to guide their work. To begin with, the law itself was of little help. Running at fourteen pages, the 1829 statute authorizing Eastern and the Pennsylvania System was one of the most detailed statutes authorizing a new state prison. But even this statute said little about actual routines and daily practices. After requiring that prisoners be fed and clothed, and kept away from everyone except official visitors, the law focused primarily on the prison's personnel – who would be employed, their general duties, and their specific duty to report to the legislature. Within this skeletal framework, it was up to the prison administrators to fill in the rest. Moreover, there was little discussion of the prison's ultimate goals – "the punishment and reformation of offenders" – or how exactly any component of the Pennsylvania System or the prison's officers (except the volunteer moral instructor) would achieve these goals.[52] Ultimately, it was up to Eastern's administrators to make those determinations.

Frustrating the administrators' efforts, the 1829 law's minimal articulation of the Pennsylvania System was vague at best and internally contradictory at worst. The original (1821) statute that authorized Eastern's construction and articulated an earlier version of the Pennsylvania System had insisted, "That the principle of the solitary confinement of the prisoners be preserved and maintained" – "always."[53] Under the newer (1829) statute, prisoners were to be held in "separate or solitary confinement,"

---

[52] Pennsylvania, "No. 204: A Further Supplement to an Act, Entitled 'An Act to Reform the Penal Laws of This Commonwealth'," in *Laws of the General Assembly of the State of Pennsylvania*. Harrisburg: Office of the Reporter, 1829, pp. 341–354, p. 347.

[53] Pennsylvania, "No. 64: An Act to Provide for the Creation of a State Penitentiary within the City and County of Philadelphia," in *Acts of the General Assembly of the Commonwealth of Pennsylvania*. Harrisburg: C. Gleim, 1821, pp. 94–97, p. 95.

receive visits from the prison personnel and authorized reformers, and perform "hard labor." The central difference between the two statutes was not the type of confinement (however different the wording), but the introduction of labor; thus, the word "labor" was nearly always included in the law's brief descriptions of the system. Confusingly to many at the time, the word "separate" was only intermittently present. Consequently, the statute was internally contradictory, variously referring to "separate or solitary confinement" and "solitary confinement."[54]

Further complicating interpretation, the legislature never explained what they meant by "separate or solitary confinement" or how "separate" confinement differed from "solitary" and thus whether these labels signified different punishments. Given the early debates and the ongoing opposition to pure solitary confinement, reformers and administrators alike intentionally used the term "separate confinement." As we shall see, they used this term to avoid the associated negative connotations by emphasizing prisoners' prosocial interactions with selected individuals while held in solitary (see Chapter 5). What "separate confinement" meant in practice, however, was unclear.

Once the prison was in operation, this legal ambiguity proved problematic. In particular, the role of the prison's cells became an item for contention as commentators sought to understand the intended form of confinement. Was it enough for prisoners to avoid other prisoners or must they remain in their cells (and attached yards) at all times? In light of the ambiguity surrounding the exact nature of prisoners' confinement – the lack of definition, details, or other guidance in the foundational

---

[54] The first page twice uses the phrase "to suffer punishment by *separate or solitary confinement* at labor." Pennsylvania, "No. 204: A Further Supplement to an Act, Entitled 'An Act to Reform the Penal Laws of This Commonwealth'," p. 341. In the second page, it switches between the phrase "the punishment by *solitary confinement* at labor" and, in the next paragraph, "*separate or solitary confinement* at labor." Ibid., p. 342. Later, it again refers to "solitary confinement at labor" and the "system of solitary confinement." Ibid., pp. 344, 347. A later statute again referred only to "solitary confinement at labor." Pennsylvania, "No. 373: An Act Declaring Obstruction to Private Roads to Be a Public Nuisance, and for Other Purposes," in *Laws of the General Assembly of the Commonwealth of Pennsylvania*. Harrisburg: J. M. G. Lescure, 1847, pp. 476–477, p. 476. A substantial revision of the penal code in 1860 (Act. No 374) authorized some convicts to "undergo an imprisonment, by separate *and* solitary confinement at labor" and others "to undergo an imprisonment, by separate *or* solitary confinement at labor" (emphasis added). Pennsylvania, "No. 374: An Act to Consolidate, Revise and Amend the Penal Laws of This Commonwealth," in *Laws of the General Assembly of the State of Pennsylvania*. Harrisburg: A. Boyd Hamilton, 1860, pp. 382–427, sect. 86, p. 404; sect. 139, p. 416.

statute – the administrators ultimately used their own discretion when implementing this system of "solitary or separate confinement."[55]

Publicly, Eastern's administrators followed a narrow reading of the statute. According to the ideal propagated in their annual reports, prisoners worked only in their cells, performing workshop-style labor (chairmaking, shoemaking, weaving, etc.); prisoners would never leave their cells except to go into their private yard.[56] In practice, as we shall see in more detail (see Chapter 7), administrators often set prisoners to work outside their cells: some prisoners worked as blacksmiths, cooks, bakers, launderers, and apothecaries, all in specially designated rooms or buildings (blacksmith shop, bake house, etc.) around the prison. Some prisoners were employed as gardeners and others as runners – taking items from one part of the prison to another. When carefully supervised, such work assignments would keep prisoners separate from one another while also allowing them to perform labor suited to their skills and accomplish necessary tasks for the prison.

As far as the administrators were concerned, this strategy, although not publicly acknowledged, was consistent with the law, as they read it. Because prisoners were kept separate from one another, they were kept in "separate or solitary confinement." Others disagreed. Very early in the prison's history, word leaked out that Eastern's prisoners were employed in this manner and the question arose: Did these assignments violate the Pennsylvania System?

During the winter of 1834–1835, the state legislature investigated this practice, as well as several other charges against the prison's administrators (see also Chapter 8). Although the investigation proved quite scandalous – featuring stories of fatal torture, routine embezzlement, and open lechery and adultery – the only charge that was sustained was the violation of the Pennsylvania System, what investigators labeled "a frequently and illegal practice in the treatment of convicts by the warden, of departing from and in effect disregarding the sentence of the courts of justice, &c."[57] As far as the legislature's investigative committee was concerned, prisoners were sent to Eastern State Penitentiary to serve

55 See also Lauren B. Edelman, "Legal Ambiguity and Symbolic Structures: Organizational Mediation of Civil Rights Law," *American Journal of Sociology* 97:6 (1992), pp. 1531–1576.
56 Or, once seasonal bathing was instituted, to walk, blindfolded, to the bathing apparatus.
57 Pennsylvania, Pennsylvania, *Report of the Joint Committee of the Legislature of Pennsylvania Relative to the Eastern State Penitentiary at Philadelphia (Mar. 26, 1835)*, p. 18.

their sentences in solitary confinement at hard labor; by letting prisoners out of their cells to perform work in other parts of the prison, the administrators had violated the Pennsylvania System. No one alleged that Eastern's prisoners were assigned to work together as occurred under their competitor (Auburn) system; indeed, the investigation's official report explained that administrators took great pains to keep the prisoners from espying each other when they were taken from their private cells. Instead, the committee argued, administrators had violated the law by removing prisoners from their cells to work, in the presence of an overseer, and thus not in solitary confinement.

From a legal standpoint, the committee was wrong: Removing prisoners from their cells did not violate the law. Although the 1829 law had variously used "solitary confinement" and "solitary or separate confinement" interchangeably, it also ordered that prisoners "shall be kept singly and separately at labour, in the cells *or work yards* of said prisons" (emphasis added).[58] In fact, several of Eastern's administrators – including Warden Wood and Inspector Bradford – had helped write the law governing the prison. They believed their practice of employing prisoners beyond their cells, but away from other prisoners, was entirely within the scope of the law's intent. As Inspector Bradford testified, he authorized these out-of-cell work assignments "under a full and perfect belief that the word and spirit of the law sustained us. I drafted the section which provides that the prisoner shall be kept singly and separately at labor in their cells or work yards and in this Mr. Wood [who had also helped lobby for the law] fully concurred."[59]

But the legislature primarily relied on various reformers' (more idealized) interpretations of the Pennsylvania System, which differed from the administrators' (more pragmatic) interpretation. According to one reformer, Francis Lieber, removing the prisoners from their cells to work in other parts of the prison, according to other reformers consulted, "would be an infringement on what I consider the system to be."[60] Specifically,

---

[58] Pennsylvania, "No. 204: A Further Supplement to an Act, Entitled 'An Act to Reform the Penal Laws of This Commonwealth'," p. 341.

[59] Pennsylvania, *Testimony from Legislative Committee to Investigate State Penitentiary for the Eastern District of Pennsylvania*, Partial Transcript. Series II, State Penitentiary for the Eastern District of Pennsylvania Records. American Philosophical Society, Philadelphia, 1835, Bradford testimony.

[60] Pennsylvania, *Report of the Joint Committee of the Legislature of Pennsylvania Relative to the Eastern State Penitentiary at Philadelphia (Mar. 26, 1835)*, p. 20.

removing prisoners from their cells violated the mandate "to keep solitude uninterrupted as much as possible."[61] As the committee explained in their report, confining prisoners to their solitary cells was crucial to the Pennsylvania System's efficacy:

It is the profound and noiseless solitude of the penitentiary cell, from which alone we can hope for that deep reflection and penitential sorrow, leading to a moral change in a mind and disposition almost wholly cancerous and depraved, with lawless passions, licentious habits, and obdurate propensities. Such a mind must be thrown back upon itself, and left without that delusive prop which wicked men derive from intercourse with their fellow men, more particularly, if that intercourse should be with those who want the extreme prudence and discretion, to say nothing of moral qualifications, which can in any case make such intercourse profitable to the unfortunate convict.[62]

Of course, nowhere in the 1829 statute (or any other piece of law) was such sentiment conveyed. So strong was the committee's conviction that neither the letter of the law nor the drafters' intent mattered as much as the ideal propounded.

When the legislature did consult the law, however, their arguments illustrate the uncertainty that surrounded the system of "solitary or separate confinement at hard labor." Ultimately, the legislature's legal interpretation rested on the rather convoluted (and almost farcical) question of whether the "or" used in the statute ("solitary or separate confinement") was conjunctive or disjunctive. The administrators' interpretation assumed a disjunctive (or as "or"), which allowed them to remove the prisoners from their cells because it meant solitary confinement was different from separate confinement and, thus meant prisoners could either remain alone in their cells (solitary) or be out of their cells but away from other prisoners (separate). The committee argued for a conjunctive (or as "and"), eventually explaining,

It is true that the disjunctive conjunction is used, but it is not used to make a distinction between two kinds of punishments in the alternative, either of which might be used at discretion, but the words "separate or solitary," are employed as descriptive of the nature of the only punishment which by the act, is established. That is, the punishment is to be not only separate but also solitary.[63]

In the end, the committee left the distinction to interpretation, but chided the administrators to leave the prisoners in their cells. The administrators

---

[61] Ibid., p. 31.   [62] Ibid., p. 20.

[63] Pennsylvania, *Testimony from Legislative Committee to Investigate State Penitentiary for the Eastern District of Pennsylvania*, p. 20.

declined to do so and continued, without another meaningful challenge, allowing prisoners to work around the prison's grounds.[64]

Muddling Through

The poorly defined and contradictory law itself complicated administrative work, briefly inviting unwanted scrutiny. But the debate over the meaning of the Pennsylvania System was only one source of legal ambiguity. In fact, myriad uncertainties arose from inserting a state prison into an existing network of a half-dozen other institutions designed for society's deviant and unfortunate. Confusion abounded over Eastern's actual jurisdiction and thus which prisoners the administrators could receive through their gates. Problematic situations were not always covered by the statutory law, but even when they were, many authorities simply ignored the law.

For example, numerous problems surrounded the types of crimes that would merit incarceration in the state penitentiary. The 1829 statute authorized Eastern to incarcerate offenders from Pennsylvania's eastern counties who had been convicted of serious offenses – "murder in the second degree, manslaughter, high treason, arson, rape, sodomy or buggery, burglary, forgery, passing counterfeit money, robbery, kidnapping, mayhem, horse stealing and perjury."[65] In practice, counties repeatedly

---

[64] There were other cases of legal ambiguity in which the law was either so poorly specified or poorly communicated with the administrators that they were unknowingly violating the law. For example, there was some uncertainty about the physician's ability to interfere with the warden's decision to punish. By law, the physician was allowed to notify the warden if the "discipline" of the prison or other "treatment" of the prisoner negatively affected the prisoner's health. Pennsylvania, "No. 204: A Further Supplement to an Act, Entitled 'An Act to Reform the Penal Laws of This Commonwealth'," p. 350. However, Eastern's first physician, Dr. Bache, testified at the 1834–1835 legislative investigation, "I never heard that the law gave me any power of directing the punishment of the prisoners." Bache also testified, however, he was "consulted ... not infrequently." He explained that Warden Wood "never consulted me as to whether such a punishment was proper or not for such a offence [sic], but he consulted me to determine in a medical point of view whether the prisoner was a proper object of punishment." Bache further clarified, "I do not mean to say that I was always consulted before a prisoner was punished, neither did I expect to be, but after a prisoner has been punished I have occasionally expressed my disapproval of the punishment on some medical ground or other." Additionally, Bache "considered it my duty when a prisoner was under punishment to watch its effects, and also a privilege to punish them myself if they misbehaved to me or in relation to my department." Pennsylvania, *Testimony from Legislative Committee to Investigate State Penitentiary for the Eastern*, Bache testimony, no page.

[65] Pennsylvania, "No. 204: A Further Supplement to an act, entitled 'An Act to Reform the Penal Laws of This Commonwealth'," p. 341.

sent convicts ineligible for confinement at Eastern, including those who had committed a crime not covered by the statute. Not quite a year into Eastern's existence, Warden Wood, after "consultations with the Inspectors," turned away "Sam Shadle from Union Co. convicted of an assault & battery with intent to kill"; the warden "sent him to Walnut St Prison, as the crime is punishable there."[66] Likewise, many people convicted of larceny arrived at Eastern for punishment even though it was not included in the 1829 statute. In late 1830, the inspectors simply decided the warden should accept Philadelphia's larceny offenders.[67] The following year, the legislature addressed these confusions with a new law. As of May 1, 1831, "any crime" previously eligible for "imprisonment in the jail and penitentiary house of Philadelphia" for one year or more would be incarcerated at Eastern instead.[68]

Even still, offenders' gender and age – or rather authorities' responses to them – complicated these directives. Prisoner No. 539, Ann Morgan, alias Elizabeth Eartlick, had been "convicted … of Larceny & sentenced to 3 years" at Eastern in 1834. Instead, she was initially brought to Arch Street Prison, where she "ha[d] been acting as nun," but she "attempted to escape" and was finally sent to Eastern in late 1835.[69] Prisoner No. 945, James Farral, was "a white boy aged 12 years"; despite his larceny conviction and two-year sentence, "the court considered him a fit object for the House of Refuge, the Sheriff took him there but they would not receive him & he then took him to a Magistrate who would not commit him." In 1838, Eastern's Warden Wood "received him with the advice of [Inspector] Tho. Bradford who was here at the time."[70] A few weeks later, the inspectors and some reformers secured an order "from Judge King for the removal of James Farrell to the House of Refuge."[71] Nearly two decades later, Warden Strickland received as Prisoner No. 3241 a

---

[66] Eastern State Penitentiary, *Warden's Daily Journal*, September 24, 1830.

[67] Ibid., December 12, 1830.

[68] Pennsylvania, "No. 119: An Act To enlarge the buildings of the State Penitentiary, for the Eastern District, and for other purposes," in *Laws of the General Assembly of the State of Pennsylvania*. Harrisburg: Henry Welsh, 1831, pp. 220–222, p. 221. When the state legislature revised the penal code in 1860, it again insisted that all sentences to hard labor and "separate or solitary labor" for one year or more should be served in one of the two state prisons. Pennsylvania, "No. 373: An Act to Consolidate, Revise and Amend the Laws of This Commonwealth Relating to Penal Proceedings and Pleadings," in *Laws of the General Assembly of the State of Pennsylvania*. Harrisburg: A. Boyd Hamilton, 1860, pp. 427–458, pp. 449–450.

[69] Eastern State Penitentiary, *Warden's Daily Journal*, December 9, 1835.

[70] Ibid., August 8, 1838.   [71] Ibid., August 29, 1838.

young man whom the Managers of the House of Refuge had "refused to receive" because he seemed "a hopeless case." The boy, "Andrew Palmer, white, convicted of Larceny, and sentenced for one year" seemed to Warden Strickland very young. "This lad, for he is such, more especially in size and appearance, than in alleged age, 18 yrs." Strickland noted, "He is evidently not bright; decidedly dull intellectually."[72] These prisoners were not explicitly within Eastern's jurisdiction, but, in the administrators' minds, the other institutions' refusal to receive them left them little choice.

The closing of Walnut Street Prison in 1835 presented other problems. Its prisoners were transferred to Arch Street Prison and Moyamensing Prison – two Philadelphia facilities that functioned as a combination of jail, debtor's prison, and workhouse – and to Eastern. The statutes authorizing these transfers had specified that Eastern should receive prisoners with two or more years remaining on their sentence. Several prisoners who had been sentenced to hard labor, but not to solitary confinement, and were transferred to Eastern submitted unsuccessful *habeas corpus* petitions challenging their relocation as an illegal change in their conditions of punishment.[73] In one case, prisoner John Reddill (alias John Reading) argued he should have been sent to Moyamensing instead. In a decision dismissing the case, Pennsylvania's Supreme Court explained, "The City and County jail is only for those convicted in the City or County, and sentenced to confinement for a period under two years." The court noted that the two-year requirement was "strange," but applied the law nevertheless: offenders who had more than two years left on their sentence were rightfully removed to the state penitentiary.[74] Nothing in the 1829 statute had restricted Eastern's population to those people sentenced to more than two years; indeed, over the years, many prisoners entered Eastern with sentences of less than two years. But among those coming from Walnut Street in 1835, only those with lengthy sentences were received.

Eastern also received federal prisoners, whose reception was (initially) entirely within Eastern's administrators' discretion.[75] Mere months after

---

[72] Ibid., February 17, 1855.
[73] *Pember's Case.* 1 Whart. 439, 1836; *Reddill's Case.* 1 Whart. 445, 1836.
[74] Ibid., p. 448.
[75] The United States did not erect a federal penitentiary until late in the century, although a penitentiary house existed in Washington, D.C. As the corpus of federal crimes was quite small – mostly mail-related crimes, piracy, and treason – the federal government did not need a large facility. However, given the space constraints and the costs of transportation,

the prison opened, the inspectors received a letter from John Conard, U.S. Marshal. Marshal Conard requested permission to temporarily inter George Wilson and James Porter, "two prisoners ... held for trial on a charge of robbing the mail." Conard also explained,

I am well aware that the Penitentiary was built for certain convicted offenders of the state and was not intended to be used as a bridewell for untried prisoners. We do not, therefore, ask this as a right, to be used as a precedent at any future time, but as a favor, and for the furtherance of justice, under the peculiar circumstances of this case, as well for keeping the prisoners safely, as also to keep them entirely separate and apart from each other; which cannot be done in any other prison in the city.

Former U.S. Senator and Pennsylvania's Attorney General George M. Dallas also wrote to the inspectors to explain "the peculiar circumstances." He explained that the two men were particularly dangerous: "Their boldness and dexterity are such as to inspire all the officers and agents of justice with an apprehension that, unless confined with more than usual scarcity, they will affect their escape before the time of trial. ... Considering the Arch Street prison as not fitted to hold such men." Dallas explained of one of the accused, "The villain is extremely desperate, and the very best precautions to secure him must be taken. There is one already lodged in Arch street, and it is deemed absolutely necessary to confine this one somewhere else." Dallas had been told the man in the Arch Street Jail "will be safe no where but" at Eastern.[76]

Conard and Dallas laid strong cases because, ultimately, the decision belonged to Eastern's administrators. Inspectors Coxe and Bradford agreed to the request, "as a matter of amicable accommodation, and not as a right to apply the Penitentiary to the purpose of keeping untried prisoners."[77] Several years later, the legislature finally formalized this issue: an Act of April 15, 1834, required the warden to accept federal prisoners sent to them.[78] Even so, the warden continued to defer to

the federal government often sent its accused or convicted criminals to be incarcerated in nearby state facilities. See Paul W. Keve, *Prisons and the American Conscience: A History of U.S. Federal Corrections.* Carbondale: Southern Illinois University Press, 1991.

[76] Eastern State Penitentiary, Minute Books of the Board of Inspectors and Board of Trustees of the Eastern State Penitentiary, March 6, 1830.

[77] Eastern State Penitentiary, Minute Books of the Board of Inspectors and Board of Trustees of the Eastern State Penitentiary, March 6, 1830.

[78] Pennsylvania, "No. 215: Supplement to the Act Entitled 'an Act Relative to the Eastern and Western State Penitentiaries, and to the Philadelphia County Prisons'," in *Laws of the General Assembly of the State of Pennsylvania.* Harrisburg: Henry Welsh, 1834, p. 473, section 3.

the Board of Inspectors for confirmation. For example, in 1835, a marshal arrived at Eastern, "& requested us to take Lyman Parke for safe keeping."[79] Warden Wood "referred him to the President of the Board of Inspectors" who, the following day, "directed me to ... receive Lyman Parke, subject to the Marshals order."[80]

Legal inconsistencies, lacunae, and ambiguities gave authorities extensive discretion. In most cases, when Eastern's administrators faced an unclear course of action, they dealt with the matter themselves – the warden queried the inspectors and the inspectors discussed the matter among themselves, deferring especially to the lawyers among them. Only occasionally did they consult outside parties.[81] The rest of the time, the administrators were on their own.

OVERSIGHT

Embedded within a still-developing criminal justice system, Eastern's administrators encountered little oversight during its first five decades. Semi-bureaucratic forms of oversight over Pennsylvania's prisons emerged slowly, and not until after the Civil War. In 1869, the legislature created a Board of Public Charities to oversee "all charitable, reformatory or correctional institutions within the state."[82] The Board's "secretary and agent" was ordered to visit each institution at least once per year; the rest of the Board was to meet every three months at the state

[79] "Safe keeping" became the term for housing someone at Eastern not under sentence, such as those awaiting trial or found mentally insane and dangerous.

[80] Eastern State Penitentiary, *Warden's Daily Journal*, March 31, April 1, 1835. Similar negotiations would again take place during and after the Civil War as the prison received men convicted of wartime (i.e., federal) offenses.

[81] One example occurred in 1838. A recurring problem occurred when prisoners escaped: should the escapee should be released at his initial expiration date or held over for the same duration he spent beyond the prison's walls. On January 6, 1838, Warden Wood wrote to the inspectors, "The time of Samuel Brewster expires on the 12th inst: when he got out of this prison he was absent five days. I wish the Board to direct whether he is to serve these 5. days beyond the expiration of the period fixed in his sentence." Eastern State Penitentiary, *Minute Books of the Board of Inspectors and Board of Trustees*, January 20, 1838. Taking a relatively rare course of action, the inspectors referred the matter to the Supreme Court, whose chief justice, the warden reported, "informed me that it was the courts [sic] opinion that I could not [hold him for those five days] & must discharge him on the day his sentence expires." Eastern State Penitentiary, *Warden's Daily Journal*, January 10, 1838.

[82] Pennsylvania, "No. 66: An Act to create a Board of Public Charities," in *Laws of the General Assembly of the State of Pennsylvania*. Harrisburg: B. Singerly, State Printer, 1869, pp. 1267–1268, pp. 91, 92.

capitol.[83] The Board was also given "full power... to look into and examine the condition" of these institutions and was instructed to identify ways to improve their management. The agent was also directed to include in his annual report information on "the causes and best treatment of pauperism, crime, disease and insanity."[84]

While Eastern's administrators saw this development as a significant incursion into their own jurisdiction (see Chapter 9), the new Board's presence was little felt in practice. Indeed, as Historian Harry Elmer Barnes has explained, "no matter how alert or vigilant the board might be, it could never pass beyond a supervisory and critical capacity, and could never assume any administrative direction or coordination of the several penal, reformatory and correctional institutions."[85] Additionally, the state legislature created a Board of Pardons in 1874, but this creation limited the governor's pardoning power rather than prison administrators' control. Thus, even with the nascent bureaucratization occurring in the 1870s, Eastern's administrators remained in control of their prison – and yet these semibureaucratic forms of oversight were much larger than any other in Eastern's earlier history.

When Eastern was founded, the inspectors themselves were intended to be the prison's major form of oversight. Eastern's Board of Inspectors was partially modeled on the Board of Inspectors for Walnut Street, and employed some of the same men. As we have seen, Walnut Street's Board of Inspectors, composed primarily of PSAMPP members, was designed in large part to ensure the jailer followed the new rules of prison governance. Likewise, the inspectors' biweekly visits to Eastern's prisoners were intended to ensure that no "oppression, peculation, or other abuse or mismanagement" had occurred, and to investigate any of which they heard,[86] while the warden's power to punish prisoners was only solidified by the "approbation" of at least one inspector.[87]

Despite their formal role as a check on the warden's power, the inspectors' oversight at Eastern was designed to be more limited than it had been at Walnut Street. Indeed, there were only five inspectors, not twelve. Importantly, with Eastern's first warden (Samuel Wood)

---

[83] Ibid., p. 90.   [84] Ibid., p. 91.

[85] Harry Elmer Barnes, *The Evolution of Penology in Pennsylvania.* Indianapolis: The Bobbs-Merrill Company, 1968 [1927], p. 195.

[86] Pennsylvania, "No. 204: A Further Supplement to an Act, Entitled 'An Act to Reform the Penal Laws of This Commonwealth'," p. 347.

[87] Ibid., p. 348.

hand-picked from the reformer community, Eastern's architects did not anticipate needing the same level of vigilance. According to Roberts Vaux, writing a few years before Eastern opened, the inspectors were expected to maintain a certain distance, literally and figuratively, from the prison, which was built on (what was at the time) the city's hilly outskirts. As he explained, "more cannot be expected [of them] than the exercise of a general control over the prison, situated at such a distance from the city *as to preclude their minute and frequent interference*" (emphasis added).[88]

In practice, the distance does not appear to have impeded or discouraged the inspectors from exercising their authority in all areas of prison life. As the body ostensibly responsible for the prison's oversight, the inspectors operated with great discretion. It was the inspectors, rather than the legislature, who made the prison's internal rules. The 1829 statute establishing Eastern's governance was sparse in its actual guidance for establishing and managing the prison. Inspectors were given the "power, if they on conference find it necessary, to make such rules for the internal government" so long as the rules were not "inconsistent with the principles of solitary confinement" as articulated in the statute.[89] These rules would also include guidelines about when, by what means, and in what quantity unruly prisoners would be punished.[90] Illustrating just how autonomous the inspectors were, they found no need to make such rules for nearly a decade; the legislature officially directed them to do so only once (following an investigation into wrongdoing), yet the inspectors still waited five years to comply. Even these rules were not firmly enforced, prompting a new generation of inspectors to write a set of rules in the late 1840s.

Official Visitors

While the inspectors were expected to provide oversight from within, the 1829 statute also allowed a range of government officials access to the prison for their own inspection. These officials included "the Governor, Speaker and members of the Senate, the Speaker and members of the House of Representatives, the Secretary of the Commonwealth,

---

[88] Vaux, *Notices*, p. 60.
[89] Pennsylvania, "No. 204: A Further Supplement to an Act, Entitled 'An Act to Reform the Penal Laws of This Commonwealth'," p. 347.
[90] Ibid., p. 348.

the Judges of the supreme court, the Attorney General and his deputies, the president and associate Judges of all the courts in the state, the mayor and recorder of the cities of Philadelphia, Lancaster and Pittsburg, [and] commissioners and sheriffs of the several counties." In addition, the statute granted PSAMPP members access to the prison, continuing the privilege they had first gained at Walnut Street. Any other person required written permission to enter the prison, and only official visitors – government officials and PSAMPP members – could speak with the prisoners.[91]

None of these official visitors, however, were *required* to visit the prison on a regular basis, and visits verged between infrequent and rare. Members of the legislature, individually or as part of a group, visited the prison on a semiannual basis; legislators, individually or in small groups (along with their families and friends), typically visited only once a year, especially over the winter recess, apparently more recreationally than formally. Governors sometimes made the trips with members of the legislature, but their visits were even less frequent.

When state representatives did come to the prison, their "visits" were remarkably social in nature, particularly when they came *en masse* rather than alone. For example, visits often included not only a tour of the prison but also a "dinner party."[92] From their descriptions, such visits offer little semblance to a formal inspection. Warden Townsend recorded one such visit in 1871:

Judges Thompson, Agnew, Sharswood, & Williams of the Supreme Court, Judge Pierce of the court of Common Pleas, & Col. J. Ross Snowden Prothonotary [sic] of the Supreme Court, with all of the Inspectors visited the Prison this afternoon, after which we had a festive dinner in the east room, having also the company of our Physician (Dr. H. Klapp) our Moral Instructor (John Ruth) and our clerk (S. S. Sheneman) ... Much pertinent & instructive conversation was indulged in, and whilst there was a good deal of pleasantry there was no compromise of dignity by any of our assembled company.[93]

Occasionally, visits were too social. During one of the state legislature's few visits to the prison, this one lasting several days in 1837, Warden Wood noted in his log, "Had the [Senate's] Committee of both houses of the Legislature & all the members from the county now chose to come, With the Governor and many more, spending the day & took dinner with

---

[91] Ibid., pp. 351–352.
[92] E.g., Eastern State Penitentiary, *Warden's Daily Journal*, April 3, 1834.
[93] Ibid., January 27, 1871.

us to the No. of 54[.] Many of whom were not invited & should not have come."[94]

Given the size of some of these groups, it seems that official visits were more often driven by curiosity than regulation. Indeed, when Governor Francis R. Shunk visited the prison in 1847, he brought along "his Son, Brother & nephew."[95] Likewise, in 1852, Governor William Bigler brought

his Lady and her sister, who were met here by the President of the Board Mr Vaux and Messrs Campbell & Brown and the Hon. Mr Campbell M.C. from Illinois also Mrs Shunk widow of the Deceased Governor, Mrs Brown & her sister. The Ladies visited the female prisoners, while his Excellency saw a number of the men, spending really four hours in viewing the different parts of the Establishment.[96]

In contrast, other visits were apparently perfunctory and short, particularly when official visitors' family members did not attend. After Governor Shunk visited Eastern in 1845, "accompanied by Jesse Miller Secretary of State and John K Kane Attorney General," Warden Thompson observed, "their visit was rather an [sic] hurried one."[97]

The most common official visitors were the grand juries associated with the various courts (Quarter Sessions, Oyer and Terminer, Mayor's Court) in Philadelphia and other counties in eastern Pennsylvania. The prison received about a half a dozen to a dozen grand jury visits per year.[98] As we have seen, grand juries historically had played an important role in prison reform. However, as with the legislature and governor, their visits to Eastern may have been based more in curiosity than formal supervision; when they did act more formally, juries had narrow interests. As Warden Wood noted of one such grand jury, "I showed them the establishment or as much as they were willing to see for they appeared to care about seeing anything but a few special prisoners."[99] Grand juries coming from outside of Philadelphia in particular spoke only with prisoners from their county.[100]

The main source of external oversight, then, came from the local penal reformers. PSAMPP assigned members of its Acting Committee – a smaller group of more active members charged with additional duties – to visit the prison, spending the time interviewing prisoners, ministering to them, and reporting any neglectful, abusive, or otherwise distasteful behavior at the prison. Serious findings could be reported in a "memorial"

94 Ibid., December 30, 1837.   95 Ibid., October 23, 1847.   96 Ibid., May 15, 1852.
97 Ibid., November 11, 1845.   98 Ibid., Calculations based on entries in the text.
99 Ibid., March 19, 1835.   100 Ibid.

and distributed to the prison administrators; general dissatisfaction might impel PSAMPP to lobby the legislature for change. Positive findings would appear in the reformers' public writings, including their annual *Journal of Prison Discipline and Philanthropy* from 1845 onward.

However, even PSAMPP's visits were sporadic. Until the mid-1840s, the "Visiting Committee" usually consisted of two people who were assigned to visit the prison during the month and then report at the monthly meeting of the Acting Committee. Many Acting Committee meetings had no report, either because the Visiting Committee members were absent or because they had failed to visit the prison that month. When reports were provided, they were generally short and quite positive – still basking in the glory of their accomplishment in establishing the new prison and its Pennsylvania System.

In the mid-1840s, the Acting Committee increased the number of members assigned to the Visiting Committee (which thenceforth ranged from a handful of men in 1847 to one dozen in 1852 to more than two dozen in the early 1860s). They also formalized the reporting procedures, assigned members to particular blocks, required written reports, and even fined members for not visiting the prison or for failing to appear at the monthly meetings.[101] Even so, their meetings' minutes often included common references to one or more members noting that their schedules prevented them from visiting the prison that month.[102] In 1848, PSAMPP's Acting Committee even passed a resolution "request[ing]" the Visiting Committee "to meet monthly ... for the purpose of conferring together ... & *encouraging one another in the faithful performance of their duty*," among other reasons.[103]

Eastern's administrators keenly noticed the paucity of these visits, too. Warden Strickland noted in early 1856,

Samuel Caley, of the Prison Society, visited to-day; Townsend Sharpless was also here. Mr C. is the only one of the Society who can be said to have visited faithfully and regularly during the past year. Several others who came on Sunday have done pretty well; but the majority of the Society['s visiting] committee have been very irregular and infrequent in their attendance.[104]

---

[101] For Visiting Committee membership, see PSAMPP, *Acting Committee Minute Books* (see May 5, 1854 for fines).

[102] PSAMPP, *Minute Books*. Vol. 2, 4, 5; Pennsylvania Prison Society Records (Collection 1946), Series I, Vol. 2–4. Historical Society of Pennsylvania. 1810–1880; PSAMPP, *Acting Committee Minute Books*, e.g., August 2, 1854.

[103] PSAMPP, *Acting Committee Minute Books*, November 10, 1848.

[104] Eastern State Penitentiary, *Warden's Daily Journal*, January 2, 1856.

Other wardens were silent on these fluctuations, allowing the absence of recorded visits in their daily log to speak for themselves.

However infrequent, visits from external parties were ultimately mediated by Eastern's administrators. In many ways, they made the prison widely available. While only official visitors could speak with the prisoners, the prison was open to the public, tens of thousands of whom entered its walls throughout this period. Visitors' guides, such as *Philadelphia as it is in 1852*, listed Eastern among Philadelphia's various attractions; the prison was "well worthy of a visit." The guide informed out-of-towners that they could buy "Tickets of admission" from "any of its Inspectors" (listing Inspector Richard Vaux's address "[f]or the accommodation of strangers"). The guide also noted, "On the Lord's day, any Christian minister, of good standing in his denomination" was permitted to "visit the convicts, and preach to them, or otherwise instruct them."[105] Additionally, the administrators extended official visitor status to a range of foreign dignitaries, including Alexis de Tocqueville and Gustave de Beaumont, who visited on multiple consecutive days in 1831 while they compiled information on U.S. prisons for a report to the French government, and Charles Dickens, who visited in 1842 while he toured the states and their various attractions.

Despite this apparent openness, the administrators carefully curated access to the prison. In May 1843, the Grand Jury visited the prison, after they had "been discharged by the court"; Inspector Richard Vaux informed them "on applying at the gate ... that they could not be recognised as a Grand Jury but he would furnish them with tickets of admission individually as citizens, this was done and they were admitted to see the interior of the prison but not the inmates."[106] While Eastern's administrators fastidiously limited access to prisoners only to *official* visitors, the guards did not always accommodate the administrators' wishes. Warden George Thompson recorded his annoyance that "Mr James Barclay Secretary of the Prison Society visited with a Friend, visited a prisoner (Alexander) without orders"; an overseer had mistakenly "suppos[ed] the Gentleman was also one of the [Visiting] Committee

---

[105] R. A. Smith, *Philadelphia as It Is in 1852: Being a Correct Guide to All the Public Buildings; Literary, Scientific, and Benevolent Institutions; and Places of Amusement; Remarkable Objects; Manufactures; Commercial Warehouses; and Wholesale and Retail Stores in Philadelphia and Its Vicinity.* Philadelphia: Lindsay and Blackiston, 1852, p. 385.
[106] Eastern State Penitentiary, *Warden's Daily Journal*, May 11, 1843.

of the Prison Society."[107] Such exceptions were unacceptable to the administration; on several occasions, Eastern's administrators sent word to PSAMPP reminding them that only members of their Society's Visiting Committee were permitted to speak with the prisoners.[108]

Even when the administrators granted official visitors access to the prisoners, this access was incomplete. A former overseer reported privately to PSAMPP member William Foulke that a prisoner, who "had been kept in irons 30 days," had been "removed from his cell to another block to keep him out of the way of the visits of the Acting Committee of the Prison Society lest he should tell something." The former overseer commented "that he was a bad prisoner, but the trick of evading the visitors was wrong."[109] On another occasion, the former overseer reported that, while visiting Eastern, PSAMPP member "George W Smith ... [was] purposely called away on some pretense, when he was going to visit a particular prisoner when it was desired that he not see ... lest he should learn something that the warden did not wish him to know."[110] By controlling access to prisoners, Eastern's administrators could limit criticism of their activities by outside parties.

Lawsuits and Investigations

While "official" visits were both relatively informal and controlled by Eastern's administrators, complaints from prisoners or prison staff could lead to formal sanctions in the form of lawsuits against prison administrators or legislative investigations into prison management. However, both outcomes were exceedingly rare and largely inconsequential. In this period – and well into the twentieth century – prisoners were considered "civilly dead," barren of rights, and courts refused to hear cases, even of alleged torture.[111] *Habeas corpus* petitions – requests for release from

---

107 Ibid., April 13, 1843.
108 PSAMPP, *Acting Committee Minute Books*, June 8, 1852
109 William Foulke, *Notebooks Concerning Prisons and Prisoners*, Box 7, William Parker Foulke Papers. American Philosophical Society, Philadelphia, 1846–1852, October 26, 1849.
110 Ibid., November 6, 1849.
111 Rebecca M. McLennan, *The Crisis of Imprisonment Protest, Politics, and the Making of the American Penal State, 1776–1941*. New York: Cambridge University Press, 2008; Eric Cummins, *The Rise and Fall of California's Radical Prison Movement*. Stanford, CA: Stanford University Press, 1994; Malcolm Feeley and Edward Rubin, *Judicial Policy Making and the Modern State: How the Courts Reformed America's Prisons*. New York: Cambridge University Press, 2000.

confinement in the absence of cause – were prisoners' only legal recourse. During this period, only a handful of prisoners submitted *habeas corpus* petitions, and the prison administrators were rarely the subject of complaint.[112]

In general, court cases were simply inconveniences to the administrators: They often arranged transportation for their prisoners to attend court and, occasionally, even testified themselves, traveling to whichever court in eastern Pennsylvania requested their presence. In some cases, the warden traveled with the prisoner, which could be both time consuming and frustrating. In 1876, Warden Townsend took Prisoner No. 7428, Mark Reinhart, to the U.S. District Court, where Judge Cadwalader postponed the hearing for one week. Townsend dutifully "went again" to the court with his prisoner, but the case "was again postponed." He "again attended" court the following week only to see the prisoner "again remanded to appear on Saturday next." Finally, after traveling to the court "again" (nearly a month after the initial trip), the warden reported the case "was again deferred until the Court sends further notice." There were no further entries about this case. Beyond Townsend's repeated use of "again," he made no private notations to express his frustration; however, someone (probably Townsend) highlighted each entry with a half circle.[113]

A few years later, his frustration piqued, Warden Townsend did express his anger. At 7:15 on the morning of March 23, 1877, Townsend received a writ of habeas corpus instructing him to deliver Prisoner No. 8706, Morris Springfield, to "court at 8 oclk" (Townsend's emphasis). Townsend later recorded, "as it was impossible to comply with that regression I declined to answer the writ." The judge was not amused and issued a "Bench warrant" for the warden. Townsend then "went before the Judge accompanied by [Inspectors] Richard Vaux & Alexander Henry," both of whom were lawyers (and former Mayors of Philadelphia). Despite their advocacy, Townsend was "charged with 'contempt of court' " and "a reprimand was discharged." Fuming into his private log, Townsend reported, "the object [of the writ] was to have Morris Springfield to attend his deceased wife's funeral, entirely unprecedented in this or any other prison, & a dangerous precedent."[114]

[112] e.g., *Pember's Case; Reddill's Case; The Commonwealth ex rel. Johnson v. Halloway.* 42 Pa. 446. 1862; *The Commonwealth ex rel. James Buchanan Crosse v. John S. Halloway,* 44 Pa. 2010. 1863.
[113] Eastern State Penitentiary, *Warden's Daily Journal,* February 8, 18, 27, March 4, 1876.
[114] Ibid., March 23, 1877.

During Eastern's first five decades, the administrators were directly challenged in court only one other time. For almost a full year, Eastern's administrators refused to enforce the Commutation Law of 1861, a law that established a new schedule for prisoners' early release in exchange for good behavior. Two prisoners who were eligible for release under the law submitted *habeas corpus* petitions. As we shall see in greater detail in Chapter 9, the Court ruled against the prisoners and struck down the law, citing several arguments raised by Eastern's administrators. They remained safe from judicial scrutiny.

In the entire nineteenth century, moreover, Eastern's administrators underwent legislative investigation only twice: once in the winter of 1834–1835 and again in 1897. In 1834–1835, the legislature investigated charges that the administrators, especially Warden Wood, had embezzled from the prison; tortured prisoners to the point of insanity and death; engaged in immoral, lecherous acts with a female employee (who was also accused of embezzlement and other inappropriate behavior); and violated the Pennsylvania System by letting prisoners out of their cells to work around the prison, among other misdeeds. Ultimately, the administrators were cleared of all charges – Warden Wood, in particular, emerged with the admiration of the investigating committee. The female employee in question was less fortunate; her employment was terminated. A minority of the legislature challenged the findings,[115] but ultimately nothing came of the investigation or its charges.[116] Indeed, no inspector (or warden) was ever removed from office by outside forces.

* * *

Throughout Eastern's first five decades, a relatively small number of men enjoyed a level of personal control over Eastern that would be unimaginable today.[117] Although these men had at most meager prior

[115] McElwee, *A Concise History of the Eastern Penitentiary of Pennsylvania Together with a Detailed Statement of Proceedings of the Committee Appointed by the Legislature (Vol. 1)*. Philadelphia: Neall & Massey, 1835; McElwee, *A Concise History of the Eastern Penitentiary of Pennsylvania (Vol. 2)*.

[116] This investigation is also discussed in Chapter 8. For a more detailed treatment, see Michael Meranze, *Laboratories of Virtue: Punishment, Revolution, and Authority in Philadelphia, 1760–1835*. Chapel Hill: University of North Carolina Press, 1996, pp. 305–328.

[117] My phrasing of "personal control" is a partial reference to James Jacobs' classic study of Stateville prison in Illinois, in which he described the "personal dominance" of Warden Joseph Ragen between 1936 and 1961. Ragen, a former sheriff with a ninth-grade

experience with criminal justice administration, they worked within a framework of minimal external controls, and thus faced few limits on their autonomy over their prison. They also faced tremendous uncertainty in their work, unable to look to the law or other prisons for guidance; instead, most decisions were left to their own discretion – and thus to their own principles and desires. They were firmly in control of their own prison, left to decide how to implement the Pennsylvania System on their own. It was these men who ultimately retained the Pennsylvania System at Eastern State Penitentiary.

education (Jacobs, *Stateville*, pp. 28–29), took over the management of Stateville prison amid widespread political corruption, under which prison administration positions – warden and later director of the Department of Public Safety – were political cherries distributed to friends of the current gubernatorial administration. See also Charles Bright, *The Powers that Punish: Prison and Politics in the Era of the "Big House,"* *1920–1955*. Ann Arbor: University of Michigan Press, 1996. By single-handedly insulating prison appointments from patronage, Ragen protected Stateville from the spoils system, but in its place he created an "authoritarian prison regime" that included shakedowns of prison staff and prisoners alike, restricted outsiders' access to the prison, and featured strategic publicity campaigns that catapulted Ragen into national appointments, including as President of the American Corrections Association. Jacobs, *Stateville*, pp. 28–51. See also Bright, *The Powers that Punish*. The parallel to Eastern is striking, even though it was an earlier era, a larger group of administrators, and a prison in which patronage apparently played no role. Both prisons witnessed administrations with immense control over their prison and worked to keep outsiders at bay, albeit in different ways. The largest difference is Eastern's administrators' commitment to benevolence, which was absent with Ragen. While Eastern's administrators sometimes engaged in despicable behavior, they seemed more committed to reform or rehabilitation as a purpose of punishment than Ragen, who only used such language publicly. In Eastern's context, "dominance" would yield incorrect connotations, and also implies a single, dominant force, rather than an evolving collectivity.

4

Criticism and Doubt

The Pennsylvania System and the Social Construction of Penal Norms

[W]e cannot believe that even Pennsylvania will any longer allow the prison at Philadelphia, with its annual train of horrors, to cast an opprobrium on the justice and humanity of the State.

A writer for the *North American Review* (1848)[1]

The friends of the separate system had not only to educate the public mind in Pennsylvania as to its real merits, but also to combat opposition in England, New England, New York, and among various gentlemen who had some general opinions on penal jurisprudence.

Inspector Richard Vaux (1872), *Brief Sketch of the Origin and History of the State Penitentiary for the Eastern District of Pennsylvania at Philadelphia*[2]

"MR. DICKENS OF ENGLAND"

The English author Charles Dickens toured the United States between January and June 1842. When he published his travelogue *American Notes* later the same year, he dedicated the book to his American hosts "who, loving their country, can bear the truth, when it is told good humouredly, and in a kind spirit."[3] Many Americans who had interacted with Dickens were instead deeply offended by his remarks.

---

[1] "*Prison Discipline in America* by Francis C. Gray," *The North American Review* 66:138 (1848), pp. 145–190, p. 190.

[2] Richard Vaux, *Brief Sketch of the Origin and History of the State Penitentiary for the Eastern District of Pennsylvania at Philadelphia*. Philadelphia: McLaughlin Brothers, Printers, 1872, p. 88

[3] Charles Dickens, *American Notes for General Circulation*. ed. Patricia Ingham. London: Penguin Books, 2000 [1842], p. 4.

Dickens was clearly not impressed by the country. Traveling to Philadelphia by train, Dickens had been disgusted by the prodigious rate of patrons spitting, a habit he witnessed throughout the country.[4] As one historian has explained, "Before Dickens arrived in Philadelphia, he had become so irritated by people's habits and idiosyncrasies that his focus shifted – from American institutions to the American people."[5] Nevertheless, being a fan of Gothic fiction, fascinated by the luckless, and drawn to prisons (his father had been held in a debtor's prison), Dickens still wanted to see Eastern State Penitentiary. Indeed, when asking permission to visit, Dickens told Eastern's inspectors, "the Falls of Niagara and your Penitentiary are two objects I might almost say I most wish to see in America."[6]

Dickens visited the prison on March 8, 1842, in the company of "a number of Gentlemen." He visited several prisoners, accompanied by two administrators, and "dined with the Inspectors."[7] His visit was uneventful and he left pleased, as far as Eastern's administrators could tell. In his published account, however, Dickens did not hold back his true opinion. He was convinced that the Pennsylvania System was "cruel and wrong."[8] He went on to describe the Pennsylvania System and Eastern in macabre detail, recounting his interviews with apparently pathetic prisoners, and spent several pages imagining what it would be like to be a prisoner at Eastern.[9] Not only was the Pennsylvania System cruel, Dickens suggested, it was also deadly and dangerous, as it likely "wears the mind into a morbid state."[10]

Dickens' conclusion added insult to injury. He remarked, "the choice is not between this system, and a bad or ill-considered one, but between it and another which has worked well, and is, in its whole design and practice, excellent; there is surely more than sufficient reason for abandoning a mode of punishment attended by so little hope or promise, and fraught, beyond dispute, with such a host of evils."[11] Thus, Dickens was not biased against all American prisons – he endorsed the Auburn

---

[4] Ibid., p. 109.

[5] Jane S. Cowden, "Charles Dickens in Pennsylvania in March 1842: Imagining America," *Pennsylvania History: A Journal of Mid-Atlantic Studies* 81:1 (2014), pp. 51–87, p. 62.

[6] Vaux, *Brief Sketch*, p. 111.

[7] Eastern State Penitentiary, *Warden's Daily Journal*, Volumes 1–2. Eastern State Penitentiary Collection, Record Group 15 (#15.50). Pennsylvania State Archives, 1829–1877, March 8, 1842.

[8] Dickens, *American Notes*, p. 111.

[9] Ibid., pp. 111–123.   [10] Ibid., p. 121.   [11] Ibid., p. 123.

System – just Eastern. Its reliance on the Pennsylvania System made Eastern an anathema.

* * *

When Eastern opened in 1829 and became the first prison to fully implement the Pennsylvania System, it theoretically could have offered a competitor model to the Auburn System. Penal reformers, prison administrators, politicians, and other social elites – like Charles Dickens – traveled to Eastern to see the system in operation firsthand. Prison visitation was a popular activity in this era, as we have seen with Auburn in the 1820s and Walnut Street in the 1790s. But while Eastern was a popular tourist destination, it did not have the same success that Auburn did. Quickly after Eastern opened, commentators revived earlier criticisms of solitary confinement and took aim at Eastern and its supporters, especially its administrators. Over the course of the 1830s and 1840s, Eastern became a deviant prison – both as one of the few American prisons to follow the Pennsylvania System and as a *heavily* criticized prison. This chapter traces that process. It introduces the origins and propagators of the most frequent calumnious myths about the Pennsylvania System and their influence on other states' and prisons' decisions to avoid or abandon the Pennsylvania System. Finally, it discusses the impact of deviance on Eastern's administrators, who were just as criticized as the system they implemented. This criticism became central in the process by which the Pennsylvania System became personally institutionalized at Eastern.

THE SOCIAL CONSTRUCTION OF DEVIANCE

As we have seen, criticism over prison discipline centered around the use and type of solitary confinement. Although the Pennsylvania System would be intrinsically linked with solitary confinement and all of its liabilities, the Auburn System also used this method of confinement. And as we have seen, in the 1820s penal commentators did not uniformly reject solitary confinement. The disaster at Auburn in the early 1820s had permanently and viscerally linked solitary confinement to mental and physical harms – but it would take more than a full decade for commentators to work out the nuances of which type of solitary confinement would be taboo. What changed to make Eastern's use of solitary confinement dangerous and illegitimate and Auburn's use of solitary confinement safe and acceptable?

Before the Fall

The Boston Prison Discipline Society (BPDS), founded in 1825, would be Eastern's most vocal and organized critic. They started out as, and would continue to be, major proponents of the Auburn System, and therefore of a modulated form of solitary confinement. In its first annual meeting (held in 1826), the BPDS passed a resolution endorsing the Auburn System as a new version of solitary confinement, noting, "That solitary confinement, at least by night, with moral and religious instruction, are an obvious remedy for the principal evils existing in Prisons."[12] They explained at length the virtues and benefits of this approach in their first annual report. Disorder was prevented – "there can be no concert" among the prisoners when they were housed separately. It aided reformation, because "solitary confinement (if any thing will do it) is likely to lead such men to reflection and remorse, which is a state of mind unfavorable to mischievous designs." It protected reformed prisoners after release because solitary "prevents prisoners from forming an acquaintance with each other" and sharing their criminal skills such as "the arts of pickpockets and thieves."[13] At the same time, they were adamant that European reports "that the solitary cells in the Prisons at Auburn, New York, are dark dungeons, such as that humanity would shudder to see persons confined in them ... is an important mistake in point of fact." In reality, "only a few are dark," the rest were well lit.[14] They also countered the concern that "solitary confinement ... is a mode of punishment which operates unequally" – harshly on the least criminal and virtually not at all on the hardened criminal. Instead, they argued that the reformative or cruel effects "depend[] more on the manner, than on the kind of punishment" and ultimately should be left to the "discretion" of prison administrators.[15]

Their opposition to solitary confinement began the following year (1827). The BPDS's previous exegesis on the value of solitary confinement notwithstanding, they turned their attention to "another mode, which we do not approve ... *Solitary confinement day and night.*"[16] The BPDS had recently learned of Maine's experiment with pure solitary confinement that lasted "about three years." The BPDS provided several graphic accounts of the results: Simeon Record spent four days in solitary before

---

[12] BPDS, *First Annual Report of the Board of Managers of the Boston Prison Discipline Society,* Fifth edition. Boston: T. R. Marvin, 1827 [1826], p. 4.
[13] Ibid., pp. 6–7.   [14] Ibid., p. 8.   [15] Ibid., p. 18.
[16] BPDS, *Second Annual Report of the Board of Managers of the Boston Prison Discipline Society.* Boston: Perkins & Marvin, 1829 [1827], p. 38.

he "hung himself to the grate of the cell with a piece of the lashing of his hammock"; Isaac Martin spent two terms in solitary – the first for 24 days and the second, after a gap of several months, for 25 days – before he "cut his throat in his cell"; Nathaniel Parsons had to be "pardoned on account of ill health" after three periods (of forty-three, eight, and twenty days) in solitary. By contrast, Asa Allen, a former soldier "accustomed to the hardships of a camp," was unaffected and unreformed when he left.[17] Contradicting their comments of the year before, the BPDS quoted that prison's superintendent, who complained "the great diversity of character, as it respects habits and temperament of the body and mind renders solitary imprisonment a very unequal punishment."[18] Likewise, they summarized New York's (recently publicized) earlier experiment with pure solitary confinement at Auburn:

> It was found, in many instances, to injure the health; to impair the reason; to endanger the life; to leave the men enfeebled and unable to work when they left the Prison, and as ignorant of any useful business as when they were committed; and, consequently, more productive of recommitments, and less of reformation, than solitary confinement at night and hard labor by day.[19]

They concluded their examination of the subject negatively: "*As the experiments have been conducted, thus far, the results are decidedly opposed to solitary confinement day and night, as the means of preventing evil communication.*" By contrast, they expressed their "*preference for solitary confinement at night, and hard labor by day, with such regulations to prevent evil communication as the case requires.*"[20] The BPDS's main concern at this point was to distinguish the Auburn System from the pure solitary confinement that had been so disastrous.

In this context, Pennsylvanians had begun to discuss revising the Pennsylvania System in time for Eastern's opening; consequently, the BPDS began paying more attention to Philadelphia in particular.[21] In their 1827 report, the BPDS was most critical of the old Walnut Street Prison and the great delay in replacing it. Referring to Eastern as the "most magnificent and costly Prison [that] has been *partially* built," they

---

[17] BPDS, *First Annual Report of the Board of Managers*, pp. 39–40.   [18] Ibid., p. 40
[19] Ibid., p. 41   [20] Ibid., p. 43; italics in original.
[21] Indeed, the 1828 report of the Pennsylvania Commissioners cited the BPDS report as evidence in their argument against solitary confinement. Charles Shaler, Edward King, and T. I. Wharton, *Report of the Commissioners on the Penal Code*. Harrisburg: S. C. Stambaugh, 1828, p. 43.

warned that the rate at which construction had proceeded was already costing lives, given the high mortality rate at Walnut Street.[22]

The following year, they took aim at Eastern again. They "rejoiced" that the Shaler, King, and Wharton Report had endorsed the Auburn System and they encouraged Pennsylvania to adopt the Commission's recommendations.[23] To support their endorsement, the BPDS wrote,

> The weight of opinion and of fact, in this country and in Europe, is so generally and decidedly opposed to solitary confinement day and night without labor, that we sincerely hope it will be abandoned in Pennsylvania, the only one of the United States in which there is any fear of its being introduced.[24]

They devoted many pages to recapping the developments in Pennsylvania and the arguments made by reformers and reform societies on both sides of the Atlantic against the Pennsylvania System in its current iteration. Underlying their attack may have been an overriding concern to clarify the "misapprehensions [that] exist in Europe, concerning prison discipline in America" – namely, that American prisons all relied on solitary confinement of the type initially used at Auburn or what was planned in Pennsylvania.[25] The BPDS was thus, in some ways, trying to protect the Auburn System from criticism abroad by condemning – and thus signaling their differences from – the Pennsylvania System.

When the Pennsylvania legislature passed the final version of the Pennsylvania System – continuous solitary confinement with labor and instruction – in 1829, the BPDS pulled back. Pennsylvania had not, as these reformers had feared, turned to pure solitary confinement. The BPDS thus muted their skepticism, noting, "Whether the Pennsylvania system with these modifications will bear the test of experience, is now to be proved."[26]

Eastern continued to get a pass for a few years. In the BPDS's next report (1830), they mentioned the Pennsylvania System's supporters' assessment that the new prison would perform with "convenience, economy, and the most favorable moral results." The BPDS chided the legislature for delaying the prison and making it too small, focusing

---

[22] BPDS, *Second Annual Report of the Board of Managers*, p. 29.
[23] BPDS, *Third Annual Report of the Board of Managers of the Boston Prison Discipline Society*. Boston: T. R. Marvin, 1828, p. 9.
[24] Ibid., p. 10.   [25] Ibid., p. 47.
[26] BPDS, *Fourth Annual Report of the Board of Managers of the Boston Prison Discipline Society, 1829*. Boston: Perkins and Marvin, 1830 [1829], p. 29.

again on the consequences for prisoners still held in Walnut Street.[27] The BPDS even advocated building another prison "on the original plan of the Eastern Penitentiary" to alleviate Walnut Street's prisoners.[28] The following year, they reprinted Eastern's first annual report and noted, "The system, as a whole, ... is so far approved in Pennsylvania, as to induce the legislature" to authorize funds to build even more cells – a plan with which the BPDS clearly concurred.[29] The BPDS also noted with approval that the legislature had further authorized a new county prison in Philadelphia to help relocate some of Walnut Street's prisoners.[30]

The following year (1832), the BPDS still appeared to give Eastern and its Pennsylvania System the benefit of the doubt. They included extracts from the Eastern's latest annual report and noted its administrators' positive assessments – "the success of their experiment thus far."[31] However, hints of the BPDS's future skepticism were beginning to show through. They referred to Eastern's "peculiar character" – their first reference to its singularity – and noted that "the number of deaths has been large for the number of prisoners."[32] Even so, in these early reports, there was none of the vitriol to come.

In these early years, the BPDS did not seem to recognize the Pennsylvania System as that different from the Auburn System. Indeed, they often grouped Pennsylvania together with New York and other states in various attempts to measure the profitability and efficacy of the new prisons. In their 1832 report, for example, the BPDS wrote, "the great principle of solitary confinement, at least by night, is now adopted in Maine, New Hampshire, Vermont, Massachusetts, Connecticut, New York, Pennsylvania, Maryland, Tennessee, Louisiana, Illinois; and great efforts are making to adopt it in New Jersey and Ohio" as well as in several jails.[33] They continued, "When we think of the progress which has been made during the last year, but more especially of that which has been made in the last five years, in regard to the application of this great and fundamental principle of all good Prison discipline, we cannot help rejoicing with great joy."[34] In 1833, they again reported an even greater

[27] BPDS, *Fifth Annual Report of the Board of Managers of the Boston Prison Discipline Society*. Boston: Boston Type and Stereotype Foundry, 1830, p. 33.
[28] Ibid., p. 34.
[29] BPDS, *Sixth Annual Report of the Board of Managers of the Boston Prison Discipline Society*. Boston: Perkins and Marvin, 1831, p. 74.
[30] Ibid., p. 75.
[31] BPDS, *Seventh Annual Report of the Board of Managers*. Boston: Perkins and Marvin, 1832, p. 51.
[32] Ibid., pp. 47, 51.   [33] Ibid., pp. 72–73.   [34] Ibid., p. 73.

list of prisons operating on the principle of solitary confinement, again including Pennsylvania in their list of Auburn-style prisons.[35] When the BPDS tabulated the number of prisons specifically on the Auburn System, they avoided any reference to Pennsylvania or its distinctive system, apparently preferring not to call attention to it.[36] As late as 1834, they included Eastern on a list of prisons that "would do honor to any country."[37] Far from insulting the Pennsylvania System at Eastern, the BPDS in these early years counted it among the country's successes.

Calumnious Myths

The turning point came in 1835, when all of the criticisms of solitary confinement – with or without labor – that had been discussed in the 1820s suddenly came roaring back. The precipitating event was the publication of Pennsylvania's legislative investigation into wrongdoings at the prison, especially a minority report written by Thomas McElwee.[38] Of particular interest in this report were the sustained accusations that Eastern's administrators violated the Pennsylvania System by removing prisoners from their cells to work around the prison.

To BPDS members, this report confirmed some of the earlier criticisms of the Pennsylvania System. In particular, it confirmed their expectation that Eastern's administrators would need to remove the prisoners from their cells (as they had earlier at Western), either for health or economic reasons, and thus imperil any chance of their reformation, which was the entire basis for their separation. Given the undisclosed nature of this practice, moreover, the BPDS immediately expressed skepticism about the veracity of Eastern's annual reports, holding them to a new level of scrutiny. In particular, the BPDS pointed out gaps in the information

---

35 BPDS, *Eighth Annual Report of the Board of Managers of the Boston Prison Discipline Society*. Boston: Perkins and Marvin, 1833, p. 6.
36 Ibid., pp. 6–9.
37 BPDS, *Ninth Annual Report of the Board of Managers of the Boston Prison Discipline Society*. Boston: Perkins, Marvin, & Co., 1834, p. 41.
38 Pennsylvania, *Report of the Joint Committee of the Legislature of Pennsylvania Relative to the Eastern State Penitentiary at Philadelphia (Mar. 26, 1835)*. Harrisburg: Welsh and Patterson, 1835. As we shall see, while the legislature cleared the administrators of wrongdoing, McElwee's report accused the main committee of favoritism and believed the charges had been sustained by the evidence. Thomas B. McElwee, *A Concise History of the Eastern Penitentiary of Pennsylvania Together with a Detailed Statement of Proceedings of the Committee Appointed by the Legislature*. Vol. 1–2. Philadelphia: Neall & Massey, 1835.

included and explicitly accused the administrators of purposeful omissions and actual lies to cover up how poorly the prison was really operating.[39] However, the BPDS would go further, helping to establish and circulate calumnious myths that would transform Eastern's status from simply a unique prison to a deviant prison.

Narratives that exaggerate (or even fabricate) the practical advantages of a new technology have long been a powerful means of convincing decision makers to adopt such technology. According to neoinstitutional theorists, these "rational myths" provide a pragmatic case for adoption. Scholars call these narratives "myths" because they often mobilize common misconceptions or inaccurate data to provide the best case for the technology, but they also become repeated, taken for granted, and widely believed.[40]

In the case of early nineteenth-century prisons, penal reformers circulated what I call "calumnious myths," or rational myths that were maliciously designed to discredit a competitor system – most often, the Pennsylvania System as a competitor to the Auburn System – to convince other states to adopt the reformers' preferred system. (It is perhaps noteworthy that these myths were systematically propagated only after Pennsylvania had finally developed a coherent alternative model, one that was beginning to gain recognition in other states.) Like other rational myths, these calumnious myths offered explanations of how the Pennsylvania System was pragmatically worse than the Auburn System. However, these calumnious myths also offered normative criticisms against the Pennsylvania System's loathsome program, thereby raising the stakes of a state's decision to adopt either system: it was not just a practical decision, but a moral decision. Finally, calumnious myths drew on earlier fears about solitary confinement and prisons generally, which gave them additional credence – it was difficult to question familiar concerns.

The BPDS reformers' primary calumnious myths specified four moral and practical problems with the Pennsylvania System – critiques that

39 BPDS, *Tenth Annual Report of the Board of Managers of the Boston Prison Discipline Society*. Boston: Perkins, Marvin, & Co., 1835, pp. 21–23.
40 John W. Meyer and Brian Rowan, "Institutionalized Organizations: Formal Structure as Myth and Ceremony," *American Journal of Sociology* 83:2 (1977), pp. 340–363; Lauren B. Edelman, Christopher Uggen, and Howard S. Erlanger, "The Endogeneity of Legal Regulation: Grievance Procedures as Rational Myth," *American Journal of Sociology* 105:2 (1999), pp. 406–454; Carol A. Heimer and JuLeigh Petty, "Bureaucratic Ethics: IRBs and the Legal Regulation of Human Subjects Research," *Annual Review of Law and Social Science* 6:1 (2010), pp. 601–626.

would be repeated by other Auburn supporters and that are still rehearsed in discussions of Eastern State Penitentiary today. First, the Pennsylvania System was too expensive and unprofitable. Building sufficiently large cells for each prisoner was prohibitively expensive, while traditional craft-style labor could not repay this expenditure. By contrast, prisoners could stay in tiny cells under the Auburn System (because they were in them only at night) while Auburn's factory-style labor was more efficient and produced higher-demand goods, which could not only counter costs but also yield profits for the state. Second, the Pennsylvania System's reliance on "solitary confinement" was dangerous to prisoners' mental and physical health. Third, the Pennsylvania System was cruel and inhumane: humans are social creatures and preventing human interaction for years was akin to torture. Finally, the Pennsylvania System was impractical and ineffective: too many problems would plague its implementation – prisoners would find ways to communicate or administrators would be forced to let prisoners socialize to prevent mental illness – while the hardest criminals would be unaffected by their conscience and not repent. The Auburn System, they argued, would not have such flaws. For all of these reasons, they argued, the Pennsylvania System was vastly inferior to the Auburn System.

By the time the BPDS first criticized Eastern in 1835, most of these calumnious myths had already been articulated episodically by early critics of solitary confinement like British reformer William Roscoe; the Pennsylvania Commissioners Shaler, King, and Wharton; and the BPDS in its first several reports before Eastern had opened and the contours of the Pennsylvania System were still being determined. But beginning in 1835, the BDPS's attack was not just on the Pennsylvania System as a theory of incarceration, but on Eastern as a prison actually run on this system. They complained that Eastern, "unlike other public institutions of a similar kind in the United States, publishes nothing concerning its pecuniary affairs, in its annual reports," which made it difficult to evaluate the profitability of "solitary labor."[41] They commented on the "communication between the convicts" and the increased rate of "recommitments" to the prison. Contradicting the promoted "mildness of the system," the BPDS noted, the "punishments [that] have been resorted to, in the Eastern Penitentiary … are more objectionable than stripes."[42] They further cautioned, without any hint of irony given their earlier endorsement of the Pennsylvania System after Eastern opened,

---

[41] BPDS, *Tenth Annual Report of the Board of Managers*, p. 21.   [42] Ibid., p. 21.

We have always felt distrustful of the system, on this ground; because we have not known, from the nature of man, how he could be confined day and night in solitude, for a short term of years, to so narrow a space, and have his cell made his work-shop, his bed-room, his dining-hall, his water-closet, his chapel, &c., without getting the air and himself into a condition unfavorable to health.

They proceeded to compare the "proportion of deaths" at Eastern and the prisons at Charlestown (Massachusetts), Wethersfield (Connecticut), and Auburn, revealing Eastern to have the worst mortality rate; they concluded, it "is not healthy compared with Prisons on the Auburn plan." The report included similar analyses of mental illness and disease, apparently seeking to correct the statement "that the system is not injurious to the mind, and does not produce insanity."[43] In the end, they decided, "These matters of record do not look very favorable to the system, in regard to its effect on the mind. There is too much about insanity, in proportion to the number of prisoners." The BPDS concluded their comments on Eastern, "On the whole therefore, we are becoming more, rather than less distrustful, of the Philadelphia system of Prison discipline."[44] As the years progressed, these criticisms would grow more extensive.

The BPDS continuously picked apart Eastern's annual reports (and any other available data) looking for any confirmatory evidence for their claims of its inferiority – which they usually found. In 1836, they began by summarizing: "it fails, in comparison with the Auburn system, in regard to health, reformation, earnings, and moral and religious instruction."[45] After detailed comparisons along each of these dimensions, they revised their statements from years earlier and stated, "we *have been* willing to see it tried; but ... *we are almost sick of the experiment*; it fails so much. ..."[46] Writing in 1838, they reported,

the Ninth and last Report of the New Penitentiary of Philadelphia is the most unfavorable ever made concerning this institution: —unfavorable in regard to deaths; unfavorable in regard to dementia; unfavorable in regard

---

43 Ibid., p. 22.
44 Ibid., p. 23. The BPDS also criticized the moral education at Eastern. The BPDS was a particularly faith-based organization, and they paid particular attention to the role of religion, the presence of bibles, and other related activities in prisons everywhere. Other actors, however, seemed to be less concerned by this critique, so I exclude it from further discussions.
45 BPDS, *Eleventh Annual Report of the Board of Managers of the Boston Prison Discipline Society*. Boston: Perkins and Marvin, 1836, p. 38.
46 Ibid., p. 40; italics in original.

to recommitments; unfavorable in regard to current expenses; unfavorable in regard to moral and religious instruction.[47]

The following year, they again reported,

The Tenth Report on the Eastern Penitentiary, by the inspectors, warden, and physician, is in excuses and opinions very fair, but in facts, AWFUL!—402 prisoners, 26 deaths; 23 recommitments, 18 cases of mania, &c., and expenses above earnings, untold by the government of the Prison, but disclosed by the treasurer of the commonwealth, to be the amount of $34,368 in a single year.[48]

While they reviewed other prisons' annual reports, the BPDS usually saved their strongest condemnation for Eastern.

Pamphlet Warfare

When the BPDS threw down the proverbial gauntlet, Philadelphia-based reformers (and Eastern's administrators, as we shall see) picked it up. They responded by defending the Pennsylvania System and criticizing the Auburn System in turn. They pointed to whipping at Auburn and derided Auburn supporters' profit motivation. They also outlined the logical advantages of fully separating prisoners from one another, arguing that silence was insufficient. Soon, a back-and-forth had begun in which the Boston reformers were responding to claims in Eastern's annual reports that had been written in response to the BPDS's critiques.[49] One third-party observer summarized the key arguments in the debate:

"You drive the prisoners mad," cries Boston, "by the long continued horrors of solitary confinement"; "You subject the criminals to the cruel and degrading punishment of the lash," shouts Philadelphia. "Your own statistics," exclaims the former, "show a fearful amount of insanity and mortality in your prisons"; "Figures prove nothing, and there is a mistake in your calculations," retorts the latter. And so it goes; the quarrel is a very pretty quarrel ...[50]

Importantly, however, the debate was not limited to Boston- and Philadelphia-based commentators.

---

[47] BPDS, *Thirteenth Annual Report of the Board of Managers of the Boston Prison Discipline Society*. Boston: Published at the Society's Rooms, 1838, p. 56.

[48] BPDS, *Fourteenth Annual Report of the Board of Managers of the Boston Prison Discipline Society*. Boston: Published at the Society's Rooms, 1839, p. 53.

[49] This most clearly begins in BPDS, *Twelfth Annual Report of the Board of Managers of the Boston Prison Discipline Society*. Boston: Published at the Society's Rooms, 1837.

[50] "Report of a Minority of the Special Committee of the Boston Prison Discipline Society, Appointed at the Annual Meeting, May 27, 1845 by S. G. Howe," *The North American Review* 64:134 (1845), pp. 257–260, p. 259.

TABLE 4.1 *The debate over prison discipline, 1830–1867.*

Author	Year
Roberts Vaux	1830
George Washington Smith	1830
George Washington Smith	1833[1]
Gustave de Beaumont and Alexis de Tocqueville*	1833
William Crawford*	1835
Edward Livingston	1836
Charles Lucas*	1837
Francis Lieber*	1838
Anon. [F. A. Packard]	1839
Charles Dickens*	1842
Dorothea Dix	1845
Samuel Gridley Howe	1846
Francis C. Gray	1848
Anon. [F. A. Packard]	1849
E. C. Wines and Theodore W. Dwight	1867

The names in this table are those of individual penal reformers, prison administrators, or commissioners who published the most well-known letters, pamphlets, and reports on "prison discipline." I exclude the hundreds of other articles published in newspapers and other periodicals. For example, penal reform societies' annual reports and their privately funded journals (e.g., the *Pennsylvania Journal of Prison Discipline and Philanthropy*) offered another forum for discussion. Both kinds of publications were also discussed in *North American Review*, a popular review. As the publication dates illustrate, the debate was most intense in the 1830s and 1840s.
Note: Starred authors were British or European. Reprinted version of 1828–1829 essays.
[1] Reprinted version of 1828–1829 essays.

The debate was extensive. As de Beaumont and de Tocqueville reported, "there is not a citizen of the United States who does not know how the prisons of his country are governed, and who is not able to contribute to their improvement, either by his opinion or his fortune."[51] While interested parties engaged in lengthy discussions during reform societies' meetings and private afternoon teas, the debate took place primarily in published documents: penal reform societies' widely circulated single-authored pamphlets, small treatises, travel diaries, and letters to and from other penal reformers on both sides of the Atlantic (see Table 4.1). Reformers and other interested parties also consumed prisons' annual

[51] Gustave de Beaumont and Alexis de Tocqueville, *On the Penitentiary System in the United States and Its Application in France,* Trans. by Francis Lieber. Philadelphia: Carey, Lea, and Blanchard, 1833, pp. 30–31.

reports, which were themselves an important part of the debate, often reciting facts to support their preferred system of prison discipline, which were then copied and published again in other publications as excerpts or appendices.[52] So prodigious and contentious was the resulting literature that historian David Rothman described these exchanges as "pamphlet warfare" between the opposing camps.[53]

Indeed, there are several important differences between the debate of the 1820s and the 1830s and 1840s. First, the later debate was more extensive, both in having a wider range of commentators and in the frequency of comments. As we have seen, the debate over solitary confinement had begun even before the Auburn and Pennsylvania Systems were implemented, let alone fully operational. But it accelerated in the 1830s and peaked in the 1840s.[54] Second, the topic had shifted. In the 1810s and 1820s, the major question had been what level or type of solitary confinement should form the foundation of incarceration, with multiple options available that varied the role of labor and the severity of the solitary confinement. By the 1830s, the debate had narrowed to the question of "prison discipline," or how prisons should be operated, and the options consisted only of the Auburn System or the Pennsylvania System.[55] The accuracy of the calumnious myths, particularly those outlined most vociferously by the BPDS, remained the primary focus. Finally, the debate of the 1830s and 1840s would have a much wider impact.

THE MYTHS' EFFICACY

The BPDS's calumnious myths were quite effective in delegitimizing the Pennsylvania System. The clearest measure of their success is the number

---

[52] As de Beaumont and de Tocqueville noted, "Their [prisons'] reports, printed by order of the legislatures, are immediately handed over to publicity and controversy; the papers, the number of which in that country is immense, republish them faithfully." Ibid., pp. 30–31.

[53] David J. Rothman, *The Discovery of the Asylum: Social Order and Disorder in the New Republic.* New York: AldineTransaction, 2002 [1971], p. 88.

[54] A commentator from the 1860s notes that the controversy peaked "from 1845 to 1849." "Art. VIII [Review of Three Works]." *The North American Review* 102:210 (1866), pp. 210–235, p. 211.

[55] As Ely Aaronson has noted, the creation of particular legal regimes has a narrowing effect on discussions, often preventing the question of alternatives. Ely Aaronson, *From Slave Abuse to Hate Crime: The Criminalization of Racial Violence in American History.* Cambridge: Cambridge University Press, 2014. See also Ryken Grattet and Valerie Jenness, "The Birth and Maturation of Hate Crime Policy in the United States," *American Behavioral Scientist* 45:4 (2001), pp. 668–696.

of states that adopted the Auburn System or the Pennsylvania System in this period. Even before the Pennsylvania System was functional at Eastern or Western, the Auburn System had become the dominant model in U.S. prisons. But this situation continued after 1829 and, as time went on, the gap between the number of prisons on the Pennsylvania System and the Auburn System grew. When states decided to build prisons, particularly states on the frontier and in the Deep South, they too followed the Auburn System. Outside of Pennsylvania, only two states adopted the Pennsylvania System – New Jersey in 1836 and Rhode Island in 1838. However, both states abandoned the Pennsylvania System – Rhode Island within six years and New Jersey somewhat later – in favor of the Auburn System. By the Civil War, every state prison outside of Pennsylvania officially followed the Auburn System. By 1867, after touring most of the country's prisons, penal reformers Wines and Dwight could state, "Everywhere, then, beyond the limits of Pennsylvania, the system of imprisonment in the United States is that which is called, indifferently, the Auburn, congregate, or silent system."[56]

Given the importance of officials' visits to prisons in order to assess their operations, the Pennsylvania System's slow start did not help its diffusion. Even though Western had opened in 1826, its architectural problems prevented a working model of the Pennsylvania System there until 1837. Eastern did not open until 1829. By that time, the Auburn System had been adopted at nine prisons, several of which had been in operation for enough years to be fully functional. Those states contemplating abandoning their old proto-prisons for a newer version of prison thus had an ample number of established Auburn-style prisons to visit and copy.

While state representatives continued to visit Auburn for information when their own prisons were being built or renovated, they increasingly toured other prisons as well; almost every such tour resulted in another state adopting the Auburn System. As Illinois poised to adopt its first state prison, Lieutenant Governor William Kinney visited established prisons on the east coast before adopting the Auburn System.[57] As time

---

[56] Enoch C. Wines, and Theodore W. Dwight, *Report on the Prisons and Reformatories of the United States and Canada Made to the Legislature of New York, January 1867.* Albany, NY: Van Benthuysen and Sons' Steam Printing House, 1867, p. 56.

[57] William Robert Greene, "Early Development of the Illinois State Penitentiary System," English. *Journal of the Illinois State Historical Society (1908–1984)* 70:3 (1977), pp. 185–195, p. 187.

went on, states made copies of copies – using more proximate replicas of Auburn. By all accounts, Connecticut's Wethersfield State Prison was the exemplar of the Auburn System, and it became the source material for several states' prisons. Louisiana's prison commissioners were "not bound to adhere to the plan of the penitentiary-house at Wethersfield," but they were instructed to use it as a model.[58] Likewise, Iowa's superintendent of construction was instructed to copy Wethersfield "as nearly as convenient and [as] may appear advisable."[59] Texas sent its prison commissioners to Mississippi's Auburn-style prison, "The Walls," before borrowing that prison's design and even its name.[60] Two of Alabama's governors wrote to other states, including Tennessee, Maine, New York, and Georgia, to learn about their penitentiaries and select the appropriate model.[61] Before finally adopting the Auburn System, Alabama's prison commissioners visited Tennessee's Auburn-style prison, which served as their model; Alabama's state prison "was almost an exact replica in size and appearance of its Tennessee model."[62] The Auburn System had spread from the Northeast through the South and across the frontier into the territories; as each new state entered the Union, it soon adopted a prison on the Auburn System.[63]

Having functional models of prisons to copy was clearly important in facilitating Auburn's diffusion. Additionally, any observer using popularity as a proxy for success would have rightly deemed Auburn the more successful model, reinforcing Auburn supporters' claims of superiority. But when officials explained their reasoning for selecting the Auburn System over the Pennsylvania System, they often cited the calumnious myths.

It is important to understand that, although the debate was centered in the Northeast, the myths reached other regions. Reform societies' annual

---

[58] Louisiana, "An Act to Amend an Act Authorizing the Erection of a Penitentiary-House, and for Other Purposes," in *Acts Passed at the First session of the Eleventh Legislature of the State of Louisiana*. New Orleans: Jerome Bayon, State Printer, 1833, pp. 104–107, p. 106.

[59] Joyce McKay, "Reforming Prisoners and Prisons: Iowa's State Prisons – The First Hundred Years," *The Annals of Iowa* 60:2 (2001), pp. 139–173, p. 141.

[60] Blake McKelvey, *American Prisons: A History of Good Intentions*. Montclair, NJ: Patterson Smith, 1977 [1936], p. 47.

[61] Robert David Ward and William Warren Rogers, *Alabama's Response to the Penitentiary Movement, 1829–1865*. Gainesville, FL: University Press of Florida, 2003, p. 37.

[62] Ibid., p. 48.

[63] Ashley T. Rubin, "A Neo-Institutional Account of Prison Diffusion," *Law & Society Review* 49:2 (2015), pp. 365–399.

reports and other writings were frequently republished or summarized by newspapers in other states and reviews and other periodicals with national circulation. As a writer for the popular *North American Review* explained, "the cause of truth and justice and humanity, as well as of policy, is deeply concerned in having both sides of the question illustrated by all the light that their advocates can throw upon them."[64]

Despite the broad publicity, reformers' messages were not equally broadcast. Auburn supporters in particular were well organized and well able to distribute their side of the argument: The BPDS had more connections "throughout the country" than PSAMPP,[65] including other states' prison administrators among their "corresponding members."[66] In 1829, the BPDS reported it had

printed about sixteen thousand copies, or 1,600,000 pages of the Annual Reports of the Society, and furnished them, at a moderate price, to the Legislatures of Maine, Massachusetts, New York, and New Jersey ... and gratuitously to the Legislators of some other States, and to benevolent individuals and Societies in America and Europe.[67]

By contrast, PSAMPP only began publishing its annual *Pennsylvania Journal of Prison Discipline (PJPD)* – its answer to the BPDS's annual reports – in 1845. Even then, PSAMPP only issued 100–300 copies of its *PJPD* in most years.[68] Beginning in 1844, the BPDS was also joined by another pro–Auburn System reform society, the New York Prison Association (NYPA), which helped spread their message.

A wider network and a stronger publication record helped the BPDS propagate their claims about Auburn's superiority across the country. Thus, when legislators, governors, and prison commissioners considered adopting a prison, they were cognizant of the arguments supporting each model. However, they were more familiar with the arguments against the Pennsylvania System.

---

[64] "Prison Discipline," *The North American Review* 60:127 (1845), p. 510, p. 501.

[65] Harry Elmer Barnes, *The Evolution of Penology in Pennsylvania*. Indianapolis: The Bobbs-Merrill Company, 1968 [1927], p. 177.

[66] Thanks to Stephen Tillotson for calling my attention to this point.

[67] BPDS, *Fourth Annual Report of the Board of Managers of the Boston Prison Discipline Society, 1829*, p. 303.

[68] PSAMPP, *Acting Committee Minute Books*, Series I, Vol. 2–6, Pennsylvania Prison Society Records (Collection 1946) Series I, Vol. 6–10. Historical Society of Pennsylvania. 1798–1883.

Navigating High Stakes and Uncertainty

State actors charged with deciding what type of prison to authorize or build in their states may have welcomed these myths: the myths clarified what was a very important choice. Implementing the wrong model might mean the death and insanity of prisoners, as occurred during Auburn's early experiments, at a time when citizens strongly opposed cruelty and suffering.[69] Alternatively, as Auburn's Agent Powers explained, "If the present mode of punishment ... fails, then the whole system must be given up in despair; the hopes of the philanthropist must perish; and scourges, the gallows, or gullotine [sic] must administer to the demands of sanguinary law."[70] This possibility was especially troubling to many reformers who believed such methods were uncivilized and barbaric. More drastically, should the chosen model later prove to be ineffective, whether by failing to deter or to reform, this could imperil the fragile Republic, which required virtuous citizens (criminals were not virtuous). As historian Michael Meranze has argued, the fate of the Republic was still uncertain and some middle-class citizens feared that (perceived) increases in urban crime, associated with the degenerating proto-prisons, foreboded the Republic's demise.[71] With these very high stakes, suggestions were helpful when navigating penal decisions permeated by uncertainty.

Despite fifty years of penal reform by the time Eastern opened, Americans faced widespread technological uncertainty. Incarceration as punishment was still a novel concept; the modern prison was a poorly understood technology that had fatal consequences during early testing. Expressing the level of unpredictability they felt, penal reformers, prison administrators, and politicians frequently referred to various prison policies and practices as an "experiment."

In their debates over prison discipline, moreover, penal actors had little evidence to rely upon; in the absence of meaningful experience or evidence, they turned to logical arguments. In 1823, the Directors of the Massachusetts State Prison wrote,

---

[69] David Brion Davis, "The Movement to Abolish Capital Punishment in America, 1787–1861," *The American Historical Review* 63:1 (1957), pp. 23–46.
[70] Gershom Powers, *A Brief Account of the Constitution, Management, & Discipline &c. &c. of the New-York State Prison at Auburn.* Auburn, NY: U. F. Doubleday, 1826, p. 34.
[71] Michael Meranze, *Laboratories of Virtue: Punishment, Revolution, and Authority in Philadelphia, 1760–1835.* Chapel Hill: University of North Carolina Press, 1996.

The subject of punishment for crime is one, on which most people have thought something and very few profoundly. Each man has his own theory, and each successive Committee of the Legislature its own favorite plan.... Opposite and conflicting expectations are entertained by different individuals, and often by the same individual.[72]

But even in the early 1830s, with only two approaches available, both recently established, both criticized by opposing parties, there was widespread uncertainty over best practices.

Underlying this technological uncertainty was widespread epistemic uncertainty as penal actors questioned the reliability of statements disseminated as truth. The prison administrators and reformers themselves only reinforced the feeling of unpredictability. The initial reports of Auburn's use of pure solitary confinement had been positive – until administrators admitted that prisoners were losing their minds and injuring or killing themselves.[73] Likewise, as we have seen, the BPDS had endorsed the Pennsylvania System before becoming one of its strongest critics after Eastern opened. Early opinions were unsettled and unreliable.

Worse, it was difficult to know what and whom to believe and trust at any point. During the debate over prison models, penal reformers and prison administrators from warring camps expressed skepticism toward each others' statements. In the BPDS's first anti–Pennsylvania System report, they wrote,

It has often been said, and generally believed, that all communication between the convicts is rendered physically impossible, in this [Pennsylvania] Prison, by the construction. If persons investigating this subject for the public benefit, would be a little more thorough in their investigations, they would find that this is not *true*.[74]

Both sides claimed their opponents doctored their statistics or otherwise hid the truth. They were correct: as historian Harry Elmer Barnes has noted, "Both [sides] were fiercely partisan and both were disgracefully unscrupulous in their use of statistics designed to support their cause or damage their opponents."[75]

---

[72] Cited in Adam J. Hirsch, "From Pillory to Penitentiary: The Rise of Criminal Incarceration in Early Massachusetts," *Michigan Law Review* 80:6 (1982), pp. 1179–1269, p. 1194.

[73] e.g., Powers, *A Brief Account*.

[74] BPDS, *Tenth Annual Report of the Board of Managers*, p. 883 (italics in original).

[75] Barnes, *The Evolution of Penology in Pennsylvania*, p. 177.

Supporters from both camps occasionally acknowledged their own or their colleagues' biases. A brief introductory note to the series of essays written by Pennsylvania System supporter George Washington Smith in 1828–1829 and reprinted in 1833 explained,

The tone of some of our comments in the following essays, appears to us at the present time somewhat more harsh than our present tempered zeal, and respect for the writer of this report, would willingly sanction. His errors were those of opinion, not of intention; errors which zeal and inexperience, however united with purity of motive, almost invariably produce. It is possible, that the critic himself may unconsciously illustrate the difficulty of avoiding similar mistakes of omission and commission; neglecting or overlooking such evidence as may be adverse, and selecting or regarding only, such testimonials as may be in unison with preconceived and approved opinions.[76]

By the 1840s, BPDS member and former Auburn supporter Samuel Gridley Howe had experienced his own crisis of confidence, explaining,

The spirit of our [BPDS Annual] Reports was so partial, the praises of the Auburn system were so warm, and the censure of the Pennsylvania prisons was so severe, that one could not help suspecting the existence of violent party feeling.... A personal inspection of the principal prisons in the United States, and reflection upon the subject, afterwards convinced me that very little reliance could be placed upon those Reports, either for facts or doctrines.[77]

With statements like these circulating, interested parties likely questioned the reliability of "facts" and were more inclined to defer to anything that appeared to be unambiguously concrete data (like prisoners' deaths and insanity during pure solitary confinement at the Auburn and Maine prisons) and to common sense (however limited and flawed).

In this context, the calumnious myths were widely believed because they built on both concrete data and common sense. BPDS members and other Auburn supporters capitalized on the early disasters at Auburn and Maine, using them to remind readers of the consequences of employing long-term solitary confinement. Additionally, their critiques built on Western's initial experience with pure solitary confinement, which confirmed many observers' worst fears about solitary confinement: the system, had it been fully implemented, would have been fatal given the prison's subpar architecture, which did not provide prisoners with enough ventilation.

[76] George W. Smith, *A Defence of the System of Solitary Confinement of Prisoners Adopted by the State of Pennsylvania*, Philadelphia: G. Dorsey, printer, 1833 [1829], p. 4.

[77] BPDS, *Report of a Minority of the Special Committee of the Boston Prison Discipline Society*. Boston: William D. Tricknor and Company, 1846, p. iii.

Of course, these precedents, and the type of solitary confinement they used, were markedly different from the Pennsylvania System authorized in 1829 and implemented at Eastern, but Auburn supporters swept these differences aside in favor of their similarities. For example, they often ignored the role of official visits at Eastern, which belied claims that prisoners never saw another living person for years on end. Additionally, the myths downplayed the role of solitary confinement used in the Auburn System and its similarity to the earlier precedents, even using the same tiny cells. Auburn supporters also ignored the possibility that lack of human interaction through silence – for much longer sentences in Auburn-style prisons – could (and did) lead to any mental or physical illness.[78]

[78] Contemporary records make it difficult to analyze comparative claims about the Pennsylvania System's greater likelihood of producing mental or physical illness with great confidence, but the data suggest little concrete evidence to support the claims. The charge that the Pennsylvania System caused insanity is easily understood, particularly in light of recent research on the effects of contemporary solitary confinement and mental decompensation in supermax prisons. (Craig Haney, "Mental Health Issues in Long-Term Solitary and 'Supermax' Confinement," *Crime and Delinquency* 49:1 (2003), pp. 124–156; Craig Haney and Mona Lynch, "Regulating Prisons of the Future: A Psychological Analysis of Supermax and Solitary Confinement," *NYU Review of Law & Social Change* 23 (1997), pp. 477–570). However, it must be remembered that Eastern was *not* a supermax. Among the important differences, prisoners at Eastern had social contact on a weekly (if not daily) basis with some combination of penal reformers and the prison's overseers, physician, moral instructor, warden, and inspectors. Prisoners also had access to fresh air and private yards, and their cells were larger than contemporary supermax facilities, which hold their prisoners in conditions of sensory deprivation. Consequently, we should not anticipate the rate of insanity at Eastern to be comparable to current rates of mental decompensation in solitary confinement. Indeed, recent research has suggested that many cases identified as insanity at Eastern were misdiagnosed and the case against the Pennsylvania System overstated. Ian O'Donnell, *Prisoners, Solitude, and Time*. Oxford University Press, 2014. Moreover, the nineteenth-century definition of insanity was somewhat unclear. Insanity was a catchall term for many ailments and use of the term itself was quite variable, often applied with racist or sexist overtones. As an example, insanity was often attributed to masturbation – such was the state of medical knowledge for some practicing physicians. Suicide rates offer the closest objective indicator: with fewer than a dozen suicides among Eastern's first 7,000 prisoners (despite ample access to items that could be used and opportunity to injure oneself without intervention), the suicide rate at Eastern was comparable to twentieth-century facilities that used a version of the Auburn System (Alcatraz, mistakenly described by the authors as a supermax) and one of the first supermaxes (U.S. Penitentiary Marion). Eastern's suicides were recorded in the inmate reception registers. For Alcatraz and Marion, see David A. Ward and Thomas G. Werlich, "Alcatraz and Marion," *Punishment & Society* 5:1 (2003), pp. 53–75, p. 65. Finally, the claim that the Pennsylvania System caused insanity diverted attention from the fact that many prisoners also became mentally ill under the Auburn System. Actual comparisons across the two systems are difficult not only because of variations in the use of the term, but also because states pardoned

However, it was more believable that continuous solitary confinement, albeit interrupted by labor and visits, was cruel and would lead to mental illness.

The Auburn System also *appeared* to have a greater potential for profit, strengthening its supporters' claims that it *was* profitable. Auburn's reliance on factory-style labor over workshop-style labor implied more efficient (and cost-effective) production. Additionally, prisoners' cells could be much smaller and, consequently, were cheaper to construct. By contrast, under the Pennsylvania System, prisoners needed large cells, with sufficient workspace (and external yards), to preserve their health. Auburn's cheaper architecture and seemingly more efficient labor were particularly attractive for states struggling to tax their citizens. What Auburn supporters failed to emphasize was that most of the profits of prisoner labor went to the contractors who managed the prison – entrepreneurs who paid a small fee to lease the prison or its prisoners and then sold the products of their labor – rather than to the state that paid for the prison's initial construction and upkeep.[79]

Given the experience and knowledge at the time, the calumnious myths appeared quite convincing to most commentators. Even if they did not believe the myths, however, state actors and penal reformers could still use the myths to guide their judgments. Because the myths offered plausible accounts of the two systems – how the Pennsylvania System would fail

---

mentally ill prisoners. If Eastern's administrators are to be believed, administrators in New York's prisons strategically obtained pardons for the mentally ill prisoners to reduce their institution's reported rate of insanity. (Eastern's administrators appear to have only done this rarely in the first several decades, only in cases where an individual appeared to be insane at the time they had entered, and mostly when the administrators could secure a spot for the prisoner at the insane asylum once it was open – before then, such prisoners were often diverted to the Philadelphia almshouse.) While some prisoners' mental illness was likely caused by either system, many convicts were already mentally ill. Even after Pennsylvania's mental asylum opened in 1841, mentally ill people who committed crimes were sent to prison rather than to hospital.

[79] Figures varied across time and state, but the Auburn System was certainly not as profitable as its supporters suggested. When some Auburn-style prisons reported some profitable years, these profits went primarily to the contractors. Rebecca M. McLennan, *The Crisis of Imprisonment: Protest, Politics, and the Making of the American Penal State, 1776–1941*. New York: Cambridge University Press, 2008; Rothman, *The Discovery of the Asylum*, p.88; Barnes, *The Evolution of Penology*, p. 177. For example, before converting to the contract system, New Hampshire's prison was reported to be "a heavy burden to the State" and had rarely turned a profit. Orlando Faulkland Lewis, *The Development of American Prisons and Prison Customs, 1776–1845: With Special Reference to Early Institutions in the State of New York*. Albany: Prison Association of New York/J. B. Lyon Company, 1922, p. 152.

and the Auburn System would succeed – and because they were widely believed, they provided cover, should anything go wrong: if a new prison followed the popular, reformer-approved system of prison discipline, it would be less vulnerable to criticism for any fatalities or failure to profit. As an example, if a prisoner experienced mental illness at a Pennsylvania-style prison, it was evidence of the myths' veracity; if a prisoner experienced mental illness at an Auburn-style prison, it was a fluke or the result of the prisoners' own inadequacies. Similarly, when prisoners in Pennsylvania-style prisons found ways to communicate with each other, it was evidence of the system's intrinsic inability to control prisoners; when prisoners in Auburn-style prisons were found talking or communicating with eye signals, it was deemed a remediable failure of enforcement. The myths shaped commentators' interpretations of how prisons functioned. Adopting the Auburn System in this context was a far safer decision even if a decision-maker did not personally believe the myths. The myths' persuasiveness was thus a strong incentive for states and prisons to adopt the Auburn System.

Conversely, these myths created substantial problems of legitimacy for those few prisons that adopted the Pennsylvania System. Indeed, pro-Auburn penal reformers, especially the BPDS, criticized not only the Pennsylvania System, but also any prison that adopted and retained the Pennsylvania System. The few Pennsylvania-style prisons were repeatedly berated by the BPDS and other pro-Auburn reformers for their misguided, but especially immoral, behavior in maintaining prisoners in such (unnecessarily) inhumane conditions. Eastern was not alone in receiving such criticism, but as the flagship prison of the Pennsylvania System it bore the brunt of this attack.[80] For example, an anonymous writer for the *North American Review* exclaimed in 1848, "[W]e cannot believe that even Pennsylvania will any longer allow the prison at Philadelphia, with its annual train of horrors, to cast an opprobrium on the justice and humanity of the State."[81] Eastern's experience in particular was a billboard warning states that, should they adopt the Pennsylvania System, they ran the risk of attracting similar labels of immorality or deviance. Few penal actors were willing to accept such stigma.

---

[80] The BPDS's attacks on the New Jersey and Rhode Island prisons were comparatively mild. For example, in 1835, they referred briefly to the planned prison in Rhode Island. The plan, they said simply, "we think [is] not as good as the Auburn." Rather than explaining their reasons, they referred readers to the section of their report on Eastern. BPDS, *Tenth Annual Report of the Board of Managers*, p. 13.

[81] "*Prison Discipline in America* by Francis C. Gray," p. 190.

As we have seen, excepting Eastern, each prison that had initially followed the Pennsylvania System abandoned it. When they did, their administrators recited the several myths to explain their decision. By their fourth year of operations, Rhode Island State Prison's Board of Inspectors requested the legislature to do a full investigation into "whether the present mode of separate confinement be not expensive to the State and injurious to the minds of the convicts." They included statistics on the high rate of insanity and other "slight symptoms of derangement."[82] After adopting the Auburn System, the warden wrote a report condemning the Pennsylvania System, reaffirming the myths.[83] In particular, he referred to "the injurious and alarming effects of solitary imprisonment upon the mental and physical condition of those who were subjects of it" and provided statistics for support.[84] In the 1840s, the New Jersey State Prison's physician and other administrators criticized the effects of the Pennsylvania System on prisoner well-being.[85] The physician described the Pennsylvania System as "the most effectual to drive him mad, or reduce him to imbecility, besides inducing organic diseases almost incurable."[86] The administrators also complained about their failure to profit and expressed a disbelief in the Pennsylvania System's reformatory power.[87]

By the 1860s, even Western State Penitentiary's administrators began to criticize the Pennsylvania System. In their opinion, the Pennsylvania System was impracticable (noting that difficulties of implementation had long superseded faithful application), ineffective at reforming prisoners, and cruel. These problems and administrators' belief in the benefits of the Auburn System and the new (in the 1850s and 1860s) Irish System of early release for good behavior led them to request authorization to abandon the Pennsylvania System.[88] In using the myths to support their request to authorize the Auburn System, the administrators across these three states, especially Pennsylvania, only strengthened the myths' persuasiveness.

Indeed, the calumnious myths about the Pennsylvania System, and their paired rational myths about the Auburn System, proved persuasive across

---

[82] Cited in Enoch C. Wines, and Theodore W. Dwight, *Report on the Prisons and Reformatories of the United States and Canada Made to the Legislature of New York, January 1867*. Albany, NY: Van Benthuysen and Sons' Steam Printing House, 1867, p. 54.

[83] Ibid., pp. 54–55.   [84] Cited in ibid., p. 54.   [85] Ibid., p. 52.

[86] Cited in ibid., p. 53.

[87] Ibid., pp. 53–54; see also Barnes, *The Evolution of Penology*, p. 173.

[88] Ibid., pp. 307–309.

the country throughout the antebellum period. Legislators, governors, and other officials, though often seriously considering both models or even initially preferring the Pennsylvania System, repeatedly cited pro-Auburn reformers' claims about the disadvantages of the Pennsylvania System and the advantages of the Auburn System. Although the myths about the Pennsylvania System's effect on prisoners' mental and physical health were often mentioned, the Pennsylvania System's cost (or its inability to profit) was the most persuasive.[89] Maryland adopted the Auburn System in 1828, complaining that the Pennsylvania System – which, at that time, still meant solitary confinement without labor – would require a prison facility too expensive to build and lacked sufficient mental stimulation for the prisoners.[90] When the Maine legislature sought to alter its Thomaston prison in 1839, they favored the Auburn System, which was thought "less expensive to build, fully as easy to administer, and, while less expensive to maintain, quite as popular among the authorities on prison discipline, as well as quite reformative."[91] When New Jersey abandoned the Pennsylvania System, it was said by other observers to be "chiefly, though not wholly, on financial considerations."[92] Widespread belief in the myths criticizing the Pennsylvania System solidified Auburn's victory in these states.

THE PAINS OF DEVIANCE

Eastern's administrators were certainly not immune to the power of the calumnious myths as well as the forces that made the myths compelling. It was difficult work to manage a heavily criticized and highly unique prison. For one thing, the same uncertainties that permeated the field were even stronger at Eastern. Particularly in the prison's early years, memories of the insanity and death that halted Auburn's early experiment with total solitary confinement – influential in shaping other penal actors' choice to adopt the Auburn System, and still fresh in the 1830s and 1840s – made Eastern's administrators nervous about their own prison. As Inspector Thomas Bradford explained early in the prison's history of the challenges when embarking on "[t]he experiment of separate confinement": "Good

---

[89] McLennan, The Crisis of Imprisonment, pp. 8, 63–64; Rothman, *The Discovery of the Asylum*, p. 88; Barnes, *The Evolution of Penology*, p. 177.

[90] Lewis, *The Development of American Prisons and Prison Customs, 1776–1845*, pp. 206–207.

[91] Ibid., p. 149.   [92] Wines, and Dwight, *Report on the Prisons and Reformatories*, p. 52.

men had doubts. None of us could say how far the body and mind could be in total seclusion from society and confinement to a cell for a length of time."[93] Bradford's comment was a rare public acknowledgment of the doubt he and other administrators felt. More typically, the administrators' anxiety was expressed more subtly, continuously referring to the Pennsylvania System or its components as an experiment – even decades into its operations.[94]

Running a unique prison meant that Eastern's administrators could not benefit from other prison administrators' examples. Most prison administrators in the country could alleviate some of the anxiety that came from the uncertainty of imposing long-term cellular confinement for the first time by copying others who were following the same plan of confinement – the Auburn System. When they faced ambiguity about their work – how to proceed in a particular situation or, more existentially, what the purpose of their work was – they could look to other prison

[93] Pennsylvania, *Testimony from Legislative Committee to Investigate State Penitentiary for the Eastern District of Pennsylvania*, no page (Bradford testimony).

[94] Noting the prison's "more than five years in actual operation," Warden Wood suggested, "I think we may now cease to call our system of discipline an experiment." Eastern State Penitentiary, *Sixth Annual Report of the Inspectors of the Eastern State Penitentiary of Pennsylvania*. Philadelphia: J. W. Allen, 1835, p. 7. Five years later, however, Wood still referred to it as an experiment, noting, "More than ten years have elapsed since this experiment was commenced." Eastern State Penitentiary, *Eleventh Annual Report of the Inspectors of the Eastern State Penitentiary of Pennsylvania*. Philadelphia: Brown, Bicking & Guilbert, 1840, pp. 9–10. It was only in the late 1840s that the administrators moved away from the appellation, referring to the earlier years as the experimental period. In 1847, the inspectors noted,

Pennsylvania has nobly set the example; she made the experiment at a time when doubts and difficulties, impediment and hindrance, were clouding the prospect – but year after year has brought to light the wisdom of the founders of the system, and added proof upon proof of its complete success. It is now no longer an experiment; but the separate system of Prison discipline speaks in the voice of experience, subjected to the test of strict trial, to the spirit of progress of the age. Eastern State Penitentiary, *Eighteenth Annual Report of the Inspectors of the Eastern State Penitentiary of Pennsylvania*. Philadelphia: Ed. Barrington and Geo. D. Haswell, 1847, p. 16.

In 1852, they again noted of the prison's early years, "It was then an experiment." Eastern State Penitentiary, *Twenty-Third Annual Report of the Inspectors of the Eastern State Penitentiary of Pennsylvania*. Philadelphia: B. Mifflin, 1852, p. 7. Indeed, writing in the early 1870s, Inspector Richard Vaux offered his own periodization of Eastern's then-forty-year history. To his mind, "The period from 1829 to 1849 was one of *experiment and experience*." Vaux, *A Brief Sketch*, p. 85. By the late 1840s, public expressions of their trepidation about their work subsided as accumulated experience helped them to feel more confident.

administrators' choices or responses.[95] They could, and did, write to other prisons' administrators for advice.

Eastern's administrators, by contrast, were alone. While they did visit other prisons, these visits provided limited information. Most prisons followed the Auburn System, and there was little in those prisons' experiences that could benefit a Pennsylvania-style prison. After visiting New York's Sing Sing prison (which followed the Auburn System) and being "shown round," Warden Wood recorded that he "did not like the appearance of the place, as well as when I was last there."[96] Decades later, Warden Thompson visited "the New York city prison ('Tombs') Black-well's Island Penitentiary & work house, Sing Sing Prison, Albany Penitentiary & the Penitentiary at Auburn." He returned "[m]ore than ever satisfied with our own Penitentiary and of its being the only reformatory Prison, that I have knowledge of."[97] For Eastern's administrators, Auburn-style prisons were inferior and thus not useful models.

Other prisons following the Pennsylvania System were not helpful examples either, because they usually did not adhere to the system in practice. At the other end of the state, Western did not follow the Pennsylvania System for the first six or so years and only partially administered it thereafter; its administrators visited Eastern for guidance more often than Eastern's administrators visited them.[98] When Eastern's administrators toured the prisons in New Jersey and Rhode Island, they were often dissatisfied with what they saw, finding in them little to learn from. Warden Scattergood spent one afternoon in 1850 at New Jersey's prison (which followed the Pennsylvania System) with "Overseers Rogers & Blundin [from Eastern] … in order to gain what information we could in regard to cane seating" (a method of making chairs by weaving long-stemmed plant parts). He noted that New Jersey's "Warden Jacob Gaddis was very kind in giving us all the information he could." But Scattergood also recorded, somewhat gloomily, "it appears evident that their profit in working arises from the use of machinery, and a departure from the

95 See also Erich M. Studer-Ellis, "Springboards to Mortarboards: Women's College Foundings in Massachusetts, New York, and Pennsylvania," *Social Forces* 73:3 (1995), pp. 1051–1070; Tricia McTague, Kevin Stainback, and Donald Tomaskovic-Devey, "An Organizational Approach to Understanding Sex and Race Segregation in U.S. Workplaces," *Social Forces* 87:3 (2009), pp. 1499–1527.

96 Eastern State Penitentiary, *Warden's Daily Journal*, August 26, 1838.

97 Ibid., January 24, 1871.

98 E. g., Ibid., November 8, 1832; December 2, 1836; July 5 and 17, 1847; May 18, 1852; December 11, 1863; May 19, 1869.

Separate System of imprisonment. We returned home in the evening."⁹⁹
Eastern was the exemplar of the Pennsylvania System; its administrators
had no model to turn to, they had nowhere to look for guidance but to
each other and their own principles.

More than the uncertainties of managing a unique prison, Eastern's
administrators also had to contend with the criticism. Public criticism of
the Pennsylvania System and their prison apparently weighed heavily on
these men: Judging by the amount of space in their annual reports devoted
to their prison's defense (see Chapters 5 and 6), Eastern's administrators
took this criticism seriously – enough to counter every claim made to
protect their institution's reputation. Indeed, the administrators knew that
others were watching their progress, looking for evidence of success or
failure. Warden Wood perceived "much interest and some anxiety" over
Eastern's experience with solitary confinement on the part of "those who
have of late years paid attention to Penal Jurisprudence in Europe and
America, as to the result of what many considered an experiment."¹⁰⁰
While this attention was simultaneously exhilarating and terrifying, the
firehose of criticism proved a significant source of anxiety.

It is important to understand that criticism of the Pennsylvania System was simultaneously a criticism of the men who implemented it. If
the Pennsylvania System was cruel and inhumane, Eastern's administrators were cruel and inhumane for implementing it. If the Pennsylvania
System was costly and inefficient, they were bad managers and bad businessmen running a bad prison. This connection was sometimes made
explicit. Charles Dickens, for example, made clear that he was not simply
criticizing the Pennsylvania System, but the men who implemented it as
well. While speaking charitably of their motivations, Dickens cautioned,
"those benevolent gentlemen who carry it into execution, do not know
what it is that they are doing. I believe that very few men are capable of
estimating the immense amount of torture and agony which this dreadful
punishment, prolonged for years, inflicts upon the sufferers."¹⁰¹ Calling
the Pennsylvania System "immeasurably worse than any torture of the
body," Dickens explained, "there is a depth of terrible endurance in it
which none but the sufferers themselves can fathom, and which no man
has a right to inflict upon his fellow-creature."¹⁰² In effect, Dickens was
calling the administrators ignorant monsters and possibly even criminals.

⁹⁹ Ibid., April 26, 1850.
¹⁰⁰ Eastern State Penitentiary, *Eleventh Annual Report of the Inspectors*, pp. 9–10.
¹⁰¹ Dickens, *American Notes*, p. 111.   ¹⁰² Ibid., p. 111.

Dickens' comments, even more than other public criticism, stung Eastern's administrators. Writing thirty years after the publication of Dickens' *American Notes* – and still smarting from its insults – Inspector Richard Vaux dedicated several pages of his momentous history of Eastern to Dickens' visit. Vaux complained, "Not one word of criticism or objection was then or there made. He did not even express a doubt of the success of separate confinement as a system of prison discipline."[103] Vaux was not alone in remembering the sting of Dickens' comments. In 1875, Warden Townsend noted the reception of Prisoner "No 8048. William Morris alias Charles Langheimer" a white man sentenced to one year for larceny. According to Townsend, "This is the ninth time this man has been in Prison & the one whom Dickens wrote so pathetically about 30 years ago."[104] Townsend had not been associated with the prison when Dickens had visited or published his notes, but as Eastern's Warden, responsible for implementing the Pennsylvania System, he was still cut by Dickens' words. More than the public embarrassment, Dickens' criticism had devastating implications for the administrators: What if they *were* wrong?

Looking for Signs

Criticism did more than simply linger in the administrators' consciousness: confounded by the novelty of their work, criticism also planted seeds of doubt. The administrators' private writings – especially during Eastern's first two decades – reveal an undercurrent of anxiety about their work. The warden's log, in particular, is full of passages reminiscent of seventeenth-century Calvinists looking for signs of their Inner Light – their promise of future salvation – so intensely did they look for evidence that their system was working.[105] For example, wardens frequently recorded improvements in their prisoners. Numerous prisoners were released having learned to read, write, or both in prison, and the wardens were careful to record this improvement. Warden Thompson noted in a typical entry, George Evans, No. 1512, "was unable to read when admitted and has learned in prison."[106] These small successes helped to strengthen the administrators' resolve and faith in the system; bigger

---

[103] Vaux, *A Brief Sketch*, p. 111.
[104] Eastern State Penitentiary, *Warden's Daily Journal*, September 9, 1875.
[105] See also Max Weber, *The Protestant Ethic and the Spirit of Capitalism*. Trans. by Talcott Parsons. London and New York: Routledge Classics, 2006 [1930].
[106] Eastern State Penitentiary, *Warden's Daily Journal*, March 1, 1843.

successes were even more powerful. Warden Wood was particularly touched after James Brown, Prisoner No. 54, voluntarily returned to the prison looking for work (see also Chapter 8). Wood recorded, "What a commentary on the system."[107] Likewise, after Warden Thompson returned from visiting New York's prisons – finding them wanting and his own prison far superior – he noted, "I feel a renewed earnestness & zeal to press forward in the good work, and with a firm reliance that the good hand will ever be underneath to support in every well directed effort."[108] Simple episodes like these reassured Eastern's administrators that their system was beneficial.

Wardens also sought evidence that their prisoners were not the worse for wear, especially during the late 1830s and 1840s when the prison faced the strongest criticism. In one interesting manifestation of their anxiety, the wardens diligently recorded prisoners' physical condition upon release, especially for those prisoners completing lengthy sentences. Warden Wood described Hugh Righten (alias William O'Donald), Prisoner No. 171, as "better in appearance & health than when he arrived here" six years previous.[109] Prisoners' weight was of particular interest to the wardens. Warden Wood recorded of Hall Holmes, Prisoner No. 621, discharged after three years' incarceration, "he was fat & in good health."[110] Warden Thompson noted that Henry Butler, Prisoner No. 1634, was not only released "in good health," he also reported that he was "well treated" and his "Food had been plenty" – indeed, his "circumference round the body had increased six inches."[111] Similarly, Warden Thompson released Jacob Ford, Prisoner No. 1740, "in good health" and he "ha[d] encreased in weight 50 pounds" despite the fact that he "came in very bad health" (he, too, was well treated and had plenty of food).[112] Warden Scattergood recorded of William Blackstone (alias Dad Miller), Prisoner No. 1790, "He is more fleshy than when admitted & in quite as good health."[113]

Conversely, wardens tried to explain away prisoners who died in prison or left in bad health. Julia Wilt, Prisoner No. 1109, died after four years at Eastern; she "came in very ill[,] she has been sick the whole time of her confinement."[114] John Rickhon, No. 1278, was discharged "in bad health having been admitted in a very reduced state and having been on the sick list during the whole time of his imprisonment or with few exceptions."[115]

[107] Ibid., December 6, 1835.   [108] Ibid., January 24, 1871.   [109] Ibid., May 8, 1839.
[110] Ibid., August 18, 1839.   [111] Ibid., January 20, 1844.   [112] Ibid., May 15, 1845.
[113] Ibid., January 22, 1846.   [114] Ibid., May 11, 1843.   [115] Ibid., May 18, 1843.

Such explanations could help to neutralize the wardens' doubts about the safety and morality of their system.[116]

Perhaps most tellingly, wardens also made special notes about prisoners others had claimed had been deranged by their time at Eastern. Warden Thompson recorded the dismissal of William Whitley, No. 1066, "in good health." The warden went on to record, "This man was alluded to by Mr Dickens as the man who made the Wooden clock and was deaf &ct, the latter impression was received by Mr D. in consequence of the prisoner having a cold in his head. His hearing was not affected."[117] Mary Lee, Prisoner No. 2331, was pardoned and left the prison "in poor health."[118] When she returned to her home county, Warden Scattergood was informed, "those acquainted with her could observe little difference in her now & when she was first committed." The frustrated warden recorded privately, "Yet here set down for Insane! by reason of the system!!."[119] These wardens were clearly angry, but reciting these cases of false accusations, even privately, could also be reassuring – their critics made baseless claims, these cases seemed to tell them, and they were on the right path. As we shall see, the administrators were even more vocal in their public efforts to challenge their own and others' anxieties about their Pennsylvania System.

* * *

The disasters at Auburn and Maine left an indelible impression in the minds of reformers and statesmen that would continue to link solitary confinement to insanity and death. Western's early failures, first beginning in 1826 and then beginning in 1829, and later the legislative investigation of 1834–1835 into problems at Eastern, seemed to confirm these early fears. Building on these examples, the BPDS and other commentators worked to continuously describe the Pennsylvania System as a system of pure solitary confinement and challenge the humanity and practicality of the Pennsylvania System as a mode of prison discipline. Their critiques persuaded most decision makers throughout the young United States to adopt the Auburn System, which minimized prisoners' time in solitary confinement within a system that assigned prisoners ostensibly profitable labor. Importantly, these myths also established Eastern – and any prison

---

[116] See also Chapter 5 and 6 for their more public strategies of neutralization.
[117] Eastern State Penitentiary, *Warden's Daily Journal*, February 19, 1843.
[118] Ibid., October 10, 1849.   [119] Ibid., October 20, 1849.

that continued to follow the Pennsylvania System – as a deviant prison. Eastern was out of sync with the rest of the country, leaving it vulnerable to extensive criticism. For at least fifty years after its opening (and even today), Eastern would be associated with mental illness and unnecessary prisoner deaths, cruelties imposed by a costly and inefficient system that would never function or reform prisoners as promised.[120] This criticism extended to Eastern's administrators, who took it to heart. With the weight of national (and some international) opinion against them, their own doubts and anxieties, and the personal cost of managing a deviant prison, why did they continue, decade after decade, generation after generation, to support the Pennsylvania System?

---

[120] Sullivan writes that the Pennsylvania System "lost out in the United States partly because of the relentless opposition of Louis Dwight and the Boston Prison Discipline Society and partly because of accusations (which were basically accurate) that pure solitary confinement induces insanity rather than penitence. More important, however, the Auburn model was less expensive to build, and its factories resulted in higher productivity in the prison and profits for the state. Among almost all reformers, a primary criterion for prison success was profitability." Larry E. Sullivan, *The Prison Reform Movement: Forlorn Hope*. Boston: Twayne Publishers, 1990, pp. 12–13.

PART II

THE ADVANTAGE OF DIFFERENCE

The Process of Institutionalization

A

THE ADMINISTRATORS' PUBLIC DEFENSE

To defend the organization is often to defend oneself. These defensive activities are aided when a set of beliefs is so fashioned as at once to fortify the special needs or interests of the organization and to provide an aura of disinterestedness under which formal discussion may be pursued.

Philip Selznick[1]

[1] Selznick, *TVA and the Grassroots*, p. 51.

5

Neutralizing the Calumnious Myths

Administrators' Public Defense of the Pennsylvania System

Before the Pennsylvania System can be said to be in full operation, each county must have a prison to confine the accused before trial, separate and alone, and those for small offences in separate cells, for all terms under two years, the System would be in perfect operation.

Warden Samuel Wood (1840), Annual Report[1]

Could I deem it at all compatible with my duties, as the medical officer of the institution, I would prefer confining my Report for the past year, to the presentation of the usual statistics; but having daily forced on my observation, suffering and death, originating in defects that have no just connection with our discipline, I feel that I should be highly culpable, were I to pass them over in silence.

Physician Robert Given (1849), Annual Report[2]

There is not a criticism which objectors to the Pennsylvania system have ever made, that the administration, in its details and from the experience thus gained, have not successfully removed or denied.

Board of Inspectors (1865), Annual Report[3]

---

[1] Eastern State Penitentiary, Warden's Report, *The Eleventh Annual Report of the Inspectors of the Eastern State Penitentiary of Pennsylvania.* Brown, Bicking & Guilbert, 1840, p. 14.

[2] Eastern State Penitentiary, Physician's Report, *The Twentieth Annual Report of the Inspectors.* Philadelphia: Edmond Barrington and Geo. D. Haswell, 1849, p. 25.

[3] Eastern State Penitentiary, Inspectors' Report, *Thirty-Sixth Annual Report of the Inspectors of the State Penitentiary for the Eastern District of Pennsylvania.* Philadelphia: M'Laughlin Brothers, 1865, pp. 16–17.

THE ANNUAL REPORTS

As required by Eastern's foundational statute, the administrators wrote annual reports on the operations of their prison. Eastern's annual reports consisted of separate reports from the Board of Inspectors, warden, physician, moral instructor, and (in some later years) schoolteacher. The Board of Inspectors' reports were written by a one- or two-person subcommittee (typically the president and/or the secretary of the board) and then presented to and, after some revision, signed by the board. The reports were occasionally debated, but they usually represented a consensus view among the inspectors, somewhat skewed toward the president's views. In the early period (1830s–early 1840s), Inspector Thomas Bradford, Jr., longtime president of the board, was a major influence; in later years (mid-1840s–1870s), Richard Vaux, first as secretary, later as the board's other longtime president, was even more influential. Notably, however, for some years in the late 1840s, Inspector Bradford refused to sign the annual reports because of his ongoing disagreement with the board (see Chapter 8). The remaining reports were written by the relevant officer of the prison – warden, physician, or moral instructor.

These reports – produced every year from 1831 onward, excepting 1874 (a deep depression year) – were officially addressed to the state legislature. In practice, they were the prison's main public relations vehicle as they were widely circulated to and read by penal reform societies, prison administrators, and legislators around – and beyond – the country. Periodicals, including daily newspapers and bimonthly or quarterly publications, such as the *North American Review*, often reprinted excerpts or summarized these (and other prisons') reports for a wider audience, as did several reform societies in their own annual reports or journals. Many international commentators and even heads of state interested in penal reform acquired copies. These reports thus offered administrators a prime opportunity to challenge the calumnious myths about the Pennsylvania System.

* * *

The annual reports represent the principal medium through which the administrators presented and defended their embattled prison. By gathering facts and statistics and constructing tables to present their data, administrators could offer concrete proof against the claims that their system was cruel and inhumane, dangerous to prisoners' physical and mental health, too expensive and unprofitable, and simply impractical and ineffective. Challenging these criticisms was exactly the purpose of this work. As the inspectors noted in the 1860s,

The yearly reports that have been made for the last quarter of a century, are testimony on the subject that are reliable, as far as they can be made so. They present more information, on penal science, or data from which penal science can be studied, than any other like institution in the country. There is not a criticism which objectors to the Pennsylvania system have ever made, that the adminis-tration, in its details and from the experience thus gained, have not successfully removed or denied.[4]

Indeed, the administrators often described this data as "the best argu-ment" against the myths.[5] They noted, "It is submitted that the truest test of our system, is to be found in this comparison, as well as that of the yearly tables of statistics, which constitute a part of the Reports made to the Inspectors. Indeed it is not well understood, how else to determine the question."[6] However, these claims not only defended the Pennsylvania System to its critics, they also defended the men who implemented it and faced criticism for doing so.

In challenging the veracity of the myths about the Pennsylvania System, Eastern's administrators relied on what criminologists Gresham Sykes and David Matza call "techniques of neutralization," or a series of accounts of their behavior that challenge the fact of, or mitigate responsibility or blame for, immoral or inappropriate behavior.[7] This chapter explores three such strategies: changing how they described the Pennsylvania System in response to criticism, denying the existence of bad outcomes through extensive logic-based and statistical evaluations, and denying the system's responsibility for bad outcomes that did occur by placing the blame on others. These strategies, in combination with the two strategies discussed in the following chapter, represent some of the most common themes of Eastern's Annual Reports. Ultimately, these techniques of neutralization enabled Eastern's administrators to neutralize the pains

---

4 Ibid., Inspectors' Report, pp. 16–17.

5 Eastern State Penitentiary, Inspectors' Report, *Fortieth Annual Report of the Inspec-tors of the State Penitentiary for the Eastern District of Pennsylvania*. Philadelphia: M'Laughlin Brothers, 1869, p. 5.

6 Eastern State Penitentiary, Inspectors' Report, *Thirty-Ninth Annual Report of the Inspec-tors of the State Penitentiary for the Eastern District of Pennsylvania*. Philadelphia: McLaughlin Brothers, 1868, p. 25.

7 Gresham M. Sykes and David Matza, "Techniques of Neutralization: A Theory of Delin-quency," *American Sociological Review* 22:6 (1957), pp. 664–670; Marvin B. Scott and Stanford M. Lyman, "Accounts," *American Sociological Review* 33:1 (1968), pp. 46–62.

of deviance and sustain the Pennsylvania System despite the criticism. Defending against the myths in this way also created a context for the Pennsylvania System to become personally institutionalized for Eastern's administrators.

NAME CHANGES

Throughout the period examined, administrators often referred to their distinctive approach as "the Pennsylvania system of prison discipline." However, Eastern's administrators also used more substantive names for the Pennsylvania System, strategically changing the names and even the definition of the Pennsylvania System over the years in order to reduce their vulnerability to the calumnious myths and thereby increase the Pennsylvania System's legitimacy. In the earliest period,[8] the administrators referred to the Pennsylvania System as the system of "solitary or separate confinement" *with* particular activities like labor, education, and religion. But after a decade or so – particularly after the BPDS decided the Pennsylvania System was an inferior system – the administrators introduced the most well-known title of the "separate system."

These changes were purely rhetorical. Indeed, there was no great shift in actual practice associated with these name changes. Instead, the administrators gradually shifted their stated definition of the Pennsylvania System, emphasizing different elements at different times. Initially, administrators emphasized the prisoner's solitude (and his opportunities for reflective reformation); later, they emphasized prisoners' separation from each other (and their opportunities for reformation). Though generally similar, these descriptions represented slightly different conceptions of the Pennsylvania System.

The administrators' changing characterizations of the Pennsylvania System were purposeful. Through these name changes, the administrators intended to demonstrate that the myths of their system's cruelty were based on a misunderstanding: it was solitary confinement *with* labor and religious instruction, not plain solitary, or it was *separate* confinement, not

---

[8] It is impossible to give exact dates at which a particular shift in nomenclature came because, in each identifiable period, administrators referred to their mode of confinement with multiple names, switching back and forth between an older moniker and the newer. However, while the dominance of a particular moniker took several years to establish, it tended to persist. In the following sections, I offer specific dates when the transitions begin, but I note the halting way in which these names took hold.

solitary confinement. If they could convince others of this misconception, it would undermine many of the standard criticisms. Sociologists Marvin B. Scott and Stanford M. Lyman, expanding on Sykes and Matza, call this technique "identity switching."[9]

The System of "Solitary or Separate Confinement," 1829–1830s

For Eastern's first decade, its administrators tended to describe the Pennsylvania System with the phrase "solitary confinement." Administrators were not fully consistent when referring to the system by name in this period or any other: In their first two reports, administrators referred to "the system of solitary confinement,"[10] "the system of solitary confinement, with labour,"[11] and "the penitentiary system of solitary confinement at labour, with moral and religious instruction."[12] Nor was solitary confinement the only description included. In the same reports, administrators referred to "this plan of the separate confinement of criminals."[13] A few years later, they referred to it as "separate or solitary confinement" or "solitary or separate imprisonment with labour."[14] While "separate confinement" became increasingly common in later decades, administrators throughout the first decade often used "solitary" to describe the Pennsylvania System. Their varied use of "solitary" was consistent with the 1829 statute, which some of that generation of Eastern's administrators had helped write (see Chapter 3).

Administrators in these early years also emphasized solitary confinement's importance for reformation. It was central to how the Pennsylvania System would work. For one thing, prisoners were kept away from each other and thus unable to contaminate each other; moreover, without an

---

9 Scott and Lyman "Accounts,"; Sykes and Matza, "Techniques of Naturalization."
10 Eastern State Penitentiary, Inspectors' Report, *The First and Second Annual Reports of the Inspectors of the Eastern State Penitentiary of Pennsylvania*. Philadelphia: Thomas Kite, 1831, p. 5.
11 Ibid., p. 4.
12 Ibid., p. 7. Another iteration included "the penitentiary system of solitary confinement at labour, with instruction in labour, in morals, and in religion." Eastern State Penitentiary, Inspectors' Report, *Report of the Board of Inspectors of the Eastern Penitentiary of Pennsylvania*. Harrisburg: Henry Welsh, 1832, p. 5.
13 Eastern State Penitentiary, Physician's Report, *The First and Second Annual Reports of the Inspectors*, p. 15.
14 Eastern State Penitentiary, Inspectors' Report, *Seventh Annual Report of the Inspectors of the Eastern State Penitentiary of Pennsylvania*. Harrisburg: Theo. Fenn, 1836, p. 7.

audience to jeer at them or goad them into backsliding, prisoners could repent. For example:

The punishment inflicted not merely on the body, but on the mind of the prisoner, uniting severity and humanity, is one which the unhappy culprit feels with all its force; ... he is soon made to feel that the horrors of his cell are the fruits of sin and transgression, and the only certain relief to be obtained is through his Redeemer. Having no one to prompt in wickedness or shame him for his tears, he becomes humbled in spirit and anxious for help in the way of truth; and I am pleased to be able to say, that I do believe that there are some who rejoice that they have been brought here.[15]

Unique to this early period, administrators emphasized the way in which solitude broke the spirit of prisoners. These comments were familiar to administrators like Warden Wood, who had been an inspector at the Walnut Street Jail, where this rhetoric was common.[16] However, administrators were less ready to emphasize this advantage in later years as fears of insanity intensified.

Indeed, administrators' word choices in this period only subtly distinguished their system from pure solitary confinement. Their designations often included specifications such as "solitary confinement at labor" or with "moral and religious instruction" to make it clear that it was not *just* solitary confinement. They also were careful to not refer to pure solitary confinement as only solitary confinement, and instead variously called it "absolute," "exclusive," or "total" solitary confinement. To further distinguish the Pennsylvania System from this kind of solitary confinement, they actively condemned such treatment as cruel and inhumane. As the inspectors noted early in the prison's lifetime,

Absolute solitude for years, without labour or moral or religious instruction, probably does bear too severely upon a social being like man, and, were such the mode of punishment in this Institution, the Board would feel little hesitation in recommending its repeal, as cruel, because calculated to undermine the moral and physical powers of the prisoner, and to disqualify him from earning his bread at the expiration of his sentence; as impolitic, because, when persisted in beyond a very limited time, it tends to harden rather than reform the offender, while it produces great expense to the public, the prisoner in no way contributing by labour to his support.[17]

---

[15] Eastern State Penitentiary, Warden' Report, *Fourth Annual Report of the Inspectors of the Eastern State Penitentiary of Pennsylvania*. Philadelphia: Printed for the Philadelphia Society for Alleviating the Miseries of Public Prisons, 1833, p. 9.

[16] Michael Meranze, *Laboratories of Virtue: Punishment, Revolution, and Authority in Philadelphia, 1760–1835*. Chapel Hill: University of North Carolina Press, 1996.

[17] Eastern State Penitentiary, Inspectors' Report, *The First and Second Annual Reports of the Inspectors*, p. 9.

By publicizing their own condemnation of this harsher form of solitary confinement, they helped to reassure their readers that the Pennsylvania System relied on a different, less severe form of solitary.

By the end of the decade, however, administrators had realized the error in continuing to refer to "solitary confinement" at Eastern. Recall that after Eastern opened, the BPDS had taken the lead in condemning the Pennsylvania System: after an initial, tentative willingness to see how it worked in practice, midway through the decade, the BPDS had changed their stance and repeated their earlier concerns that the Pennsylvania System was nothing more than solitary confinement and was, therefore, dangerous. The label "solitary" routinely generated visions of prisoners going insane, mutilating themselves, dying, or killing themselves after spending months in the cramped solitary cells – stories that were repeated even in the 1860s.[18]

In response to such concerns, Eastern's administrators reassured their readers that the Pennsylvania System did not cause prisoners to go insane. As they explained in their 1836 report, "The expectation hitherto expressed by the board [of inspectors], that solitary or separate imprisonment with labour, has no unfavorable influence upon the mind or body of the prisoner, is fully confirmed by the experience of another year."[19] They also increasingly reminded their audience that solitary at Eastern included "labour, with moral and religious instruction." But this clarification was insufficient to stop the criticism. Almost forty years later, administrators were still conscientious of their predecessors' error, complaining, "Nearly all the objections which have ever been urged against this Penitentiary discipline arose entirely from the name by which it was first known."[20] But even by the late 1830s, it was clear that the word "solitary" was too much of a liability.

The "Separate System," 1840s–1860s

Beginning in the 1840s, Eastern's administrators rarely used the word "solitary" when referring to the Pennsylvania System. Instead, they

---

[18] Enoch C. Wines, and Theodore W. Dwight, *Report on the Prisons and Reformatories of the United States and Canada Made to the Legislature of New York, January 1867.* Albany, NY: Van Benthuysen and Sons' Steam Printing House, 1867.

[19] Eastern State Inspectors' Report, Inspectors' Report, *Seventh Annual Report of the Inspectors*, p. 7.

[20] Eastern State Penitentiary, Inspectors' Report, *Forty-Fifth Annual Report of the Inspectors of the State Penitentiary for the Eastern District of Pennsylvania.* Philadelphia: Sherman & Co., 1875, p. 27. See also: Eastern State Penitentiary, Inspectors' Report, *Thirty-Sixth Annual Report of the Inspectors*, p. 90.

referred to the Pennsylvania System as "the separate system" or the "system of separate confinement." These new designations became (and continued as) the dominant name until the 1860s with few exceptions. The administrators sometimes also included "with labor" as part of the title[21] following the early practice, but references to "moral and religious instruction" as part of the system's name were dropped by 1841.[22]

With this transition in official nomenclature from "solitary" to "separate" confinement, the administrators cautiously avoided the association between their system and the failed experiments at Auburn, Maine, and, less fatally, Western. Eastern's administrators were not the first penal actors to use this technique of circumlocution. Historian Michael Ignatieff has described how English reformers in the 1780s also strategically shifted from solitary to separate confinement to avoid opposition to the new approach; Eastern's administrators borrowed this tactic from them. Moreover, the practice continues today as prison administrators use a panoply of names – administrative segregation, disciplinary segregation, secure housing, restrictive housing, lockdown, isolation – to avoid the phrase "solitary confinement."[23]

But Eastern's administrators did not rely on names alone. In the 1840s, Eastern's administrators increasingly reminded their readers that separate confinement did not mean prisoners were isolated from *all* human contact. For example, the inspectors explained,

The prisoners in the separate or solitary prisons have the same intercourse with all, but their fellow convicts, ... and the idea that prisoners are shut up, and shut out, from all intercommunication with the good and the instructive, is an error – a gross error. They have that, at all times, besides almost hourly intercourse with their overseers and other officers of the prison.[24]

---

[21] e.g., Eastern State Penitentiary, Inspectors' Report, *Fifteenth Annual Report of the Inspectors of the Eastern State Penitentiary of Pennsylvania*, Philadelphia: Joseph and William Kite, 1844, p. 11.

[22] The final reference to "moral and religious instruction" was in Eastern State Penitentiary, Warden's Report, *Eleventh Annual Report of the Inspectors of the Eastern State Penitentiary of Pennsylvania*, Philadelphia: Brown, Bicking & Guilbert, 1840, p. 10.

[23] Michael Ignatieff, *A Just Measure of Pain: The Penitentiary in the Industrial Revolution, 1750–1850*. New York: Pantheon Books, 1978, p. 142; Ashley T. Rubin and Keramet Reiter, "Continuity in the Face of Penal Innovation: Revisiting the History of American Solitary Confinement," *Law & Social Inquiry* 43:4 (2018), pp. 1604–1632.

[24] Eastern State Penitentiary, Inspectors' Report, *Sixteenth Annual Report of the Inspectors of the Eastern State Penitentiary of Pennsylvania*. Philadelphia: Ed. Barrington and Geo. D. Haswell, 1845, p. 15.

Essentially, the term "solitary" could be misleading if taken too literally, they argued.

In these years, the administrators started to explain why they used such a misleading term: their reliance on the terms "solitary" or "separate" was intended to distinguish their mode of confinement from the congregation of prisoners under the Auburn System. The inspectors explained in the same report, "It may be proper here to remark, that the term 'solitary or separate confinement,' refers to the fact that each prisoner is alone, in contradistinction to the 'aggregate confinement,' or 'silent system,' where prisoners are in gangs, or together in large or small numbers."[25] Nearly two decades later, administrators continued to emphasize this difference, referring to "the separate as contradistinguished from the congregate system of punishment."[26] Thus, the "separation" of prisoners became the key designation, not their solitude. For example, administrators explained, "The prisoners are separated from each other at all times. They never see one another. From the moment they come into prison, they are separated and alone, only as regards their fellow prisoners. The system is properly called therefore the separate system."[27] The naming practices thus shifted as administrators sought to distinguish the Pennsylvania System from absolute solitary confinement and emphasized instead its differences from the Auburn System.[28]

---

[25] Ibid., p. 15.
[26] Eastern State Penitentiary, Inspectors' Report, *Thirty-Third Annual Report of the Inspectors of the State Penitentiary for the Eastern District of Pennsylvania*. Philadelphia: M'Laughlin Brothers, 1862, p. 24. See also Eastern State Penitentiary, Inspectors' Report, *Forty-Fifth Annual Report of the Inspectors*, p. 27.
[27] Eastern State Penitentiary, Inspectors' Report, *Seventeenth Annual Report of the Inspectors of the Eastern State Penitentiary of Pennsylvania*. Philadelphia: Ed. Barrington and Geo. D. Haswell, 1846, p. 7.
[28] Administrators offered a lengthy account of its history in the 1872 report:

A few words, it is hoped, will show that no such cruelty enters into the actual treatment. Our system is properly called the separate or solitary. To describe it properly would be to denominate it the system of individual treatment. But the separation or the solitude is relative not absolute. This is evident from the historical origin of these descriptive terms. They were originally suggested at a time when the congregational system prevailed, and they were employed to contradistinguish the new system from the old, so the words separate or solitary simply signify anti-congregational. The subsequent practice at the Penitentiary has conformed to this explanation. It is a separation or solitude as respects other convicts, not as respects other connections or relationships of the prisoner which may be beneficial to him. It is considered of the utmost importance that association or fellowship or intercourse with other criminals should by all means be guarded against, and that to this extent the imprisonment should be separate or solitary. But otherwise,

In these later years, the administrators developed another strategy to explain how their system differed from older practices. Still haunted by the association between the Pennsylvania System and a system of total solitary confinement, they turned their gaze to Eastern's early years. In the 1850s and 1860s, administrators often criticized the earlier operations at Eastern as a system of (unqualified) solitary confinement to further emphasize that their current system was not one of solitary confinement. In a representative example, the Physician explained that the mortality and incidences of mental illness were lower than they had been previously because the administrators had abandoned its earlier, more "stringent" system of solitary confinement:

In reviewing the medical records of the institution during the early years of its existence, it will be perceived that the amount of physical, and especially of mental disease, was much greater than at present. This was no doubt owing to the peculiarly stringent discipline in vogue at the time, when solitary confinement was an appropriate designation. This term has become obsolete, and separate confinement, more properly describes the condition of the prisoner. The former existed at a time when a criminal was considered as divested of the attributes of humanity, and the object was more to punish than reform. At this time a lunatic was treated more like a beast than an unfortunate human being. He was caged and chained, starved and beaten. The spread of more enlightened opinions has changed all this, and the insane are shown all kindness and consideration consistent with safety. The prisoner too, although debarred from intercourse with his fellows, has the benefit of visits from the Inspectors, Warden, Physician, Moral Instructor, Teacher, Overseers, and Keepers, also the members of the Prison Discipline Society, from whom he receives much kindly advice and instruction, tending to render him a more respectable and useful member of society.[29]

A review of the annual reports and private records from the earlier period suggests more fiction than truth in this description. Indeed, it is

the prisoner's door is open to every other influence that may ameliorate his condition or benefit himself. He is constantly visited by those who have his interest at heart. His overseer visits him; the Moral Instructor visits him; the Secular Instructor visits him; religious people from without visit him; the physician visits him; the teacher of his trade or handicraft visits him; he corresponds with his family, and may make them the recipients of a portion of the profits of his labor; books and newspapers are supplied to him from the library; the Inspectors grant special permits to see him; they themselves visit him, and the Warden is in constant intercourse with him. It thus appears that the separation or solitude is to be understood relatively to other convicts. Inspectors' Report, Eastern State Penitentiary, *Forty-Third Annual Report of the Inspectors of the State Penitentiary for the Eastern District of Pennsylvania*. Philadelphia: McLaughlin Brothers, 1872, pp. 25–26.

[29] Eastern State Penitentiary, Physician's Report, *Thirty-Sixth Annual Report of the Inspectors*, pp. 66–67.

important to emphasize that there is no apparent shift in either actual practice or what administrators claimed to do that suggests there was a difference in the use of solitary confinement in these early years. However, administrators' willingness to critique their forerunners illustrates the desperation in their efforts to renounce solitary confinement – but *not* the Pennsylvania System. Indeed, as we shall see in this and the next chapter, this was far from the administrators' only effort to rewrite the history of their prison.

Summary

Naming trends can be important statements of an organization's identity.[30] Administrators' name changes for the Pennsylvania System were not simply responses to fads or the administrators' own whims. Instead, these naming practices were strategic attempts to protect the legitimacy of the Pennsylvania System, a defense against reformers' calumnious myths. Both names enabled administrators to convey the idea that the Pennsylvania System was not merely solitary confinement. While administrators explicitly and implicitly rejected this idea in other ways, the names and definitions of the Pennsylvania System emphasized the distinction between what their system did and the failed experiments at Auburn and elsewhere. While some commentators adopted the administrators' preferred title, it did not convince many that, as the administrators argued, the Pennsylvania System was different from solitary and avoided its associated dangers and other problems. Of course, naming practices were not their only technique to neutralize criticism.

EVALUATION

Eastern's administrators allocated large portions of their Annual Reports to evaluating their prison. Their evaluations took the form of logical, summary, and comparative analyses along the dimensions on which the Pennsylvania System was challenged most – health and mortality, cost and profitability, and efficacy in reforming prisoners and reducing crime rates. These evaluations often included comparisons to previous years, but the administrators also offered detailed comparisons of the mortality rates, costs, and (apparent) recidivism at Eastern and elsewhere. These

---

[30] Mary Ann Glynn and Rikki Abzug, "Institutionalizing Identity: Symbolic Isomorphism and Organizational Names," *Academy of Management Journal* 45:1 (2002), pp. 267–280.

evaluations provided evidence that the Pennsylvania System did not cause harm – it did not harm the prisoners, it did not increase the taxpayers' burden, and it did not increase citizens' vulnerability to crime victimization – what Sykes and Matza, call "denials of injury."[31]

Prisoner Health and Well-Being

Administrators' evaluations focused foremost on medical assessments. Here they received the harshest criticism, so here they expended the most ink refuting the criticism. The administrators used several tactics to illustrate the healthfulness of their prison environment. At the most general, they called special attention to their low disease and mortality rates. In 1862, Warden Halloway noted,

The mortality is so small that it cannot be regarded otherwise than exceptional, as a greater one must certainly be due amongst the class of persons who form a prison population. And yet while this is the fact, it only furnishes additional evidence of the general healthfulness of the institution, and the nice adaptation of the diet and general hygeinic [sic] arrangements of the house for the preservation of health.[32]

The administrators also pointed out that their prison was at times healthier than free society – or what one would expect given the diseased state of free citizens at the time. Physician Newbold clarified in 1858, "Although a large proportion of the convicts received during the past year were infirm in health, the mortality has been exceedingly small."[33] Likewise, in several years with widespread epidemics in Philadelphia, the administrators made sure to note the prison was largely unscathed. Warden Townsend crowed in 1872, "Although the small-pox epidemic has fearfully prevailed in the city and throughout the country, I am able to say, with feelings of gratitude, that we have been almost exempted from it. There have been only three cases within our walls – the first proved fatal – the other two have entirely recovered."[34] Such claims suggested that the prison was not only healthy for a prison, but it was healthy for any population cluster.

[31] Sykes and Matza, "Techniques of Naturalization."
[32] Eastern State Penitentiary, Warden's Report, *Thirty-Third Annual Report of the Inspectors*, p. 46.
[33] Eastern State Penitentiary, Physician's Report, *Twenty-Ninth Annual Report of the Inspectors of the State Penitentiary for the Eastern District of Pennsylvania*. Philadelphia: F. Pierson, 1858, p. 25.
[34] Eastern State Penitentiary, Warden's Report, *Forty-Third Annual Report of the Inspectors*, p. 93.

While these remarks were useful flourishes, the administrators primarily rejected their prison's reputation for poor health by comparing their prison to other prisons. Since other prisons lacked Eastern's reputation for mortality, commentators paid less attention to deaths at those prisons; at Eastern, however, every death seemed to confirm its reputation. Eastern's administrators therefore used the statistics of other prisons to proclaim that their own mortality statistics were on par with Auburn-style prisons (see Figure 5.1).

Mortality rates were often similar, but small differences up or down were treated as though significant. When mortality rates were lower at Eastern, the administrators crooned. In 1844, Physician Hartshorne observed, "By a comparative estimate with five State Prisons on the Auburn plan, two of which are more favourably suited than this, it is shown ... that our mortality has been less than theirs."[35]

When mortality rates were unfavorable to Eastern, its administrators accused the other prisons' administrators of poor reporting strategies that disadvantaged the Pennsylvania System. For example, Eastern's administrators claimed that other prisons' administrators solicited pardons for their insane prisoners, which artificially reduced their mental health and mortality numbers. Eastern's administrators, by contrast, denied engaging in such practices. Warden Thompson explained in 1845,

to my knowledge, no prisoner has been pardoned that would have been likely to have added to the mortality if he had remained during the year: this fact should always be ascertained in examining prison records of mortality, as a few pardons, humanely interposed by the Executive, would entirely alter the per centage, and lead to great error in comparing the mortality of different prisons.[36]

Consequently, comparisons unfavorable to the Pennsylvania System, they argued, were misleading.

Eastern's administrators made similar arguments regarding insanity at Eastern and elsewhere. For example, the administrators often claimed they were more fastidious in recording cases of insanity, while clear cases of insanity went unreported in other prisons like Connecticut's Wethersfield State Prison. Eastern's administrators also accused supporters of the Auburn System of doctoring their records or misrepresenting the

---

35 Eastern State Penitentiary, Physician's Report, *Fifteenth Annual Report of the Inspectors*, p. 28.
36 Eastern State Penitentiary, Warden's Report, *Sixteenth Annual Report of the Inspectors*, p. 20.

For those anxious to compare the mortality occurring in the Separate with that of the Auburn System, I annex the following table
which is taken from all the reports that I have received for the last
year.

AUBURN SYSTEM.

Penitentiary.	No. of Prisoners.	Deaths.	Pardons, remissions, &c.
Massachusetts . . .	384	2	31
Michigan	130	1	8
Auburn	975	14	34
Sing Sing	1069	33	38
Maryland	387	21	12
SEPARATE SYSTEM,	2945	71	123
Eastern S. Penitentiary,	487	11	15

per cent.

Per centage of deaths in five prisons on Auburn Plan, ... 2.41
Ditto of pardons, &c. in the same, ... 4.17
Ditto of deaths in Eastern State Penitentiary, (Separate System,) 2.25
Ditto of pardons in "   "   " 3.08
The deaths in the five prisons (Auburn System) as above,

1843, p. ct. 2.41

Ditto   in three Separate, viz :

Eastern S. P. Pa. ⎫
Western,   do. ⎬ 1843,   p. ct. 1.96
Trenton, N. J. ⎭

FIGURE 5.1 Official comparison of mortality rates as presented in an annual
report.

Source: Eastern State Penitentiary, *Fifteenth Annual Report of the Inspectors of the
Eastern State Penitentiary of Pennsylvania*. Philadelphia: Joseph and William Kite, 1844,
p. 14. Scanned by Google. Available at books.google.com (last accessed December 1,
2018).

data.[37] As Physician Given explained in 1849, "the superiority of one
or other system can never be justly established, unless the respective
partisans of both, are as faithful in reporting what contradicts, as they

---

[37] In an 1846 minority report and later pamphlet, Samuel Gridley Howe, of the BPDS,
accused his colleagues of just such partisan-inspired data manipulation. Samuel Gridley
Howe, *An Essay on Separate and Congregate Systems of Prison Discipline*. Boston:
William D. Ticknor and Company, 1846.

are ready to publish what supports, their cherished views."[38] Second, most prisons did not offer annual reports that were as detailed as those produced at Eastern, preventing appropriate comparisons. In 1871, the inspectors promised that once prisons are "require[d to produce] yearly, full reports, and investigations into those subjects which are directly connected with penal science, ... then the Pennsylvania system of discipline will be placed where it belongs, in the advance of a progress, philosophic and practical."[39] Eastern's reputation, they argued, was thus damaged by other prisons' reporting practices, which enabled those prisons to continue to enjoy their more positive reputations.

A third problem was disagreement in diagnoses – Eastern's administrators claimed to be more likely to diagnose prisoners as insane. Physician Given explained in 1848 that there was no "mutual understanding ... as to what really constitutes" insanity in American prisons. He continued, "there is reason to believe that what in our Penitentiary is deemed evidence of mental alienation, is in others considered the effect of moral turpitude; hence, no just comparison can be made on this basis as to the effect of either system." But all was not lost. He made sure to add that had he used the standard used at other prisons – when the insane prisoner's "delusions or excitement interfere with the performance of his daily task" – then this standard "would have enabled me to reduce the number that I report for the last year very greatly," putting the system on par with its competitors.[40] These comparisons helped to counter the calumnious myths that the Pennsylvania System was dangerous to the prisoners' mental and physical health.

Costs and Profit

The administrators also routinely evaluated their costs and profitability, another proclaimed weakness of the Pennsylvania System. During Eastern's first several years, its administrators could claim their system made some measure of profit. "The inspectors feel great satisfaction in

---

[38] Eastern State Penitentiary, Physician's Report, *The Twentieth Annual Report of the Inspectors*, p. 28.
[39] Eastern State Penitentiary, Inspectors' Report, *Forty-Second Annual Report of the Inspectors of the State Penitentiary for the Eastern District of Pennsylvania.* Philadelphia: McLaughlin Brothers, 1871, pp. 45–46.
[40] Eastern State Penitentiary, Physician's Report, *The Nineteenth Annual Report of the Inspectors of the Eastern State Penitentiary of Pennsylvania.* Ed. Barrington and Geo. D. Haswell, 1848, p. 41.

announcing that the profits of the past year meet the expenses of the Institution, excepting the salaries, and we entertain the belief heretofore expressed, that when the entire plan shall be completed, and the prison fully occupied, a revenue will arise from the labour of the convicts."[41] In fact, the coming years were less economical than they had hoped, and their attention turned to lower-than-expected costs and comparisons to other prisons.

One strategy in this later period was to point out that these other prisons were not as profitable as their proponents claimed. For example, in 1861, following a year when "the excess of maintenance over productions ... [wa]s $8\frac{1}{2}$ cents per diem" in their own prison, the inspectors spent several pages comparing their finances to those of New York prisons. After reviewing various New York prisons' financial records for the year, the inspectors noted, "If they [the figures] accurately express the entire cost, and all the earnings and the whole population; congregate labor, under the contract plan, or any other adopted in these institutions, is certainly not a paying system of convict labor."[42] Because Eastern was expected to be unprofitable, greater costs than returns was seen as evidence of its failure; by illustrating a similar unprofitability elsewhere, they countered the calumnious myths that only focused on the Pennsylvania System's inability to profit and the mistaken assumption that the Auburn System was profitable.

Although the administrators could not demonstrate greater profitability, they subtly shifted the comparison to argue the Pennsylvania System was more "economical" than its competitor system. By demonstrating the Auburn System's high costs, they also countered the myth that the Pennsylvania System was overly expensive. The inspectors noted in the same report from 1861,

From the report of the New York State Penitentaries [sic], for the year '58–9, it appears, that $32\frac{1}{3}$ cents per diem per capita, is the average cost of maintenance of their convicts. This is found from the official returns from those prisons.

The same sources of information from our Penitentiary show, that for the past year, with all its embarrasments, $28\frac{1}{2}$ cents is the similar cost in this Institution. These expenditures are as $32\frac{1}{3}$ to $28\frac{1}{2}$ cents, and the difference is in favor of the

[41] Eastern State Penitentiary, Inspectors' Report, *Fourth Annual Report of the Inspectors*, pp. 5–6.
[42] Eastern State Penitentiary, Inspectors' Report, *Thirty-Second Annual Report of the Inspectors of the State Penitentiary for the Eastern District of Pennsylvania*. Philadelphia: M'Laughlin Brothers, 1861, p. 48.

separate system. …The Inspectors would be fully justified, relying on all the facts contained in this report, to assume, that a more economical or productive system of prison discipline is not shown in a large majority of State Penitentiaries on the congregate plan.[43]

These comparisons not only helped to refute the calumnious myths that the Pennsylvania System was unprofitable (and that the Auburn System was profitable), but also to designate their system as superior.

Efficacy

The administrators argued that theirs was the superior system across the board, but they most emphasized its superior ability to reform prisoners – the one area where they had a clear advantage, logically speaking. The separation of offenders was central to their claims. As Warden Halloway explained in 1851,

Ours is a rule of reason rather than of fear or coercion; and herein consists one of the chief excellencies of our mild and rational system. The separate convict uninfluenced by the bad example, and secured from the sneers and taunts of his fellows, soon yields himself to the better feelings of his nature, and becomes ready to listen to the salutary counsels extended to him by the Inspectors and other officers of the prison, aided by the visits of those benevolent gentlemen, who seek in this unobtrusive way to promote the general good.[44]

By contrast, under the Auburn System, prisoners were not separated from one another and could be subjected to "sneers and taunts," and they lacked such "salutary counsels." Such differences, the administrators argued, made the Auburn System vastly inferior in its ability to reform. Eastern's inspectors made the implicit critique more explicit in 1859 when they explained of the Auburn System,

Contracting for the labor of the convicts, by which individuals may become rich on the toil of the unfortunate and degraded, and blending together the innocent, the young offender, and the hardened criminal, are, it would seem, producing their proper fruits, by augmenting to repletion the population of prisons, where every thing is thus done to foster habits, which naturally produce crimes, or educate criminals.[45]

---

[43] Ibid., p. 46.
[44] Eastern State Penitentiary, Warden's Report, *Twenty-Second Annual Report of the Inspectors of the Eastern State Penitentiary of Pennsylvania*. Philadelphia: Kite & Walton, 1851, p. 9.
[45] Eastern State Penitentiary, Inspectors' Report, *Thirtieth Annual Report of the Inspectors of the State Penitentiary for the Eastern District of Pennsylvania*. Philadelphia: M'Laughlin Brothers, 1859, pp. 19–20.

This argument undermined claims that the Pennsylvania System was comparatively ineffective, particularly when the administrators could offer statistical evidence to support their claims of efficacy.

Their favorite metric of efficacy in reforming prisoners was recidivism. Analyzing recidivism in the nineteenth century was, of course, much more difficult than it is today. Administrators used the rate at which prisoners returned to their prison or the size of their state's prison population relative to the overall population, both of which are highly problematic measures for many reasons – including high mobility across state lines, differences in sentence lengths (leading to bigger prison populations), flexibility and bias in prison and jail commitments, and unobserved criminality that was never caught or convicted – but were the preferred metric of the day. For example, the inspectors boasted in 1859,

Without desiring to be invidious, it is justice to our State Penitentiary System to remark, that while, under the congregate plan, the several state prisons of New York are full, and overflowing with inmates, our two State Penitentiaries have hardly an increased number, in proportion to the ratio of the increase of population. But ten per cent. of re-convictions appear on our records since the opening of the institution.[46]

By these rough estimates, they could claim to have a more effective prison.

The administrators also compared the recidivism rates of offenders who had spent time under the Pennsylvania System alone and those who had been incarcerated under the Auburn System. The underlying logic was that prisoners who had served time under the Auburn System had been tainted and would have a higher recidivism rate, even after they spent time at Eastern. One typical evaluation from Warden Halloway in 1852 read:

Twenty-two years have now elapsed since the admission of the first prisoner into this institution; during that period, 2846 have been the subject of its discipline. Of this number, 2290 have been discharged by expiration of sentence, pardon and otherwise; of whom there have been 287 re-convictions, and, of this latter number, 169 had been the inmates of other prisons, previous to their confinement here, leaving 118 as the number of those who, so far as our information extends, had never been the subjects of any other system of prison discipline; being equal to $5\frac{1}{2}$ per cent.[47]

---

[46] Ibid., p. 19.
[47] Eastern State Penitentiary, Warden's Report, *Twenty-Third Annual Report of the Inspectors of the Eastern State Penitentiary of Pennsylvania*. Philadelphia: B. Mifflin, 1852, p. 11.

In many cases, administrators found favorable assessments.

The most rewarding comparisons, however, came from the administrators of other prisons or from pro-Auburn penal reformers. In one report, Eastern's administrators gleefully repeated the findings of Massachusetts' Board of State Charities, "OUR PRISONS DO NOT DIMINISH CRIME."[48] Eastern's inspectors smugly noted, the finding "is not very creditable to Massachusetts" or the Auburn System.[49]

However, Eastern's administrators also supported these statistics with more qualitative measures – either their own assessments of how rehabilitated prisoners were when they left or their own knowledge of former offenders living in Pennsylvania. For example, the inspectors noted in 1849, "In their occasional official visits, the Inspectors have been called to witness the triumph of the Gospel of Peace, in the heart of many a child of sorrow. From the couch of many a prisoner, a light has beamed, fitted to obscure the splendor of the highest human attainments."[50] Likewise, Moral Instructor Larcombe explained in 1840, "Several prisoners have been discharged during the year, of whose reform a confident impression is entertained; of the permanency of their good dispositions, time only can determine."[51] These additional measures could sometimes override administrators' more quantitative findings, as in 1836 when Warden Wood explained, "although out of the one hundred and eighty-nine prisoners discharged from the opening of the institution to the first of this year, sixteen have been reconvicted, we feel little discouragement on that account, knowing as we do, that many who have been inmates, are living correct and exemplary lives, and demeaning themselves as good citizens."[52] With arguments like these, the administrators sought to undermine the calumnious myth that the Pennsylvania System was simply ineffective at reforming criminals.

---

[48] Eastern State Penitentiary, Inspectors' Report, *Thirty-Seventh Annual Report of the Inspectors of the State Penitentiary for the Eastern District of Pennsylvania*. Philadelphia: McLaughlin Brothers, 1866, p. 23.

[49] Ibid., p. 22.

[50] Eastern State Penitentiary, Inspectors' Report, *The Twentieth Annual Report of the Inspectors*, p. 11.

[51] Eastern State Penitentiary, Moral Instructor's Report, *Eleventh Annual Report of the Inspectors*, p. 42.

[52] Eastern State Penitentiary, Warden's Report, *Seventh Annual Report of the Inspectors*, p. 11–12.

Effusive Praise

These evaluations enabled the administrators to praise their system extensively. Most reports contained some version of what became a virtual boil-
erplate endorsement of their system – that it was the best, most humane
system known to man. A fairly common version of this theme was the
administrators' endorsement of the system based on "another year's experience," their miscellaneous experience with the system, or its demonstrated record. Thus, in 1847, Warden Scattergood reported, "A year's
further experience has served to fasten still more deeply in my mind the
conviction of the humanity, and the advantage of the separate system of
confinement for the reformation of offenders."[53] Another form of this
endorsement was the administrators' congratulations to all involved in
the system or, as Warden Wood remarked in 1836, that all should be
gratified with the "experiment thus far made."[54] In some cases, the administrators called for more than gratification, as did the inspectors in 1844:
"The Inspectors, in common with all the friends of practical philanthropy,
can but rejoice in the great change which is thus being effected in the
treatment of the outcast prisoner."[55] Their reports sometimes contained
more hyperbolic statements. For example, the inspectors stated in 1865,
"The system of punishment which belongs exclusively to Pennsylvania,
as it is now administered, which had its origin in our State, and is known
over the civilized world as peculiarly Pennsylvanian, demands a yearly
tribute to its value and success."[56] The administrators had no shortage of
glowing praise for their system.

At their boldest, these endorsements took the shape of a kind of dare or
invitation to review the prison for oneself. Thus, in one case, the Warden
Wood exclaimed in 1835,

To the philanthropist, to all who earnestly wish for the well being and improvement of society; to all who look forward to so desirable an end as the reformation
of those deluded, misguided, miserable beings who are under our charge, I would

53 Eastern State Penitentiary, Warden's Report, *Eighteenth Annual Report of the Inspectors of the Eastern State Penitentiary of Pennsylvania*. Philadelphia: Ed. Barrington and Geo. D. Haswell, 1847, p. 35.
54 Eastern State Penitentiary, Warden's Report, *Seventh Annual Report of the Inspectors*, p. 11.
55 Eastern State Penitentiary, Inspectors' Report, *Fifteenth Annual Report of the Inspectors*, p. 11.
56 Eastern State Penitentiary, Inspectors' Report, *Thirty-Sixth Annual Report of the Inspectors*, p. 5.

exhibit fully and fairly the discipline of the Institution; and ask them to examine thoroughly its condition and every branch of its operations; to view the convicts at their various employments, to witness their health, their cleanliness, their general cheerfulness, and with very few exceptions their willing industry; to learn from their own lips the manner in which they are treated by the Inspectors, the Warden and Officers; to ascertain from them their feelings toward those who have the immediate care of them, to speak to them of their future intentions, and in short to inquire minutely into the whole effect of the system on both body and mind.[57]

Such effusive praise challenged the calumnious myths globally, and their meticulous evaluations made this praise possible.

SCAPEGOATING

The statistical evaluations did not, however, always favor the Pennsylvania System, even in comparison to other prisons. When the administrators had to acknowledge failures, they constructed narratives that displaced the blame for physical and mental illness, death, high expenses, and recidivism onto conditions, individuals, or groups – but not the Pennsylvania System. To insulate the Pennsylvania System from blame for the system's visible failures, administrators centered their explanations on state actors (the legislature, governor, and judges), state and local policies, the economy, and even the prisoners themselves (particularly African-American prisoners). Sykes and Matza, refer to such narratives as "denials of responsibility":[58] the administrators conceded that bad outcomes did happen, but they claimed these scapegoats, not intrinsic flaws in the Pennsylvania System, were responsible.

Prisoner Health and Well-Being

Disease, death, suicide, and mental illness among the prisoners were not uncommon at Eastern. However, the administrators were clear – and it was important to them that readers understood – that the Pennsylvania System was not responsible for these bad outcomes. As Physician Given explained in 1849,

Could I deem it at all compatible with my duties, as the medical officer of the institution, I would prefer confining my Report for the past year, to the presentation of the usual statistics; but having daily forced on my observation, suffering

---

57 Eastern State Penitentiary, Warden's Report, *Sixth Annual Report of the Inspectors*, p. 9.
58 Sykes and Matza, "Techniques of Naturalization."

and death, originating in defects that have no just connection with our discipline, I feel that I should be highly culpable, were I to pass them over in silence.[59]

Humanity as well as respect for the Pennsylvania System, he and other administrators believed, demanded an explanation that correctly allocated the blame.

The administrators often blamed negative health outcomes – particularly their mental health outcomes – on state actors and policies. One of their largest complaints was the claim that people known to be insane were routinely sent to prison – especially to Eastern – instead of to an appropriate facility where they could be cared for properly – and where they could be kept without hindering the institution's proper functioning. Administrators assumed (perhaps correctly) there was little they could do for these prisoners – and later argued that the Pennsylvania System made them worse. In making this argument, however, the administrators were not condemning the Pennsylvania System; rather, they argued that Eastern was not the proper place for such prisoners, who were inappropriate subjects for the Pennsylvania System. By sending such prisoners to Eastern, state actors were effectively sabotaging the Pennsylvania System.

In these accounts, the administrators often chided the Legislature and Judiciary first for not having a public insane asylum for these prisoners and then, after one was built, for not sending these prisoners to the asylums where they could be better looked after. To illustrate their point, administrators often included information about specific cases where a prisoner was previously known to have been insane, but was sent to Eastern anyway – contributing to its mythologized high insanity rates. After describing two such cases in detail, Physician Lassiter reflected in 1852,

I may be asked, why dwell upon the cases of Nos. 2153 and 1978? I have dwelt upon them in order to call attention to the fact that much of our mortality is composed of prisoners, who, first go deranged, and then, like Bajazet, literally dash out their brains against the bars of their cage. When will this terrible cruelty end? I had hoped that the remedy was at hand, but I regret to learn that the prospect of transferring our insane to the State Asylum seems as yet far distant. In their behalf, however, I shall make a last appeal. In the name of justice and mercy, let it be no longer necessary for the friends of the institution to deplore, or in the

---

[59] Eastern State Penitentiary, Physician's Report, *The Twentieth Annual Report of the Inspectors*, p. 25.

power of its opponents to boast that a number of helpless lunatics are immured within the cells of the Eastern Penitentiary.[60]

Although framed as a plea for justice and humanity, and advocacy on the part of the helpless, the physician's complaint was also an attempt to protect Eastern. Without these problematic prisoners, Eastern – and its statistics – would fare much better.

Notably, these assessments were simultaneously strategic and genuine. In 1855, Warden Strickland privately recorded his views after discharging Prisoner "No 2605 Benjamin Bender," an "insane" man who had been admitted to Eastern "for safe keeping under an order of the Oyer & Terminer of Perry." Strickland had worked to remove Bender from the prison, writing to "Judge Graham, some ten days ago, calling his attention to the case and urging him to bring it before the Perry County Court, [which] had the desired effect." Strickland's view was clear:

His removal will be a great relief of trouble to the Institution. ... The Asylum is the proper place for him, and his continuance here was disgraceful to his county and the State. It has the time and conveniences to do more for his physical comfort, than a Prison, and God grant that it may be able to do something for his mental improvement.[61]

It was an injustice to such prisoners to keep them confined in a prison, but insane prisoners also threatened the functioning of the prison.

While the administrators often challenged their state policies and blamed politicians for hamstringing the prison, they placed most of the blame for bad health outcomes on the prisoners. The administrators argued that those prisoners on the sick list had entered the prison in a particularly weakened or diseased state; consequently, their illnesses or deaths should not count against the Pennsylvania System as it did not cause them. For example, Physician Newbold cautioned in 1858, "of the three deaths which have occurred from natural causes, two were the result of chronic affections existing prior to their admission into the prison."[62] More commonly, the administrators claimed that the prisoners' prior bad habits – intemperance, debauchery, unclean living – had taken their toll and made them more susceptible to disease. For example, examining

---

[60] Eastern State Penitentiary, Physician's Report, *Twenty-Third Annual Report of the Inspectors*, p. 30.

[61] Eastern State Penitentiary, *Warden's Daily Journal*, April 12, 1855.

[62] Eastern State Penitentiary, Physician's Report, *Twenty-Ninth Annual Report of the Inspectors*, p. 25.

the tabulated medical statistics in his report, Physician Klapp explained in 1871,

> These facts confirm what has, again and again, been stated in previous Reports, i.e., the impaired health of prisoners when received in the Penitentiary; their habits, previous to conviction, together with the exigencies of a life at variance with the law, having a powerful tendency to produce both physical and mental disease. The percentage of mortality therefore, and of mental disorders, small as it is, cannot be fairly charged against the System.[63]

Regardless of the precise reason, the implication was clear: with prisoners coming in sick already, it would be impossible to reduce the illness and mortality rates.[64]

Most colorfully, administrators claimed that the prisoners were making themselves insane by excessive masturbation (or "self-abuse," "mst.," "the secret vice," "erotic enervation," etc.). For example, Physician Darrach reported in 1840, "seventy-three items [i.e., cases of sickness] were owing to self-abuse."[65] Likewise, in 1845, Physician Given reported the "mental alienation" of prisoner "No. 1796, [who] was notorious for the practice of self-abuse."[66] Physician Newbold attributed one of the six prisoner deaths in 1859 to "de-bility, caused by the habit of self-abuse."[67] According to beliefs at the time, masturbation could produce disease, mental illness, and even death. As the Pennsylvania System insisted on the separation of all prisoners, administrators were particularly sensitive to the fact that their system provided prisoners the requisite privacy for their immoral (and dangerous) actions. Again, the administrators implied, it was not the system's fault, but the prisoners' predisposition to vice.

In addition to blaming prisoners as a group for negative health outcomes, administrators specifically targeted African Americans as problematic prisoners. Beginning in the late 1830s, coinciding with

---

[63] Eastern State Penitentiary, Physician's Report, *Forty-Second Annual Report of the Inspectors*, p. 117.

[64] Physician Newbold explained in 1858, "I do not deem it possible, by any additional sanitary regulations, to reduce the average of mortality below what it has been for several years past." Eastern State Penitentiary, Physician's Report, *Twenty-Ninth Annual Report of the Inspectors*, p. 25.

[65] Eastern State Penitentiary, Physician's Report, *Eleventh Annual Report of the Inspectors*, p. 26.

[66] Eastern State Penitentiary, Physician's Report, *Sixteenth Annual Report of the Inspectors*, p. 52.

[67] Eastern State Penitentiary, Physician's Report, *Thirty-First Annual Report of the Inspectors of the State Penitentiary for the Eastern District of Pennsylvania*. Philadelphia: M'Laughlin Brothers, 1860, p. 45.

the arrival of Physician Darrach, the prison began distinguishing its health statistics by race (White and Black or "Coloured"). African Americans were often reported to have a higher mortality rate, which led to widespread speculation and scapegoating based on common racist beliefs and stereotypes of the time. In one of the earliest references to this issue, Physician Darrach noted in 1838,

> this Penitentiary is burdened with a sickly inefficient coloured population, which by self-abuse, become debauched in mind and body, and diseased, and make 3–5 of its mortality, yet during a period of 7 years and 3 months, there has been no more than 51 deaths, of whom only 17 are of the white prisoners, making of the total average of such a per centage of 1 80–100.[68]

The administrators had several explanations for such discrepancies: African Americans, they argued, were particularly vulnerable to disease because they had an inferior constitution. Moreover, African Americans, particularly those from the South but generally all whose ancestors hailed from Africa, were not acclimated to Philadelphia's cooler climate and suffered accordingly, the administrators argued. Finally, African Americans were an overly sexual people, they argued, who masturbated to excess, accounting for their disproportionate mental illness and death rates. In these ways, African-American prisoners were viewed as especially prone to illness, insanity, and death; they were thus the cause of the prison's unexpectedly high mortality rates.[69] With these explanations, the administrators blamed increases in mortality in the late 1830s and early 1840s on the increase of African-American prisoners at Eastern.

The administrators extended this argument, however, by comparing their situation to that at other prisons. Eastern's administrators believed that their prison was uniquely susceptible to the challenges from their African-American prisoner population. In his report from 1840, Warden Wood complained about "the peculiar situation of Pennsylvania as the frontier State, between the slave and free States, and hence the recipient of a worthless clan of coloured persons, which was the cause of our having so large a portion of coloured prisoners."[70] No similar remarks

[68] Eastern State Penitentiary, Physician's Report, *Ninth Annual Report of the Inspectors of the Eastern State Penitentiary of Pennsylvania*. Philadelphia: William Brown, 1838, p. 12.

[69] e.g., Eastern State Penitentiary, Inspectors' Report, *Seventeenth Annual Report of the Inspectors*, p. 11.

[70] Eastern State Penitentiary, Warden's Report, *Eleventh Annual Report of the Inspectors*, p. 13–14.

were made about Irish or German prisoners – two categories that were also stigmatized at the time in different ways – or any other ethno-racial group. Indeed, race became a kind of catchall scapegoating category that could be blamed for a number of problems. For example, in the same year, Physician Darrach blamed the "increasing disproportionate number of coloured prisoners in the Eastern Penitentiary … for its sickness, mortality, medical expense and labour."[71] As we shall see, administrators' racist beliefs about African Americans also informed their explanations for the prison's costs and (un)profitability.

Costs and Profit

In administrators' explanations for economic failures, prisoners again bore the brunt of the blame. For the prison to make any profit, or simply to offset its costs, prisoners needed to be productive workers. However, some prisoners were too old, diseased, insane, or otherwise infirm to work at all, let alone to work well. For his report on 1831, a year in which most prisoners were able to repay their expenses, Warden Wood singled out "one old man, [and] the diseased" among several "exceptions."[72] There was little administrators could do about the aged and diseased among incoming prisoners, but they did request the state to relocate mentally ill prisoners – if not for humanity's sake, then for cost savings. Warden Scattergood complained in 1846,

until some provision is made by our State to relieve us of the number of insane and imbecile that are now from time to time committed to our charge, I fear, that however successful we may be in the introduction of labour, we shall still fall short of producing a sufficient amount to maintain our prisoners free of cost to the Counties.[73]

By implication, it was the composition of the prisoner population, not the prison's economy, that accounted for these shortfalls.

Exacerbating the effects of weak prisoners was, once again, Eastern's geographic location. As Warden Wood exclaimed in 1840, Eastern contained "the most worthless, ignorant, and least profitable inmates of any prison in the union."[74] Many factors went into forming this unique

---

[71] Ibid., Physician's Report, p. 16.
[72] Eastern State Penitentiary, Warden's Report, *Report of the Board of Inspectors*, p. 10.
[73] Eastern State Penitentiary, Warden's Report, *Seventeenth Annual Report of the Inspectors*, p. 24.
[74] Eastern State Penitentiary, Warden's Report, *Eleventh Annual Report of the Inspectors*, p. 13–14.

population. For one, Eastern had more prisoners from urban counties than rural ones, and "[p]risoners from large cities will not be found as productive labourers as those from country districts." Eastern suffered from other geographical disadvantages. There was "a more intelligent and better class" of prisoners found "in the New England States, and at Auburn, than at Sing Sing and Philadelphia; they are therefore much more easily taught trades, are more healthy, and are abler to do work."[75] This unique set of circumstances explained why Wethersfield (in Connecticut) and Auburn showed positive returns on all fronts, while Sing Sing (New York's other prison) and Eastern did not. This explanation cleverly reminded readers that not all Auburn System prisons showed positive returns while still emphasizing the unique disadvantages Eastern faced due to its geographical position – not its system of prison discipline.

The biggest consequence of Eastern's geographic position, according to its administrators, was its susceptibility to an influx of qualitatively different African-American prisoners – freed slaves. These prisoners were, the administrators complained, simply bad workers: they were lazy, poorly trained, or their diseased state continually prevented them from working. Warden Wood continued his exegesis, explaining,

Pennsylvania being bounded by three slave States, (being the Frontier between the slave and Free States,) is the recipient of discontented free blacks, of worthless slaves set free by their masters, and of runaway slaves. All acquainted with this neglected class know how helpless, ignorant, and of course worthless, they generally are, and how prone they are to commit depredations. Thus we find that about forty per cent. of the inmates of the Eastern Penitentiary are coloured persons. It is difficult to provide productive labour for them; and many enter the prison in so diseased a state that for some time they cannot be set to work. It is to this class that we must attribute the small amount of the earnings in proportion to the number of our prisoners.[76]

African-American prisoners generally, the inspectors noted in 1840, were not only bad workers, but their frequent illness also made them "a burthen to the Institution." Such prisoners not only failed to offset their costs, but required additional medical expenses and thus cost much more to maintain than the average (white) prisoner.[77] As the inspectors explained

---

75 Eastern State Penitentiary, Warden's Report, *Tenth Annual Report of the Inspectors of the Eastern State Penitentiary of Pennsylvania*. Philadelphia: Brown, Bicking & Guilbert, 1839, p. 10.

76 Ibid., p. 10.

77 Eastern State Penitentiary, Inspectors' Report, *Eleventh Annual Report of the Inspectors*, p. 5.

more explicitly the following year: "The coloured prisoners are a burthen to the system, both because it does not and cannot operate as beneficially on them as on the white prisoners, and because they are more diseased, and less capable of being made profitable in confinement."[78] Under such circumstances, Eastern's increase in costs in the late 1830s and early 1840s should not be understood as a blemish on the Pennsylvania System – or so the argument went – but a consequence of its unique prisoner population.

Prisoners were not the only group at fault, however. As with their explanations for bad health outcomes, administrators also targeted state actors. When Eastern did not turn a profit or had greater-than-typical costs, they often blamed a combination of underfunding, a lack of resources, and a general need for more investment from the legislature. Thus, in 1831, Warden Wood stated,

I am therefore sanguine in the belief, that if the proper machinery, &c. were provided, this Penitentiary would not only produce the great good which we all so ardently desire to the unfortunate inmates, but would also relieve the several counties who send them, of the great burthen which they have hitherto borne in the support of convicts.[79]

After several years of operations with still no increase in funds, the administrators grew more aggressive. More combative this time, Warden Wood explained in 1835,

It was hoped that the Legislature of the last year would have appropriated a sum of money as a capital to be invested in our manufacturing department, particularly as a committee of the House of Representatives who came and examined into the various branches, advised it in their report. We have, and must continue to labour under serious loss and great disadvantage for want of capital; and therefore cannot compete with other institutions who have their forty, fifty, and some upwards of one hundred thousand dollars capital. Had this grant been made, a different result in our pecuniary affairs would have been shewn. It is very desirable that the Legislature should grant not only a sufficient sum to enable us to properly conduct our manufacturing, but also to complete the whole establishment in building and machinery; as the system cannot be conducted satisfactorily until this is done, and all the workmen are out of the yard.[80]

---

[78] Eastern State Penitentiary, Inspectors' Report, *Twelfth Annual Report of the Inspectors of the Eastern State Penitentiary of Pennsylvania*. Philadelphia: E. G. Dorsey, 1841, p. 4.

[79] Eastern State Penitentiary, Warden's Report, *The First and Second Annual Reports of the Inspectors*, p. 14.

[80] Eastern State Penitentiary, Warden's Report, *Sixth Annual Report of the Inspectors*, p. 10–11.

The message was clear: the Pennsylvania System can function effectively and profitably if only the legislature provided the requisite investment; because the legislature had failed to act, the Pennsylvania System could not be blamed for its underperformance.

The administrators also blamed their lack of profitability on sentencing practices in the state. Administrators often complained, particularly in the first two decades or so, that prisoners' sentences were too short for prisoners to learn a trade. In 1831, Warden Wood explained the problem with the frequency of one-year sentences:

> a novice cannot always be taught in that period, a business that will be of service to him. The cases of numbers 38 and 39 may be mentioned in support of this opinion, lads of 18 and 19 years of age, sentenced to one year only, might, if their sentences had extended to 3 years, have been taught shoemaking or weaving, and thus have been enabled to support themselves, when discharged.[81]

Wood's interest was not only benevolence toward the prisoners: longer sentences had financial advantages for the prison. Teaching a prisoner a trade took time and it also cost money; consequently, during their first year or two, prisoners cost the institution more than they made. The administrators argued, however, that with sufficiently long sentences, prisoners could pay back the institution for the losses; but many prisoners were released before serving two full years, preventing the prison from recouping its losses. The problem was especially acute for prisoners who came in with no trade: as the inspectors explained in 1834, "a convict sentenced for a short term of years, if he be ignorant of a trade, can rarely produce a profit by his labor."[82] Longer sentences were necessary if Eastern was to profit.

The general economic climate was another recipient of administrators' blame. When demand was low, or they lacked enough raw materials, prisoners were left idle, in violation of the Pennsylvania System, and system expenses increased. But such problems were not the Pennsylvania System's fault – it was the economic conditions that made profitability impossible: as the inspectors explained following the Panic of 1837, "no opportunity has existed for making sales."[83] A few years before, in 1834,

---

[81] Eastern State Penitentiary, Warden's Report, *The First and Second Annual Reports of the Inspectors*, p. 17.

[82] Eastern State Penitentiary, Inspectors' Report, *Fifth Annual Report of the Inspectors of the Eastern Penitentiary of Pennsylvania*. Harrisburg: Welsh & Patterson, 1834, p. 3.

[83] Eastern State Penitentiary, Inspectors' Report, *Ninth Annual Report of the Inspectors*, p. 6.

Warden Wood explained, "Although the vicissitudes of trade have not allowed us to realise as much as it has cost to maintain the prisoners, and pay all incidental expenses, (except salaries), yet we have abundant evidence to satisfy us, that in ordinary times we shall be able to do this."[84] Similarly, when prices went up for basic necessities, the cost of housing prisoners necessarily increased as well. Following the Panic of 1873, and in the midst of the ensuing depression, the inspectors reflected,

The average cost per diem per capita for the keep of convicts for 1840, was $23\frac{58}{100}$ cents; 1850, $21\frac{71}{100}$ cents; 1860, 20 cents; 1870, 34 cents; for the year 1874, 31 cents.

The annual cost for fuel and light is included in the above cost. It is to be observed that in the latter of these items the cost is fixed, and as to the former but small reduction in price is to be obtained. This explains the increase of cost from 1870 to 1875.

The cost of coal for the (5) five years ending December 31st, 1874, was $38,700.17.

The cost of gas for the (5) five years ending December 31st, 1874, was $24,865.45.[85]

These external factors, they argued, made profitability unlikely at Eastern, its perfect system of prison discipline notwithstanding.

Administrators also carefully complained that the *type* of labor pursued under the Pennsylvania System made profitability difficult. Superficially, this argument was exactly the same one made by its critics: workshop-style labor is far less efficient, more costly, and overall less profitable than factory labor. However, Eastern's administrators were careful not to attack any features of the Pennsylvania System; instead, they focused on the conditions that made this work unprofitable. For example, the inspectors explained in 1859,

The year just closed, like the one preceding, in the pecuniary operations affecting the labor of this institution, has been below the just expectations of the Inspectors. The demand for the peculiar kind of work within the scope of our employments has been limited. Great care is required to select purchasers whose business facilities enable them to make short and cash payments. These causes have produced less return for labor than is equivalent to cost of maintenance.[86]

[84] Eastern State Penitentiary, Warden's Report, *Fifth Annual Report of the Inspectors*, p. 5.
[85] Eastern State Penitentiary, Inspectors' Report, *Forty-Fifth Annual Report of the Inspectors*, pp. 7–8.
[86] Eastern State Penitentiary, Inspectors' Report, *Thirtieth Annual Report of the Inspectors*, pp. 12–13.

It was not that workshop-style labor was inefficient; rather, it was that demand for workshop-style labor was too low.

Similarly, later in the period examined, administrators complained about shifts in the market due to mechanization. During 1870, the prison had lacked "sufficient employment for our men." Warden Townsend explained the cause: "Weaving was once a very important branch of manufacture; now a few hands can accomplish all that can be procured." He had diverted the excess prisoners to shoemaking, but this stopgap was not enough. Townsend continued,

> Much thought has been given to the subject of introducing other branches of industry into the Institution, but there are very few of the mechanic arts that can be pursued with which we can successfully compete with labor outside. This subject will continue to claim serious consideration, and if any means can be devised to increase the labor of our convicts without violation of the law which prevent unjust competition with outdoor labor they will be adopted.[87]

It was these larger factors related to shifts in the economy – supply of and demand for materials, the labor market, mechanization, and resistance from nascent worker unions – rather than the Pennsylvania System's reliance on crafts-style labor that was the problem.[88]

Efficacy

Finally, accounting for the prison's occasionally high recidivism statistics, administrators again blamed state actors and policy for the prison's failings. According to Eastern's administrators, the Pennsylvania System was virtually guaranteed to prevent the spread of crime because prisoners were separated from each other and incapable of cross-contamination. Unfortunately, administrators pointed out, the county jails still relied on confinement styles from the colonial and Early Republican eras. Jail inmates were generally housed in large rooms together with little work and no separation, allowing older, hardened offenders to contaminate young, fresh, impressionable offenders. By the time prisoners reached Eastern, the administrators argued, the damage had already been done. Thus, Warden Wood argued in 1840, "Before the Pennsylvania System

---

[87] Eastern State Penitentiary, Warden's Report, *Forty-Second Annual Report of the Inspectors*, p. 111–112.

[88] For more on the opposition of organized free labor to prisoner labor, see Rebecca M. McLennan, *The Crisis of Imprisonment: Protest, Politics, and the Making of the American Penal State, 1776–1941*. New York: Cambridge University Press, 2008.

can be said to be in full operation, each county must have a prison to confine the accused before trial, separate and alone, and those for small offences in separate cells, for all terms under two years, the System would be in perfect operation."[89] Until such changes were made, the Pennsylvania System should not be blamed for its failure to reform prisoners and reduce recidivism. As jails remained unreformed for much of the nineteenth century, the administrators repeated this argument for decades.

Two other penal policies – sentencing and pardoning – also negatively affected prisoners' chances at reformation, according to the administrators. Unlike their discussion of jail policy, however, administrators primarily used these arguments in the first two decades of the prison's history. First, repeating their earlier remarks, administrators claimed that judges were far too lenient on offenders: their sentences were too short. Administrators often disaggregated their recidivism statistics to show the role of short sentences. For example, Warden Wood explained in 1835, "Since the Penitentiary has been in operation, one hundred and four prisoners have been discharged; of this number only three have returned to this prison re-convicted, two of whom had served less than one year, and one two years."[90] Short sentences caused recidivism because, administrators claimed, reformation takes time, and prisoners were released before they were ready.

Specifically, Warden Wood explained in 1834, short sentences prevented prisoners from receiving the proper portion of training and mentorship:

I must express my firm belief that if any material benefit is to be afforded to those who are brought here, that their sentence should extend to two years or more: no great benefit will result to any who have a shorter period to serve. One year is not sufficient to learn a trade, to eradicate old and fix new habits; and the period is too brief, that the impression made on their minds, will very soon be obliterated. I have little doubt, that when we receive convicts for a second conviction to this penitentiary, that they will prove to be those who have had on their first sentence, but one year.[91]

Careful to clarify his own benevolence, Wood added, "In thus recommending an extension of the term from one to two or three years, I am not actuated by a desire to punish the unfortunate culprits, but by a

---

[89] Eastern State Penitentiary, Warden's Report, *Eleventh Annual Report of the Inspectors*, p. 14.

[90] Eastern State Penitentiary, Warden's Report, *Sixth Annual Report of the Inspectors*, p. 10.

[91] Eastern State Penitentiary, Warden's Report, *Fifth Annual Report of the Inspectors*, p. 7.

decided belief that it will promote their ultimate good."[92] Longer sentences, although seemingly punitive, would ultimately benefit the prisoners and society, because they would enable the Pennsylvania System to work as intended.

Administrators made similar arguments about pardons, which shortened sentence length and thus interfered with the Pennsylvania System's proper functioning. In a characteristically lengthy exegesis on pardons in 1841, Warden Wood deployed several arguments administrators typically used in the 1830s and 1840s to illustrate their point. To begin with, administrators in this early period frequently stated their opposition to pardons and highlighted the fact that they did not recommend any sane prisoners for pardon. Thus, Warden Wood summarized the year's exits: "Of the 71 pardoned, I believe only three or four have had the sanction of the Board of Inspectors or myself, and there is certainly no cause for either of us abandoning our opposition to this practice." As in his argument about sentence length, Wood was careful to emphasize that his opposition to pardons did not result from a punitive instinct; rather it spawned from the awareness that frequent pardons stifled the good of society. The warden complained, "[i]t appears necessary that this power should be placed somewhere as the last resort; but if the happiness and good of the mass were consulted, the power would, I am persuaded, be abrogated, if the existing evil attending its exercise be inseparable from it."[93] Their most basic argument, then, was that pardons frustrated the social good by increasing recidivism.

Administrators also relied on more traditional arguments. The use of pardons in capital punishment had long been criticized by penal reformers concerned with deterrence; Eastern's administrators relied on this history to defend their prison. To sustain their claims, they referred to the Beccarian adage that the certainty of punishment was more important than its severity.[94] Wood thus explained, "There is nothing more certain than that the certainty of punishment is of more importance than its severity."[95]

[92] Ibid.

[93] Eastern State Penitentiary, Warden's Report, *Twelfth Annual Report of the Inspectors*, p. 13.

[94] Cesare Beccaria, *An Essay on Crimes and Punishments, Translated from the Italian of Caesar Bonesana, Marquis Beccaria*. Trans. Edward D. Ingraham. Second American Edition. Philadelphia: Philip H. Nicklin, 1819 [1764].

[95] Eastern State Penitentiary, Warden's Report, *Twelfth Annual Report of the Inspectors*, p. 14. As another example, he explained in 1838, "A moderate sentence, with the certainty of having to serve the entire period, is much more beneficial than twice the

Building on this logic, administrators argued that the hope of pardon, nurtured by news of its frequent use, prevented offenders from taking reformation seriously. Deploying this argument as well, Wood explained,

The prisoner is promised by his friends, immediately on conviction, that their influence will be exerted, and he very soon liberated, and by these means he is encouraged to keep up his spirits. The sheriff, in whose custody he is, not wishing him to attempt an escape, gives him all the encouragement he can; and thus he goes into the Penitentiary with a full belief that he is scarcely to set there before his pardon will arrive. Disappointment succeeds hope, and the man is kept all the time restive and unhappy, and finally thinks he is utterly neglected by his friends, or that he has not one left in the world.[96]

Additionally, administrators complained, pardons were given out inconsistently across offenders. Warden Wood bemoaned the overuse of pardons for the undeserving: "others more guilty, who have powerful friends, scarcely occupy their cells before they are liberated, and in many instances directly return to their former habits."[97]

Each of these arguments led to one bottom line: pardons interfered with Eastern's operations. So long as prisoners held out hope for a pardon, administrators argued, the prison could not be expected to effectively reform its prisoners, encourage them to learn a trade or how to read and write, or improve them through religious and moral training. Warden Wood emphasized in 1841,

Our penal system will never be perfect until our governors cease to pardon, except in those few cases where innocence can be proved or some circumstances that could not be on their trial. Of all that have been pardoned since my knowledge of prisons, I know of very few that would not have been decidedly better if they had been allowed to remain until their terms expired, and I know of many who have been very much injured by it. ... Too much pains cannot be taken by the friends of reform to discourage the pardoning power as it has been exercised.[98]

Pardons, and not the Pennsylvania System's inability to reform, were thus responsible for recidivism – and it was the administrators' duty as good

---

number of years accompanied by the constant hope of receiving a pardon." Eastern State Penitentiary, Warden's Report, *Ninth Annual Report of the Inspectors*, p. 9. This was a particularly ingrained belief. In a later report, the administrators noted, "society gains its ends by the certainty, and not by the quantity of punishment." Eastern State Penitentiary, Warden's Report, *Thirty-Sixth Annual Report of the Inspectors*, p. 87.

[96] Eastern State Penitentiary, Warden's Report, *Twelfth Annual Report of the Inspectors*, pp. 13–14.

[97] Ibid., p. 14.   [98] Ibid.

humanitarians and public servants to bring the truth and consequences of this misguided policy to the legislature's attention.

REACTION

By explaining how these various actors, groups, policies, and conditions prevented the Pennsylvania System from achieving its expected results, administrators sought to displace any blame from their system. To construct particularly compelling explanations (either strategically or because they reflected their own feelings), administrators relied on central beliefs that would resonate with their audience – for example, stereotypes about African Americans, the preference for certainty over severity, and the importance of investment for financial solvency. Indeed, some of their arguments, like the overuse of the pardon or the problems of incarcerating the mentally ill, may still resonate with us today. However, administrators' empirical evaluations and explanations for failure were not readily received by opponents of the Pennsylvania System.

As we have seen, beginning in the 1830s, members of the opposing BPDS, and other defenders of the Auburn System, challenged the methodology, operationalization, and even honesty of the figures produced at Eastern (see also Chapter 4). Indeed, the BPDS routinely used Eastern's annual reports – including the administrators' defenses to this criticism – to condemn the Pennsylvania System. As an example, the BPDS was particularly amused by the administrators' (and their testators') claims that insanity at Eastern was often a product of masturbation. In one annual report, the Boston reformers cited at length their own "letter ... addressed to Dr. Woodward of the Insane Hospital at Worcester," his response, and the replies of other doctors weighing in on this and other issues. Although these doctors did not refute the claim that masturbation caused insanity or dementia (a type or effect of insanity), they all agreed that the rate of insanity and dementia were too high at Eastern.[99] This disproportionality, they found completely natural and attributable to the Pennsylvania System. As another doctor consulted, William H. Rockwell, explained, "It is also the natural tendency of the solitary cell to produce an increase both of masturbation and dementia."[100] This was useful ammunition to the Boston reformers, who concluded "the Ninth and last Report of the New

[99] Boston Prison Discipline Society, *Thirteenth Annual Report of the Board of Managers of the Boston Prison Discipline Society*. Boston: Published at the Society's Rooms, 1838, pp. 50–53.
[100] Ibid., p. 53.

Penitentiary of Philadelphia is the most unfavorable ever made concerning this institution: – unfavorable in regard to deaths; unfavorable in regard to dementia; unfavorable in regard to recommitments; unfavorable in regard to current expenses; unfavorable in regard to moral and religious instruction."[101]

Indeed, the BPDS examined the same data Eastern's administrators did and often came to very different conclusions. In one report, they noted, "These matters of record do not look very favorable to the system, in regard to its effect on the mind. There is too much about insanity, in proportion to the number of prisoners."[102] The BPDS and others would continue to push back against the claims in Eastern's annual reports, shredding their excuses and explanations while denying claims of parity across the systems and overlooking the fallacies in their own claims. However, the more opponents pushed back, the more justification it gave Eastern's administrators to continue their defense of Eastern.

* * *

Eastern's administrators fervently defended their prized Pennsylvania System throughout the period examined. The administrators conscientiously used their reports to defend the Pennsylvania System against the challenges from the field. Indeed, their responses to the myths that the Pennsylvania System was cruel and inhumane, dangerous to prisoners' physical and mental health, too expensive and unprofitable, and simply impractical and ineffective represented the largest share of the annual reports. It was no accident that they evaluated their prison's functioning along the dimensions on which it was most heavily criticized. By reframing their use of solitary confinement; finding their medical, fiscal, and penal outcomes to be on par with, or better than, those under the Auburn System; and explaining away bad outcomes, the administrators sought to undermine the calumnious myths' veracity. If successful, this endeavor would not only help protect the prison from criticism and incursion, but it would also help reassure Eastern's administrators that they were right to maintain the Pennsylvania System. Most grandly, their defenses often gave the administrators the opportunity to claim the excellence or superiority of their prison and even of themselves.

[101] Ibid., p. 56.
[102] Boston Prison Discipline Society, *Tenth Annual Report of the Board of Managers of the Boston Prison Discipline Society*. Boston: Perkins, Marvin, & Co., 1835, p. 885.

6

Combatting the Pains of Deviance

Organizational Defense As Self-Defense

The mode of treatment in the Eastern Penitentiary is of a mild character. The severity used in other prisons, in which large bodies of men are to be kept in subjection by force or power, is not required here.

Board of Inspectors (1833), Annual Report[1]

Long may the institution continue to be administered by such faithful Inspectors, long may its unhappy inmates receive the blessings of your kindness and care, and thus prove a blessing to the State in which it is erected, and spread its philanthropical principles to the remotest corner of the globe.

Warden George Thompson (1841), Annual Report[2]

That such superiority now exists is a fixed fact – it is beyond cavil, beyond doubt – and since the effective operation of the State Penitentiary has been examined and investigated, and understood, the separate system has made advocates, converted the incredulous, strengthened the opinions of its friends in its favor, and convinced the most enlightened inquirer after that mode of prison discipline and reform, which is best calculated to promote the greatest good of the greatest number of those who are unfortunately to be subjected to its infliction.

Board of Inspectors (1847), Annual Report[3]

---

[1] Eastern State Penitentiary, Inspectors' Report, *Fourth Annual Report of the Inspectors of the Eastern State Penitentiary of Pennsylvania*. Philadelphia: Printed for the Philadelphia Society for Alleviating the Miseries of Public Prisons, 1833, p. 4.

[2] Eastern State Penitentiary, Warden's Report, *Twelfth Annual Report of the Inspectors of the Eastern State Penitentiary of Pennsylvania*. Philadelphia: E.G. Dorsey, 1841, p. 16.

[3] Eastern State Penitentiary, Inspectors' Report, *Eighteenth Annual Report of the Inspectors of the Eastern State Penitentiary of Pennsylvania*. Philadelphia: Ed. Barrington and Geo. D. Haswell, 1847, pp. 17–18.

A year's further experience has served to fasten still more deeply in my mind the conviction of the humanity, and the advantage of the separate system of confinement for the reformation of offenders.

> Warden Thomas Scattergood (1847), Annual Report[4]

there are higher objects to gain in the treatment and discipline of convicts, than profit from their labor.

> Board of Inspectors (1858), Annual Report[5]

The system of punishment which belongs exclusively to Pennsylvania, as it is now administered, which had its origin in our State, and is known over the civilized world as peculiarly Pennsylvanian, demands a yearly tribute to its value and success.

> Board of Inspectors (1865), Annual Report[6]

CONFRONTING THE PAINS OF DEVIANCE

While the administrators diligently worked to distinguish the Pennsylvania System from mere solitary confinement, illustrate the lack of bad outcomes at Eastern, and explain away their occurrence, Eastern was still an outlier within the field, making its administrators social deviants for continuously rejecting field-wide norms. Indeed, even apart from claims of high prisoner mortality, unnecessary expense, and ineffectiveness, the Pennsylvania System was still synonymous with cruelty and inhumane treatment. At the heart of this myth was an objection to the Pennsylvania System's basic premises: long-term solitary (or "separate") confinement, which – even with labor, education, and occasional visits – deprived prisoners of human contact for a large portion of their prison sentence.

Eastern's administrators were doubly vulnerable to criticism. Squarely in the minority, their system was recognized as a deviant approach and, without the safety of numbers, criticism of their system was more salient. The easiest way of ending the criticism was to abandon the Pennsylvania System, adopt the Auburn System, and thereby demonstrate conformity

[4] Ibid., p. 35.
[5] Eastern State Penitentiary, Inspectors' Report, *Twenty-Ninth Annual Report of the Inspectors of the State Penitentiary for the Eastern District of Pennsylvania*. Philadelphia: F. Pierson, 1858, p. 7.
[6] Eastern State Penitentiary, Inspectors' Report, *Thirty-Sixth Annual Report of the Inspectors of the State Penitentiary for the Eastern District of Pennsylvania*. Philadelphia: M'Laughlin Brothers, 1865, p. 5.

with other prisons and their established norms. But Eastern's administrators never did – and as we shall see (Chapter 9), they resisted local and state-level attempts to alter the Pennsylvania System. This retention presented a dilemma: So long as they retained the Pennsylvania System (and as long as no more prisons followed suit), the standard method of signaling conformity to the larger environment was unavailable to Eastern's administrators. Their only alternative was to demonstrate conformity to those values that permeated penal reform and prison administration without adopting the Auburn System. This strategy would require separating the norms and values of the field from the Auburn System.

* * *

This chapter examines two rhetorical strategies Eastern's administrators used in their annual reports to challenge one of the most effective – and personally detrimental – myths: the cruelty and inhumanity of the Pennsylvania System. To undermine this myth, Eastern's administrators characterized the Pennsylvania System, and themselves, as kind, benevolent, and humane, while arguing that the Auburn System and its supporters were the opposite – profit-mongers willing to resort to cruel practices. The administrators again turned to several techniques of neutralization to make these arguments. More than the other techniques of neutralization discussed in Chapter 5, however, these techniques allowed the administrators to defend not only the Pennsylvania System but also themselves against charges that *they* were engaging in cruel and inhumane behavior. More than establishing their system's superiority through evaluation and scapegoating, these techniques allowed the administrators to clothe themselves in positive descriptions. Because of their defensive posture, however, the administrators could sublimate their own self-praise into the defense of the prison – organizational defense, as Selznick explains, "provide[d] an aura of disinterestedness" for this self-praise.[7] Thus, administrators' statements defending the Pennsylvania System against claims of its cruelty and inhumanity were often as much about the administrators themselves as the system they sought to defend. Indeed, the ability to constantly issue these statements incentivized Eastern's administrators to maintain the Pennsylvania System for as long as they did. These claims were the largest anchor keeping the Pennsylvania System personally institutionalized for Eastern's administrators.

---

7 Philip Selznick, *TVA and the Grassroots.* Berkeley: University of California Press, 1949, p. 51.

CHARACTERIZATIONS

In a common theme within their annual reports, Eastern's administrators characterized the Pennsylvania System as a humane, benevolent, mild, and kind approach to punishment. They offered detailed descriptions of the system's treatment of prisoners to illustrate its kindness or mildness and its appeal to humanitarian reformers. They described each other – the prison's administrators and other affiliates – as exceedingly benevolent people. To further their case, they emphasized the role of prisoner reformation as an especially important goal of Eastern's Pennsylvania System. Finally, they offered creation myths about punishment in early Pennsylvania and the origin of the Pennsylvania System to characterize it as a uniquely humane system that the state had pursued continuously despite criticism and others' reluctance to expend resources for the good of prisoners and society.

In these ways, the administrators were "appealing to higher loyalties" – calling on values of greater importance than those (fiscal) values on which they were judged. As Sykes and Matza, explain, deviants can reject some social obligations – here, adopting the Auburn System – in favor of others that may be deemed more important.[8] In this case, Eastern's administrators could implicitly argue that their commitment to positive social values was more important than the field's understanding of how to achieve those values. This technique allowed administrators to simultaneously challenge the calumnious myths about the Pennsylvania System and display their conformity to the most important values in the penal field – values that (they claimed) the Auburn System and its supporters had rejected.

Beyond protecting the prison's reputation, these statements also insulated the administrators themselves from their own self-doubts. *They* were humanitarian, benevolent, progressive individuals who supported the more humane system. *They* were affiliated with the prison that uniquely sought and achieved the most admirable goals. If they could believe their own statements, they could not only neutralize the personal cost of maintaining the Pennsylvania System, but also *revel* in their difference – a difference they could only retain if they kept the Pennsylvania System.

---

[8] Gresham M. Sykes and David Matza, "Techniques of Neutralization: A Theory of Delinquency," *American Sociological Review* 22:6 (1957), pp. 664–670.

The System

Eastern's administrators were adamant in their annual reports that the Pennsylvania System was a morally irreproachable system. It was not harsh, but mild. It was not cruel, but kind. It was even progressive and benevolent. These words – "mild," "kind," "humane," "benevolent," "progressive," and other similar terms – heavily populated the reports. For example, the inspectors noted in 1835, "The Pennsylvania system is emphatically a mild and humane system."[9] Likewise, in 1846, the inspectors explained, "While the distinguishing features of this system are to prevent crime, deter from its commission, and to reform and improve the prisoner, its administration and discipline are based upon kindness and gentleness, tempered with firmness and impartiality."[10] Statements like these – simply proclaiming the Pennsylvania System's mildness, kindness, and humaneness – were commonplace in the annual reports.

While many such claims were simply grand statements, administrators also pointed to specific aspects of their system – including specific descriptions of their treatment, their personnel, their goals and motivations, and the history of the Pennsylvania System – to explain, at length, just how their system qualified for these positive descriptors. For example, the inspectors expounded in 1835,

Where do we place them [the incoming prisoners], and how do we treat them? They are taken to the bath and cleansed of outward pollution, they are new clad in warm and comfortable garments, they are placed in an apartment infinitely superior to what they have been accustomed, they are given employment to enable them to live by their own industry, they are addressed in the language of kindness, interest is shown in their present and future welfare, they are advised and urged to think of their former course and to avoid it, they are lifted gently from their state of humiliation; self-degradation is removed, and self-esteem inducted. Pride of character and manliness is inculcated, and they go out of prison unknown as convicts, determined to wrestle for a living in the path of honesty and virtue. Is not this humane?[11]

---

[9] Eastern State Penitentiary, Inspectors' Report, *Sixth Annual Report of the Inspectors of the Eastern State Penitentiary of Pennsylvania*. Philadelphia: J.W. Allen, 1835, p. 4.

[10] Eastern State Penitentiary, Inspectors' Report, *Seventeenth Annual Report of the Inspectors of the Eastern State Penitentiary of Pennsylvania*. Philadelphia: Ed. Barrington and Geo. D. Haswell, 1846, p. 16.

[11] Eastern State Penitentiary, Inspectors' Report, *Sixth Annual Report of the Inspectors*, pp. 4–5.

This emphasis on kindness, beyond a refutation of cruelty, was central to their claim of humanitarianism.

Administrators also extended their arguments into effusive praise. Cognizant of the possible shame the criticisms of the Pennsylvania System brought to its namesake state, administrators argued that the Pennsylvania System was an asset rather than a liability. So benevolent and progressive was the Pennsylvania System, they argued, that it reflected very well on the state. The 1829 legislation authorizing the Pennsylvania System, the inspectors exclaimed in 1837, "will render her [i.e., Pennsylvania's] character for philanthropy pre-eminent."[12] In 1845, they further described Eastern as "an institution, which will stand a monument of the benevolence and wisdom of Pennsylvania, and the glory of her people."[13] Indeed, the prison was a beacon of Pennsylvania's humanitarianism, according to Warden Wood in 1841:

Long may the institution continue to be administered by such faithful Inspectors, long may its unhappy inmates receive the blessings of your kindness and care, and thus prove a blessing to the State in which it is erected, and spread its philanthropical principles to the remotest corner of the globe.[14]

Such glowing praise could do more than counteract the shame of their prison's deviance – it elevated the administrators themselves as admirable human beings.

In another method of overcoming claims that their system was cruel and inhumane, administrators explicitly aligned their system with philanthropists and humanitarians. Its humanity, the administrators argued, was so great that all benevolent persons should endorse the Pennsylvania System. The inspectors noted of themselves in 1845,

They [i.e., the inspectors] believe, that all the friends of practical philanthropy, in examining this system, as it has been developed, and can be tested by the experience of so long a period of time, do rejoice in the great change which is thus being effected in the treatment of the outcast prisoner – kindness and compassion, and a desire for their improvement and reform, accompanied by the means to produce both, are supplanting cruelty and contempt.[15]

---

[12] Eastern State Penitentiary, Inspectors' Report, *Eighth Annual Report of the Inspectors of the Eastern State Penitentiary of Pennsylvania*. Philadelphia: J. Thompson, 1837, p. 4.

[13] Eastern State Penitentiary, Inspectors' Report, *Sixteenth Annual Report of the Inspectors of the Eastern State Penitentiary of Pennsylvania*. Philadelphia: Ed. Barrington and Geo. D. Haswell, 1845, p. 18.

[14] Eastern State Penitentiary, Warden's Report, *Twelfth Annual Report of the Inspectors*, p. 16.

[15] Eastern State Penitentiary, Inspectors' Report, *Sixteenth Annual Report of the Inspectors*, pp. 16–17.

Through statements like this one, administrators forged a link between humanitarianism, benevolence, progressiveness, philanthropy, and support for the Pennsylvania System. By corollary, those who opposed the Pennsylvania System were not as humanitarian and philanthropic as its supporters.

Indeed, administrators were not content to simply claim their system's humanitarian status to deny opposing penal reformers' claims. The administrators also sought to make it clear that their system was *the most humane* system. Thus, as they were fond of saying, as Warden Thompson did in 1841, "As to its [i.e., the Pennsylvania System's] humanity, if the term of imprisonment is justly proportioned to the offence, no system can claim precedence."[16] The administrators described the Auburn System as mere punishment that lacked reformatory influences and that did not seek to improve the offender or help him; the Pennsylvania System, they argued, did all of this and more. As the inspectors noted in 1865,

The separate system regards these reformatory influences as essential elements of punishment, if that is to be a restorative infliction, for the good of the convict, and the benefit of the State. Mere deprivation of liberty, with labor, is not all of punishment. It may be, only in so far as it restrains or detains the offender in a fixed place. But that is the external or physical idea. Has punishment only this one phase? Secure a convict in a place removed from society, and can we then proclaim that the social relations between the secluded and society end till the days of his sentence are ended, and be satisfied that his punishment is complete? Have benign philosophy, christian benevolence, civilization, penal and social science and jurisprudence, no better teachings, no higher aims? The Pennsylvania system reaches to the confines of a truer humanity. It preserves, cultivates, teaches the individuality of the convicts; their personal relations to society and their fellow man, and the God of that newer dispensation which seeks for the soul of a man, not that of a class, and proclaimed that it were better, individually, to receive the whole promise of the gospel, than gain a world without it.[17]

Although they began from a position of defense, administrators finished by taking an offensive position in many such comments. Thus, after one lengthy description of the system in practice in 1835, the inspectors noted, "The nature of this report forbids a longer indulgence in this strain of remark, but it appears to us only to be necessary to turn the current of thought in the proper channel, and the real difference between this and all

---

[16] Eastern State Penitentiary, Warden's Report, *Twelfth Annual Report of the Inspectors*, p. 8.

[17] Eastern State Penitentiary, Inspectors' Report, *Thirty-Sixth Annual Report of the Inspectors*, p. 16.

other known systems must be apparent."[18] The message was clear: Our system is humane; these other systems do not compare.

Indeed, Eastern's administrators described their system as a model for the country (and world). Although they could partially claim international success by the 1840s, it appears that they were more anxious about securing domestic success. Its humanitarian features, the administrators argued, made it particularly well suited to the United States. As the inspectors explained in 1846,

France, England, Prussia, Sweden and Austria, have adopted our plan of penitentiary reform, as the basis of their own, and it is the hope of the Board that it may become general in the States of the Union. It is certainly most in unison with the principles of our Institutions, for it seeks to benefit those who are the objects of its operation – and while it protects society and punishes crime; it not only deters from its commission and prevents its increase; but in its humanity, does not forever brand the prisoner, as one of a class to be regarded with repugnance – and thus deny him the opportunity of commingling with the virtuous – which in the wise economy of Providence, is secured to all the children of men.[19]

The challenge was convincing their opponents of the Pennsylvania System's superiority.

To make this case, the administrators occasionally relied on the testimony of their own prisoners. In their 1833 report, the inspectors exclaimed, "The mode of treatment in the Eastern Penitentiary ... has been called, by one who was once a subject of its wholesome regulations, 'a humane institution;' and we believe many more are prepared to unite in the same testimony."[20] Indeed, in several reports, administrators included letters from former prisoners praising the Pennsylvania System. While the spelling, grammar, and word choice make these letters fairly suspect,[21]

---

[18] Eastern State Penitentiary, Inspectors' Report, *Sixth Annual Report of the Inspectors*, p. 5.

[19] Eastern State Penitentiary, Inspectors' Report, *Seventeenth Annual Report of the Inspectors*, p. 18.

[20] Eastern State Penitentiary, Inspectors' Report, *Fourth Annual Report of the Inspectors*, pp. 4–5.

[21] A letter from the 1833 Annual Report used words like "immured" and referred to Eastern as "that terrific prison." Ibid., Inspectors' Report, p. 4. One former prisoner published a book of poems that he dedicated to the warden. In the preface of the book, the former prisoner wrote of himself,

He regards his confinement at Cherry Hill the happiest event of his life. It has dissolved improper connections, remodelled [sic] his tastes, improved his mind, and, he trusts, made better his heart. He is neither morose, imbecile, dispirited, or deranged, and whatever reformation his imprisonment may have produced, he can attribute it to the

their inclusion was part of administrators' arsenal for challenging characterizations of their system as cruel and inhumane.

Benevolent Motivations

Administrators could further describe their system, and their personnel, in positive terms by discussing their motivations and the goals of the Pennsylvania System. The administrators routinely claimed that their underlying motivations were benevolent – they wanted the prison to benefit its prisoners and society, and they believed it would. For example, Warden Wood recorded in 1832, "I humbly hope by divine aid, that it [i.e., the penitentiary] will prove a blessing to most, if not to all, of the unhappy persons who are brought within its walls."[22] Focusing on society as another primary beneficiary, Moral Instructor Larcombe noted in 1841, "Upwards of two years' acquaintance with the institution and its discipline has confirmed in my mind the opinion, that it is in every respect better adapted than any other system for the reform of offenders, and for the peace and security of society."[23] Often, however, administrators pointed to specific policies or goals that demonstrated their upright motivations.

Administrators used their commitment to reformation as one of the features that most defined the Pennsylvania System as a progressive system: Its "remedial and reformatory influences," the inspectors explained in 1860, "attest the enlightened, benevolent, and indeed philosophic treatment, by society, of those few, who have violated its laws. They mark the

separate seclusion from evil example and worse precept, which must necessarily follow the indiscriminate congregation of offenders, in place of punishment. ... Philadelphia, July 25, 1843. Harry Hawser, *Buds and Flowers of Leisure Hours*. Philadelphia: George W. Loammi Johnson, 1844.

A comparison to handwritten letters from Eastern's prisoners, however, offers a marked difference. One possibility is prisoners who wrote the more public letters did so with great assistance from highly educated reformers and administrators. Another possibility is the prisoners who wrote the public letters did so themselves, but they came from a higher class and educational background (e.g., occasionally bankers and lawyers were incarcerated for white-collar offenses like forgery or counterfeiting) and thus were not representative of the general prison population.

[22] Eastern State Penitentiary, Warden's Report *Report of the Board of Inspectors of the Eastern Penitentiary of Pennsylvania*. Harrisburg: Henry Welsh, 1832, p. 10.

[23] Eastern State Penitentiary, Moral Instructor's Report, *Twelfth Annual Report of the Inspectors*, p. 28.

progress of penal science. The separate system is its most signal and *sui generis* realization."[24]

There was occasionally some confusion about whether reformation was the primary goal or simply a desirable goal,[25] but prisoner reformation was a common theme in the report. Thus, administrators often wrote about the ways in which the Pennsylvania System enabled rehabilitation. For example, the inspectors wrote in 1847,

the distinctive features of the Pennsylvania plan ... are – separation of the prisoners from each other at all times – moral and intellectual improvement – honest and persuasive efforts to reform and reclaim the prisoners. Prevention, by this constant separation from each other of the evil of contamination and the prejudicial influence which must arise from the association of the more or less hardened offenders. The prevention by separation of the acquaintance and knowledge which the community of evil-minded persons obtain of each other by association in the place of punishment. The ability which is afforded by the separation of offenders, to individualize the corrective and reformatory treatment best suited to their peculiar characters. The almost certain consequence which results from the separate system, of making these no worse who cannot be made better by the infliction of the punishment they undergo. The addition of all improvements which experience and not mere theory suggests in the improvement of the moral and physical condition of the prisoners. These are the principles on which the Pennsylvania system is based, these rendered it antagonistical to the congregate system.[26]

That their prison was distinctive in the field in its commitment to rehabilitation made it uniquely humanitarian.

---

[24] Eastern State Penitentiary, Inspectors' Report, *Thirty-First Annual Report of the Inspectors of the State Penitentiary for the Eastern District of Pennsylvania*. Philadelphia: M'Laughlin Brothers, 1860, pp. 6–7.

[25] In the same year (1850), two separate administrators filed reports offering different views of the role of reformation. One noted, "While reformation is not the sole or even main object of punishment, it is, nevertheless, a most desirable effect of it." Eastern State Penitentiary, Inspectors' Report, *The Twenty-First Annual Report of the Inspectors of the Eastern State Penitentiary of Pennsylvania*. Philadelphia: Edmond Barrington and George D. Haswell, 1850, p. 5. The other noted, "in an age which declares the reformation of the convict to be the chief motive for his incarceration, and under a system of discipline which professes to accomplish this desirable result more effectually than any other. ..." Ibid., Physician's Report, p. 28. Throughout the entire period, however, administrators were usually concerned with reformation to some degree, and often more than any other purpose of punishment.

[26] Eastern State Penitentiary, Inspectors' Report, *Eighteenth Annual Report of the Inspectors*, p. 17.

Creation Myths

More than describing the humane, benevolent excellence and superiority of their system, the administrators also deployed "creation myths,"[27] or narratives of Eastern's origin, to counteract criticism of their system's inhumanity. Administrators' narratives of Eastern's history often took a rather heroic tone. These creation myths often described the Pennsylvania System as facing tremendous odds to succeed and the reformers and administrators who nurtured the system as extraordinary, benevolent humanitarians who bore the criticism but were not dissuaded from doing the right thing. For example, the inspectors reflected in 1837 on their prison's founding the previous decade,

The experiment at the time was a bold one, and was attended with difficulties at its commencement that would have damped the courage of any set of men less persuaded of the practicability or a plan which years of deliberation had decided to be the true one. Opposed at home by a respectable number of our fellow citizens, who, with views quite as honest, held adverse opinions; its main principles questioned by a commission of our own state especially instituted to examine the subject; assailed by the official agent of an influential and indefatigable society of a sister State, because it conflicted with his favourite system: Attacked from abroad by persons of high consideration in the moral and political world, who had become endeared to America by their military and other services, the friends of the Pennsylvania system held their course unchecked, and with a steadiness and perseverance worthy the cause, made their opinions public sentiment, and the State at length passed the law which will render her character for philanthropy pre-eminent.[28]

Notably, these descriptions emphasized the perseverance of the Pennsylvania System's supporters, including the inspectors writing this praise, and their close colleagues.

Descriptions of their efforts to face and overcome challenges became even more Herculean as time went on. Decades later, in 1869, the inspectors offered an even more impressive creation myth:

Half a century ago, when the Pennsylvania system of Penitentiary Reform was established by the Legislature, the theory of separate Imprisonment of convicts was attacked by earnest men in Massachusetts, New York and England, with a

---

[27] Carol A. Heimer and JuLeigh Petty, "Bureaucratic Ethics: IRBs and the Legal Regulation of Human Subjects Research," *Annual Review of Law and Social Science* 6:1 (2010), pp. 601–626.

[28] Eastern State Penitentiary, Inspectors' Report, *Eighth Annual Report of the Inspectors*, p. 3.

series of objections, which in themselves were thought to be fatal to its successful administration. Then, penal science, as an element of social science, was almost unknown. Thinkers and students had avoided it as repulsive and incapable of development. There were no data, there was no knowledge, nor experience, from which to deduce a reasonable conclusion as to its results. Its opponents resisted it on several grounds. They assumed that it would be, if carried out, destructive to health, injurious to the mind, and useless in its influences on those under its discipline. Against that system they set up the congregate plan, of commingling convicts by day at work, in prison, separating them at night. The distinction between these systems was radical. The separate system rested on the philosophy that punishment was a separation of the convict from society, to be treated for his crime as his individual character required; to produce that regret which might cause an amended life; to aid or induce reformation; to protect society; to prevent discharged criminals from organizing into a class in the community to prey on it with success, and by acquaintance with each other, made in prison, thus recruit the number and prevent any from returning to honest pursuits, or forming domestic ties. This was the basis on which the separate confinement of convicts was placed. These were the reasons which induced the founders to press it to a practical trial.[29]

Creation myths like these offered a different take on Eastern's singularity in the field. Pennsylvania pursued a new, more humane system, at great personal and material expense, while other states turned to simpler, less humane approaches.

Indeed, as the inspectors continued their retrospective in 1869, they contrasted the Pennsylvania System with the Auburn System:

The theory of the congregate system, on the other hand, may be thus stated: that as convicts were associated with society, association on conviction was obedience to social law, and in prison, therefore, they should work together; that each knew his degredation [sic], and that crime was its cause; yet legal punishment was complete when thus inflicted, though measured alone by the period of this degradation [sic], and that on its termination the convict was either a better man or a worse one, society only requiring crime to be punished and the criminal sentenced to a prison. The effects on the individual which his punishment produced, were never considered, except so far as that it should not injure his health nor his mind; and it was not cruel, because these convicts worked together all day, and went to separate cells at night. A Penitentiary as a place of reformatory penance for crime, may represent one system; a Factory, as a place of primitive manual labor, may represent the other. This is plainly stating the opposite theories of the two systems at the time to which we refer.[30]

[29] Eastern State Penitentiary, Inspectors' Report, *Fortieth Annual Report of the Inspectors of the State Penitentiary for the Eastern District of Pennsylvania*. Philadelphia: M'Laughlin Brothers, 1869, pp. 6–8.
[30] Ibid., pp. 6–8.

In this creation myth, the Pennsylvania System's difference from the Auburn System was admirable, not something to be criticized.

Notably, these myths did more than characterize the Pennsylvania System as uniquely humane. These myths also characterized its supporters and administrators as particularly benevolent for eschewing the less humane, albeit more common, approaches. This was a theme the administrators expanded on in other ways.

Eastern's Benevolent Administrators

The administrators habitually referred to themselves and others associated with the Pennsylvania System with the same language of humanitarianism, progressiveness, and benevolence. Instances of personnel turnover were ripe opportunities to heap praise on incoming or outgoing wardens, inspectors, and other administrators. Thus, when Eastern's first warden left his post in 1840, the inspectors eulogized his tenure in their annual report: "Much praise is due to this gentleman, for his judicious organization and arrangement of an important and united system of Penitentiary punishment, and for his humane and kind treatment of the prisoners under his care."[31] Likewise, when Warden Thomas Scattergood assumed office in 1845, the outgoing Warden George Thompson recognized, "[t]he benevolent and highly respectable gentleman now Warden, [who] induced by his own views of duty and the solicitations of many of the best friends of the Pennsylvania System, consent[ed] to assume the office."[32] Such comments, however, were not restricted to moments of turnover.

Praise for the administration and staff was routine in the annual reports. For example, the inspectors noted in their report in 1851, "To the kindness, firmness, and humanity of the Warden, Overseers, and Matron, we are chiefly indebted for the order, obedience, and contentment which have prevailed, and which continue to prevail, throughout the prison."[33] Likewise, as part of his annual report the previous year, Physician Given reported, "I cannot refrain from expressing my high sense of the intelligence and humanity that have been invariably displayed by

---

[31] Eastern State Penitentiary, Inspector's Report, *Twelfth Annual Report of the Inspectors*, p. 5.

[32] Eastern State Inspectors' Report, Warden's Report, *Seventeenth Annual Report of the Inspectors*, p. 20.

[33] Eastern State Penitentiary, Inspectors' Report, *Twenty-Second Annual Report of the Inspectors of the Eastern State Penitentiary of Pennsylvania*. Philadelphia: Kite & Walton, 1851, p. 7.

the officers of the different departments."[34] Occasionally, the prison's overseers were singled out for the administrators' praise. In his first annual report in 1842, Warden Thompson noted,

The officers of the institution under my control have, by attention to their duties, deserved the confidence reposed in them; I have the most conclusive proofs of their humanity and kindness to the prisoners, by the unbiased statements to that effect made at the period of their discharge, when no motive can exist for a perversion of truth.[35]

Everyone who worked at the prison deserved praise.

Sometimes this praise extended to those involved with, but not employed at, the prison. In the prison's first several decades, the administrators praised the penal reformers who voluntarily spent time with the prisoners. For example, the inspectors noted in 1850,

On the minds of some [prisoners], a permanent impression for good is not unfrequently produced. To those instrumental in achieving this result, and particularly to the occasional visiters [sic], whose only object is the highest welfare of their fellow men, the thanks of the community are emphatically due.[36]

Virtually any individual associated with Eastern was bequeathed the administrators' praise as humanitarian and philanthropic.[37] However, the administrators received the bulk of this type of praise.

Flowery descriptions of administrators' humane benevolence helped to establish them as progressive men who would never consent to supervising or imposing a cruel system of punishment. Indeed, the administrators were cautious to publicize their abhorrence for anything resembling cruel punishment as a way of emphasizing their system's humanity. As we have already seen, the administrators condemned the use of pure solitary confinement to emphasize its difference from confinement under the Pennsylvania System; as we shall see below, they also showcased their opposition to whipping prisoners and using prisoners for profit.

The administrators also established their own commitment to humane treatment by condemning other instances of inhumane treatment closer to

---

[34] Eastern State Penitentiary, Physician's Report, *The Twenty-First Annual Report of the Inspectors*, p. 22.

[35] Eastern State Penitentiary, Warden's Report, *Thirteenth Annual Report of the Inspectors of the Eastern State Penitentiary of Pennsylvania*. Philadelphia: Mifflin & Parry, 1842, p. 9.

[36] Eastern State Penitentiary, Inspector's Report, *The Twenty-First Annual Report of the Inspectors*, p. 5.

[37] We shall see temporary and strategic exceptions to this trend in Chapter 9.

home, including the confinement of mentally ill prisoners. Warden Wood explained in 1841,

In a future age it will scarcely be believed, that in the nineteenth century, in a Christian land, in a State containing throughout its extent innumerable monuments of piety, of intelligence and benevolence, that those whom Providence, in its mysterious dispensations, had visited with the most grievous [sic], the most appalling calamity, the deprivation of reason, and consequently of responsibility – that indigent lunatics should be deprived of all sympathy, of all justice, by the cruelty or negligence of their fellow men – should be consigned to a prison appropriated only to felons of the vilest degree, where no friend or relative could visit them or alleviate their distress, and where almost every surrounding circumstance is hostile to their repose, their comfort, or their restoration to reason. ... I hope, I trust, that the great State of Pennsylvania, which is inferior to none in wealth, which has already done so much to ameliorate the miseries of prisons, will not refuse to do justice to her lunatics, by imitating, even at this late day, the institutions of her rival sisters.[38]

Their opposition to inhumanity not only helped to demonstrate their own humanitarian bonafides but also to challenge the identification of the Pennsylvania System as a cruel system.

Summary

In these several ways, Eastern's administrators sought to establish their prison, its methods and purpose, its heritage, and its personnel as humanitarian, progressive, and benevolent. Relying on this claim to benevolent humanitarianism throughout their descriptions was no accident. Emphasizing the benevolent and humanitarian aspects of the Pennsylvania System helped to counter the calumnious myth that the Pennsylvania System was cruel and inhumane. Through these arguments, Eastern's administrators crafted an identity for their prison that directly challenged several of the criticisms leveled at it – especially its particularly harsh and cruel character. Administrators characterized their organization with terms that represented the opposite of cruelty, deployed creation myths emphasizing the benevolent origins of the prison, and emphasized their unique status within the field as a prison that sought – and successfully achieved – prisoner reformation. In these ways, administrators marketed their organization's difference, turning deviant status into an asset, showing how its highly criticized Pennsylvania System could achieve goals

---

[38] Eastern State Penitentiary, Warden's Report, *Twelfth Annual Report of the Inspectors*, p. 13.

not possible through alternative means. Along the way, administrators were able to characterize themselves in positive terms that were salient to their (reform-oriented) audience. Defending the prison allowed them to defend themselves, but also to give themselves an identity as superior gentlemen reformers – an identity unavailable under the Auburn System.

UNDERMINING THEIR CRITICS

While Eastern's administrators presented themselves and their prison as benevolent and humanitarian, they also argued that their opponents were not. In particular, the administrators pointed out contradictions in their critics' claims that the Pennsylvania System was a cruel and inhumane system when the Auburn System, their critics' favored approach, could be criticized along these same lines. The administrators pointed especially to the Auburn System's use of whipping and, inverting one of their critics' central arguments against the Pennsylvania System, the moral impropriety of using profitability to evaluate criminal punishment. Sykes and Matza, called this strategy – undermining one's critics in order to undermine their criticism – "condemnation of the condemners."[39] While each of the administrators' other strategies was primarily defensive with an undertone of offense, this strategy primarily positioned them on the offense and their critics on the defense.

Rejecting the Whip

When Eastern's administrators emphasized their own kind treatment of their prisoners, they were depicting the Pennsylvania System as a humane system. More strategically, however, they were implicitly labeling the Auburn System, not particularly known for its kind treatment, as the cruel system. As the inspectors explained in 1844, "Any treatment of prisoners, which has for its object imprisonment and reform, and is not based on principles of *kindness*, is worse than useless; indeed, it is a cruelty, a wrong, and a prevention of benefit."[40] This seemingly generic statement was a thinly veiled critique of the Auburn System.

---

[39] Sykes and Matza, "Techniques of Neutralization."
[40] Eastern State Penitentiary, Inspectors' Report, *Fifteenth Annual Report of the Inspectors of the Eastern State Penitentiary of Pennsylvania*. Philadelphia: Joseph and William Kite, 1844, p. 5.

Eastern's administrators often described their treatment in opposition to treatment under the Auburn System. By positively evaluating their own treatment, they implicitly criticized the treatment under the Auburn System. For example, it was a point of pride among Eastern's administrators that they did not use the whip to instill discipline in their prison. The whip, especially associated with Southern slavery, was a symbol of inhumane treatment and cruelty. Thus, Eastern's administrators frequently emphasized the "mildness" of the punishments they did use not only to reject claims of their system's cruelty but also as a kind of code for their refusal to resort to whipping. In one early explanation in 1833, the inspectors noted,

The mode of treatment in the Eastern Penitentiary is of a mild character. The severity used in other prisons, in which large bodies of men are to be kept in subjection by force or power, is not required here. The warden and his officers are considered by our prisoners, not as tyrants or cruel oppressors, but as their friends. The voice of kindness is that which reaches their ears, and most successfully affects their hearts; suitable labour, daily exercise, cleanliness in their persons and apartments, with wholesome diet, and above all, religious instruction by personal conversation and the public preaching of the Gospel, all combine to produce health of body, and moral renovation of the mind.[41]

Explaining their penal philosophy in 1844, the inspectors stated their personal mandate: "Reason with the convict, do not whip him; condole with him, don't aggravate him; bring him back to the standard of integrity, don't debase him below the degree of a felon," presumably referring to the status of a slave.[42] Statements like these sought to simultaneously establish Eastern's administrators and their Pennsylvania System as benevolent and humane and their pro–Auburn System opponents as "tyrants and cruel oppressors," much like the whip-loving slave owners of the South.

To bolster the contrast between the two systems, administrators often included accounts of how much misconduct occurred at Eastern and what punishment they had meted out in the course of the year. For example, the inspectors noted in 1842, "During the past year the conduct and deportment of a very large majority of the prisoners have been good. Few cases have required any other than humane treatment, and where any such cases have occurred, the mildest form of punishment the Inspectors could

[41] Eastern State Penitentiary, Inspector's Report, *Fourth Annual Report of the Inspectors*, p. 4.
[42] Eastern State Penitentiary, *Fifteenth Annual Report of the Inspectors*, p. 6.

adopt, has been resorted to."[43] The whip, they argued, was unnecessary at Eastern. Following "a year of peace, of order, and of good feeling, on the part of the prisoners, both towards the Warden, and the other officers engaged in their more immediate supervision," Moral Instructor Larcombe noted in 1849, "Coercive measures are rarely needed, and I believe, are never resorted to, until moral influences have been fully tried, and prove ineffectual. When such measures are adopted as a final resort, they are never severe."[44] When the prison later became overcrowded after the Civil War, Physician Klapp made sure to point out to readers of his 1868 Annual Report that even this challenge did not push their resolve against inhumane punishments: "Oppressed by numbers, perfect discipline is observed, without resort to any but the milder degrees of punishment."[45] By not using the whip, Eastern's administrators could concretely argue their system was more humane than the Auburn System; ultimately, it was the Auburn System that deserved censure.

In practice, administrators – especially the warden and physician, sometimes after consulting the inspectors – imposed a number of additional (sometimes quite severe) punishments on recalcitrant offenders. Over the years, the warden imposed a range of punishments: Prisoners were punished with a stint in the "dark cell," a period of "short allowance" (food restriction, usually bread and water), or the loss of work (considered a privilege for alleviating monotony). More rarely – though the practice became fairly common under Warden Wood (1829–1840) – prisoners were kept in a "straight jacket," subjected to a "shower bath" or "ducking" (buckets of water repeatedly dropped on the prisoner), the "tranquilizing chair" (prisoners subjected to sensory deprivation while restrained in a chair), or the "iron gag" (a metal bar placed in the prisoner's mouth and connected to their hands tied behind their back).[46] These punishments were often combined, particularly a stay in the dark cell on short allowance or loss of work and short allowance. Very occasionally, the more severe methods were combined as well.

43 Eastern State Penitentiary, Inspectors' Report, *Thirteenth Annual Report of the Inspectors*, p. 4.

44 Eastern State Penitentiary, Moral Instructor's Report, *The Twentieth Annual Report of the Inspectors*. Philadelphia: Edmond Barrington and Geo. D. Haswell, 1849, p. 33.

45 Eastern State Penitentiary, Physician's Report, *Thirty-Ninth Annual Report of the Inspectors of the State Penitentiary for the Eastern District of Pennsylvania*. Philadelphia: McLaughlin Brothers, 1868, p. 101.

46 For an extended discussion on these devices, see Michael Meranze, *Laboratories of Virtue: Punishment, Revolution, and Authority in Philadelphia, 1760–1835*. Chapel Hill: University of North Carolina Press, 1996.

The more extreme punishments were rarely discussed in the annual reports. Indeed, publicly, the administrators claimed to have stopped using every punishment but removing one's work, "short allowance" of food, and the dark cell; in practice, the wardens sometimes still used other punishments, including the straitjacket and more rarely the shower bath.[47] The discredited shower bath continued to be used in almost every year that the Pennsylvania System remained in effect.

Rejecting the Pursuit of Profit

Eastern's administrators also reversed one of the most persuasive (and pervasive) criticisms of their system to condemn their opponents' cruel inhumanity: the question of profitability. Initially, however, this strategy began as another variant of their appeal to higher loyalties. From the prison's first years in operation, Eastern's administrators challenged the myths that Eastern was too expensive and unprofitable by reframing their willingness to expend resources on prisoner reformation as a mark of humanitarian qualification rather than as a point of criticism. Reflecting in 1837 on the not-so-distant origins of the Pennsylvania System at Eastern, the inspectors noted,

> The experiment at the outset was attended with an expense which even a *great nation* has paused to incur, and is only to be reconciled by the prevalent humanity of the people of Pennsylvania, which yearned to ameliorate the condition of her criminals, and to substitute a moral and wholesome atmosphere in lieu of the vicious miasma which pervades great communities.[48]

This claim, which reframed an established weakness as a strength, was repeated throughout Eastern's history.

Years later, for example, they continued to demonstrate their prioritization of moral over fiscal benefits. Thus, commenting on the influx of prisoners at the close of the Civil War, the inspectors wrote in 1866,

> Attention is called to the number of unapprenticed convicts and minors which the tables appended show have been received during the past year. It is of far greater advantage to these individuals and to society, to teach, to improve, or reform them, than to waste vain regret at the per centage of profit their manual labor

---

47 Eastern State Penitentiary, *Warden's Daily Journal*, Volumes 1–2. Eastern State Penitentiary Collection, Record Group 15 (#15.50). Pennsylvania State Archives, 1829–1877, March 5, 1839; July 5, 1839; November 13, 1840; March 10, 1841; June 11, 1859.

48 Eastern State Penitentiary, Inspectors' Report, *Eighth Annual Report of the Inspectors*, p. 4.

would produce during the time they are undergoing punishment for crimes. The punishment is inflicted, and they are placed in a position to avoid crime thereafter, as a necessity. If new impulses are given to the life of a majority of these convicts, Pennsylvania will have gained far more permanent moral benefits, than the saving of a few dollars which without this benefit, would have been realized.[49]

Rather than focusing their efforts on maximizing profits, a good prison should expend the money necessary to help its prisoners and society more generally.

The administrators were careful to note, however, that they were not fiscally irresponsible; indeed, they frequently endeavored to clarify their fiscal responsibility. After "rejoicing" in his state's rejection of profit, Warden Wood carefully added, "Nevertheless, sufficient time has elapsed to satisfy me of the correctness of an opinion I have long believed and asserted, 'that a prisoner who has two years or upwards to serve, can in his solitary cell earn sufficient to clear all his expenses from the time of his admission to his discharge.'"[50] Likewise, decades later, while the inspectors touted their legacy of rejecting profit concerns, they clarified in 1858, "Economy in their maintenance is the duty of all to secure, who are entrusted with their [prison's] custody and care."[51] That is, just because they rejected profit as a reasonable goal did not mean they were profligate custodians of the prisons.

These claims were part of a particularly strategic tactic that did more than confirm the administrators' humanitarian intentions. Embedded in these claims was an implicit, at least initially, critique of their critics. Challenged from the beginning about their prison's cost, administrators did not know at the outset whether Eastern would be profitable, self-sufficient, or an extremely expensive endeavor. Describing pecuniary interests as a lowly and inappropriate incentive for penal or social policy helped to insulate them from potential charges of undue expense should things not go their way. Thus, in his first report to the legislature, Warden Wood noted in 1831,

I rejoice that it never has been the policy of the legislature of this state, to sacrifice the safety of the community and the welfare of the convict for apparent pecuniary

49 Eastern State Penitentiary, Inspectors' Report, *Thirty-Seventh Annual Report of the Inspectors of the State Penitentiary for the Eastern District of Pennsylvania*. Philadelphia: McLaughlin Brothers, 1866, p. 26–27.
50 Eastern State Penitentiary, Warden's Report, *The First and Second Annual Reports of the Inspectors of the Eastern State Penitentiary of Pennsylvania*. Philadelphia: Thomas Kite, 1831, p. 13.
51 Eastern State Penitentiary, Inspectors' Report, *Twenty-Ninth Annual Report of the Inspectors*, p. 7.

gain. They have taken a higher, a more dignified and nobler ground. They have provided that labour shall be furnished the convict in his cell, and not for the sordid purpose of reimbursing the Commonwealth the expense of his maintenance.[52]

By implication, those critics who overlooked such considerations were inhumane and should not be taken seriously.

Indeed, explaining that benefit to the convict and to society was more important than profit allowed the administrators to explain away losses or the failure to profit as irrelevant considerations. The inspectors explained in 1834,

Weaving and shoemaking have been the principal employments. In the former, some loss has been sustained in the past year, from the depreciation in the value of goods. In the latter, the aggregate profit has been small. If, however, we can ensure the steady employment of the prisoners, in trades which must eventually benefit them, and tend to divert them from the commission of crime, when restored to society, the main design will be fulfilled.[53]

The long-term benefits to society, they argued, outweighed the short-term unprofitability.

Rejecting the profit motivation thus augmented the system's humanitarian status, excused fiscal failures, and criticized those supporting the Auburn System. Eastern's administrators, whether savvy or sincere, thus made their weaknesses into strengths and made their opponents' strengths into weaknesses: Eastern may or may not make a profit, but it was an improper concern for humanitarian, benevolent prison administrators. Notably, the administrators were well aware of the inversion they were attempting. Referring to the warden's annual report, the inspectors noted in 1849,

This document will show that the Commonwealth is not an immediate pecuniary gainer by the maintenance of the present system of discipline – a fact of which constant use is made by a class of writers, as proof of the defects of the system, as well as of the obtuseness of the popular mind in tolerating it, but which, to the apprehension of the undersigned, constitutes much stronger evidence of that stable, straight-forward and effective benevolence, which has ever distinguished the people of Pennsylvania.[54]

Proclaiming fiscal disinterest helped to establish their system's humanitarian nature and their superiority over other systems.

---

[52] Eastern State Penitentiary, Warden's Report, *The First and Second Annual Reports of the Inspectors*, p. 13.

[53] Eastern State Penitentiary, Inspectors' Report, *Fifth Annual Report of the Inspectors of the Eastern Penitentiary of Pennsylvania*. Harrisburg: Welsh & Patterson, 1834, p.3.

[54] Eastern State Penitentiary, Inspectors' Report, *Twentieth Annual Report of the Inspectors*, p. 9.

These claims, however, were belied by their own attempts to make the prison more cost-effective, as we will see in Chapter 7. Throughout the Annual Reports, administrators indicated that they were indeed concerned with their prison's pecuniary faring. When they did discuss profitability, they often noted that it was not their "primary" concern. For example, after offering a favorable account of the year's finances, Warden Wood noted in 1833, "This result is satisfactory; for, although it never was contemplated to make profit a primary object, yet it is desirable that the convict should not be a burthen to the state."[55] This posture enabled administrators to publicly justify labor tasks in light of reformation, and feign pleasant surprise when they did more than break even. But profit and cost were far from the irrelevance that they often publicly made it out to be. Indeed, as we will see in Chapter 7, cost-effectiveness was, privately, often the greater concern, even competing with rehabilitation and other penal goals. Their public stance toward profitability was thus part of their larger strategy to not only defend Eastern and themselves against criticism but also to elevate their prison and themselves against their competitors.

While this overall theme of reframing fiscal concerns continued throughout the prison's history, in the 1850s a new variation emerged in which the rejection of profit moved beyond appealing to higher loyalties. In this context, their criticism of their critics became more apparent. As Eastern's administrators explained in that decade, the common tendency in other states to consider the profitability of one's prison was truly base. It was morally imperative, the inspectors wrote in 1859, to "regard[] man, even criminal and in prison, as worthy of higher consideration, than a mere money-making agent for the people of the Commonwealth."[56] However, other states were not simply *concerned* with profit; rather, it was their *primary concern* – according to the inspectors writing in 1856, "the profits of prisoners' labor" were "paramount to every other principle of Penitentiary discipline."[57] No longer were Eastern's administrators content to tout their willingness to expend resources

55 Eastern State Penitentiary, Warden' Report, *Fourth Annual Report of the Inspectors*, p. 10.
56 Eastern State Penitentiary, Inspectors' Report, *Thirtieth Annual Report of the Inspectors of the State Penitentiary for the Eastern District of Pennsylvania*. Philadelphia: M'Laughlin Brothers, 1859, pp. 12–13.
57 Eastern State Penitentiary, Inspectors' Report, *Twenty-Seventh Annual Report of the Inspectors of the Eastern State Penitentiary of Pennsylvania*. Philadelphia: King & Baird, 1856, p. 8.

on prisoner reformation; now, they reframed the fiscal arguments by implicitly condemning those who did care about expense and profitability.

Although, as we have seen, profitability was indeed a pressing concern for Eastern's administrators in their first several decades, by the 1850s part of their claim to superiority was their claim that they were, by contrast to other prisons' administrators and Auburn supporters, unconcerned with profit – and *never had been*. For example, Eastern's inspectors emphasized in 1858, "The Inspectors have never from the earliest dawn of reformatory efforts in prison discipline, been taught to regard a profit-paying penitentiary, as a primary purpose of that true philanthropy, which originated our system of penitentiary punishment."[58]

In making these arguments, Eastern's administrators continued to quite literally appeal to higher loyalties. For example, in 1856, the inspectors "advocated and successfully practiced *far higher aims*" (emphasis added).[59] Indeed, they repeated this theme that "there are higher objects to gain in the treatment and discipline of convicts, than profit from their labor."[60] This argument thus referred back to their other claims of benevolence and humanitarian treatment, which they described as part of these "higher aims."

Notably, these remarks from the 1850s, and those remarks that followed in later years, conveniently overlooked the fact that they had in fact been quite concerned with the profitability of their prison earlier in its history, as seen in their evaluations and scapegoating efforts discussed in Chapter 5. As we shall see in Chapter 7, the administrators continued to be concerned with profit considerations privately as well. Their remarks decrying profitability as a criteria for evaluating prison systems were entirely strategic.

Delegitimizing profit as a criteria of evaluation undermined conclusions about Eastern's inferiority derived from dominant evaluations. Given the disparity between humanity and profitability, Eastern's administrators claimed that their critics were using inappropriate criteria to evaluate the two systems. As the inspectors explained in 1866,

[58] Eastern State Penitentiary, Inspectors' Report, *Twenty-Ninth Annual Report of the Inspectors*, p. 7.

[59] Eastern State Penitentiary, Inspectors' Report, *Twenty-Seventh Annual Report of the Inspectors*, p. 8.

[60] Eastern State Penitentiary, Inspectors' Report, *Twenty-Ninth Annual Report of the Inspectors*, p. 7.

In the several States of America, it can be truly said, the objective point of their penitentiary plans is pecuniary gain to the State out of its convict population. All other ameliorations are incidental to this primary purpose. ... "Self-supporting" is the test of their prisons and penitentiaries, and those systems are regarded best, which yield the largest pecuniary returns from convict labor. The larger the number working together, the greater the facilities to supervise and render them the more productive.

Clearly, this was a problematic, even inhumane, approach, as the administrators saw it. It was, the inspectors continued, part of "the sordid and the selfish among the false doctrines of that material dispensation which idolises gain, and denies to man the inherent right, even in his convict condition, to every beneficial influence which christianity or civilization has in its power to bestow."[61] It was entirely unbecoming a progressive, humane prison; in any contest between the Auburn System and the Pennsylvania System, the latter should win.

EFFECT

The administrators' rhetorical defense served multiple purposes. Most clearly, it could (if successful) convince their opponents, critics, and other interested parties (including their allies) that the Pennsylvania System (and its administrators) were not so bad. They could (if successful) possibly even convince other states' decision makers to adopt the Pennsylvania System for their prisons. After the 1840s, however, the administrators' defense was unsuccessful in this regard. Where they were more successful, at least for a while, was in protecting the Pennsylvania System at home from local incursions – when they could convince the local reformers, state legislature, governor, and supreme court of their system's superiority and that the Pennsylvania System was a source of pride rather than of embarrassment (see Chapter 9).

More subtly, their public, rhetorical defense offered Eastern's administrators several personal benefits that explain how and why the administrators continued to maintain the Pennsylvania System despite their ongoing deviant status. As the flagship prison of the Pennsylvania System, Eastern bore the brunt of the field's criticism. Unlike other administrators at other prisons that followed the Pennsylvania System, Eastern's administrators never requested an end to their highly criticized system and

---

[61] Eastern State Penitentiary, Inspectors' Report, *Thirty-Seventh Annual Report of the Inspectors*, p. 17.

they never criticized the system themselves. For decades, they withstood criticism without buckling. Indeed, of the four American prisons that followed the Pennsylvania System at any time, Eastern's administrators had the strongest need to constantly defend the Pennsylvania System and themselves. I argue that it was precisely this need to constantly defend the Pennsylvania System that created the ideal conditions to personally institutionalize it. Eastern's location at the center of criticism made the Pennsylvania System unexpendable because it offered the administrators something more than technical value.

The administrators' public defense of the Pennsylvania System offered two benefits that encouraged their commitment. First, their defenses of the prison offered a kind of salve against the vicious criticism coming from their opponents. As administrators of the flagship prison of the heavily criticized Pennsylvania System, they were in a sense living effigies of their organization's deviance. To withstand criticism, Eastern's administrators had to reconcile what so many in the field thought of them with how they envisioned themselves. Their defense in the annual reports gave the administrators a means of rejecting the criticism of their work and allowing their own self-conceptions to reign. Indeed, techniques of neutralization were first identified as a way for juvenile delinquents to reconcile their beliefs about their own virtue with the fact of their criminal behavior, and mitigate the shame of being labeled "deviant." Such techniques enable the delinquent to persist in her criminal activity while continuing to think of herself as a good person.[62] In the present case, Eastern was a deviant organization and its administrators, berated for imposing an inhumane, ineffective system, were stigmatized as a result. In such context, techniques of neutralization offer deviant-organizational actors a way to challenge their deviant identity.

At the most basic level, the administrators' rhetorical defense allowed them space to undermine claims about their own inhumanity and inferiority. Repeatedly issuing positive statements about their system and themselves allowed the administrators to internalize these statements. If they could convince themselves that they were truly in the right, their defenses could insulate them from any doubts that might linger about whether they were, as Dickens had claimed, subjecting their prisoners to an unimaginable torture. Consequently, as with non-organizational deviants (i.e., deviant individuals), techniques of neutralization provided

[62] Sykes and Matza, "Techniques of Neutralization."

Eastern's administrators a way to withstand the criticism, overcome the pressure to adopt the Auburn System, and persist in their commitment to the Pennsylvania System.

Second, their defenses of the prison provided a legitimate outlet for them to define and display their own superiority both as prison administrators but also as men. More than simply neutralizing the criticism, the administrators' defense took on a life of its own. Their need to defend the Pennsylvania System gave the administrators a platform for describing themselves in extremely positive terms: rather than being cruel social deviants, they were benevolent, progressive gentlemen responsible for administering the nation's – nay, the world's – most humane and effective prison.

In defending the Pennsylvania System, they were able to describe themselves in these glowing terms and enjoy the status that came with administering – what they identified as – a superior prison. Ostensibly for their prison's benefit, Eastern's administrators could describe themselves as humanitarian, benevolent gentlemen. Their affiliation with the superior prison gave them a basis from which to claim an exalted status within the field while their need to defend it gave them the opportunity to proclaim this status. These defenses of the Pennsylvania System thus provided the administrators with a means of creating a unique identity that no other administrators could claim. Defending the Pennsylvania System thus allowed administrators to bolster their own status in a seemingly "disinterested" manner.[63]

It is important to recognize the strategic nature of the administrator's public defense. The Pennsylvania System had become an important source of status to these gentleman reformers, and they had to save it by any means necessary. They were not, however, simply "true believers"; for Eastern's administrators, convincing the world to recognize that they were running a humane prison under a superior system was more important than it was for them to actually run such a prison in practice. Indeed, as we shall see, Eastern's administrators, including the most vocal supporters among them, routinely violated the Pennsylvania System behind closed doors. While these violations sometimes served their own personal gain, it was much more common for administrators to violate the Pennsylvania System strategically – to save its public reputation.

* * *

[63] Selznick, *TVA and the Grassroots*, p. 51.

Eastern's administrators fought, and fought hard, to defend and keep their Pennsylvania System. In addition to their evaluations and scapegoating efforts, the administrators sought to undermine the calumnious myths about the Pennsylvania System by offering positive characterizations of their prison, its system, and themselves that challenged claims of its (and their) cruelty. Moving from defense to offense, they also pointed out contradictions in their opponents' support for a potentially crueler system that saw prisoners as sources of profit rather than as reformable members of society. These claims may have helped to insulate Eastern from local incursions for a while by reminding their state that it should be proud of its uniqueness. But – more importantly – these claims helped Eastern's administrators remain committed to the Pennsylvania System, despite the criticism it invited, and resist ever publicly criticizing their system. Ultimately, the basis for their commitment to the Pennsylvania System was provided by their unique need to defend it against rampant criticism; the process of repeatedly defending it, and themselves, personally institutionalized the Pennsylvania System at Eastern.

B

BEHIND THE SCENES

[The insecure organization] had to feel its way. This required the formulation of a policy that would reassure external elements and would so educate its own ranks as to maximize the possibilities of social acceptance.

Philip Selznick[1]

---

[1] Selznick, *TVA and the Grassroots*, p. 49.

7

Strategic Manipulations

Acceptable and Unacceptable Violations of the Pennsylvania System

Over the head and face of every prisoner who comes into this melancholy house, a black hood is drawn; and in this dark shroud, an emblem of the curtain dropped between him and the living world, he is led to the cell from which he never again comes forth, until his whole term of imprisonment has expired. He never hears of wife and children; home or friends; the life or death of any single creature. He sees the prison-officers, but with that exception he never looks upon a human countenance, or hears a human voice. He is a man buried alive; to be dug out in the slow round of years; and in the mean time dead to everything but torturing anxieties and horrible despair.

Charles Dickens (1842), *American Notes*[1]

James J. Barclay reports having visited the prisoners in this Block and saw 16 in their cells – 2 or 3 of the cells have two prisoners in each of them. ... Richard Williams ... [reports] Many of the prisoners, particularly those under his charge, were out of their cells, in the workshops and other places.

PSAMPP's Acting Committee (1854), Meetings Minutes[2]

your liquer done me good to night for when i got up to my sell my head whirld like atope and i throde up all of my dinner and fell some what beter now dear.

Elizabeth Velora Elwell to Albert Green Jackson, prisoners at Eastern (1862)[3]

---

[1] Charles Dickens, *American Notes for General Circulation*. ed. Patricia Ingham. London: Penguin Books, 2000 [1842], pp. 112–113.

[2] PSAMPP, *Committee for Eastern, Minute Books*, Vol. 1–3; Pennsylvania Prison Society Records (Collection 1946), Series I, Vol. 27–29. Historical Society of Pennsylvania, 1854–1885, 5 Mo 31, 1854; 8 Mo 2, 1854.

[3] Elizabeth Velora Elwell, *Elizabeth Velora Elwell Correspondence*. Series III, State Penitentiary for the Eastern District of Pennsylvania Records. American Philosophical Society, Philadelphia, 1862, May 7, 1862.

THE PENNSYLVANIA SYSTEM IN PRACTICE

If we are to believe public accounts of the Pennsylvania System – whether from supporters like PSAMPP or critics like Charles Dickens – Eastern's prisoners were interred within their cells, never seeing a living soul beyond a handful of reformers and prison staff, for years on end. Apart from these visitors, according to Dickens, the prisoner "never looks upon a human countenance, or hears a human voice." Like many visitors, Dickens described Eastern as a deathly silent prison: "the dull repose and quiet that prevails, is awful."[4] Adding a flare for the dramatic, commentators sometimes described how prisoners were first brought to their cell hooded – "this dark shroud, an emblem of the curtain dropped between him and the living world" in Dickens' view – in order to protect their identity against chance sightings by prison staff and workmen engaged in the prison's endless construction. Once within his cell, the prisoner "never again comes forth, until his whole term of imprisonment has expired." In the interim, the prisoner worked alone, driven by boredom, and, according to Dickens and some other commentators, slowly losing his mind from "torturing anxieties and horrible despair." Prisoners' total confinement within their individual solitary cells and the complete absence of social contact – "he is a man buried alive" – was the primary emphasis among critics and supporters alike.[5]

Both critics' and supporters' descriptions of what the Pennsylvania System looked like in practice were rarely accurate. Although critics occasionally heard and repeated rumors of deviations from the system's rules, they mostly focused on theoretical arguments – the Pennsylvania System constituted torture, it was dangerous to mental and physical health, it was too expensive, and, ultimately, its central mandate of solitary confinement would have to be bent in order to preserve prisoners' health or buoy the prison's bottom line. Supporters likewise counteracted these claims and argued that the Pennsylvania System functioned well – and when it did not, that there was a clear impediment that, once removed, would no longer cause failure. As we have seen, Eastern's administrators in particular offered eloquent defenses of the Pennsylvania System – and their prison's continued reliance on it – by challenging the veracity of

---

4 In this period, silence was often seen as the mark of a good prison. See, for example, Louis Dwight's description of his visit to Auburn and its "silent system," described in Chapter 4. However, in critics' accounts of Eastern, silence became a marker of its gothic horrors.

5 Dickens, *American Notes*, p. 113.

these various myths. But relying on either group's descriptions of the Pennsylvania System would yield a highly inaccurate understanding of how the Pennsylvania System functioned in practice. Importantly, a behind-the-scenes look at how Eastern functioned reveals much about its administrators' commitment to the Pennsylvania System.

* * *

This chapter describes what the Pennsylvania System looked like in practice, focusing on how Eastern's administrators' implementation choices deviated from the Pennsylvania System's idealized regimen that they so vehemently defended. If Eastern's administrators publicly presented themselves as fully confident in the Pennsylvania System, their private actions said otherwise. Quite at odds with their extensive public proclamations of their system's excellence, the administrators often subverted the Pennsylvania System's ultimate goals or directly broke its most central rules.

This chapter makes sense of the administrators' apparently para-doxical behavior by demonstrating that these deviations were part of a behind-the-scenes effort to reduce the Pennsylvania System's vulnerability to further criticism. Importantly, most of these actions were never acknowledged in Eastern's annual reports and the administrators' other public writings. Indeed, their management decisions at the prison were intensely pragmatic, guided not by a perfect belief in the Pennsylvania System or even penological goals, but by the desire to reduce expenses and prevent insanity – the Pennsylvania System's biggest weaknesses according to its critics. Administrative violations were never enough to betray the entire system; consequently, even when violating the rules or subverting its goals, the administrators could still convince themselves that they were not violating the system. Whatever they called it, the administrators sought to prevent worse manifestations of the calumnious myths so they could continue to claim their system's superiority and protect their own status as benevolent, humane gentlemen running a model prison – a status that kept the Pennsylvania System personally institutionalized at Eastern.

SUBORDINATING PENAL GOALS

Officially, every element of the Pennsylvania System was designed to prevent crime through a disciplinary form of reformation. Prisoners' separation was, at its most basic, intended to prevent cross-contamination among prisoners that might hinder reformation. Additionally, separation allowed for privacy that protected prisoners' identities, so that, after completing their sentences, they would be able to reenter society without stigma or the recognition from a society of criminals. More aspirationally, separation was intended to provide prisoners with time for reflection and, possibly, repentance. Given enough time, they would come to long for a task to perform and thereby become grateful for the work provided as it mitigated the realities of solitary confinement. Moreover, specific work tasks were expected to teach prisoners technical skills in a particular craft, while hard labor itself would instill self-discipline in prisoners; these skills would help prisoners secure regular employment after their incarceration. Primary education would enable prisoners to achieve a greater potential in life and to fully engage society as citizens of the republic. Religious and civic mentorship would likewise shape individual prisoners' personality, and morality, thereby encouraging them to follow a better path. In sum, the Pennsylvania System was intended to enable prisoners to become "honest, industrious, and useful members of society."[6] (Officially, other goals, like economic self-sufficiency, were secondary, as we have seen.) The Pennsylvania System was a complete package and alterations were unnecessary – indeed, Eastern's administrators argued that alterations, would hinder its ability to achieve these goals.

In practice, however, the administrators themselves subordinated penological goals to pursue other goals – most notably, minimizing costs and maximizing profits. This subordination is most apparent in administrators' decisions about what kinds of labor prisoners should be instructed in and how to punish refractory prisoners. In both cases, penal goals were, at best, simply left unmentioned and, at worst, actually subverted.

Labor

Over the years, as we have seen, administrators repeatedly stressed that profitability was secondary to the goal of prisoner reformation and the benefits that would accrue to prisoners by learning a trade. However unprofitable for the prison, such vocational training was essential to the Pennsylvania System. In practice, however, the economic goal that

---

[6] Eastern State Penitentiary, Inspectors' Report, *The First and Second Annual Reports of the Inspectors of the Eastern State Penitentiary of Pennsylvania*. Philadelphia: Thomas Kite, 1831, p. 4.

prisoners should defray the cost of their confinement frequently competed with the penal goal that prisoners should receive beneficial training in a useful trade. Specifically, administrators evaluated trades based on their profitability and related benefits to the prison, rather than their benefit to prisoners' reformation.

Following a visit to Eastern, PSAMPP member William Foulke recounted in his journal administrators' assessments of the various trades. Warden Scattergood and Inspector Vaux had informed him, "That a trial of hinge-making had just been begun; but it was yet to be seen how far it would succeed." "Success" was determined by profitability; indeed, they were also contemplating "harness work" for this reason. However, other factors could interfere: it "might be profitable; but the smithing part would require more than one hand in the shop ..." They did not make it explicit whether the concern about the additional "hand" had more to do with needing to employ two prisoners to a room, in violation of the Pennsylvania System, or the added expense of maintaining a designated overseer with a prisoner doing the smithing. However, they were also discouraged by the prospect of fighting organized labor's growing influence and opposition to prisoner labor in this period.[7] Underlying all of these decisions, however, was the need to offset costs. As Foulke recorded, "Mr. Vaux stated to me that in making business calculations at the prison, the cost of keeping a convict was rated at 19 or 20 cts per day – probably an average of three years would give 20 cts per day[.] This rate was assessed by him in his estimate of the probable advantage of hinge-making."[8] Notably, "advantage" was economically, rather than penologically, defined. The cost-effectiveness of a particular trade – not its utility to prisoners and their ability to desist from crime in the future – was the dominant focus in decisions about introducing new trades within the prison.

Economic goals also outweighed penal goals when determining the tasks assigned to specific prisoners. In the previously discussed conversation with William Foulke, Warden Scattergood had explained to Foulke,

---

[7] For a national account of this phenomenon, see Rebecca M. McLennan, *The Crisis of Imprisonment: Protest, Politics, and the Making of the American Penal State, 1776–1941*. New York: Cambridge University Press, 2008.

[8] Apparently, however, even these assessments were optimistic as the figure of 20 cents was "exclusive of the allowance from the state which would make it about 25 cts per day says Mr. Vaux." William Foulke, *Notebooks Concerning Prisons and Prisoners*, Box 7, William Parker Foulke Papers. American Philosophical Society, Philadelphia, 1846–1852, October 13, 1849, emphasis in the original.

"that <u>one</u> restriction upon the choice of trade was the <u>value of materials</u> which were wasted by learners, especially if unwilling ..." The expense was not worth the benefit of instruction. Another restriction he noted was the prisoners' sentence length: The cost of training prisoners made training inefficient for those serving short sentences, as they were not present long enough to pay back the prison. The administrators also made these complaints in the prison's annual reports, as we have seen; but more than requesting longer sentences, the administrators let economic concerns shape their decisions to not instruct those prisoners who would cause an economic loss for the prison. Foulke explained, "the warden told me that persons received in short sentences (e.g., one year) are set at <u>bobbin winding</u> because of the time being too short to teach them a trade with advantage."[9] Bobbin-winding was a particularly tedious task and was considered to be "unskilled" labor. Prisoners performing this task thus received no training in a useful trade; instead, they effectively performed manual labor for the duration of their sentence in the service of preserving the prison's bottom line.

Punishment

The warden's discretion to punish refractory prisoners was one area of daily practice in which penal goals were apparently most influential. Most centrally, we observe the role of reformation, especially discipline, as measured by subordination to authority and a willingness to perform one's tasks – both were goals of punishing refractory prisoners.[10] However, other goals were also influential in these decisions. Indeed, in many cases of prisoner punishment, isolating the influence of penal goals from economic goals is difficult given the records available. For example, one reason a prisoner could be punished, according to Inspector Bradford, was "destroying their work" or generally refusing to work,[11] a common occurrence throughout the prison's history. Whether punishment was intended

---

[9] Ibid., October 13, 1849, emphasis in the original.

[10] For a discussion of how reformers and administrators' desire to have prisoners submit to authority shaped early punishments, see Michael Meranze, *Laboratories of Virtue: Punishment, Revolution, and Authority in Philadelphia, 1760–1835.* Chapel Hill: University of North Carolina Press, 1996.

[11] Pennsylvania, *Testimony from Legislative Committee to Investigate State Penitentiary for the Eastern District of Pennsylvania,* Partial Transcript. Series II, State Penitentiary for the Eastern District of Pennsylvania Records. American Philosophical Society, Philadelphia, 1835.

more to prevent material loss to the prison or to punish a rule violation is unclear. As labor was integral to the Pennsylvania System, refusing to work was evidence of insubordination and willingness to work was evidence of penal success; but because the prison relied on prisoner labor to defray its costs, insubordination also meant reporting greater economic losses.

Even if penal goals were the ultimate goal of punishment, however, they were not the dominant consideration for how punishment was meted out. Instead, the impact on a prisoner's ability to work (and thus defray the costs of the system) was an important factor in shaping decisions to punish. During his 1835 testimony, Inspector Bradford explained the choice of different punishments available. He testified,

As to the Straight Jacket, I always approved of it as one of the least injurious and most operative modes of punishment we have in use. It produces submission sooner than starvation or short allowance and *it does not affect the health or strength of the prisoner, added to which he does not lose more than a day from his work.* (emphasis added)[12]

While the penal goal could be accomplished either way, it was important to avoid impacting the prisoner's productivity by either reducing his strength or keeping him long from work. Bradford offered other evidence for the straight jacket's positive characteristics. Bradford reported that a prisoner had told him "that he had never met with anything which broke him down so much as the Jacket." The prisoner, Bradford said, compared it favorably to the solitary confinement "on bread and water" he experienced at Walnut Street, which the prisoner told him severely affects the prisoners' strength. Bradford reminded the legislative committee to which he was testifying that the straight jacket "would have produced ... no loss of strength."[13] In these cases, the economic goal of ensuring prisoners' productivity became one of the determinants of punishment.

TACTICAL RULE VIOLATIONS

Decisions about what labor tasks to assign prisoners and how to punish them were discretionary; when administrators based their decisions more on non-penal goals than penal goals, they had not technically violated the Pennsylvania System even if they departed from the beliefs underlying it. However, non-penal goals also motivated deviations from the prison's

[12] Ibid.   [13] Ibid.

formal rules, but in these cases as well, the administrators' motivations were strategic. When Eastern's administrators authorized violations of the Pennsylvania System, they did so to improve the prison's economy and to preserve prisoners' health rather than to achieve penal goals; this is illustrated by two semi-routine practices at Eastern, both of which violated the Pennsylvania System. Perhaps the most surprising of these two practices was their decision to temporarily double-cell selected prisoners. This decision was not an attempt to deal with overcrowding, as occurred during the prison's later years (see Chapter 10); its primary motivation was, in fact, the desire to preserve prisoners' mental health in spite of the possible consequences for penal goals. Their other noteworthy practice was the decision to assign prisoners to labor outside their cells. Throughout the period examined, prisoners were assigned to tasks that took them out of their cells for reasons of cost-effectiveness and to preserve prisoners' health; however, these decisions were also informed by understandings about race and the general uncertainty surrounding carceral punishment at the time. These work assignments also jeopardized penal goals. Prisoners' authorized excursions often enabled various forms of prisoner misconduct and other outcomes that frustrated the penal goal of prisoner reformation. Ultimately, administrators were so driven to protect the Pennsylvania System's visible success at Eastern that they violated its foundational features and most cherished goals.

Double-Celling

The single most important feature of the Pennsylvania System was the separation of prisoners through long-term solitary confinement. As we shall see, the years following the Civil War witnessed overcrowding for the first time in the prison's history, making it necessary to house dozens (and later hundreds) of prisoners two per cell. Eastern's administrators loudly condemned the practice they were forced into, arguing that it was a violation of the Pennsylvania System and jeopardized their ability to reform prisoners. The administrators begged the legislature for relief (see Chapter 10). However, double-celling prisoners was a long-standing practice that began well before overcrowding forced the administrators' hands.

Since the 1840s at least, prison administrators had authorized select prisoners to be housed together. Though a seemingly rare occurrence, mentally ill prisoners were provided with a roommate – another prisoner – with the hope of alleviating any aspect of their mental illness that was caused by their solitary confinement. In 1846, Foulke recorded in his journal parts of his conversation with prisoner No. 2153, "a young man." The prisoner informed Foulke that "he was put in a cell with Daniel or David Heath, an old criminal who was unwell; and 2153 was put in with him to attend him."[14] Several years later, Foulke recorded his conversation with an overseer at Eastern, Mr. Roe, who indicated that this coupling was a fairly routine practice at Eastern. Roe explained to Foulke (in Foulke's words)

that whenever a prisoner's mind becomes a little unsound, another prisoner is selected and put with him for company ... Mr. Roe ... is [in] favour of the association in this way in cases in which the mind is likely to fail.[15]

It is unclear from the records when this practice began or for how long it persisted.[16]

In 1852, the state legislature passed a statute that some of Eastern's administrators interpreted as authorizing this practice. The statute authorized "altering and improving of part of" some of the prison's buildings "for the suitable accommodation of prisoners, whose mental or physical condition requires, in the opinion of the Inspectors, a temporary relaxation of the separate confinement system." The statute further authorized the inspectors to petition to remove prisoners with "such marked insanity as to render their continued confinement in said Penitentiary improper, and their removal to the State Lunatic Hospital necessary to their restoration."[17] Notably, this violation of the Pennsylvania System was expected to be temporary rather than continuous, and it was expected

---

[14] Foulke, *Notebooks Concerning Prisons and Prisoners*, November 15, 1846.

[15] Ibid., November 1, 1851. Reference was also made in the Foulke prison diaries to the same practice occurring at Western State Penitentiary (Ibid., May 29, 1851).

[16] The first reference appears in the 1840s. The records that are available from the 1834–1835 investigation do not discuss the practice. The Meeting Minutes for PSAMPP offer a useful ongoing audit of the system; however, the most relevant minutes were those of the Committee for Eastern State Penitentiary, which are only available starting in 1854. From then until 1862 – which overlaps with the primary period in which Foulke visited the prison – the minutes provide a detailed look at Eastern's behind-the-scenes practices. After 1862 PSAMPP's minutes become much less detailed. The general meeting minutes are also useful, but one crucial volume (1832–1851) is missing. PSAMPP's Acting Committee's meeting minutes are available throughout the whole period; by the late 1850s, however, although their reports of their visits to the prison became more common and systematic, they often focused on summary details, including how many visits they made and how many books they loaned the prisoners.

[17] Pennsylvania, "An Act to provide for the ordinary expenses of government, the repair of the public canals and railroads, and other general and special appropriations," in *Laws of the General Assembly of the State of Pennsylvania*. Harrisburg: Theo. Fenn & Co., 1852, pp. 542–562, p. 551.

to be restricted to a part of the prison such as the medical ward. In reality, the practice had predated this statute and was not restricted to one designated space.

After the statute, double-celling apparently became more common. Indeed, PSAMPP's visiting committee often discovered the practice throughout the 1850s. During one meeting, a volunteer visiting the third cell block, "James J. Barclay reports having visited the prisoners in this Block and saw 16 in their cells – 2 or 3 of the cells have two prisoners in each of them."[18] PSAMPP reported more instances of this practice than occurred in the warden's daily journal for this period: for the most part, routine double-celling went unrecorded, while the wardens typically recorded their efforts to double-cell prisoners who had been particularly violent, which necessitated greater care.

Warden Strickland reported on November 20, 1854, for example, that a young black prisoner, No. 2936, George Henson (or Hinson), was "violent and outrageous in his conduct, shortly after dinner, tearing up his bunk, bed & bedding, and assailing with pieces wood, brick &c whoever appeared at his cell door." Henson had to be removed to the second block (the location of the dark cells) for punishment; Strickland blamed the behavior on "self-abuse" and feared "that he may be a troublesome prisoner." By January, however, it was clear that Henson was mentally ill. Strickland put him "at work, to-day, under the care and instruction of no 2986 a steady and well disposed prisoner, with a view of restoring the mind of the former and discouraging and preventing him from self-abuse." The practice continued for two weeks, during which time "No 2936 had, with an occasional manifestation of debility and unruly spirit, got along at work with No 2986, pretty well." But on January 23, "he exhibited a violent and dangerous disposition, from the time he entered the working cell in the morning, until a short time before he was removed, in the evening, to his lodging cell." Warden Strickland concluded, "I fear there is much trouble and no little danger awaiting us with this man, as he is one of great muscular but little mental power; of strong animal passions, and given to excessive masturbation." The arrangement was apparently called off. After five years and eight months at Eastern – Henson had been convicted of rape and sentenced to eleven years and nine months, a long sentence by the standards of the time – Henson died of "debility

---

[18] PSAMPP, *Committee for Eastern, Minute Books,* Vol. 1–3; Pennsylvania Prison Society Records (Collection 1946), Series I, Vol. 27–29. Historical Society of Pennsylvania, 1854–1885, 5 Mo 31, 1854.

and general prostration" under the watch of Warden Halloway. Halloway reported that "he has been insane for the last 3 or 4 Years."[19] Like many others, Henson was never removed to the State Lunatic Asylum.

Other violent, mentally unstable prisoners were also kept two to a cell, but Henson's experience seems to have inspired caution. A month after Henson's double-celling was called off, Physician Lassiter, "under the direction & approbation of Visiting Inspectors Vaux & Bacon," ordered "the association of No. 2016 and No 2605, both sent here as Insane, with a hope of somewhat improving at least one, 2605. The association is to be but for an hour or so in a day, and keepers to be with them, to prevent violence."[20] Prisoner No. 2605, Benjamin Bender, was sent to Eastern to be held in "close custody. He being a Lunatic."[21] Prisoner No. 2016, John Billman, was a special case, however.

When Billman was first admitted to the prison – more than a decade before his association with Bender – Warden Thompson reported that the sheriff who had delivered the prisoner believed him "to be idiotick"; for his part, Thompson believed Billman's "mind is very weak."[22] Billman was sentenced to two years for horse stealing, but he would remain for much longer. Little more than a year into his confinement, Billman murdered the prison's nurse, James Gaston, and then escaped from his cell. Billman "struck [Gaston] with the board on the side of the head and then across the forehead." Once Gaston was dead, Billman "took off his cloths [sic] and dressed himself in them except the coat which he tore getting off. He then went down to the Gate" and was soon taken back into custody. The Coronor and a grand jury were soon summoned, and witnesses were immediately questioned. Billman "with out hesitation related the particulars of the affair stating that he was sorry he had killed Gaston." Apparently, Billman wanted to go out into the Gallery for exercise and Gaston had said no. Warden Thompson explained to Billman that "there was a sick prisoner walking in the Gallery at the time and that each sick man must have their turn." Billman responded "that if Gaston had told him there was a sick man out, he would not have killed him."[23]

Almost a year later, during most of which time Billman remained at Eastern, the trial jury "pronounced him a Lunatic" and he was

[19] Eastern State Penitentiary, *Warden's Daily Journal*, Volumes 1–2. Eastern State Penitentiary Collection, Record Group 15 (#15.50). Pennsylvania State Archives. 1829–1877. November 20, 1854; January 15, 1855; January 23, 1855; June 19, 1858.
[20] Ibid., February 28, 1855.   [21] Ibid., April 30, 1850.
[22] Ibid., September 13, 1843.   [23] Ibid., November 1, 1844.

returned "to the Eastern State Penitentiary to be kept in close custody at the expense of Philada County, untill [sic] the further order of the Court. I received him as Prisoner 2016 John Billman, Lunatic," Warden Thompson recorded on October 24, 1845.[24] A few weeks after his return, Billman had apparently laid a trap for his overseer. Billman had placed "straw thrust thro' the peep hole." Having noticed the straw, Overseer Merrill, "open[ed] the wicket" when Billman "called his attention to the wetness of his cell, asserting 'that his privy was running over.'" To obtain a better view, Merrill "introduced his head part way thro' the wicket" when he realized that Billman was holding one end of a rope, "made out of his blanket" – "much to [Merrill's] alarm the other part [was] fix'd with a slip knot &c, nicely adjusted around the inside of the wicket, so that upon the introduction of his head, it would have been an easy matter to have noosed him & strangled him without any one knowing it."[25]

A decade later, when Warden Strickland was reviewing Dr. Lassiter's order to pair Billman with Bender, the warden was well aware of Billman's violent past. The memory of Henson's violence still fresh, Strickland personally objected to double-celling Billman with another prisoner. Strickland recorded,

The fact that such an effort has to be made in the Penitentiary, and not in the State Lunatic Asylum, is certainly not very creditable to the latter Institution, or to the State! The movement has my consent but not my approval, because I believe that No 2016 is and will continue to be a most dangerous man, always disposed to take life whereas an opportunity of doing so presents itself, and that whatever benefits may be realized by 2605, could have been as certainly afforded by active exercise, and association with a sane man.

They proceeded nevertheless, and "[t]he experiment to-day passed off quietly and satisfactorily." Several days later, Strickland again reported, "The association of 2016 and 2605 was continued yesterday and to-day, a portion of each afternoon, under the observation of two keepers." The practice continued for at least another several days.[26]

Almost a month later, however, Bender was discharged. Warden Strickland had written to Judge Graham of Perry County who then "revoked" the order for Bender's "safe keeping" at Eastern and a new order was issued to send him to the State Lunatic Asylum. Bender "appeared to be pleased with the change." Billman was less fortunate. Eventually, he was taken "very ill" and finally died "from gradual wearing out of the

[24] Ibid., October 24, 1845.   [25] Ibid., November 10, 1845.
[26] Ibid., February 28, 1855; March 2, 1855; March 5, 1855.

system."[27] He had been at Eastern for most of the preceding fourteen years. Neither would be the last prisoner paired with another to preserve their mental health. Two years after Billman died, an internal report from PSAMPP indicates that the practice still persisted: "In a few cases two prisoners have been together during a short time; on some occasions a very few days. This has been where the depressed state of feeling of a prisoner has given cause to fear its continuance would be permanently injurious."[28]

Occasionally, prisoners were double-celled for reasons beyond mental health. In some cases, double-celling prisoners was economically motivated. During a PSAMPP Acting Committee meeting, the Visiting Committee for Eastern summarized their monthly reports, noting that one member's report

states that in two instances two men were in a cell together. In one case they were both Germans, one of whom could not speak English; and it was said the overseer found it difficult to instruct him in making shoes, and was obliged to place him with one acquainted with the language. The other two were finishing Boots. It was stated that it was so because the duty could be better performed than when separated.[29]

Indeed, labor-related considerations would motivate other violations of the Pennsylvania System.[30]

Out-of-Cell Work

The Pennsylvania System did not simply mean the separation of prisoners from each other. As we have seen, the idea that prisoners would never leave their cell was also integral to the Pennsylvania System – the prison was designed in such a way that the prisoner could work, eat, pray, and

27 Ibid., August 25, 1856; June 9, 1857.
28 PSAMPP, *Acting Committee Minute Books*, Series I, Vol. 2–6, Pennsylvania Prison Society Records (Collection 1946) Series I, Vol. 6–10. Historical Society of Pennsylvania, 1798–1883, July 1, 1859.
29 Ibid., November 4, 1853.
30 This practice apparently also occurred at Moyamensing Prison, Philadelphia's county prison where the local government was trying to impose the Pennsylvania System, often noticeably imperfectly. At one PSMAPP meeting, that prison's visiting committee reported, "Mr. Hacker also stated that at his last visit during the week, some of the cells contained two convicts each, and that an officer in charge of the shoemaking assigned to him as a reason for this duplication of inmates that 'the convicts could instruct one another.' Mr Hacker said that this was not an unusual arrangements; and that in several cases of this kind he had observed a manifest deterioration of the dispositions of the convict after being placed in a cell in company with another." Ibid., May 13, 1851; see also, June 10, 1851, and November 13, 1846.

sleep without ever leaving his cell; when he needed additional exercise, he[31] could enter his attached private yard to breathe fresh air and walk around in the minimal space. However, administrators routinely assigned prisoners to work that took them out of their cells. It was not a common practice that affected most prisoners – only 5–20 percent of prisoners were employed in this manner at any given time – but it was a practice that persisted throughout the Pennsylvania System's reign at Eastern.[32]

This practice began early in the prison's history. In the Legislature's Investigation into official misconduct at the prison, testimony from late 1834 to early 1835 and the official report indicated that several dozen prisoners had been assigned tasks that took them out of their cells.[33] Inspector Thomas Bradford's testimony offers a snapshot of these tasks:

The first prisoner admitted to the Institution was suffered for a time to work in the large yard during the day under the watch of a keeper and at night returned to his sleeping room .... [W]e erected a blacksmith's shop in the South Western side of the Center building in which a convict was kept at work during the day singly and separately from any other prisoners and then returned to his cell at night. Afterwards a convict was employed in the same shop as a cook and treated in like manner. Another was placed in the upper room of the Center Building, at warping and beaming and treated in like manner. Another was employed in the dye house, another at making the fire and breaking the coal, taking care of the house occasionally and splitting wood .... At different periods, convicts have been employed as bakers and cooks and on two occasions one has been taken down to the front to wait on table when the member of the Legislature or Judge dined in the Institution after having come out to pay an official visit to the Penitentiary.[34]

These various employments were all outside prisoners' private cells. Indeed, at least one prisoner, John Gurren, was even set to work "outside of the External Wall" according to Overseer John Coxe.[35]

---

[31] The several female prisoners who entered the prison each year were generally assigned to cells on the second floor of a cellblock and thus did not have access to a yard.

[32] This practice also seems to have occurred at Western State Penitentiary. Foulke notes that at a State Medical Conference in 1851, he heard from that prison's physician, "That the prisoners at the Western Penitentiary generally are confined wholly to their cells, a few get out to sweep the passages and do necessary work about the establishment; but the number of these is very small." Foulke, *Notebooks Concerning Prisons and Prisoners*, May 29, 1851.

[33] Pennsylvania, *Testimony from Legislative Committee to Investigate State Penitentiary for the Eastern District of Pennsylvania*; Pennsylvania, *Report of the Joint Committee of the Legislature of Pennsylvania Relative to the Eastern State Penitentiary at Philadelphia (Mar. 26, 1835)*. Harrisburg: Welsh and Patterson, 1835.

[34] Pennsylvania, *Testimony from Legislative Committee to Investigate State Penitentiary*, January (day not specified), 1835.

[35] Ibid., January 6, 1835.

Sending prisoners to work outside of their cells was not a continuous practice, nor was it widespread. Especially after a few years of operations, the majority of prisoners were employed within their cells, or at least in their yards. Bradford explained,

Since the commencement of the new cell building we have employed several of the convicts at blacksmithing and carpentry, necessary in the erection of the cells and to this end workshops have been erected in the cell yards and assistants have been hired to work with the convicts in the shops. Twenty four convicts are employed in shops connected with their cells, working in the day time in their shops under the supervision of an overseer or an assistant and at night locked up in their cells.

Bradford and other personnel also explained that the practice of out-of-cell work assignments was at least temporarily halted before the 1834–1835 legislative investigation, except in a few cases of prisoners working as blacksmiths. At the time of the investigation, "owing to his great skill as a workman," one of the several prisoners "engaged as blacksmiths in the manner stated ... is still engaged in work connected with the building of new cells, which as your committee understood sometimes required that he should be employed out of his cell."[36] As we have seen (Chapter 3), the investigative committee did not condone the practice of assigning prisoners work outside of their cells. Such assignments violated the principles of separate confinement, the committee stated.[37] The committee suggested that it would tolerate the practice to continue so long as the prison remained under construction, but that the practice should cease thereafter.[38]

However, the practice of assigning prisoners to out-of-cell work was to continue for decades to come. Records for the work performed by 359 prisoners on December 31, 1843, and by 351 prisoners on August 14, 1844 – the two days for which such records exist – indicated that on both days, 4 prisoners were designated as "Runner[s]." Two prisoners were also employed as "Baker" and "Cook," while several were also employed as "blacksmiths," "fireman," and "wood warping" – jobs that would be difficult to carry out within one's cell and were previously performed in other parts of the prison beyond prisoners' cells.[39] There is some

[36] Pennsylvania, *Report of the Joint Committee (Mar. 26, 1835)*, 18.
[37] Ibid., pp. 19–20.   [38] Ibid., p. 22.
[39] Pennsylvania, *Overseer's Roll*. Series I, State Penitentiary for the Eastern District of Pennsylvania Records. American Philosophical Society, 1843; Pennsylvania, *Overseer's Roll*. Series I, State Penitentiary for the Eastern District of Pennsylvania Records. American Philosophical Society, 1844.

evidence that prisoners assigned to work outside of their cells were "trusty" prisoners – prisoners selected for jobs that require a certain amount of trust because of the freedoms entailed. In his journal, Foulke wrote of a prisoner, No. 1814, who also worked beyond his cell: "His keepers told me that he is one of the best in prison – a trustworthy man. [H]e picks oakum and works about the corridors."[40] This characterization appears to be generally the case for other out-of-cell workers. The labor records from 1843 and 1844 list the prisoners' character: those employed as runners were generally prisoners of "Good" or "Very Good" character; only one Runner employed in 1843 was listed as having a "Bad" character, and may have been employed for health reasons – the records did not specify why these prisoners were selected for this work. However, an internal report from PSAMPP noted, "In one or two of the shops, the work requires two persons at times. Care is used to place the most suitable persons, whenever it is requisite it should be so," and character is a likely test of "suitability."[41]

In the 1850s and 1860s as well, some version of out-of-cell work was still ongoing. PSAMPP's Visiting Committee recorded that some prisoners continued to leave their cells for work. For example, in the entry for August 2, 1854, (8 Mo 2, 1854,) Richard Williams, the member assigned to visit the sixth block, reported that "Many of the prisoners, particularly those under his charge, were out of their cells, in the workshops and other places." This entry was not very common. No such report came from the other blocks for that meeting, nor was a similar found for other meetings held in surrounding months. But this was not the last such entry. For example, during the February 1862 meeting, the member charged with visiting the "Third Block and Fourth Block Gallery" met with "40 prisoners in their cells and shops."

Evidence of out-of-cell labor comes from another source in the 1860s. A series of contraband prisoner letters – written by a surprisingly literate female prisoner, Elizabeth Velora Elwell, to her lover, Albert Green Jackson, also incarcerated at Eastern – refers to other out-of-cell work. In one such reference, Elwell wrote, "I am very sory you can not be in the yard eney more."[42] She also refers to having the trust of the overseers and matron and to the lovers' efforts to maintain that trust – and certain privileges with it. Indeed, during the two months during which their

[40] Foulke, *Notebooks Concerning Prisons and Prisoners*, May 24, 1846, p. 85.
[41] PSAMPP, *Acting Committee Minute Books*, July 1, 1859.
[42] Elwell, *Correspondence*, Elwell to Jackson, April 22, 1862.

relationship was documented, Elwell and Jackson were able to rendezvous at various times (as we shall see) in part because of limited supervision during their out-of-cell assignments, again suggesting a certain level of trust placed in those prisoners given such work.

What accounts for such a significant and, as we shall see, consequential violation of the Pennsylvania System? When asked about these practices, administrators explained their decisions primarily in terms of two goals: maintaining a cost-effective prison and maintaining prisoners in good health. Interwoven in these accounts, we also see understandings of race (e.g., the perceived unique health and skills of African-American prisoners) and the role of uncertainty. What was largely (and perhaps surprisingly) absent from these explanations, however, was reference to penal goals (e.g., reformation) – goals that were imperiled by out-of-cell labor's consequences, at least according to beliefs at the time.

Economic goals were a dominant factor in decision making at the prison, including the decision to assign prisoners to tasks outside of their cells. During his testimony, Inspector Bradford explained the decision retrospectively: "[W]e were induced to permit some of the convicts to work out of their cells ... from principles of economy, and in one or two instances from a desire to preserve the health of some who were suffering under the effect of confinement." After further testimony, he clarified the calculus that justified these decisions: "Laborers cost us from 75 [cents] to $1 per day while the average value of convict labor ... was only 25 [cents per day]."[43] In their final report, the investigative committee concluded, "Economy seems to have been the chief motive for this departure from the spirit and letter of the law."[44] Indeed, the investigative committee was somewhat moved by the economic goal. Though disapproving out-of-cell work assignments generally, the committee did, however, leave open the possibility that this practice could continue for a short duration on this basis. "Perhaps it may be expedient owing to the great saving which such employment of the convicts produces to permit it to continue until their work is no longer needed in the building of new cells, but when this takes place, it should be altogether abandoned."[45] Thus, again for economic reasons, deviation from the practice could be allowed to continue until the construction of the new cells was completed, and only for some jobs.

Health goals also motivated administrative decisions, including the authorization of out-of-cell work assignments. Administrators often

---

[43] Pennsylvania, *Testimony from Legislative Committee to Investigate State Penitentiary.*
[44] Pennsylvania, *Report of the Joint Committee (Mar. 26, 1835)*, p. 19.   [45] Ibid., p. 22.

implicitly referred to their belief that prisoners' ability to leave their cells for some period of time would be beneficial to prisoners in poor health. Indeed, health concerns were a motivating factor at least when the administrators began the practice, as the previously mentioned Bradford testimony illustrates. However, these concerns persisted over the years while the practice expanded. On October 24, 1849, Foulke noted that he met with No. 1533, a "Coloured man ... He has been in about 7 years – on a sentence of 10 years. His health becoming impaired he was made a runner in the 6th block, but grew worse." Health was also a reason behind sending prisoners to work in the prison's gardens:

Mr. Scattergood [the current warden] informed me ... that during the last 2 or 3 weeks an average of 20 prisoners per diem had had exercise ... in the space between the cells[.] That 5 or 6 were out at one time, of whom one was of the most infirm invalids under the [illegible] charge of the assistant nurse; and the others worked in the garden patches under the direction of the gardener.[46]

Allowing prisoners to leave their cell for a variety of work assignments was thus motivated in part by health goals as well as economic goals.

Racialized beliefs interacted with these goals of economy and prisoner health. As we have seen (Chapter 5), Eastern's administrators throughout this period believed that African Americans would respond poorly to confinement; this belief further informed decisions based on the organizational goal of preserving prisoner health. In his testimony on out-of-cell work assignments, Inspector Bradford noted, "In one or two instances of coloured prisoners I recommend that they should be put to splitting wood in an open yard for the benefit of health of which the Doctor approved. Solitary confinement affects people of colour more than it does the white."[47] Thus, the need to prevent disease among African-American prisoners, and the belief that they were particularly susceptible to disease within prison, made administrators more willing to assign these prisoners to out-of-cell labor.

Years later, Warden Scattergood, operating on an economic goal, was also influenced by understandings of racial differences to different ends. Foulke summarized a long list of points made by the warden, including

5th that when a prisoner had learned a trade before admission, which is practiced in the prison, he is set at that if possible, for obvious reasons. 6. [sic] That as respects blacksmiths and carpenters, there are not many so engaged at any one

---

[46] Foulke, *Notebooks Concerning Prisons and Prisoners*, October 13, 1849.
[47] Pennsylvania, *Testimony from Legislative Committee to Investigate State Penitentiary*.

time; and those have previously learned those trades; which also accounts for whites being selected for them.[48]

Thus, racialized differences in who was trained in certain trades before prison were exacerbated by other organizational concerns within the prison: Administrators believed that it was wasteful to teach new trades to prisoners serving sentences of one or two years, so many prisoners were set to work at profitable but unskilled labor, as we have seen. The administrators' unwillingness to train new prisoners in more skilled trades (because it was not cost-effective) then reinforced the racial hierarchy by failing to train African Americans in trades that may have been useful to them.[49] Racial goals, combined with economic and health goals, thus structured decisions to assign prisoners to work that took them beyond their cells, as well as what types of work they were (or were not) given.

Underlying all of these decisions was the administrators' general uncertainty, which made these goals more salient. As we have seen in Chapter 3 and Chapter 4, there were multiple sources of uncertainty at Eastern and in the field more generally. The proper interpretation of an ambiguous law and the unknown effects of the new technology informed decision making, particularly in the 1830s when the prison was still new. How safe and how expensive the Pennsylvania System would be was unknown, and administrators felt compelled to build in assurances around these matters. Meanwhile, legal ambiguity and technical uncertainty provided cover for the more questionable efforts toward these ends.

Inspector Bradford summarized these various concerns during his 1835 testimony. He explained to the legislature that out-of-cell work assignments were authorized "under a full and perfect belief that the word and spirit of the law sustained us. I drafted the section which provides that the prisoner shall be kept singly and separately at labor in their cells or work yards and in this Mr. Wood [the warden] fully concurred." He contextualized this decision within the uncertainty we saw in Chapter 4:

The experiment of separate confinement by day and night was about to be made. Good men had doubts. None of us could say how far the mind and body could be in total seclusion from society and confinement to a cell for a length of time.

---

[48] Foulke, *Notebooks Concerning Prisons and Prisoners*, October 13, 1849; emphasis in original.

[49] This stratification in labor tasks based on past skill sets continues in U.S. prisons to this day. Michael Gibson-Light, "The Prison as Market: How Penal Labor Systems Reproduce Inequality." PhD thesis, University of Arizona, 2019.

We knew that the great evil of the old system was the association of convicts by which they encouraged each other in crime and banished reflection from the mind – and that separation from each other would remove the excitement and growth of vice and prepare the mind for reflection on their past conduct.... We therefore did not consider the system infringed although some of the convicts were permitted to work out of their cells, more especially as we were enabled to employ them in a manner which produced a considerable savings to the Institution.[50]

For Bradford, the prisoner health goal was particularly salient in this context of uncertainty and helped to motivate the decision to send prisoners to work outside of their cells, while the economic goal encouraged and reinforced the decision.

The law's ambiguity, however, allowed administrators to offer a justification for the violation and perhaps emboldened their willingness to violate the Pennsylvania System. They could argue that penal goals could still be accomplished because the mere separation of prisoners from each other would (in theory) be retained despite the out-of-cell nature of their work. While this explanation may have satisfied the legislative committee, it was largely a fiction, again reflecting the subordination of penal goals. Repeated evidence that penal goals were jeopardized by this practice did not prevent administrators from continuing the practice. Moreover, the uncertainty about how prisoners would react to separate confinement should have diminished after several decades of practice (and the mass of statistics generated by prison administrators). Yet the practice continued, despite more evidence that the average prisoner was unaffected by the Pennsylvania System, a mandate from the legislature to stop this practice after the ongoing construction ended, and evidence that the practice imperiled penal goals. Instead, they continued the practice in order to shore up their economic and health-related bottom lines – despite its consequences for their penal goals – and thus protect the Pennsylvania System's external image.

CONSEQUENCES

While the administrators violated the Pennsylvania System in order to preserve its external image, these violations had negative consequences

---

[50] He noted elsewhere about the authorization of out-of-cell work, "In so doing the Warden and Inspectors did not conceive that the provisions of the law or the design of the system were violated or defeated." To illustrate this point, he noted, "The orders of the warden were that these men should be kept singly and separately at labor and in no instance to be suffered to converse with a fellow prisoner or even to see them." Pennsylvania, *Testimony from Legislative Committee to Investigate State Penitentiary* (Bradford testimony).

not only for penal outcomes (at least according to contemporary beliefs), but also for internal prison management. In the following text, I examine the unintended consequences of the long-standing practice of assigning prisoners to work outside of their cells. While this practice was limited to only a small population of prisoners in each year, it sometimes had larger unintended consequences. In the following paragraphs, I discuss four consequences of this practice, each of which constituted a further violation of the Pennsylvania System, potentially jeopardizing its penological goals, and (in some cases) potentially damaging the Pennsylvania System's reputation. Out-of-cell labor may have been unusual in its numerous, problematic, and unintended consequences; however, as an extreme example, it brings into focus the ripple effects of administrative behavior that otherwise occur on a smaller scale.

Chance Encounters

Out-of-cell work assignments often created situations in which prisoners had unapproved contact with visitors to the prison, workmen, and other prisoners. Despite Warden Wood's orders, given in the prison's first few years, that "in no instance ... [should prisoners] be suffered to converse with a fellow prisoner or even to see them,"[51] prisoners (perhaps inevitably) did indeed lay eyes on one another. Inspector Bradford mentioned one case in his 1835 testimony to the legislative committee, stating "We had reason to believe from the investigation had before the Inspectors that these orders had not been strictly complied with so far at least as one prisoner for a moment in seeing another and that as to these employed in cooking and baking some evils had taken place."[52] After hearing the testimony of all of their witnesses and closing the investigation, the legislative committee concluded,

Care seems to have been taken in this employment of convicts out of their cells, to keep them entirely separate from each other. This was certainly strictly enjoined by the warden, and if it was in any case departed from, it was the result of accident, not design, or grew out of the nature and manner of the employment of the convicts.[53]

However, additional "accidents" continued to occur.

[51] Ibid.   [52] Ibid.
[53] Pennsylvania, *Report of the Joint Committee of the Legislature* (Mar. 26, 1835), pp. 18–19.

Out-of-cell work assignments also occasionally enabled unauthorized personnel to learn prisoners' identity. The prison's grounds saw near-constant traffic from construction workers repairing or constructing new structures, and these men sometimes laid eyes on the prisoners. In his journal entry on April 5, 1846, Foulke recorded his observation that "No. 1896 (who was to be discharged the next week) was working in the garden between the 5th and 6th blocks. Three cart loads of dirt came in, and the drivers saw the convict, and he joined them in emptying the loads. The gardiner [sic] was present but still the thing was wrong."[54] No additional details about this incident were included in the record, but the smoothness with which the event seems to have taken place perhaps implies the regularity of its (or similar incidents') occurrence.

Rendezvous

Beyond chance encounters, out-of-cell work assignments sometimes enabled prisoner rendezvous. Throughout April and May 1862, Elizabeth Velora Elwell, a prisoner at Eastern, sent about a dozen letters (that we know of) to her fellow prisoner and lover, Albert Green Jackson; only one of his letters survives, and it is unclear how long their relationship lasted beyond the two months documented by their letters. Her letters imply, however, that on at least several occasions the two prisoners had secret rendezvous while outside of their cells.

In Elwell's first surviving letter, she wrote from her "lonesome sell ... to In form you that my heart was very sad after leaving you to Night but hope to see you every day." It is clear from the writing that these were unsanctioned meetings. She noted, "my dear albert there is a time coming when we will not have to run when anyone is coming. But my dear we can be like cats to play hide and seek and run when the dogs come to bark at us."[55] Similarly, in her next available letter, she wrote "Dear Albert, I was glad to see you and get your note ... Oh dear one if we were out we wood not have to creap in the holes to talk one minet. ... I am so fraid they will catch me I all most die."[56] Indeed, these rendezvous appear to be rather frequent. A few days later, she wrote "My dear i am most dead every night When I come up to the old sell and leave you my dear honey.... But you are more and more to me every day that I see you.... [M]ay we see the

54 Foulke, *Notebooks Concerning Prisons and Prisoners*, April 5, 1846.
55 Elwell, *Correspondence*, Elwell to Jackson, April 18, 1862.
56 Ibid., Elwell to Jackson, April 22, 1862.

time my dear that we will Not have to go to the cole seller to talk one word."⁵⁷ Such rendezvous appear to have continued at least into May 1862, the date of the last available letters. These later letters also indicate that other prisoners met out of their cells for their own rendezvous, but the information is too sketchy to provide further detail.

Elwell's letters indicate that some of their rendezvous were enabled by work assignments that took the prisoners out of their cells. For example, Elwell warned Jackson "I will have to clean up stone to morow you not let them hear you speek of me my dear. There is but one thing that you must be careful not to let them catch you standing at the gate for they will mistrust us...."⁵⁸ Sometimes their work assignments were too heavily guarded or cut short. In one letter, she lamented, "My dear love it is with pleasure and love that I answer your not for I am very lonly to night for I had to come up before I had time to talk to you."⁵⁹ Their interactions were thus structured by their work schedule.

That prisoners on work assignment were able to speak to one another indicates some sort of failure on the part of their overseers in charge of supervising their activities, or possibly a complicit role for these guards. However, Elwell's anxiety about being caught indicates that their meetings were indeed clandestine, unaided by complicit guards. Indeed, on one occasion Elwell was caught, apparently with other female prisoners seemingly on their way to meet other prisoners, too. As she explained to Jackson,

i have got the horror to day for juley and cate is all the time hollering to me and mr Samuel deal [an overseer] caught us so i am afridad they will shut me up ... i can tell you who got the worden to have the gate shut up old wright [another overseer] was the one that done all of that good to us he was on the tower and saw you come to the window so he told old peck [the matron] of it and *the worden don't want to shut me up if he can helpe it* dam old deal if I had him by the neck he wood not never tell on eny of the rest of the prisnors and i could kill all of the rest of them so they will not make three horse carts of me if they try if it had not bin for you my dear i wood of told him to put his mark on my door but i said oh you wont do it this time mr deel *he told me if i wanted to keepe my situation i had got I had beter not be caught again* that is all he said to me (emphasis added).⁶⁰

⁵⁷ Ibid., Elwell to Jackson, April 25, 1862.   ⁵⁸ Ibid., Elwell to Jackson, April 18, 1862.
⁵⁹ Ibid., Elwell to Jackson, April 28, 1862.
⁶⁰ Ibid., Elwell to Jackson, May 11, 1862. The listing of officers for that year's Annual Report reveals that Samuel B. Deal was an overseer at the prison, while Abigail Peck was the prison's matron in charge of female prisoners. Eastern State Penitentiary, *Thirty-Fourth Annual Report of the Inspectors of the State Penitentiary for the Eastern*

That several prison employees – Overseers Deal and Wright, as well as Matron Peck – did report the women indicates that at least these employees were not complicit in the arrangement. Moreover, this passage again seems to indicate that Elwell's "situation," possibly referring to an out-of-cell work assignment but certainly a revocable privilege, enabled such meetings.

Intoxication

Out-of-cell work assignments also gave prisoners access to contraband. A few references in the primary source material indicate that prisoners had access to alcohol and became intoxicated while incarcerated. In her correspondence, Elwell asked Jackson "[C]an you tell me where I can get a drop of gin."[61] Presumably, Jackson told her or gave her some alcohol himself because in a later letter she wrote to him, "your liquor done me good to night for when i got up to my sell my head whirld like atope and i throde up all of my dinner and fell some what beter now dear."[62] The record does not indicate where Jackson obtained the liquor.

Another brief story of prisoner intoxication indicates not only the repeated nature of such access, but also one possible source of alcohol within the prison. In his testimony for the legislative investigative committee on January 6, 1836, former overseer John Coxe explained, "I have seen one convict intoxicated. A yellow man who had been taken down to act as a waiter in front. He came up to the Center House slagging round the Center house, did not know where to go."[63] (This may be the "evil" that took place in the kitchen that Inspector Bradford had reported in his previously mentioned testimony before the legislative committee.) As we have seen, prisoner intoxication was not entirely rare, and while it was sometimes enabled by guards, it sometimes resulted from out-of-cell labor assignments. Indeed, as early as 1830, a prisoner was caught using tobacco (an illicit substance in the prison's early decades) and claimed "he found the piece of segar in the entry when he was employed

District of Pennsylvania. Philadelphia: M'Laughlin Brothers, 1863. Although not listed in the annual reports, Warden Halloway noted in his daily log that Henry Wright was a temporary overseer for Seventh Block from June 1858 to June 1862. Eastern State Penitentiary, *Warden's Daily Journal*, June 30, 1862.

[61] Elwell, *Correspondence*, Elwell to Jackson, April 18, 1862.
[62] Ibid., Elwell to Jackson, May 7, 1862.
[63] Pennsylvania, *Testimony from Legislative Committee to Investigate State Penitentiary.*

in cleaning."[64] Whether the cigar was found, pilfered, or provided, the prisoner apparently obtained it while out of his cell.

Escapes

Finally, and most dramatically, out-of-cell work assignments made escape possible. During Inspector Bradford's testimony to the legislative investigative committee in early 1835, he discussed five escapes from the prison that had occurred thus far. One of these "was that of No. 94, who was employed as a baker in the front building and who escaped over the top of that building."[65] Bradford's testimony implied that the prisoners' assignment as a baker put him closer to the exterior of the prison and gave him access to a means by which he could get over the prison's thirty-foot-high walls, enabling his escape. Another prisoner who had been "employed in a shop out of his cell had walked out unobserved among the [construction] workmen."[66] Latitia Hennard, "Prisoner No '209," escaped while she was "employed by the matron to do her house work."[67] Likewise, "prisoner No 2447 an insane man who worked in the ware room" escaped by "secret[ing] himself behind a cart that was passing out and escaped into the Street."[68] Working outside of one's cell made escape much easier.

Any escape from the prison was embarrassing when administrators were obliged to report it or when the public learned of it in other ways. In 1867, Warden Halloway noted privately, "I again have the mortification to record the passage of a prisoner through the front gate at about a quarter before 2 O'Clock to day."[69] Escapes were not common at Eastern – in most years at least one prisoner attempted to escape, but few were successful. Even successful escapees were often returned. Nevertheless, escapes rarely went unnoticed by those watching the prison. So why did administrators tolerate practices that allowed such mortifying events to occur?

Escapes made possible by work assignments were a small fraction of the total number of escapes or escape attempts, the majority of which

---

[64] Eastern State Penitentiary, *Warden's Daily Journal*, January 26, 1830.
[65] Pennsylvania, *Testimony from Legislative Committee to Investigate State Penitentiary*; Warden's Daily Journal, July 22, 1832.
[66] Ibid., May 18, 1833.   [67] Ibid., April 29, 1840.   [68] Ibid., January 10, 1853.
[69] Ibid., February 8, 1867. Using similar language five years later, Warden Townsend reported, "I have the extreme mortification to record" three escapes. Ibid., August 1, 1871.

began in prisoners' cells, often aided by the prison's architecture or prisoners' work tools.[70] Their overall infrequency, relative to the advantage of prisoner labor (much of which functioned smoothly, or at least inconspicuously, enough) may explain why Eastern's administrators continued the practice despite these unintended consequences. But why did the administrators tolerate the violations at all, given their deep commitment to the Pennsylvania System?

ACCOUNTING FOR THE VIOLATIONS

Perhaps what enabled administrators to tolerate these unintended consequences of their violations of the Pennsylvania System was that they did not perceive these practices as violations. In the language of social science, Eastern's administrators suffered from cognitive dissonance: holding conflicting or contradictory beliefs.[71] On the one hand, they championed the Pennsylvania System as perfect and therefore beyond the need for change; on the other, they privately manipulated the Pennsylvania System, subordinating its underlying penal goals and actively violating its most central rules. The administrators reconciled these contradictory stances by simply convincing themselves that double-celling their prisoners or sending prisoners to work around the prison were not violations – according to the administrators, these practices fit within the letter of the law. This rationalization was acceptable as long as no one found out about their behind-the-scenes practices. And as these practices were often temporary and not widely utilized, few people did find out. When someone did find out, however, it forced the administrators to explain the contradiction. One such episode illustrates the depths of administrative cognitive dissonance.

In the mid-1850s, around the same time that Warden Strickland was overseeing the double-celling of Henson, Bender, and Billman to preserve their mental health, an article in the *Philadelphia Sunday Dispatch* emerged discussing this practice and the use of out-of-cell labor. According to Warden Strickland, the article was "doubtless" written by the former Overseer Thomas A. Roe, who had also been Foulke's trusted

---

[70] Ashley T. Rubin, "Resistance as Agency? Incorporating the Structural Determinants of Prisoner Behaviour." *British Journal of Criminology* 57:3 (2017), pp. 644–663.
[71] Leon Felstinger, Henry Riecken, and Stanley Schachter, *When Prophecy Fails*. Minneapolis: University of Minnesota Press, 1956.

source.[72] As Strickland pointed out, he had fired Roe "in June last, because of his unfaithfulness to duty and the discipline of the Prison" and the article was "his special effort to prejudice those who read his essay, against 'the present administration' of the Institution." However, there was more than a grain of truth in Roe's account; but Strickland objected to Roe's characterizations and explanations of these illicit practices. Strickland privately complained, "This assertion that 'men are associated, often, for the purpose of making their labor more profitable', and that he has 'seen six or eight together', are wholly unfounded & false, *in the sense in which his language will be understood by the general reader*" (emphasis added).[73] Again, appearances mattered more than the reality: What Roe described was accurate, but it would be misinterpreted and used to condemn the Pennsylvania System, Strickland complained.

Moreover, according to Strickland, such activities were legally authorized rather than *illegal* violations of the Pennsylvania System:

He appears to have overlooked the fact, or not be aware of it, that the Act of 1852 authorizes "a temporary relaxation of the separate confinement system", in the cases of convicts "whose mental or physical condition require" it, a provision by which I endeavor to conform in all association of prisoners, so far as practicable, within the means allowed me, and with the outside labor necessary to be done, and to be done promptly, at occasional periods of the year. Without designing to reflect, in the least, upon any of my predecessors, I may say, and do say, that the separate system has been as rigidly and faithfully maintained, (and is now maintained,) as it was under any of my predecessors since the introduction of shop and garden labor; and I am perfectly willing that my administration, in this respect, may be subjected to the most searching and thorough investigation.[74]

Thus, for Strickland – as well as the other administrators – they had done nothing wrong: the Pennsylvania System remained intact. Moreover, a "relaxation" of the system was consistent with "rigid and faithful" application.

As it turns out, Roe was not exaggerating (at least, not greatly) about the practices at Eastern. Continuing his tirade, Strickland reported,

If Mr Roe were here to-day, he might see the Gardener with three men in his employ or care, occasionally all together. A few weeks back, he might have seen him with four men. Yet of all the convicts, there was but one of sound mind, and

---

two of them are the Nos 3000 & 3163 mentioned in Mr Roe's article. Should the Gardener and these men pass, as they necessarily must, sometimes, a varnishing shop at the end of 2nd or 3rd block, where two men (one sound & the other unsound) are at work, and perhaps at the time, setting their work out in the air to dry, Mr Roe might say there would be six convicts "together", which would, perhaps, be technically true, and at the same time virtually false, in the sense intended by the language of his article.[75]

Recalling the investigation of 1834–1835, such congregation was a violation not only of the law, but also of the administrators' early (if false) claims that prisoners performing out-of-cell work were still kept separate. But to Strickland and the other administrators, who were continuously manipulating the Pennsylvania System to fit their needs, it was not a violation.

Strickland concluded his remarks by suggesting that "[s]hould anyone be curious on the subject" and visit the prison, "he would find" in the prison's cells more than two hundred male prisoners for whom "the separate system was strictly maintained." Others were at work in the prison's workshops, where the system was also upheld, "except in cases where an unsound man is worked with a sound one; the latter is also the case with the man under the Gardener, as above stated; and both these are clearly within the meaning & spirit of the Act above referred to."[76] None of these combinations were reported elsewhere in the warden's log, suggesting such violations were more common than the record allows. Moreover, Strickland himself appears to have been unaware that these alterations, which began before his own tenure at the prison, were instituted well before the law authorized them and were not restricted to concerns about prisoners' health, as we have seen.

Strickland railed into his journal, but he did not share this intimate look at behind-the-scenes practices with the public. While Eastern's administrators did not believe these practices violated their system, they did not publicly admit to their existence; for example, they were not discussed in the annual reports where they could be used against the Pennsylvania System. The administrators' testimony during the investigation of 1834–1835 was the closest to a public admission of these practices, but the response from the legislature and local and national reformers taught the administrators to keep quiet in the future.

As we will see in more detail in Chapter 9, both the local reformers and state legislators continued to criticize the administrators' implementation

75 Ibid.   76 Ibid.

of the Pennsylvania System, including what they saw as clear violations of the Pennsylvania System. Illustrating the extent of the administrators' cognitive dissonance, when local reformers and state legislators changed their positions and sought to formally enact these and other alterations to the Pennsylvania System, the administrators (who persisted in these practices) publicly opposed their suggestions. In their mind, the Pennsylvania System did not need alterations – and they certainly did not want others to think it needed alterations.

* * *

The reality of the Pennsylvania System diverged sharply from both critics' and supporters' gothic descriptions of it. In practice, the Pennsylvania System was violated frequently and in a variety of ways. Most surprising, Eastern's administrators themselves – who fervently defended the Pennsylvania System as a perfect system that did not need alterations – routinely created large gaps between the Pennsylvania System's theory and practice. They prioritized non-penal goals, such as reducing costs and maximizing profit, at the expense of the penal goal of rehabilitation underlying the Pennsylvania System. They routinely authorized violations of the Pennsylvania System, including sending prisoners to work in different parts of the prison or housing two prisoners within a single cell to preserve prisoner health. Administrators' manipulations of the Pennsylvania System were not common in the sense that they affected many prisoners – perhaps 5–20 percent of the population at any given time was affected by the double-celling and out-of-cell labor practices combined. However, these manipulations were strategic: The administrators manipulated the system along its most vulnerable dimensions to prevent the calumnious myths from manifesting in ways they could not hide – the annual cost of the prison or the annual number of mentally ill prisoners – so they could continue to praise the Pennsylvania System and derive status therefrom. Although they made these calculations consciously, the administrators did not consider these manipulations violations of the Pennsylvania System. Instead, they were able to rationalize these activities to themselves as being consistent with the rules and spirit of the Pennsylvania System, however much local reformers and state legislators disagreed when they found out. As we shall see, strategic manipulations were not the administrators' only blind spot in their efforts to preserve the Pennsylvania System as a source of status.

8

Turning a Blind Eye

Reputation and the Limits of Administrative Commitment

Doctor Darrach, Mr Larcombe, myself, the Officers and Overseers were assembled and addressed by Mr Bradford in an eloquent and impressive speech of upwards of an hour. The Law as relates to ourselves and the Inspectors was read and explained, my election was announced, the imperative duty We were all under, of entertaining the best feeling towards each other, of uniting our efforts to promote the interest and honour of the Institution, of forbearance, tenderness, and firmness in the treatment of the prisoners was strongly impressed upon us. Mr Samuel Wood who was present was congratulated on the imperishable honour he had obtained in being one of the originators of the system and so ably conducting it for the period of eleven Years an Institution which had excited the attention of Philanthropists of all Nations.

Warden George Thompson (1840), Warden's Daily Log[1]

In the earnest hope that the blessings of health may still be continued, and the opening of the New Year may find us all sincerely desireous [sic] of promoting the best interests of the Institution we close our remarks for the year 1845.

Warden Thomas Scattergood (1845), Warden's Daily Log[2]

CONFRONTING THE JANUS FACE OF EASTERN'S ADMINISTRATORS

Christmas Day, 1834, was a "gloomy one" for the warden of Eastern State Penitentiary. On that day, Warden Samuel R. Wood recorded in his

---

[1] Eastern State Penitentiary, *Warden's Daily Journal*, Volumes 1–2. Eastern State Penitentiary Collection, Record Group 15 (#15.50). Pennsylvania State Archives, 1829–1877, July 1, 1840.

[2] Ibid., December 31, 1845.

daily journal, "Never knew what trouble was before."[3] Wood was in the midst of a month-long investigation into his role perpetrating "abuses" at the prison he had helped create and vigorously defended. Three weeks earlier, during his Annual Message to the Assembly, Pennsylvania's Governor George Wolf had announced "the unpleasant information." The allegations were several and wide-ranging: the misappropriation of public funds and prisoner labor, the use of "cruel and unusual punishments," and inappropriate behavior, including "gross immoralities" performed by the prison's administrators and staff.[4] At home in Philadelphia when the governor gave his address, Warden Wood was unaware of its content. He only learned of the governor's message while on his way to Harrisburg to request more funds for the prison. Before leaving for the state capital, the warden had heard rumors, which he then conveyed to Eastern's Board of Inspectors, that some unknown person had made disconcerting allegations to the governor. The inspectors instructed Wood to go to Harrisburg to discuss the matter – and to request more money for the prison "to carry on the manufactory business,"[5] which proved a poorly timed request indeed. Wood's discovery *en route* came as a "great surprise for I had not the slightest idea that the governor would have introduced this matter, whatever it might be in his annual message." Sensing a taste of the shame, embarrassment, and humiliation to come, he "regretted I had left home."[6]

* * *

While Eastern's administrators worked hard to protect the Pennsylvania System both through their public defense and private manipulations, their commitment had its limits. Specifically, their dedication to the Pennsylvania System and the status it provided competed with baser instincts, like interpersonal animosities and financial self-interest. Eastern's administrators were, in effect, Janus-faced: like the Roman god of that name, they presented one face to the world – a face of benevolence and undying commitment to the Pennsylvania System – and another face more privately – a face that was entirely different. This chapter highlights

---

3 Ibid., December 25, 1834.
4 George Wolf, "Annual Message to the Assembly—1834," in *Pennsylvania Archives. Fourth Series. Papers of the Governors, Vol. VI. 1832–1845*, ed. George Edward Reed. Harrisburg: Wm. Stanley Ray, 1901 [1834], pp. 183–213, p. 212.
5 Eastern State Penitentiary, *Warden's Daily Journal*, December 3, 1834
6 Ibid., December 4, 1834.

several extreme cases in which some of the most apparently committed devotees of the Pennsylvania System jeopardized the prison's operations because of their own pettiness. While their self-centered actions put these men in the minority among Eastern's administrators, their behavior was tolerated by their colleagues, who rarely intervened until circumstances became dire – such as when the administrators' private bad actions ran the risk of public embarrassment, which might jeopardize their collective reputation as benevolent gentlemen managing a superior prison.

This chapter thus reconciles the administrators' Janus-face character by arguing that one thing mattered to Eastern's administrators even more than maintaining the Pennsylvania System: maintaining their own reputations. For men whose reputation as benevolent, humanitarian gentlemen was integral to their self-image, acknowledging their own or their colleagues' occasional (if highly problematic) bad acts would be extremely damaging. Both the men who behaved badly and the men who enabled them had to ignore these behaviors or risk shattering the facade they had worked so hard to construct and maintain by retaining and defending the Pennsylvania System.

CONFLICTS

It is important to understand that, while Eastern's administrators presented a unified front to the world, they did not always act as one coherent bloc behind the scenes. Conflicts among the administrators – both between and among the various inspectors, wardens, and physicians – were especially common during the first two decades of the prison's history.

Early Tensions and Exits

During the first few years, turnover among the inspectors was quite high: Of the seven men appointed throughout 1829, only Thomas Bradford stayed for more than six years, dying in office in 1851. By contrast, Inspectors Roberts Vaux and Josiah Randall resigned without serving out their first year (1829); Inspector John Swift resigned after his two-year term, and his colleague Daniel H. Miller died the same year (1831); Inspectors Charles Sydney Coxe and Benjamin W. Richards, who (after Bradford) lasted the longest of those appointed in 1829, resigned early, both in 1835. While there is little information surrounding these early resignations, it seems at least some of them were driven by fissures that would still be driving conflicts up to twenty years later: a combination of discordant personalities and personal animosities that fell first along ideological lines and later along generational lines.[7] These fissures were exacerbated by the ongoing need to translate the theory of managing a prison into practice, thus making the prison's early years particularly tumultuous.

When men joined Eastern's administration, they held differing views about punishment and how the Pennsylvania System should function. While their views would generally converge over time, those men whose views did not converge left the prison. Problems of divergence were most apparent in times of transition, including the first several years at the prison. Just as Pennsylvania had its rival factions in the 1820s when reformers and politicians around the state debated appropriate approaches to confinement, so too did the first generation of Eastern's administrators. The winning faction was somewhat more punitive and inflexible than the others, and they did not tolerate incursions into their autonomy: They preferred to rule with an iron fist, benevolently bestowed, and did not want their choices questioned.

One incident in Eastern's first few years illustrates these tensions. It involved a disagreement over the right amount of punishment for a prisoner, "a coloured man No. 40 who had been a convict in Walnut Street Prison sentenced to the Penitentiary." After entering the prison, "He very soon refused to work. The Warden put him in a dark cell on short allowance. After he had been there for a few days, the Visiting Inspectors [Coxe and Richards], having visited him, were induced by his profession of future obedience to request the Warden to take him out." However, both Warden Wood and another inspector, Thomas Bradford,

---

7 To the extent that it is possible to identify sides, one clear group consisted of Inspectors Bradford (1829–1851), Bacon (1831–1859), Hood (1831–1842), and, to some extent, Bevan (1834–1849). These men also were aligned with Wardens Wood (1829–1840) and Scattergood (1845–1850) and Physicians Bache (1829–1837) and Darrach (1837–1844). With the exception of Scattergood, Bevan, and Darrach, all of these men had been PSAMPP members before 1830 (although Scattergood and Darrach may have been members). On the other side, two generations sparred with Bradford and his friends: Inspectors Coxe (1829–1835) and Richards (1829–1834) and, later, Inspectors Patterson (1835–1847) and (Richard) Vaux (1842–1895). Aligned with Patterson and Vaux were Warden Thompson (1840–1845) and Physician Hartshorne (1843–1844). While Coxe and (Richard) Vaux had been PSAMPP members by 1830, the others were not, although some (including Vaux) had immediate family or relatives as members. These two distinct groups eventually merged to some degree, but tensions remained visible. Beyond alliances apparent in the records, friendships can also be inferred by the frequency with which certain inspectors teamed up to act as visiting inspectors; as cooler feelings developed, one can observe shifts in these groupings.

disagreed with the visiting inspectors, warning them, "in a day or two he will be as bad as ever." But Inspectors Coxe and Richards did not listen. As later recounted by Inspector Bradford,

the man was taken out of the dark cell and put to work. After a few days he became more obstreperous than before, when the same Inspectors, Mr. Coxe and Richards, said to the Warden take him and punish him according to your own judgment. He did so and the result was that he became one of the most obedient prisoners in the house.

Bradford added that the prisoner himself found his punishment to be "the most beneficial thing that had ever occurred to him."[8] Whether or not the prisoner's words were apocryphal, this small example offers a glimpse into how conflict manifested in the early years.

Although this disagreement was not discussed further, it reflects an underlying fissure among some of the administrators. Indeed, Inspectors Coxe and Richards, the two men Bradford had disagreed with, both resigned in 1835. Only Coxe's reasons for leaving were made clear, although his reasons may have also influenced his friend, Richards. In 1833, at least one convict and several guards who had been fired made allegations of wrongdoing against Warden Wood. The board was sufficiently moved by the evidence to pass a resolution stating, "That without intending to indicate the source from which they have flowed, it is the opinion of this board, that abuses have broken in upon the Government of this penitentiary to an extent that is alarming, and which requires a full, fair, and fearless investigation."[9] Inspectors Coxe and Bradford became a two-person committee to investigate.

At some point during their investigation, Coxe and Bradford developed diverging views. Coxe, called Judge Coxe by his associates, had been president of the board since 1830, but in 1834, he resigned his post. He sent a letter to the board on February 1, 1834, stating,

---

[8] Pennsylvania, *Testimony from Legislative Committee to Investigate State Penitentiary for the Eastern District of Pennsylvania*. Partial Transcript. Series II, State Penitentiary for the Eastern District of Pennsylvania Records. American Philosophical Society. 1835 (Bradford testimony).

[9] Eastern State Penitentiary, *Minute Books of the Board of Inspectors and Board of Trustees of the Eastern State Penitentiary*, Volumes 1–4. Eastern State Penitentiary Collection, Record Group 15 (#15.44). Pennsylvania State Archives, 1829–1885, December (unspecified day) 1834.

Satisfied that abuses exist in the Government of the State Penitentiary to an alarming extent, and, that all efforts on my part, during a period of several months, to remove them, have been fruitless, I can no longer allow my name to be used to authenticate the Acts of the Board of Inspectors, nor consent to preside over its deliberations. It will, therefore, be necessary for you to Elect another President; I resign that office.[10]

Inspector Richards stepped in as president *pro tem.* Just a few days before, Warden Wood had recorded in his private log, "The board met yesterday in town and had a stormy time as Judge [Inspector] Coxe was disposed to accuse [Inspectors] Bacon & Hood as being partial oweing to their connexion with me."[11] The disagreements persisted for several months.[12]

In the end, the board cleared Wood. At Inspector Bacon's suggestion, the board passed a resolution stating, "That the charges exhibited against Samuel R. Wood ... do not appear to be substantiated, & that he stands justly acquitted of the immoral and criminal offences alleged against him."[13] Several months later, however, Inspector Richards resigned both his newly appointed position as president and his seat on the board, and Inspector Bradford became president; Inspector Coxe was formally replaced in June the following year.[14] With Coxe and Richards gone, and Bradford president, his friends Bacon and Hood became Treasurer and Secretary, respectively.[15] With this bloc in power, and new, unassuming inspectors in the minority, tensions among the administrators subsided for almost a decade.

Adding a Resident Physician

In the 1840s, new challenges in prison administration arose, creating new debates among the administrators. Underlying these debates was a particular divide among the old guard, or first-generation administrators who had started as PSAMPP reformers and helped bring the Pennsylvania System into existence (Bradford and his friends), and a newer guard, or second-generation administrators who had joined the prison's

---

[10] Ibid., February 1, 1834.
[11] Eastern State Penitentiary, *Warden's Daily Journal*, January 29, 1834.
[12] In April, the warden recorded in his private log that when the board met the previous day, only three men were present, including Coxe who "refused to act as secretary"; with Bacon as treasurer and Richards as president, there was no one else so, unable to fill all positions, the board "failed to organise." Eastern State Penitentiary, *Minute Books of the Board of Inspectors and Board of Trustees*, April 5, 1834.
[13] Ibid., June 7, 1834.   [14] Ibid., August 2, 1834; June 9, 1835.   [15] Ibid., June 9, 1835.

administration several years or more following its establishment and were less connected to PSAMPP.[16] In this case, "old guard" and "new guard" do not refer to how long an administrator had been appointed at Eastern. Indeed, length of service did not perfectly correlate with which side each administrator was on. While inspectors appointed in 1835 or later (Patterson and Vaux) were more clearly new guard, as was the prison's second warden (Thompson), the prison's second physician (Darrach) was part of the old guard. The alliances can instead be understood better as divisions between the men who had helped create the Pennsylvania System (whether or not they were part of its administration in the first decade) and second-generation reformers who had not been involved in creating or establishing it at Eastern (although some of their fathers and other male relations had been).

By the late 1830s and early 1840s, the old guard had to share their administrative duties with the new, and each group had different views over how to manage their prison. In particular, the old guard remained wedded to the original policies implemented in Eastern's early years and, as creators or originators of the Pennsylvania System, they continued to expect deference to their views. By contrast, the new guard, entering the administration without a strong commitment to the way things were done initially, recognized that as the prison population grew and the prison matured, small alterations to existing policies would become necessary.

One such fissure, emerging in the early 1840s, was a debate over the propriety of having a *resident* physician. At issue was whether the prison should require its staff physician to live on the prison's premises. Before this time, the physician lived in town and continued to work in his private practice, making calls at the prison only on certain days or when a rider came to request his presence for an emergency. The distance sometimes caused delay and, occasionally, the physician simply could not (or would not) come. Indeed, by the 1840s, the prison population was somewhat greater than in the early days but also disproportionately more sickly, which necessarily expanded the physician's workload into a full-time job.

The debate over a resident physician arose directly from failings with the prison's second physician, William Darrach (1837–1843). Although

---

[16] Teeters also refers to the middle generation of PSAMPP reformers and Eastern administrators active during the 1840s and 1850s as part of an "Old Guard." Negley K. Teeters, *They Were in Prison: A History of the Pennsylvania Prison Society, 1787–1937.* Philadelphia: The John C. Winston Company, 1937, p. 209.

joining the prison's administration after it was in full swing, Physician Darrach was a member of the old guard; he had even been considered for the prison physician position back in 1829.[17] Upon joining the administration, however, he appears to have treated his position at the prison less like a job and more like a commitment to a social reform society – an obligation, but one that could be repeatedly deferred if other matters proved more pressing.[18] Indeed, Darrach scheduled his formal visits to the prison to coincide with his social calendar: throughout 1837 and 1838, when Darrach attended the prison for his weekly visits, he mostly appeared on the days when reformers (especially the Ladies Committee of the Female Prison Society) also visited the prison.[19]

In the prison's earliest days, Darrach's approach would have been sufficient.[20] However, by the 1840s, his lackluster attendance proved problematic, particularly for the increasing number of the prisoners who needed immediate medical assistance. After "No 629 in attempting to talk [through his cell's skylight] from the top of his loom fell and broke his leg above the ancle [sic]," Warden Wood himself "went into the City" only to discover "Dr. Darrach was out of town." Darrach had failed to follow standard protocol whereby the physician would provide an alternate when he would be unavailable. Instead, Inspector Bradford tracked down the prison's first physician, Dr. Bache, who treated the injury.[21]

Neither Inspector Bradford nor Warden Wood – the most active and long-serving administrators during Eastern's first decade – complained about Darrach's absences from the prison. Their silence appears to have resulted from some combination of friendship and ideology. Darrach, Bradford, and Wood had all been members of PSAMPP and had a long

---

[17] Eastern State Penitentiary, *Minute Books of the Board of Inspectors and the Board of Trustees*, June 3, 1829.

[18] A review of PSAMPP's meeting minutes illustrates this tendency. Given penal reformers' apparent commitment to their work, their repeated absences from the monthly or quarterly meetings is striking. Moreover, some ad hoc committees sometimes had to be "continued" for years on end because they had not done even simple tasks assigned to them.

[19] Eastern State Penitentiary, *Warden's Daily Journal*, e.g., September 11, 1837; January 28, 1839; November 9, 1840; April 26, 1841.

[20] Indeed, the prison's first physician, Franklin Bache, visited occasionally. Inspector Coxe alone had pointed out that "the Physician does not visit each of the prisoners twice a week but only those who are reported to him as sick by Officers." Eastern State Penitentiary, *Minute Books of the Board of Inspectors and the Board of Trustees*, May 4, 1833. Bache responded by letter and nothing more seemed to come of this complaint.

[21] Eastern State Penitentiary, *Warden's Daily Journal*, May 14, 1837.

history together. It was Bradford who had unsuccessfully nominated Darrach to be the prison's first physician.[22] When Darrach did not accompany the Ladies Committee on their visits to the prison, he joined Bradford at the prison.[23] When Darrach's wife passed away, Bradford missed his usual trip to the prison, presumably to attend to Darrach.[24]

Besides their friendship with the delinquent physician, Wood and Bradford may not have believed more dedication was necessary. Their experience at the prison during its earliest years – when the number of prisoners was manageable and weekly visits were sufficient – was formative. It left a lasting impact on their approach to and expectations for prison management. After more than a decade out of office, Warden Wood expressed his opposition to the idea of a resident physician when asked by penal reformer William Foulke, who had joined PSAMPP after Wood and Bradford's time. Foulke recorded that Wood "could not see any necessity for the medical officer to reside in the prison; and moreover he was of opinion that it must be productive of inconvenience to the administration." Wood's opinion was quite strong: "He added that he would not submit to it, if he were warden."[25] Regardless of the reason, Darrach's absences from the prison went uncommented upon until George Thompson, a member of the new guard, became the prison's second warden in 1840.

Early in Thompson's wardenship, the necessity of a resident physician became clear. Little more than a year into his tenure, Thompson had to call for a prisoner with medical knowledge to attend to a prisoner who had "been afflicted with fits." The latter was "taken very ill" and "the urgency of the case did not allow time to send for the visiting physician."[26] By this time, the prison's population was larger and incoming prisoners were more sickly than previously. Just as the physician's presence became

---

[22] Eastern State Penitentiary, *Minute Books of the Board of Inspectors and the Board of Trustees*, June 3, 1829.

[23] Eastern State Penitentiary, *Warden's Daily Journal*, e.g., July 10, 1839, January 1, 1840, March 21, 1841.

[24] Ibid., July 18, 1841. Bradford and Wood were also closely allied. When Wood retired as Warden, "Mr Bradford ... [gave] an eloquent and impressive speech of upwards of an hour." Ibid., July 1, 1841. No other warden received such serenading.

[25] William Foulke, *Notebooks Concerning Prisons and Prisoners*, Box 7, William Parker Foulke Papers. American Philosophical Society, Philadelphia, 1846–1852, October 15, 1849.

[26] Eastern State Penitentiary, *Warden's Daily Journal*, July 24, 1841.

increasingly necessary, Darrach appears to have extended his absences, attending the prison less frequently.

Darrach's distance from the prison, delays in arrival, and other absences proved deadly. In early 1842, a prisoner died while waiting for Darrach to arrive at the prison.[27] The following week, a prisoner attempted suicide and was revived by a physician who happened to be visiting the prison; the warden sent for Darrach, who arrived two hours after the messenger was dispatched – as the warden was careful to record.[28]

Unlike Warden Wood, Thompson was noticeably dissatisfied with Darrach. After Thompson had "[s]ent for Doctor Darrach to visit the Sick," which he did not, Thompson noted that "many of the sick" were in "a state of much suffering."[29] In another case, Thompson noted that Darrach had visited the prison, but "the greatest portion of the sick were not visited."[30] A few days later, Thompson reported that Darrach had come to the prison but "refused" to visit the sick prisoners and "left without seeing them."[31] Their interactions continued to deteriorate.[32]

While Thompson's patience with Darrach was wearing thin, the Board of Inspectors began the process of authorizing a resident physician. They had initially broached the topic in 1841, passing a resolution to hire a resident physician, but "owing to peculiar circumstances" they had never acted on it.[33] The inspectors eventually admitted that their inaction stemmed from "a sincere respect for the feelings of the President [of the board, Inspector Bradford] to whom the attending Physician [Darrach] was so closely allied."[34] However, "Prolonged experience seemed to demand that a change in the administration of the Medical

---

[27] Ibid., February 1, 1842.   [28] Ibid., February 10, 1842.

[29] Ibid., March 14, 1843.   [30] Ibid., March 19, 1843.   [31] Ibid., March 23, 1843.

[32] After reviewing the Doctor's Journal, Thompson found "a notice of his visit of that time containing a given falsehood evidently designedly put upon record to convey false impression the remainder of the notice has the appearance of being the production of a disordered mind. Shall call upon witnesses and require a hearing of them and examination into the case by the Inspectors." Ibid., March 23, 1843. Thompson reported the passage to Inspector Bevan (a friend of Bradford), who "called upon [Darrach] and he had determined to erase said entry as it was made under excitement and wrong impressions. This being satisfactory no further action on the matter is necessary." Ibid., March 27, 1843.

[33] Eastern State Penitentiary, *Minute Books of the Board of Inspectors and Board of Trustees*, May 1, 1841, January 28, 1843.

[34] Ibid., February 2, 1844.

department should be made and it was accordingly made."[35] But change proceeded slowly.

When the board returned to the issue in early 1843, the inspectors disagreed about the necessity of a resident physician and especially what his duties would be – whether he would replace the "Physician" required by law or whether the two would work in tandem, the resident physician available for emergencies and the regular physician for the duties required by law, including weekly visits. The disagreements initially fell along generational lines: Inspector Vaux, the newest member of the board (appointed in 1842), pushed for replacing the physician with a resident physician; Inspectors Bradford (appointed in 1829) and Bacon (appointed in 1831) opposed this effort. Inspectors Bevan and Patterson (appointed in 1834 and 1835, respectively) were divided at first – Patterson initially allied himself with Vaux and Bevan with Bradford – but both eventually sided with Vaux and were later joined by Bacon; Bradford remained the lone holdout.

After postponing the vote for a resident physician several times, the inspectors finally elected Dr. Edward Hartshorne, who had been endorsed by several "eminent and distinguished physicians."[36] However, they did not eject Darrach from his post. Despite the recent economic downturn and the need to cut costs at the prison, the inspectors determined to support two physicians. This solution immediately proved problematic: Hartshorne was officially an adjunct to the regular physician, rather than someone hired according to statutory obligation and, as such, his responsibilities were unclear. In one meeting, Inspector Vaux offered a resolution to give the resident physician all "the duties enjoined by Law on the physician of this Institution," but Bradford, Bacon, and Bevan rejected this resolution. Vaux then offered a simpler resolution that would "require the Physician of this Penitentiary, to discharge all and each of those duties enjoined on said Physician, by the laws applicable to and regulating the said Officer." In turn, Bradford called for a vote to postpone voting on Vaux's resolution, which the remaining triad approved.[37]

Inspector Bradford then became ill for several months, giving Vaux and Patterson the opportunity to bypass his objections. Thus, a few days after electing Hartshorne the Resident Physician, the board held a meeting without Bradford (and Bacon, who was also ill). Taking advantage

35 Ibid., February 2, 1844.   36 Ibid., February 4 and 7, 1843.
37 Ibid., February 8, 1843.

of their two-to-one majority, Vaux and Patterson passed a resolution designating Physician Darrach the "Consulting Physician."[38] The following month, with Bradford still absent, the four inspectors present had "a long and serious deliberation" about the rules governing the resident and consulting physicians. At this point, the inspectors openly recognized that Bradford had not been objective in his previous opposition to change. Accordingly, they unanimously adopted a resolution introduced by Vaux that essentially gave the physician's standard duties listed in the statute, with some further specifications, to the resident physician. The consulting physician's only responsibility was to be available for consultation – and he was "required to attend at the Prison on receiving ... written Notice from either the Warden or Resident Physician or any of the Inspectors."[39] They had effectively downgraded Darrach's (the Consulting Physician's) role while still making him answerable to the other administrators.

When Bradford returned a few months later, he was seething. After serving as one of two visiting inspectors for June and July 1843, he wrote a "report" on the functioning of the prison during that period. In this report, he charged the inspectors with impropriety and denigrated the changes made to the prison's "medical department," among other changes enacted by Warden Thompson (to which we shall return shortly). Bradford's report was not addressed until February the following year by a committee composed of Vaux and Bacon, Bradford's good friend. The report defended the board's actions and lauded the benefits their changes had induced, including a reduced rate of disease and mortality. As they explained,

The Committee regret that the report of Mr Bradford contains remarks that would imply strong censure on his follow members, and they would feign [sic] hope that upon a review of it & a careful examination of its contents, he will see its bearing and be made sensible that his expressions were hastily indulged, and without a proper estimate for the feelings of those who differ so widely from him in their opinions upon this important subject.[40]

At the end of the month, when it was time for their semi-annual elections, the inspectors did not re-elect Bradford to his position as president of the board. The board also declined without comment to re-elect Darrach to any position at the prison.[41]

---

[38] Ibid., March 7, 1843.   [39] Ibid., April 1, 1843.
[40] Ibid., February 2, 1844.   [41] Ibid., February 28, 1844.

The drama was not yet over. A few months later, Dr. Hartshorne resigned his position at the prison because of continued harassment from Inspector Bradford. The inspectors felt compelled to recognize Hartshorne's "Medical skill, fidelity, and close attention" to the prisoners, noting that "the Inspectors have every reason to be satisfied" with his work. They attributed to him (and "divine providence") the "great reduction in the number on the sick list, with the present improved health of the prisoners as compared with their health under the former system." Finally, without mentioning Bradford by name, they noted, "we regret the necessity that causes him to withdraw from a station that he has filled with great credit to himself and advantage to the State." In response to this resolution, Bradford "demanded" a vote on the resolution, which passed four to one; Bradford was the sole "Nay" vote.[42]

As this episode illustrates, by the mid-1840s, ideological and generational divisions had mostly subsided as necessities required policy changes. Inspectors Bacon and Bevan, though members of the old guard, recognized the need for change and had come around to join their newer colleagues in changing the way things were done at the prison. Only Inspector Bradford objected. Thus, earlier divisions had deteriorated into problems of discordant personalities, or rather of one in particular.

The Personality Conflict between Inspector Bradford and Warden Thompson

The prison's physician was not the only casualty of Bradford's reticent personality in this period. For reasons that are not apparent in the record, Bradford did not get along with Warden George Thompson. Bradford's behavior toward Thompson may have been retaliation for the warden's role in Physician Darrach's dismissal. Indeed, there was no record of their discord until after Darrach's position at the prison had been jeopardized. In the summer of 1843 – when the inspectors made their end run around Bradford to demote Darrach – the relationship between Thompson and Bradford soured.

The precipitating incident that certainly turned Thompson against Bradford occurred in July 1843, when Bradford was acting as one of the visiting inspectors. One morning, an overseer reported that a prisoner "had prepared a spear for the purpose of piercing the eye of the

---

[42] Ibid., May 7, 1844.

Watchman."[43] Bradford was present as the visiting inspector; as such, the warden asked for instructions on how to proceed. According to Bradford, "the Warden 'under a high excitement of temper at the time, addressed me in a very rough and impolite manner saying, Here is a negro who has a spear with which he threatens &c &c; what shall I do with him?"[44] Ultimately, Bradford "ordered [Thompson] to have the man removed from his cell and punished,"[45] but Bradford wished to speak to the man first.[46] During the "interview," Bradford told the prisoner that "he must submit to punishment."[47] When it was time to remove the prisoner, Thompson undertook the responsibility himself, fearing the prisoner, now knowing punishment was forthcoming, would resist and injure his men. Sure enough, Thompson "received a blow from the prisoner which broke one of his fingers and otherwise injured the hand."[48] Later, Thompson "declared very confidently, that if he had been allowed simply to carry into effect the order for punishment, without any interview between Mr Bradford and the prisoner, ... that he could have done it very readily, and without the peril of life & limb which ensued."[49] Whatever their relationship had been before this, it deteriorated quickly thereafter.

In Bradford's report for June and July – the angry report he wrote, upon returning to duty after his long absence from the board's monthly meetings, offering a scathing attack on the changes to the medical department – he charged Warden Thompson with disregarding instructions from the inspectors regarding the erection of a greenhouse. In particular, Bradford objected to "the extravagant expenditure of money ... and the construction of a useless & expensive pond in front of it."[50] He also implied that Thompson had embezzled, demanding an inquiry into "whether any exchanges of Iron belonging to the Institution have been made for materials for the erection of the Green House or for other purposes, and whether the same have been regularly entered on the Books of the Institution."[51] (As we shall see, Bradford had previously defended

---

43 Eastern State Penitentiary, *Warden's Daily Journal*, July 7, 1843.
44 Eastern State Penitentiary, *Minute Books of the Board of Inspectors and Board of Trustees*, February 2, 1844.
45 Eastern State Penitentiary, *Warden's Daily Journal*, July 7, 1843.
46 Eastern State Penitentiary, *Minute Books of the Board of Inspectors and Board of Trustees*.
47 Ibid., February 2, 1844.
48 Eastern State Penitentiary, *Warden's Daily Journal*, July 7, 1843.
49 Eastern State Penitentiary, *Minute Books of the Board of Inspectors and Board of Trustees*.
50 Ibid., February 2, 1844.   51 Ibid., October 7, 1843.

Warden Wood against a very similar claim of which Wood was cleared but likely guilty.) Bradford further condemned several alterations in the prison's management Thompson had conducted "without any authority from the Board."[52]

The board formed a two-person committee to address Bradford's accusations. The committee – consisting of Inspectors Bevan and Bacon, Bradford's sometime-allies on the board – patiently explained that while the initial order had been to build the greenhouse without exceeding $300 on its construction, conditions had changed, necessitating the greater expense. The initial estimate was based on the expectation that Inspector Patterson "would furnish the glass for the Sashes on certain conditions, which upon after [sic] consideration it was thought best to decline." The expense increased when they had to find another supplier. When Thompson used some "old iron" to purchase the materials, "the Committee found regular entries made of it in a memorandum book showing the weight, as well as the date of its delivery when parted with," suggesting he did not misappropriate it. Further, the warden was not only authorized to build a pond, but he "paid the cost of this pond out of his own funds." The committee determined that the pond was "not only ornamental but altogether necessary and useful"; therefore, "such cost ought to be refunded to him." Finally, the committee determined that "the alterations and experiments made by the Warden ... were made in good faith, and with the best reference to economy." They defended other changes as well. Changes Warden Thompson made to the laundry department produced "an immense saving of time, labor and inconvenience, in the washing & drying the Clothing, bed liner &c has taken place, well worthy the favorable notice of the Board." Further, some of the changes "may not have been authorised in a formal manner, but generally they had the sanction of one or more Members of the Board, and hence the Committee think he is not so obnoxious to censure, as the [Bradford] report would seem to imply."[53]

After addressing Bradford's concerns, the committee took the unprecedented step of addressing the "antagonistical views" between Bradford and Thompson that "have unfortunately too long existed." The committee noted,

It is no secret to the Members of the Board and it is also known out of our immediate circle, that an unfortunate and injurious disagreement, accompanied

---

[52] Ibid., February 2, 1844.   [53] Ibid., February 2, 1844.

at times with highly excited feelings and strong and uncourteous language has for some time past existed and still continues to exist between the President of the Board and the Warden.

Passing over the cause for their disagreement, and demanding its resolution, the committee offered one of the most insightful discussions of how the administrators perceived their role at the prison:

We are all engaged in a common cause, a cause of benevolence and of charity. In carrying out the principles of this work of benevolence and humanity, we ought to be bound together as brethren, as Christians acting in a holy and religious cause doing unto one another as we would be done by, and if a brother offend, forgive him, once, nay seven times.

Our Penitentiary is viewed by the world at large as a model can [sic] that model be considered a fit one to copy from, if unhappily its principles be injured, or become at all defective by discordant differences having an injurious tendency, and which, if persisted in will result in mischievous & ruinous consequences.

Let us, therefore, one and all forget every thing that has pass'd bury in the deepest recesses of oblivion, every unkind sentiment and excited feeling, and if in thought or deed we have given cause of offence to a brother, whatever his station may be, let the hand of reconciliation be proffered and accepted, for this no more than a christian duty, we may then press onward with unity and alacrity in extending the principles and merits of the noble cause of the reformation of the imprisoned Convict.

In closing, the committee suggested that Bradford withdraw his report and "all proceedings in relation be expunged from the Minutes."[54] (Thankfully, record of this disagreement remained in the inspectors' minutes books.)

Although the inspectors removed Bradford from his position as president of the board, and despite their request for peace, it appears that Bradford's relationship with Thompson did not improve. When it came time to (re-)elect the warden (every six months), Bradford routinely voted against Thompson.[55] By September of 1845 – a year and a half after Bradford had been told to cease his feud – Thompson resigned his position as warden, citing "Circumstances which are paramount to all other

---

54 Ibid., February 2, 1844.
55 Ballots were anonymous in the records, but of the four elections after this incident, the only two yielding unanimous support for Thompson were meetings of the board from which Bradford was absent (February 28, 1844, and August 28, 1844). The other two yielded one vote for Thomas Scattergood, another friend of Bradford's (January 3, 1845, and September 5, 1845). See Ibid. In later months, the board noted, "it is believed that Thomas Bradford Esq voted on said occasions for Thomas Scattergood for Warden." Ibid., September 9, 1845.

considerations (to wit, the well being of the Institution)." In a pointed reference to Bradford, Thompson acknowledged "the support and invaluable advice of *four fifths* of the members of the Board[.] I return to them my sincere thanks and with the greatest respect" (emphasis added). At Vaux's suggestion, the board passed a resolution stating,

> That whilst this Board believes that this Institution has thus been deprived of the services & abilities of a chief Executive Officer, by reason of unfriendly relations and a spirit of animosity long existing towards Mr Thompson on the part of one of the members of this Board; it is called upon now by a sense of justice to Mr Thompson to record as the conviction of the members of this Board of Inspectors of the E.S. Penitentiary their full and entire confidence in the integrity, humanity, & fidelity & ability with which George Thompson has always discharged all his duties as Warden of this Penitentiary.

Bradford voted against this statement and the resolution to which it was attached – sending a copy of the board's statement to Thompson.[56]

By all accounts, Bradford had been in the wrong. It was later reported that when Thompson resigned, he believed "Mr. Bradford would be left out of the Board" in the future.[57] After all, Bradford, Thompson believed, was "the chief obstacle in the way of reform," and his resistance to various changes made in the early 1840s apparently confirms Thompson's belief.[58] However, Bradford would remain on the board until his death in 1851. Indeed, after the board had insulted Bradford by explicitly acknowledging his role in Thompson's departure, they offered a conciliatory gesture by electing Bradford's choice of warden, Thomas Scattergood, another member of PSAMPP and one of Bradford's friends.[59] Even still, Bradford continued to be a thorn in many administrators' sides. While other old-guard inspectors had finally recognized the need for change, Bradford objected to almost every resolution and election, routinely voting "nay" to any vote that had the majority's support for years, beginning in the late 1830s and continuing throughout his tenure.[60]

---

56 Ibid., September 9, 1845.
57 Foulke, *Notebooks Concerning Prisons and Prisoners*, October 24, 1849.
58 Ibid., October 24, 1849.
59 Eastern State Penitentiary, *Minute Books of the Board of Inspectors and Board of Trustees.*
60 Despite his ongoing minority voting, Bradford's relationships eventually improved in the few years before his death. In those years in particular, Bradford appeared to be on better terms with Inspector Vaux. Indeed, writing several decades later, Vaux described Bradford as "one of the early champions of the separate system" and "one of the

Bradford's behavior aside, tensions generally continued to subside, from the 1840s onward, as the first-generation administrators were increasingly replaced with second- and even third-generation administrators, especially those men who had not first been members of PSAMPP. As the prison was increasingly stripped of the old guard, and the uncertainty of translating the theory of the Pennsylvania System into practice diminished over time, the second half of Eastern's history was, internally at least, somewhat more stable than the first. But for its first two decades, divisions along ideological and generational lines complicated the business of managing Eastern, demonstrated most clearly when Bradford's intransigence made retaining administrators quite difficult.

BAD ACTORS

Bradford's intransigence – and his willingness to frustrate the prison's administration for personal vendettas despite his intense, and apparently genuine, commitment to the Pennsylvania System – indicates a recurring theme of Eastern's private history. Remarkably, some of the staunchest supporters of the Pennsylvania System, both in public and private, were also some of the the most self-interested men who degraded the system for personal gain and other private motivations, jeopardizing the system they otherwise sought to protect. No administrators more embodied this contradiction than Wardens Samuel Wood (1829–1841) and Thomas Scattergood (1845–1850).

Investigating Warden Wood

Warden Samuel Wood, the "great apostle" of penal reform and Eastern's first warden, was a Quaker, a member of PSAMPP prior to his appointment, and a vociferous supporter of the Pennsylvania System. Nearly twenty years after he resigned his position at the prison, Wood still defended and endorsed the Pennsylvania System to interested parties. Foulke recorded a conversation with the former warden in the late 1840s. Wood repeated the system's peculiar advantage: "by individualizing the prisoners, it enabled the observer to detect slight indications which

most devoted friends of the Pennsylvania system." Richard Vaux, *Brief Sketch of the Origin and History of the State Penitentiary for the Eastern District of Pennsylvania at Philadelphia*. Philadelphia: McLaughlin Brothers, Printers, 1872, p. 83. Of course, Vaux left out any mention of the disputes Bradford had instigated behind the scenes.

would escape the notice of observers in prisons where the men are grouped." Moreover, Wood continued to defend the Pennsylvania System against accusations that it was harmful to the prisoners' health, noting, "there were only two prisoners for whose state of health he could not account independently of the discipline" during his more than ten years as warden.[61] Although an apparent true believer, Warden Wood also jeopardized, in several ways, the prison he helped establish.

Despite his sterling reputation, in the winter of 1834–1835, Warden Wood was suddenly embroiled in an unsavory investigation into his character and conduct as warden. The earlier investigation by the Board of Inspectors into "abuses" at the prison – the investigation whose outcome prompted Inspectors Coxe and Richards to resign their positions – had cleared him. Nevertheless, someone (possibly Judge Coxe, who appeared most perturbed and least convinced by the investigation's conclusion) had reported the allegations to state officials. The allegations were made public for the first time in the Governor's annual address. Not two weeks later, the legislature traveled to Philadelphia and held an investigation between December 16, 1834, and January 22, 1835. More than sixty witnesses were called.[62] Attorney General George M. Dallas examined the witnesses, asking about details of the prison's operations, the character and demeanor of the Warden and other administrators, and specific facts surrounding certain events. Witnesses hailed from very different walks of life, including a veritable list of Philadelphia's Who's Who in penal reform, former employees of the prison, and those who had done business with the prison (e.g., buying goods made by the prisoners or selling raw materials, building materials, and food to the prison). In the course of the month-long investigation, the Warden's laudable reputation was both challenged and reaffirmed.

The investigation centered on five charges, but three were particularly scandalous: torture, embezzlement, and sexual intrigue.[63] Most famously,

---

[61] Foulke, *Notebooks Concerning Prisons and Prisoners*, October 15, 1849.

[62] Pennsylvania, *Report of the Joint Committee of the Legislature of Pennsylvania Relative to the Eastern State Penitentiary at Philadelphia (Mar. 26, 1835)*. Harrisburg: Welsh and Patterson, 1835, p. 7.

[63] Allegations of financial impropriety and torture were not uncommon in nineteenth-century prisons, even those prisons managed by men and some women known for their zeal for progressive reform. Reformers-turned-administrators around the country were, like their counterparts at Eastern, known for their benevolence – their eloquent accounts of and support for their progressive facilities won them tremendous praise. Nicole Rafter, *Partial Justice: Women in State Prisons, 1800–1935*. Boston: Northeastern University Press, 1985; Alexander Pisciotta, *Benevolent Repression: Social Control and the American Reformatory-Prison Movement*. New York University Press, 1994.

the investigation examined the conditions surrounding the punishment of two prisoners and whether these punishments constituted "cruel and unusual punishment."[64] Seneca Plumly or Plimly, a refractory prisoner, had been punished through the "water bath" (or "cold ducking") – pouring buckets of water repeatedly over his head. Many commentators considered this punishment somewhat distasteful when they heard about it. More problematic, Seneca was punished this way in the middle of a Philadelphia winter; the buckets were full of "extreme cold water … [and] partly froze on his head and person."[65] Seneca became "insane," soon after his water bath and was subsequently discharged, "having been pardoned, [while the administrators] procured on an order … to admit him in the almshouse."[66]

Another prisoner, Matthias Maccumsey, was subjected to the "iron gag," an iron bit inserted into his mouth connected to hand restraints. One could speak while wearing the gag,[67] but the device made movement difficult. However, Maccumsey, who had been gagged at least "20 or 30 times" was known for his ability to somehow remove the gag, necessitating a tighter application.[68] Maccumsey died during his punishment with the gag.

That the men had suffered severely from these punishments was significant enough, but the very fact of their usage itself was abominable to penal commentators. Both of these punishments were used therapeutically for mentally ill patients of the Pennsylvania Hospital, as well as punitively in the military for refractory soldiers and at Walnut Street Jail, but this practice was not common knowledge. Instead, these punishments were fairly shocking to the public and were considered unbecoming for a prison – particularly in this context where prisons were believed to be more humane than the corporal punishments of old. As we have seen, one of Eastern's many claims to superiority was the absence of whipping, on which so many other prisons relied. That Eastern's administrators resorted to physical punishments beyond shortening food rations or

[64] For another account of these punishments, see Michael Meranze, *Laboratories of Virtue: Punishment, Revolution, and Authority in Philadelphia, 1760–1835*. Chapel Hill: University of North Carolina Press, 1996.
[65] Eastern State Pennsylvania, *Testimony from Legislative Committee to Investigate State Penitentiary*, p. 12.
[66] Eastern State Penitentiary, *Warden's Daily Journal*, February 10, 1832.
[67] Thomas B. McElwee, *A Concise History of the Eastern Penitentiary of Pennsylvania together with a Detailed Statement of Proceedings of the Committee Appointed by the Legislature (Vol. 2)*. Philadelphia: Neall & Massey, 1835, p. 26 (Baen testimony).
[68] Ibid., pp. 26–27.

placing a prisoner in a "dark cell" was considerably embarrassing in light of their own criticism of corporal punishments elsewhere. These punishments did not comport with the image of Eastern – that of a humane prison – that its supporters, both reformers and prison administrators alike, had carefully constructed.

Ultimately, however, the investigation did not sustain the charges that the administrators had improperly tortured their prisoners. Although some commentators argued that Seneca's insanity and Maccumsey's death were direct consequences of these punishments, the investigative committee found that these punishments were applied without ill intent. At most, it described these punishments as "indiscreet" and "only to be condemned on account of the indiscretion of using it at a time when the weather was so cold."[69]

Another set of charges were particularly personal. The warden, Samuel Wood; the clerk, John Halloway; an overseer, Richard Blundin (or Blunden); and his wife, Mrs. Blundin, were accused of various forms of inappropriate behavior. The more mild accusations involved stories of drunkenness and parties. Witnesses repeatedly reported observing Mrs. Blundin intoxicated, sometimes hosting parties at her residence inside the prison. At one party, it came out, a prisoner waited table and was subsequently found drunk. These "entertainments," held "with the knowledge and connivance of the warden" were deemed "subversive" of the prison's "order, regularity, and security."[70] The more severe accusations involved charges of "licentious and immoral" behavior "attested by indecent conversations, gross personal familiarities, sexual intercourse, and the existence of a filthy disease [i.e., a sexually transmitted disease]."[71] The investigative committee's official report only included certain details, leaving out the most lurid details, to avoid tarnishing Warden Wood's reputation or publishing immoral material. The testimonies, however, were filled with salacious and prurient information.

Witnesses reported that Mrs. Blundin was were overly familiar with Warden Wood and Mr. Halloway. Former overseer Issac Coxe testified that he had constantly seen Mrs. Blundin in Wood's private quarters. At another time, during a presumed lovers' quarrel, she yelled at Wood, "[kiss] my arse you damned old Quaker son of a bitch." Continuing

---

[69] Pennsylvania, *Report of the Joint Committee of the Legislature*, p. 13.
[70] Ibid., p. 6.   [71] Ibid., p. 5.

the theme of indecency, Coxe testified provocatively, "I recollect that I have seen Mrs. Blunden sit on a chair along side of M. Holloway with her head laying on his lap and she expressed herself that she had an easy place to lay. Then she said she thought it was getting very hard and then she would raise up."[72] The investigation also explored whether Mrs. Blundin had the "filthy disease." A former employee of the prison testified that he had seen "some clothes down at the wash-house which indicated the venereal." He did not know whose clothes they were, but they were women's clothing, "a smock and a petticoat," implying that they could have been Mrs. Blundin's clothes.[73] In light of the allegations, the Warden's personal physician was asked to testify whether the Warden had ever had a venereal disease.[74]

In the end, Warden Wood, Mr. Halloway, and the other administrators emerged largely unscathed; the Warden's moral character, in particular, was found to be above reproach. Mrs. Blundin was chided for behaving in ways "entirely unbecoming her sex and condition."[75] The report almost celebrated the fact that Mrs. Blundin had "long since removed from the institution" and thus no longer presented a problem.[76]

Finally, Warden Wood was also charged with embezzlement, as was Mrs. Blundin. Mrs. Blundin was charged with "embezzling provisions, groceries, &c."; that charge was ultimately sustained, but one question was whether Warden Wood or his assistant, Mr. Blundin, knew of her behavior.[77] Additionally, Warden Wood was accused of contracting with his private business, setting prices favorably to himself, and using prisoner labor to create products used in his farm and "manufactory."

The investigation failed to sustain this charge. The legislative committee did acknowledge evidence that the warden had at the very least given the appearance of impropriety by contracting with his own business. Moreover, they explained, "There is an obvious propriety in avoiding the mingling of private accounts and business with that which belongs to the

---

[72] Pennsylvania, *Testimony from Legislative Committee to Investigate State Penitentiary for the Eastern District of Pennsylvania*, Partial Transcript. Series II, State Penitentiary for the Eastern District of Pennsylvania Records. American Philosophical Society, Philadelphia, 1835.

[73] McElwee, *A concise history (Vol. 2)*, p. 28 (Bean testimony).

[74] Ibid., p. 23 (Coates testimony).

[75] Pennsylvania, *Report of the Joint Committee of the Legislature (Mar. 26, 1835)*, p. 8.

[76] Ibid., p. 18. Her husband stayed on for years, continuing to act as the warden's most trusted overseer.

[77] Ibid., p. 10.

public."[78] But they did not formally censure the warden or contend that he had done more than create an appearance of impropriety.

Ultimately, there were no consequences from the investigation. Warden Wood was cleared of all charges except the practice of removing prisoners from their cells (as we saw in Chapter 3). In the course of the investigation, a theory emerged that several former overseers, disgruntled employees, had collaborated to ruin Warden Wood's good name; one overseer in particular had hoped to obtain the position for himself in the process.

The investigation, rather than damaging Warden Wood's reputation, was an opportunity for a number of penal reformers and others among Philadelphia's social elite to praise Wood. He was deemed one of the leading experts on prisons. The prominent jurist and penal reformer Francis Lieber testified,

I never found a superintendent of any Penitentiary, more humanely disposed, and whom I considered of a clearer mind, as to all that relates to Penitentiary systems. I must add here, that I have received from no one more sound and practical knowledge about Penitentiary-systems in general, than from Mr. Wood: – and I have never become acquainted with a person whom I thought equally fitted for that station.[79]

Another man testified that "Mr. Wood has devoted much time to the subject of prison discipline – he is considered as unusually well informed on the subject."[80] A member of PSAMPP, James Barclay, testified, "I have never known any body whom I thought so well acquainted with prison discipline – so thought Mr. Crawford, the English commissioner ... In the Prison Society his opinions are highly respected."[81] William Fry referred to Wood as "the great apostle of Penitentiary reform."[82] Wood was also praised for his work as warden of Eastern. The prison's Physician testified, "Mr. Wood took great interest in the affairs of the institution ... I think he was very much devoted to the institution – he was very zealous for the success and discipline of it."[83] Barclay testified that Wood "appeared devoted to the institution and its interests."[84] Barclay also testified that Wood's "conduct ... appeared marked by firmness and humanity."[85]

Warden Wood's good character, not only his knowledge, was also reinforced. Dr. Benjamin Coates, a physician at the Pennsylvania Hospital

---

[78] Ibid., p. 11.   [79] McElwee, *A Concise History (Vol. 2)*, pp. 55–56.
[80] Ibid., p. 15 (Yarnell testimony).   [81] Ibid., p. 14.   [82] Ibid., p. 17.
[83] Ibid., p. 11.   [84] Ibid., p. 14.   [85] Ibid., p. 13.

and member of PSAMPP, testified of Wood, "His general character has been of the best I have ever known."[86] Another member, William Fry, testified, "Until this investigation, I have never even heard the breathing of suspicion against his moral character or kindness or disposition."[87]

Not everyone was convinced by this testimony: A minority committee disagreed with Wood's exoneration and suggested his friends in high places had protected him.[88] But the official report verified that Wood's character remained untarnished in their eyes. Indeed, five years after the investigation was closed, and Warden Wood resigned from the prison, he "was congratulated on the imperishable honour he had obtained in being one of the originators of the system and so ably conducting for the period of eleven Years an Institution which had excited the attention of Philanthropists of all Nations."[89] His reputation remained intact and perhaps even strengthened.

Although Wood was cleared of all (serious) charges and the blame, it appears he was not, in fact, blameless. As other commentators have noted, in the most flattering scenario, Wood was unconscionably sloppy with his bookkeeping, failing to fully separate his personal accounts from the prison's accounts.[90] But even in the years after the investigation, Wood continued to engage in questionable economic practices. While warden and even thereafter, Wood conducted business deals with the prison – he was a partner in R.W. Richardson and Co. – and failed to pay the money he had promised in exchange for goods (purchased on credit). Just two years after leaving office, Wood filed for bankruptcy, prompting the inspectors to try to recover the debts. Although he repaid part of the debt, Wood never repaid it entirely. Over the years, the inspectors attempted, unsuccessfully, to get their money back.[91] By late 1851, Wood still owed the prison a personal debt of $3,559 and a business debt of $13,428.[92] Eventually, after Wood's death, the inspectors concluded that they would never recover the funds. His long-standing debt further

---

[86] Ibid., p. 23.   [87] Ibid., p. 17.

[88] See Thomas B. McElwee, *A Concise History of the Eastern Penitentiary of Pennsylvania Together with a Detailed Statement of Proceedings of the Committee Appointed by the Legislature*. Vol. 1–2. Philadelphia: Neall & Massey, 1835.

[89] Eastern State Penitentiary, *Warden's Daily Journal*, July 1, 1840.

[90] See also Meranze, *Laboratories of Virtue*, Jen Manion, *Liberty's Prisoners: Carceral Culture in Early America*. Philadelphia: University of Pennsylvania Press, 2015.

[91] Eastern State Penitentiary, *Minute Books of the Board of Inspectors and Board of Trustees*, July 29, 1842, August 31, 1842, October 15, 1845.

[92] Ibid., December 27, 1851.

burdened an already cash-strapped prison known for its inability to remain solvent.

Warden Scattergood's Misconduct

Thomas Scattergood was Eastern's warden from 1845 to 1850. A Quaker and a member of PSAMPP prior to his term as warden, Scattergood (much like Wood) appears to have cared deeply about the prison, preaching and enacting the administrators' particular brand of benevolence. His annual reports offered some of the strongest defenses of the Pennsylvania System, while his private notes in the warden's log portray a man who fervently believed in his work. As with other wardens, Scattergood recorded prisoners' reports of their treatment, his own assessment of their improvement (or lack thereof) during their confinement, and his hopes or fears for prisoners upon their release – whether they would do well or return to confinement. His log included short asides of gratitude to Divine Benevolence and, particularly at the years' beginnings and ends, short prayers for the success of the prison. After only a few months in office, and having weathered a smallpox epidemic, he expressed his gratitude in his journal on New Year's Eve and wrote, "the opening of the New Year may find us all sincerely desireous [sic] of promoting the best interests of the Institution." The following day, he elaborated, "May [the new year's] end find all engaged in the administration of the affairs of the Institution harmoniously labouring for its good."[93] Several years later, his yearly tributes were less extensive, but he still expressed his wish, "May [the year's] end (if spared to see it) find us still more faithful in the performance of duty."[94]

In practice, however, Scattergood himself occasionally neglected the good of the institution, subverting its policies or abusing his privileges for his own benefit. Several instances of Scattergood's misconduct were relayed by W. O. B. Merrill, a former overseer at the prison, to Foulke, who recorded their conversations in his "prison diary." As Foulke recorded, Merrill "was satisfied Scattergood regarded his own interests more than those of the institution," and he offered several examples to illustrate. Merrill reported "That he [Scattergood] skimmed the cream from the milk and gave the skimmed milk to the infirmary, that he sent the cream

---

[93] Eastern State Penitentiary, *Warden's Daily Journal*, December 31, 1845; January 1, 1846.
[94] Ibid., January 1, 1849.

to the city to some of his friends." Merrill also informed Foulke that Scattergood had sent "vegetables from the Prison garden" into the city. On one occasion, a prisoner "had been ordered by the Doctor to take a cold … bath for a disease with which he had been afflicted." Once "Scattergood had seen the bathing apparatus" he "[took] it from the prisoner and applied it to the use of a member of his own family, and Merrill had to saw a barrel in half for the prisoner." [95] For his own part, Merrill felt the warden had abused him as well. Merrill reported "that his reason for leaving the Penitentiary was that Scattergood employed him excessively during the day, and would not relieve him as to night duty – that his labour was greater than any other officer … and that Scattergood had been very harsh and ungentlemanly in his treatment and therefore he [Merrill] resigned."[96] Even a prisoner warned Merrill to "look out" for the warden.[97] Unlike some overseers who criticized the prison's administrators who fired them, Merrill appears to have been a reliable source: Several of Merrill's other revelations were confirmed by other sources. Moreover, Merrill had worked under two wardens, and neither warden listed any complaints about him. Indeed, Warden Scattergood's own records note that Merrill had resigned his position (and gave notice ahead of time, unlike some overseers who simply ceased attending their work) and not been fired.[98] Ultimately, Foulke put great stock in Merrill's private testimony.

Additional data suggest these episodes, if they did indeed occur as Merrill reported, were not Warden Scattergood's only acts of misappropriation. In mid-1848, the inspectors passed a resolution reminding the warden that "the resolution of November 15th 1843" restricted the use of the prison's horse-drawn carriage and asked him "to take measures to prevent in future any violation of said resolution."[99] Although it is not stated explicitly in the record, their exchange indicates that Scattergood had been in the practice of misusing the prison's carriage for personal, rather than official, business.

It also seems that Scattergood had acted without permission when he diverted cream and vegetables to friends in the city, although not everyone considered this a form of embezzlement. Soon after entering office,

[95] Foulke, *Notebooks Concerning Prisons and Prisoners*, October 26, 1849.
[96] Ibid., October 26, 1849.   [97] Ibid., November 6, 1849.
[98] Eastern State Penitentiary, *Warden's Daily Journal*, August 31, 1847.
[99] Eastern State Penitentiary, *Minute Books of the Board of Inspectors and Board of Trustees*, June 3, 1848.

Warden Halloway (Scattergood's successor) asked the inspectors to formally sanction the ongoing "custom" of the warden taking a supply of vegetables from the prison's garden for his family as had occurred under Scattergood.[100] After discussing whether the new warden should pay for his vegetables, the inspectors granted him the privilege; they made no note of Scattergood's illicit use.[101]

While the inspectors overlooked some of Scattergood's activities, his tenure encouraged them to rethink certain accommodations and liberties allowed to wardens. When Scattergood became warden, he accepted on the condition that he could continue to engage in his own personal business while warden, a condition that had "required a part of the then established rules rescinded." However, Scattergood's tenure revealed the problems with this accommodation. By 1850, Scattergood's final year in office, the inspectors noted that "the productive industry of the Prison" had suffered "and the number of unemployed prisoners having increased to the probable injury of both mental and bodily health"; clearly, the prison required "the undivided attention of the Warden." Moving forward, the inspectors declared, wardens could "exercise 'no other calling, trade or business whatever,'" as had been initially thought best. Scattergood was given one month "to dispose of his tanyard or other business;"[102] Scattergood, in turn, requested time to think it over.[103] The inspectors ultimately decided for him.

It was at this juncture that the inspectors voted a sitting warden out of office for the first and last time in the nineteenth century. The inspectors held elections for the prison's warden, physician, and clerk every six months. Almost every case of turnover between 1829 and 1900 was voluntary. Most wardens (who did not die in office) tendered their resignation, and the inspectors worked to find a replacement while the resigning warden stayed on for several months if necessary until a replacement was found. By a vote of three to two, the inspectors reelected George Thompson, Scattergood's predecessor.[104] For his part,

---

[100] Ibid., October 5, 1850.

[101] Eastern State Penitentiary, *Warden's Daily Journal*, November 2, 1850.

[102] Eastern State Penitentiary, *Minute Books of the Board of Inspectors and Board of Trustees*, April 6, 1850.

[103] Ibid., July 6, 1850. Foulke reported a similar series of events, but about Warden Thompson. It is unclear whether he had been misinformed about which warden behaved this way or if both wardens did.

[104] Prior to the election, a group of men – "W. J. Mullen, J. Jones, J. Bouvier, and others" endorsed John Dungan for Warden "in case of a vacancy by Thomas Scattergood

Scattergood did not go easily. As Dr. Given, the prison's then-physician, explained it to Foulke, "incumbent T. Scattergood had held over and manifested an indisposition to leave his place."[105]

In practice, Scattergood was ousted from the prison as gently as the inspectors could manage to protect his reputation. First, they allowed Scattergood to remain as warden "until the time at his early convenience he may be unable to make such arrangements in the removal of his family and his retirement from official duties as shall be agreeable to him and George Thompson the Warden elect."[106] Second, to mitigate the sting of this lack of confidence in the current warden, the board passed a resolution formally stating their "kindest feelings for Thomas Scattergood" and that they were "impressed with a just regard for the excellent qualities he possesses." The inspectors likely passed the resolution to help Scattergood save face – they rarely passed resolutions stating their confidence in an administrator unless there was some shadow cast on that administrator's reputation that they sought to counter. At Eastern, even an ousted administrator's reputation had to be protected.

* * *

For Eastern's administrators, preserving the Pennsylvania System was as much about their own reputations as about their internalized belief in the superiority of the system. As we have already seen, they were willing to manipulate the Pennsylvania System to preserve its reputation – and by extension their own. But these complex men were also willing to manipulate the Pennsylvania System, and take advantage of their privileged positions at Eastern, to satisfy baser urges like retaliation and material gain. Generally, these activities were small enough that they did

---

leaving the said office." Ibid., July 6, 1850. How they knew that a vacancy was forthcoming is unclear, but suggests that dissatisfaction with Scattergood was known beyond the prison.

[105] Foulke, *Notebooks Concerning Prisons and Prisoners*, September 16, 1850.

[106] Eastern State Penitentiary, *Minute Books of the Board of Inspectors and Board of Trustees*, July 9, 1850. As it turned out, Scattergood was allowed to remain for several months because, after some delay, Thompson declined his election to warden. He did not wish to "extricate himself" from his "business engagements," the new rule passed because of Scattergood's malfeasance. Foulke, *Notebooks Concerning Prisons and Prisoners*, October 17, 1850. Thompson's refusal prompted a second vote, at which the inspectors unanimously elected John Halloway warden. Eastern State Penitentiary, *Minute Books of the Board of Inspectors and Board of Trustees*, September 21, 1850. On September 23, Scattergood turned the prison over to Halloway.

not threaten the viability of the system; everyone – the administrators behaving badly and their colleagues – could tolerate or overlook these misdeeds, however much these acts contradicted the principles they collectively (and publicly) endorsed. But sometimes the administrators went too far. It was in such times that their colleagues, Eastern's other administrators, stepped in and chided or removed their miscreant colleagues from their positions of authority to prevent such actions from actually jeopardizing the careful image they had collectively cultivated and benefited from by maintaining the Pennsylvania System.

PART III

FORCED TO ADAPT

*The Conditions for and Process of
Deinstitutionalization*

A

LEFT BEHIND IN A NEW ERA

To institutionalize is to *infuse with value* beyond the technical requirements of the task at hand. The prizing of social machinery beyond its technical role is largely a reflection of the unique way in which it fulfills personal or group needs. Whenever individuals become attached to an organization or a way of doing things as persons rather than as technicians, the result is a prizing of the device for its own sake. From the standpoint of the committed person, the organization is changed from an expendable tool into a valued source of personal satisfaction.

Philip Selznick[1]

---

[1] Selznick, *Leadership in Administration: A Sociological Interpretation*, p. 17.

9

An Alternative Status

Administrators' Transition from Gentleman Reformers to Professional Penologists

The Inspectors have in former reports made many suggestions on the subject of jurisprudence and penitentiary discipline, which the examination of the facts thus collected has heretofore required or justified. Each year adds proof confirmatory of the suggestions contained in those reports. Public attention to them has been so often invited, and as yet with but so little interest excited in them, that they feel best satisfied yearly to increase the amount of this information, trusting that when these Reports shall be considered by earnest men, their labors will be thereby greatly aided in those investigations which will be regarded as of primary importance in deciding on attainable modifications or necessary changes in penal codes, penitentiary discipline, crime prevention, and the punishment of offenders against law.

Board of Inspectors (1868), Annual Report[1]

If the Act of May 1st, 1861, had relation to penal laws or jurisprudence, crimes or penal code, the views of the Inspectors in regard to it, might be of no importance or value. But the law relates entirely to *prison discipline*. ... It should have received full consideration before applying it to a system, working its way as a successful experiment, under the supervision of a body, directly conversant with its principles. ... To adapt this law to our system of prison discipline, or to mould any system to it, is no easy task. Its principles are very questionable. Its judicious application to the separate system is at present, a very grave question – because it embraces its propriety, its usefulness, its applicability, and its liability to engender discontent, disputes, and confusion between and among the convicts and the overseers.

---

[1] Eastern State Penitentiary, *Thirty-Ninth Annual Report of the Inspectors of the State Penitentiary for the Eastern District of Pennsylvania.* Philadelphia: McLaughlin Brothers, 1868, pp. 23–24.

It may impair our present carefully created system, without yielding a single beneficial provision in return.

Board of Inspectors (1862), Annual Report[2]

ADMINISTRATIVE REBELLION

In 1861–1862, Pennsylvania's prison administrators staged a small rebellion against the state legislature. On May 1, 1861, the Pennsylvania legislature passed a "Commutation Law," which required administrators at the two state penitentiaries and local jails to release prisoners early for good behavior.[3] Several months later, upon hearing of the law's passage, Pennsylvania's prison administrators, led by Eastern's Board of Inspectors, announced their refusal to enforce the law. It was, they argued, a bad law, which the benighted legislature would have known had it consulted the prison administrators before passing the law.[4] The Commutation Law remained unenforced for almost a year before the administrators' actions were subjected to judicial review. On April 21, 1862, the Supreme Court of Pennsylvania agreed with the administrators' assessment, and even chided the legislature for interfering with the work of experts.[5]

The court's judgment in *The Commonwealth ex rel. Johnson v. Halloway* was a substantial symbolic victory for Eastern's administrators. The court's statements were only dicta – the formal ruling was grounded in a constitutional argument about the separation of powers – but these statements recognized in Eastern's prison administrators a status they had long sought. For decades, they had presented themselves as professionals – men whose unique command of a specialized knowledge grants them autonomous control over all related matters. Their claims were often designed to distinguish themselves – primarily Eastern's Board of Inspectors, but also the prison's warden, physician, and moral instructor – from other parties who shaped penal policy, particularly those critics, reformers, and legislators who threatened Eastern's autonomy.

---

[2] Eastern State Penitentiary, *Thirty-Third Annual Report of the Inspectors of the State Penitentiary for the Eastern District of Pennsylvania*. Philadelphia: M'Laughlin Brothers, 1862, pp. 8–9.

[3] Pennsylvania, "No. 430: An Act Relative to Prison Discipline," in *Laws of the General Assembly of the State of Pennsylvania*. Harrisburg: A. Boyd Hamilton, 1861, pp. 462–463.

[4] Eastern State Penitentiary, Inspectors' Report, *Thirty-Third Annual Report of the Inspectors*, appendix.

[5] *The Commonwealth ex rel. Johnson v. Halloway*, 42 Pa. 446. 1862.

The administrators' refusal to enforce the 1861 law, and their condemnation of the legislature for passing it, represented their most forceful – and successful – expression of their authority as *professional* penologists since the prison's opening in 1829.

* * *

This chapter traces the origins of the administrators' claims to professional status and its consequences for the Pennsylvania System. As we have seen (Chapter 3), Eastern's administrators enjoyed near-total control over their prison. However, their autonomy was challenged directly by occasional incursions from the local penal reform society (PSAMPP), and indirectly by the state legislature's lackluster patronage. These challenges became much more invasive in the 1850s, peaking in the 1860s. In response, Eastern's administrators sought to establish jurisdiction over *their* prison by proclaiming their own special expertise and insisting on deference in matters that would affect Eastern.

By the 1870s, however, penal actors on the national stage were likewise proclaiming their own expertise and professional status, while Eastern's administrators felt increasingly irrelevant. In response to these national-level developments, the administrators further developed their claims to professional status. Although the administrators enjoyed some brief victories against local challengers, they were generally ignored by the larger field. Moreover, they continued to lose control over Eastern as criminal justice became increasingly professionalized and bureaucratized – at least by nineteenth-century standards. In this context, the administrators' claims to professional status provided them a more promising path to self-aggrandizement than continuing to proclaim the Pennsylvania System's superiority. Consequently, the administrators' annual reports in this period shifted away from defenses of the Pennsylvania System, including their emphasis on their own humanitarian benevolence, toward discussions of their status as professional penologists. It was this shift from defense to professionalization that deinstitutionalized the Pennsylvania System at Eastern.

INTERLOPING REFORMERS

PSAMPP reformers had long been strong advocates of the Pennsylvania System. They had been responsible for many of Pennsylvania's penal reforms, including the first state prison (Walnut Street Prison), Western and Eastern State Penitentiaries, and the Pennsylvania System itself.[6] Both reformers and administrators alike gave credit to PSAMPP for these developments.[7] Beginning in the late 1840s and 1850s, however, these reformers began to worry that the Pennsylvania System might cause insanity, just as many Auburn supporters had suggested. In January 1848, PSAMPP passed a resolution complaining that "the percentage of insanity and mortality at the Eastern Penitentiary is increasing to an alarming degree."[8] Indeed, insanity among the prisoners was the topic of several meetings and investigations between 1848 and 1852.[9] They complained in an 1849 memorial forwarded to Eastern's Board of Inspectors "that the condition of the convicts in the Eastern State Penitentiary in respect to health of body & mind is far from what it should be."[10] However, the reformers did not believe the Pennsylvania System was inherently harmful,[11] and they still believed it was the best available system. In an 1859 pamphlet, PSAMPP reported, "At no period during this long interval, has there been the slightest distrust of, or divergence from the great principle which was first espoused – INDIVIDUAL SEPARATION AND EMPLOYMENT FOR ALL PRISONERS AND ALL GRADES OF PRISONS."[12]

In order to reconcile their doubts about prisoners' health with their support for the system, PSAMPP criticized the system's implementation by Eastern's administrators. In their 1848 resolution, PSAMPP claimed that increased mortality and insanity at the prison resulted "in a great measure

---

[6] Negley K. Teeters, *They Were in Prison: A History of the Pennsylvania Prison Society, 1787–1937.* Philadelphia: The John C. Winston Company, 1937; Harry Elmer Barnes, *The Evolution of Penology in Pennsylvania.* Indianapolis: The Bobbs-Merrill Company, 1968 [1927].

[7] e.g., PSAMPP, *Sketch of the Principal Transactions of the "Philadelphia Society for Alleviating the Miseries of Public Prisons," from Its Origin to the Present Time.* Philadelphia: Merrihew & Thompson, Printers, 1859; Richard Vaux, *Brief Sketch of the Origin and History of the State Penitentiary for the Eastern District of Pennsylvania at Philadelphia.* Philadelphia: McLaughlin Brothers, Printers, 1872.

[8] PSAMPP, *Acting Committee Minute Books,* Series I, Vol. 2–6, Pennsylvania Prison Society Records (Collection 1946) Series I, Vol. 6–10. Historical Society of Pennsylvania. 1798–1883, January 14, 1848. See also Teeters, *They Were in Prison,* p. 198.

[9] See PSAMPP, *Acting Committee Minute Books;* PSAMPP, *Committee for Eastern, Minute Books,* Vol. 1–3; Pennsylvania Prison Society Records (Collection 1946), Series I, Vol. 27–29. Historical Society of Pennsylvania, 1854–1885; William Foulke, *Notebooks Concerning Prisons and Prisoners,* Box 7, William Parker Foulke Papers. American Philosophical Society, Philadelphia, 1846–1852.

[10] PSAMPP, *Acting Committee Minute Books,* December 4, 1849.

[11] For example, Teeters, *They Were in Prison,* p. 199.

[12] PSAMPP, *Sketch of the Principal Transactions,* p. 22.

from the neglect of the prescriptions and directions of the physician."[13] Likewise, in their 1849 memorial, PSAMPP's Acting Committee noted that they "have been for a long time impressed with the importance of some change in the administration of the discipline of the Institution under your care, and members of our committee have not unfrequently nor equivocally intimated these impressions to members of your Board." They then enumerated several recommendations for changes, hoping "that you [the Board] will not think it obtrusive in us to express to you in this official & formal manner our fears that the mental & bodily health of the Convicts is greatly endangered for want of certain sanitary safeguards which every prison should provide and which are perfectly consistent with a strict maintenance of individual separation."[14] It was not the Pennsylvania System itself, then, but the failure of its administrators to ensure the health of the prisoners.

In this period as well, the reformers scrutinized the prison's administration. PSAMPP's meeting minutes from this period include frequent references to complaints following their monthly observations of the prison. Members of PSAMPP's visiting committee often complained about observing prisoners doubled up in their cells, finding prisoners outside their cells, or seeing the cell doors open.[15] Indeed, the visiting committee's reports in this period (the late 1840s and 1850s) increasingly noted the members' displeasure at various situations at the prison that they had previously acknowledged but said little else about.[16]

After issuing several "memorials" to Eastern's administrators requesting certain changes, PSAMPP tried more public routes. In their 1859 pamphlet, PSAMPP warned,

It should be a subject of ceaseless concern with us to seek the improvement of the resident officers of our public prisons. Like other men, they are liable to become inured to a round of duties, and to forget that those they have to do with are men of like passions with themselves, and though guilty and degraded, are not without claims to sympathy and tenderness. A single sharp word, inconsiderately uttered, may rouse resentments in a prisoner's mind which his very helplessness and degradation will aggravate and keep alive, — no one knows how long, — and thus defeat some of the most important ends of his imprisonment ...[17]

---

[13] PSAMPP, *Acting Committee Minute Books*, January 14, 1848. See also Teeters, *They Were in Prison*, p. 198.

[14] PSAMPP, *Acting Committee Minute Books*, December 4, 1849.

[15] PSAMPP, *Committee for Eastern, Minute Books*, e.g., 5 Mo 31, 1854.

[16] PSAMPP, *Acting Committee Minute Books*, e.g., March 13, 1849.

[17] PSAMPP, *Sketch of the Principal Transactions*, p. 29.

PSAMPP also repeatedly approached the legislature, lobbying for changes to the Pennsylvania System and greater access to the prison, with varying success.

Experience and Expertise: Confronting PSAMPP

Confronting PSAMPP in the 1840s and 1850s was difficult at first. The administrators turned to a strategy they had first used against their external critics like the BPDS and others: undermining their critics (see Chapter 6). In this case, however, their critics were long-time allies and men not so dissimilar to themselves. The administrators could not point to their rejection of the whip or their abhorrence of the profit motive as they did for Auburn supporters. But the administrators could rely on another claim: they knew more about their prison and the Pennsylvania System than anyone else; therefore, comparatively ignorant or misinformed others should defer to their opinion. To establish this claim, the administrators emphasized their experience as a source of expertise throughout the nineteenth century.

The administrators began to establish their expertise through experience first with penal reform, then with prisoners and punishment. In the 1830s, they primarily touted their work in penal reform – advocacy, keeping up to date on the latest debates, and occasionally visiting jails and prisons – rather than prison management. For example, in their first report to the legislature, the inspectors described the process by which they had selected the prison's warden, Samuel Wood. They "anxiously looked around for an individual possessing the requisite talents, experience, and standing, to fill that station."[18] In the same volume, they reminded the legislature of their own "[m]any years [sic] experience, in the practical operation of the penal laws, and prison discipline."[19] Later in the decade, they described themselves as "the friends and associates of the promoters of the [Pennsylvania] system" (members of PSAMPP); consequently, the inspectors "were in the habit of discussing the subject of Penitentiary relations in all its bearings. They were fully imbued with the principles and views of its advocates, and the majority of them took an active part in calling into operation the schemes of those who felt the necessity of a

---

[18] Eastern State Penitentiary, Inspectors' report, *The First and Second Annual Reports of the Inspectors of the Eastern State Penitentiary of Pennsylvania*. Philadelphia: Thomas Kite, 1831, p. 7.
[19] Ibid., p. 12.

reform in the criminal jurisprudence of the State."[20] This "experience" with penal reform provided the primary basis of their expertise as prison administrators during Eastern's first decade.

When Eastern's administrators found themselves in direct confrontation with PSAMPP, reference to their own work as penal reformers was no longer sufficient to establish administrators' particular bona fides. Compared to PSAMPP members, Eastern's administrators had little independent basis for their claims to professional status. They shared similar backgrounds and, while working as penal reformers and politicians themselves, had rubbed shoulders with their attackers. The administrators had to confront this important detail early on in establishing their professional identity.

Beginning in the late 1840s, the administrators stopped pointing to their experience with penal reform, which was useless in establishing their credentials against the reformers. The administrators turned instead to their situational experience at Eastern, which gave them unique knowledge that others lacked. In the process, they initiated a recurring strategy: elevating themselves above unqualified others by claiming that the specificities of their experience as prison administrators established unparalleled credentials. Eastern's administrators used their claims to expertise in their larger effort, discussed in Chapter 6, to discredit any critics of the Pennsylvania System, including reformers from Boston and New York. If such critics lacked the relevant knowledge (that only Eastern's administrators possessed), then their critiques must be groundless. However, the administrators used this tactic most strategically to discredit PSAMPP reformers.

Administrators' situational experience provided a sound basis for their claims of distinct expertise and of reformers' status as being unqualified to judge. No other Pennsylvanians had continuous, firsthand experience with prisoners, the administrators argued, including the local penal reformers; therefore, no one else was qualified to make suggestions or offer alterations to penal policy. The inspectors referred to themselves as "[t]hose, whose constant intercourse with convicts enables them to form an opinion on the subject."[21] By implication, those who did not

---

[20] Eastern State Penitentiary, Inspectors' Report, *Eighth Annual Report of the Inspectors of the Eastern State Penitentiary of Pennsylvania*. Philadelphia: J. Thompson, 1837, p. 3.

[21] Eastern State Penitentiary, Inspectors' Report, *Twenty-Sixth Annual Report of the Inspectors of the Eastern State Penitentiary of Pennsylvania*. Philadelphia: B. F. Mifflin, 1855, p. 6.

frequently interact with prisoners were insufficiently knowledgeable and unqualified to engage in debates about punishment. Likewise, Reverend John Ruth, Eastern's third Moral Instructor, touted his "own experience – having been brought into contact with criminal character almost hourly every day for the last eight years" to condemn the role of deterrence as a purpose of punishment.[22] Experience was a prerequisite for engaging in penal debates.

In one of their strongest arguments against the penal reformers' inexperience, Eastern's administrators asserted that the penal reformers did more harm than good when visiting with the prisoners, even undoing the progress the administrators had made. After ten years on the job, Reverend Thomas Larcombe, the prison's first moral instructor, warned about "[i]njudicious visiters [sic]," a not-so-subtle reference to PSAMPP's visiting committee, the group of reformers who visited prisoners on a semi-regular basis. Though they had "the best intentions," they were "but a small part of the many untoward influences" that the moral instructor had to "overcome by patient and prayerful effort." How could such well-intentioned people "do much harm"? Quite simply, they lacked the requisite experience. They "cannot be acquainted with the peculiarities of a prisoner's position or disposition," so when they visited with prisoners, they could easily do or say the wrong thing, thereby undoing the moral instructor's own work.[23] Such statements undermined penal reformers' attempts to shape penal policy against the prison administrators' wishes. If PSAMPP reformers could derail a prisoner's reformation, how could the group be trusted to inform penal policy over the wishes of those knowledgeable men who worked with prisoners on a daily basis?[24]

Unfortunately for the administrators, the reformers' arguments were more persuasive. PSAMPP experienced two victories that were particularly unwelcome to Eastern's administrators. First, in 1861, the legislature – at PSAMPP's behest – passed what became known as the Commutation Law, which required administrators at the two state

---

[22] Eastern State Penitentiary, Moral Instructor's Report, *Forty-First Annual Report of the Inspectors of the State Penitentiary for the Eastern District of Pennsylvania*. Philadelphia: M'Laughlin Brothers, 1870, p. 111.

[23] Eastern State Penitentiary, Moral Instructor's Report, *The Twentieth Annual Report of the Inspectors of the Eastern State Penitentiary of Pennsylvania*. Philadelphia: Edmond Barrington and Geo. D. Haswell, 1849, p. 35.

[24] Ironically, by 1859, PSAMPP themselves would borrow this argument to criticize Eastern's administrators, especially the moral instructor. PSAMPP, *Sketch of the Principal Transactions*, p. 29.

penitentiaries and local jails to release prisoners early for good behavior, as I discuss in a subsequent section.[25] Second, in 1869, the legislature gave PSAMPP formal authority over Eastern though the formation of a Board of Charities and Corrections, a precursor to modern-day departments of corrections, but with jurisdiction over the state's prisons, jails, insane asylum, and other "charities."[26] These acts only exacerbated a weakening relationship between Eastern's administrators and the legislature.

AN UNRESPONSIVE LEGISLATURE

Pennsylvania's legislature had long shown a lackadaisical orientation to the Pennsylvania System. A common theme throughout Eastern's first five decades was the lack of funds to fully put the Pennsylvania System into operation. For nearly ten years into the prison's operations, Eastern did not employ a moral instructor, as required by the 1829 statute: as the legislature expected someone would volunteer his time, the statute had designated this position to be unpaid – the only unpaid position at the prison, excepting the PSAMPP visitors (who were given access to the prison but had no specific obligations). During this period, a number of penal reformers and local ministers volunteered their time to preach in the hallways of the prison's cellblocks and to mentor the prisoners in their cells. However, no one had volunteered to be *the* moral instructor and "the degree and extent of instruction imparted to the prisoners [wa]s not such as to satisfy the inspectors."[27]

The administrators felt the moral instructor's absence acutely during its first decade. During that period, as we have seen, the Pennsylvania System was also called the system of solitary or separate confinement with labor and moral and religious instruction. The inspectors complained in one early report, "Moral and religious instruction form one of the most important features of the system, and will require the faithful, unremitting, and undivided time of a Chaplain, or religious instructor."[28] The inspectors saw their need for a permanent moral instructor as a substantial violation of the system: "[A] fair experiment of the system of solitary confinement,

---

[25] Pennsylvania, "No. 430: An Act Relative to Prison Discipline."

[26] Barnes, *The Evolution of Penology*, 194–195, p. 395.

[27] Eastern State Penitentiary, Inspectors' Report, *Fifth Annual Report of the Inspectors of the Eastern Penitentiary of Pennsylvania*. Harrisburg: Welsh & Patterson, 1834, pp. 3–4.

[28] Eastern State Penitentiary, Inspectors' Report, *Report of the Board of Inspectors of the Eastern Penitentiary of Pennsylvania*. Harrisburg: Henry Welsh, 1832, p. 4.

with labour, cannot be made without moral and religious instruction."[29] Years later, a Select Committee appointed by the legislature agreed: "the system, in its practical operation, must remain imperfect, until a moral instructor is employed."[30] At long last, the legislature finally provided "a sum not exceeding eight hundred dollars per annum" to support a moral instructor.[31] In 1838, Eastern hired its first moral instructor – the significant violation of the Pennsylvania System was finally resolved, after nine years of operations, by legislative action after repeated requests from Eastern's administrators.

Although Eastern's administrators had other complaints about the material constraints imposed on them by the legislature, the administrators' relationship with the legislature was almost sanguine in these early years. Optimistic about the Pennsylvania System's potential, the administrators saw a number of hurdles that the legislature and other state actors could clear to help the prison succeed; to this end, the inspectors, wardens, physicians, and moral instructors issued myriad requests and recommendations during the first few decades of Eastern's existence. The administrators repeatedly asked the legislature and local judges for prison sentences of different lengths.[32] The administrators further decried the situation in local jails, which were not run under the Pennsylvania System, arguing that prisoners' time spent in the local jails did irreparable damage to prisoners' ability to reform and undermined the good work at Eastern.[33] Additionally, the administrators

---

[29] Eastern State Penitentiary, Inspector's report, *The First and Second Annual Reports of the Inspectors*, p. 4.

[30] Pennsylvania, *Report of the Select Committee Appointed to Visit the Eastern Penitentiary and the Philadelphia County Prison*. Harrisburg: Thompson & Clark, 1838, p. 10.

[31] Pennsylvania, "No. 19: Resolution Relative to the State Library, and for other purposes," in *Laws of the General Assembly of the Commonwealth of Pennsylvania*. Harrisburg: Theo. Fenn, 1838, pp. 689–691, p. 690.

[32] In the 1830s and early 1840s, they requested longer prison sentences. e.g., Eastern State Penitentiary, Warden's Report, *The First and Second Annual Reports of the Inspectors*, pp. 16–17; Eastern State Penitentiary, Inspectors' Report, *Eleventh Annual Report of the Inspectors of the Eastern State Penitentiary of Pennsylvania*. Philadelphia: Brown, Bicking & Guilbert, 1840, p. 5; by the late 1840s, they felt sentences were too long. e.g., Eastern State Penitentiary, Inspectors' Report, *The Nineteenth Annual Report of the Inspectors of the Eastern State Penitentiary of Pennsylvania*. Philadelphia: Ed. Barrington and Geo. D. Haswell, 1848, p. 5; Eastern State Penitentiary, Inspectors' Report, *Nineteenth Annual Report of the Inspectors*, pp. 41–42.

[33] E.g., Eastern State Penitentiary, Physician's Report, *Seventeenth Annual Report of the Inspectors of the Eastern State Penitentiary of Pennsylvania*. Philadelphia: Ed. Barrington and Geo. D. Haswell, 1846, p. 55.

recommended that the state build an insane asylum and stop sending mentally ill criminals to Eastern because these prisoners were skewing the prison's insanity and mortality statistics.[34] Administrators also made recommendations about children's education and vocational training to reduce juvenile crime.[35] In each case, the administrators tended to implore the legislature rather than lambaste them.

Despite their many and repeated requests, the administrators rarely succeeded in changing these policies and practices. As time went on, they grew increasingly vexed by the legislature's failure to listen to them. In 1855, for example, the inspectors "ventured again to invoke Legislative attention to the subject" of youthful and first-time offenders. The inspectors encouraged the legislature to consider revising its penal code and to do so with the inspectors' advice and guidance. They contrasted this endeavor with the more typical method through which penal policy was adopted: occasionally and without their guidance. These "[s]poradic reforms are worse than useless." The principal cause of such reforms' failure was their passage without advice: "labors of those who are required to learn while they attempt to teach, are vain."[36] The legislature needed to learn from those who knew better, namely Eastern's administrators. Tirades like this one became more common as the prison administrators grew disillusioned with the legislature's unresponsiveness.

But from the late 1850s onward, the legislature veered between unresponsive and interventionist, sometimes at PSAMPP's urging and sometimes driven by other forces. In 1858, the legislature authorized a commission to alter the existing penal code,[37] the revised form of which passed in 1860. While the legislature did not consult prison administrators to redefine the penal code, they did listen to those administrators who criticized the Pennsylvania System. In 1858, Armistead

---

34 E.g., Eastern State Penitentiary Physician's Report, *Twenty-Second Annual Report of the Inspectors of the Eastern State Penitentiary of Pennsylvania*. Philadelphia: Kite & Walton, 1851, p. 28.

35 E.g., Eastern State Penitentiary, Warden's Report, *Fifth Annual Report of the Inspectors of the Eastern Penitentiary of Pennsylvania*. Harrisburg: Welsh & Patterson, 1834, p. 6; Eastern State Penitentiary, Inspectors' Report, *Eighth Annual Report of the Inspectors*, p. 5; Eastern State Penitentiary, Inspectors' Report, *Eleventh Annual Report of the Inspectors*, p. 6.

36 Eastern State Penitentiary, Inspectors' Report, *Twenty-Sixth Annual Report of the Inspectors*, pp. 6–7.

37 Pennsylvania, "No. 14: Resolutions Relative to a Revised Penal Code of Pennsylvania," in *Laws of the General Assembly of the State of Pennsylvania*. Harrisburg: A. Boyd Hamilton, 1858, pp. 523–524.

Beckham, the longtime warden of Western, died; his death ended the long-time administrative verbal support for the Pennsylvania System at Western. Soon thereafter, Western's inspectors began requesting a shift away from the Pennsylvania System.[38] In 1866, with the distraction of the Civil War over, administrators at Western State Penitentiary blasted the Pennsylvania System as dangerous, expensive, and impractical, requesting permission to abandon the system. The following year, in 1867, the legislature authorized a commission to investigate the appropriate system of prison discipline that the state's penitentiaries and jails should adopt.[39] Although the Commission reported that the state penitentiaries' respective systems were adequate,[40] in 1869, the legislature granted Western's administrators' request to abandon the Pennsylvania System at their prison and adopt the Auburn System.[41] Clearly uncommitted to the Pennsylvania System, the legislature also starved the system at Eastern of material necessities to the point of devastation. Overcrowding struck in 1866, forcing prison administrators to double-cell their prisoners in violation of the Pennsylvania System (see Chapter 10). After repeated requests to divert prisoners to the less crowded Western penitentiary or to local jails and for more funds to extend the prison's capacity, the legislature slowly acquiesced, but by then it was too little, too late. As we shall see, the Pennsylvania System would never recover at Eastern, although its administrators fought to protect it, taking aim at the party most responsible for endangering their prison – the legislature.

Establishing Jurisdiction: Wrestling with the Legislature

Throughout the 1860s and 1870s, Eastern's administrators, feeling besieged by the legislature, became increasingly aggressive in their

---

[38] Eugene E. Doll, "Trial and Error at Allegheny: The Western State Penitentiary, 1818–1838," *The Pennsylvania Magazine of History and Biography* 81:1 (1957), pp. 3–27, p. 27.

[39] Pennsylvania, "No. 4: Joint Resolution Authorizing the Governor to Appoint a Commission to Inquire into the Various Systems of Prison Discipline," in *Laws of the General Assembly of the State of Pennsylvania*. Harrisburg: Singerly & Myers, State Printers, 1867, p. 1338.

[40] John White Geary, "Annual Message to the Assembly—1870," in *Pennsylvania Archives. Fourth Series. Papers of the Governors, Vol. VIII. 1858–1871*, ed. George Edward Reed. Harrisburg: Wm. Stanley Ray, 1902 [1870], pp. 1001–1041, p. 1032.

[41] Pennsylvania, "No. 18: An Act Authorizing the Congregating of Convicts in the Western Penitentiary for Labor, Learning and Religious Services," in *Laws of the General Assembly of the State of Pennsylvania*. Harrisburg: B. Singerly, State Printer, 1869, p. 18.

description of themselves as experts and of the legislators as dilettantes interloping in penal affairs. Their modal argument encouraged the legislature to examine Eastern's annual reports prior to passing legislation. Legislators' "careful investigation" of the reports was, according to the inspectors, "necessary for wise legislation."[42] The administrators pointed to the reports' "information in relation to crimes and their causes, as well as the classes of criminals."[43] The statistics in the reports were "worthy of the jurist, the statesman, and the legislator."[44] More specifically, these statistics would "enable statesmen to have a clearer conception of the social condition and its needs than superficial theories or crude conceptions may yield." Invoking the mantle of scientific inquiry, the inspectors explained, "these statistics, held like a mirror before the face of veneered civilization, will show what manner of face it really has. Testing penal systems by facts thus ascertained, will, it is believed, teach the one-idead [sic] man."[45] Thus, the administrators encouraged the legislature to review the reports "whenever more enlightened progress in penal science, shall demand a revision of the laws."[46] Legislators "can hardly fail to recognize the necessity of such data for any propositions predicated on ascertained results, or from which they can be deduced, or which may test merely inductive speculations."[47]

When the legislature enacted penal policy that was inconsistent with the administrators' recommendations, Eastern's administrators criticized the interference unsparingly, again emphasizing their own jurisdiction over penal policy. While the legislature was considering a new penal code, for example, the administrators sought "respectfully to present to the Legislature of Pennsylvania, the propriety, as well as policy, of checking

---

[42] Eastern State Penitentiary, Inspectors' Report, *Forty-Fifth Annual Report of the Inspectors of the State Penitentiary for the Eastern District of Pennsylvania*. Philadelphia: Sherman & Co., 1875, p. 8.

[43] Eastern State Penitentiary, Inspectors' Report, *Thirty-Fourth Annual Report of the Inspectors of the State Penitentiary for the Eastern District of Pennsylvania*. Philadelphia: M'Laughlin Brothers, 1863, p. 7.

[44] Ibid., p. 23.

[45] Eastern State Penitentiary, Inspectors' Report, *Thirty-Fifth Annual Report of the Inspectors of the State Penitentiary for the Eastern District of Pennsylvania*. Philadelphia: M'Laughlin Brothers, 1864, p. 13.

[46] Eastern State Penitentiary, Inspectors' Report, *Thirty-Fourth Annual Report of the Inspectors*, p. 7.

[47] Eastern State Penitentiary, Inspectors' Report, *Thirty-Sixth Annual Report of the Inspectors of the State Penitentiary for the Eastern District of Pennsylvania*. Philadelphia: M'Laughlin Brothers, 1865, p. 91.

crude or special legislation on penal jurisprudence, as applied to prison discipline, which is not in harmony with these ascertained principles and their systematic developments."[48] After the legislature authorized the commission to investigate the appropriate system of prison discipline, the administrators argued that "any legislation not based on the knowledge" derived from their own annual reports "must be in itself of doubtful value."[49] The year after the legislature authorized the Auburn System at Western, Eastern's administrators wrote,

> It would not be presuming too much to believe that you, Gentlemen of the Legislature, will invoke the experience of this State Institution before enacting into laws measures relating to convict discipline, penal jurisprudence, or crime cause either for prevention or punishment. Surely the knowledge of facts, and the practical working of principles or theories on penal science for a period of 40 years, might be important to test either new propositions, or determine the proposed benefits that the love of change always promises as the undoubted results thereby to be attained.[50]

Each of their responses to the legislature's interference offered the same message: Defer to our years of experience and special expertise in these matters.

The administrators' biting remarks may not have brought the legislature over to their side, but the administrators were successful in protecting their prison from reformers and legislature's incursion on at least one occasion. Upon hearing of the Commutation Law's passage in 1861, Pennsylvania's prison administrators, led by the Board of Inspectors at Eastern State Penitentiary in Philadelphia, announced their refusal to enforce the law. While any legislation passed without their suggestions was unwelcome, the administrators saw the Commutation Law as a particularly powerful blow. By successfully convincing the legislature to pass a law that changed penal policy, PSAMPP had succeeded where Eastern's administrators had frequently failed. Moreover, the law directly affected the prescribed duties of the prison administrators. The law came at a low point for the administrators: The legislature had just authorized

---

[48] Eastern State Penitentiary, Inspectors' Report, *Thirty-First Annual Report of the Inspectors of the State Penitentiary for the Eastern District of Pennsylvania*. Philadelphia: M'Laughlin Brothers, 1860, p. 10.

[49] Eastern State Penitentiary, Inspectors' Report, *Thirty-Ninth Annual Report of the Inspectors*, p. 25.

[50] Eastern State Penitentiary, Inspectors' Report, *Forty-Second Annual Report of the Inspectors of the State Penitentiary for the Eastern District of Pennsylvania*. Philadelphia: M'Laughlin Brothers, 1860, p. 36.

changes to the penal code that a commission, not the administrators, had recommended. Adding insult to injury, Eastern's administrators were not even notified of the law's discussion or passage; as they explained, they only learned of the law "from the lips of a convict under their care."[51]

Administrators from both Eastern State Penitentiary and Western State Penitentiary (which was still following the Pennsylvania System in the early 1860s) wrote to the legislature, but Eastern's Board of Inspectors took the lead in voicing their disapproval of – and disregard for – the law. The inspectors argued the law was "unnecessary" and deeply flawed.[52] The inspectors further questioned the legality and internal coherence of the law, bemoaning its "looseness of expression, its conflicting provisions, the difficulty of reconciling its language with any proposed purpose." They added pointedly, "The law itself is drawn by a most inexpert pen."[53] In the inspectors' view, the legislature had been misguided by penal reform amateurs. They compared the present legislature unfavorably to earlier bodies "too wise, to be led blindly by any zealous, though uninformed innovator."[54] That the legislature had listened to PSAMPP members who had written and "caused the Act ... to be enacted into a law" was particularly aggravating to the inspectors.[55] The legislature, the inspectors argued, should have consulted *them* before passing the law. As prison administrators, *they* were experts in all penal matters; *they* should have been accorded the decisive role in shaping penal policy, as they had been earlier in the prison's history when "wise legislation" had been passed "in conformity with suggestions in the Eighteenth Annual Report of the Inspectors."[56]

Perhaps most importantly for the inspectors, had the legislature consulted the prison administrators, it would have learned the Commutation Law was entirely inappropriate for Pennsylvania's unique prisons. The Commutation Law had been modeled on the increasingly popular "Irish System," a predecessor to parole that involved early release for good behavior. As Eastern's inspectors argued, the Commutation Law, or the Irish System more generally, was necessary only for prisons that had adopted the Auburn System. Those prisons maintained prisoners for longer sentences than were typical at Eastern. There was no need, the inspectors argued, "to further shorten sentences" in Pennsylvania.

---

[51] Eastern State Penitentiary, Inspectors' Report, *Thirty-Third Annual Report of the Inspectors*, appendix, p. 9.
[52] Ibid., appendix, p. 24.   [53] Ibid., appendix, p. 9.   [54] Ibid., appendix, p. 26.
[55] Ibid., appendix, pp. 27–28.   [56] Ibid., appendix, p. 8.

The law was therefore unnecessary. Moreover, the law would "create so extreme a change in our prison discipline" as to be harmful to the Pennsylvania System.[57] Early release would prevent the conditions necessary for reformation, encouraging prisoners to feign reformation rather than actually transform themselves.[58] After recounting their objections to the law, Eastern's inspectors issued a general declaration that they would not enforce it.

Understandably troubled by the administrators' refusal to enforce the law, two Eastern prisoners, William Johnson and Charles Langhammer, independently submitted *habeas corpus* claims to the Supreme Court of Pennsylvania, arguing that they were being held illegally and should have been released under the law. The court disagreed and, in the combined case of *Johnson* v. *Halloway* (1862), found the law unconstitutional.

The court's opinion repeated the arguments made by Eastern's inspectors, sometimes verbatim.[59] This was no accident; the court referenced the "printed report" submitted by Eastern's inspectors "with the entire concurrence of their colleagues of the Western [Penitentiary]."[60] The court's opinion was sympathetic to the administrators, their claims, and the Pennsylvania System. Justice George Washington Woodward, writing for the court, began the opinion with a brief description and history of Pennsylvania's "admirable system of penitentiary punishment."[61] It was a system, he wrote, that "by reason of the excellence of the conception and the fidelity of administration, has commanded the attention of the civilized world."[62] Echoing the inspectors, Woodward repeatedly stated that the 1861 Act would threaten the Pennsylvania System.[63]

More than repeating the inspectors' arguments, the court recognized their claims to expertise. According to Woodward, Eastern's administrators' "experience had qualified them for advising wisely in respect to the proposed measure."[64] No one, including the legislature, knew better than their administrators how to manage Pennsylvania's unique prisons.

---

[57] Ibid., appendix, p. 21.   [58] Ibid., appendix, p. 24.

[59] The only area in which the court disagreed with the administrators was the legal argument. The inspectors had also argued that the legislature had unconstitutionally usurped the power of the executive branch by placing the governor's pardoning power in the hands of prison administrators. The court noted that this was incorrect; it was an unconstitutional interference with the state's *judicial* branch. However, the constitutional argument was less persuasive to the justices than the idea that the administrators' discretion should be respected.

[60] *The Commonwealth ex rel. Johnson v. Halloway*, p. 447.   [61] Ibid., p. 447.

[62] Ibid., p. 447.   [63] Ibid., e.g., p. 447, p. 449.   [64] Ibid., p. 447.

Other states' experience was irrelevant because those states followed the Auburn System; as Woodward explained, "The letters from other states in reference to the operation of similar statutes, under different systems of punitive discipline, do not weigh very much with us. Our own experience under our peculiar system is opposed to all such attempts at alleviating prison discipline, and we think it may be safely trusted." Foreshadowing later courts' deference to prison administrators around the country,[65] the court itself deferred to the prison administrators' judgment: "They [the prison's administrators] say it [the Commutation Law] would derange the system of administration long pursued ... We will not overrule their reasons nor control their discretion."[66]

Finally, the court recognized the inspectors' prerogative to be consulted before the legislature altered penal policy, or at least the wisdom of the legislature consulting them. Justice Woodward noted, "It is much to be regretted that the legislature of 1861" passed the Commutation Law "without consulting any of the officers to whom the system had been intrusted for administration."[67] In effect, the court acceded to the prison administrators' authority over the countervailing efforts of the legislature and local penal reformers. While Philadelphia penal reformers and the state legislature had been attracted to other developments in the field, Eastern's administrators successfully convinced the state's Supreme Court of the uniqueness and superiority of the Pennsylvania System, the execution of and control over which was best left to the experts.

---

[65] See *Bell* v. *Wolfish. 441 U.S. 520. 1979; Spain* v. *Pecunier. 600 F.2d 189. 1979; Hudson* v. *Palmer. 468 U.S. 517. 1984; Wilson* v. *Seiter. 501 U.S. 294. 1991; Farmer* v. *Brennan. 511 U.S. 825.* 1994. For contrasting trends, see Mikel-Meredith Weidman, "The Culture of Judicial Deference and the Problem of Supermax Prisons," *UCLA Law Review* 51 (2003–2004), p. 1505. The courts long exercised a "hands-off" doctrine when confronting issues of prisoners' rights. Prisoners were considered "civilly dead" and devoid of rights. While this posture was reversed in the middle decades of the twentieth century, especially for Southern prisoners, courts increasingly redefined prisoners' rights issues as questions of prison administration, an area in which judges claimed to feel uncomfortable adjudicating. See Malcolm Feeley and Edward Rubin, *Judicial Policy Making and the Modern State: How the Courts Reformed America's Prisons.* New York: Cambridge University Press, 2000. For recent reversals, see Jonathan Simon, *Mass Incarceration on Trial.* New York: The New Press, 2014. For a sociological analysis of judicial deference to corporations, see Lauren B. Edelman, Christopher Uggen, and Howard S. Erlanger, "The Endogeneity of Legal Regulation: Grievance Procedures as Rational Myth," *American Journal of Sociology* 105:2 (1999), pp. 406–454; Lauren B. Edelman et al., "When Organizations Rule: Judicial Deference to Institutionalized Employment Structures," *American Journal of Sociology* 117:3 (2011), pp. 888–954.

[66] *The Commonwealth ex rel. Johnson* v. *Halloway*, p. 449.　　[67] Ibid., p. 447.

Unfortunately for Eastern's administrators, a national audience would be more difficult to convince.

CONFRONTING AN UNSCIENTIFIC FIELD

By the 1860s, Eastern's administrators had spent about thirty years grounding their claims to expertise in the situational experience provided by their appointments at the prison. Unlike most groups claiming professional status throughout history (e.g., clergy, lawyers, doctors), the administrators lacked an independent basis for their claims, beyond this experience. Traditionally, professionals use various formal structures – including training and specialized education, national networks, licensing requirements, and a code of ethics – to maintain jurisdiction over their work, perpetuate their prized knowledge, recruit additional members, or create barriers to entry.[68] Nevertheless, experience alone was sufficient to distinguish Eastern's administrators from local penal reformers and legislators, and combat (to some degree) these groups' incursions. In the 1860s, however, Eastern's administrators found an external basis to strengthen their claims: science.

Science was a burgeoning field in the nineteenth century, its popularity exploding after the Civil War.[69] As historian Dorothy Ross and others have argued, science provided a new basis for the authority of social elites, whose position in society was challenged by rapid postwar changes.[70] The emerging science of penology became central to administrators' claims to expertise, and to their defense of the Pennsylvania System, by

---

[68] Andrew Abbott, *The System of Professions: An Essay on the Division of Expert Labor.* University of Chicago Press, 1988; Samuel Haber, *The Quest for Authority and Honor in the American Professions, 1750–1900.* University of Chicago Press, 1991; Thomas L. Haskell, *The Emergence of Professional Social Science: The American Social Science Association and the Nineteenth-Century Crisis of Authority.* Urbana: University of Illinois Press, 1977; Magali Sarfatti Larson, *The Rise of Professionalism.* Berkeley: University of California Press, 1977; Harold L. Wilensky, "The Professionalization of Everyone?" *American Journal of Sociology* 70:2 (1964), pp. 137–158.

[69] For example, the American Social Science Association was founded in Boston in 1865. See Robert H. Wiebe, *The Search for Order, 1877–1920.* New York: Hill and Wang, 1966; Haskell, *The Emergence of Professional Social Science*; Dorothy Ross, *The Origins of American Social Science.* New York: Cambridge University Press, 1991; Howard Schweber, "The 'Science' of Legal Science: The Model of the Natural Sciences in Nineteenth-Century American Legal Education." *Law and History Review* 17:3 (1999), pp. 421–466.

[70] Ross, *Origins*, p. 62. See also Nicole Hahn Rafter, *Creating Born Criminals.* Chicago: University of Illinois Press, 1997, pp. 55–72.

fortifying their attacks on local penal reformers, the state legislature, *and* their national critics. While Eastern's administrators continued to tout their situational experience, they increasingly grounded their arguments in a particular knowledge that they had cultivated through diligent study. In case their claim was too subtle for their audience, the administrators made sure to frame these discussions with explicit references to science.

The Utility of Penal Science

Those interested in penal reform (and in governance more broadly) had long used the language of experimentation, while penal reformers and prison administrators fastidiously collected statistics about prisons' functioning and their apparent effects on crime. But while penal reformers' and prison administrators' methodologies do not appear markedly different in the 1860s and 1870s, their language saw a significant transformation as they embraced the new "penal science."[71] This transition was especially noticeable at Eastern, where the administrators saw their own and their prison's salvation in penal science.

Prior to the 1860s, science was not absent from Eastern's annual reports, but it was muted and different from the type of science they later identified. References to the "moral science," for example, could be found in their earlier reports, but this term generally referred to philosophical considerations rather than to a branch of physical or social science. "Science" as such was not an explicit concern in the first dozen reports. Like others in the field, however, Eastern's administrators had routinely used the language of experimentation and produced annual reports with tabulated statistics for decades (see Chapter 5).

Perhaps more than other prisons, Eastern's administrators had anxiously compiled statistics, including data on their prisoners' health and mortality, prisoners' apparent reformation and recidivism (measured by

[71] Most historians place the emergence of "penal science" in the 1870s with the adult reformatory movement, the first American prison congresses, and the National Prison Association. For example, Alexander Pisciotta, *Benevolent Repression: Social Control and the American Reformatory-Prison Movement*. New York University Press, 1994; Larry E. Sullivan, *The Prison Reform Movement: Forlorn Hope*. Boston: Twayne Publishers, 1990. However, the first references occurred before the Civil War. See for example, Francis C. Gray, *Prison Discipline in America*. London: John Murray, 1848. Also, "As the science of prison discipline might be considered in its infancy, it was regarded as their duty to endeavour, by discussion, to diffuse such light as was practicable, upon the several questions which it embraced." Eastern State Penitentiary, Inspectors' Report, *The Nineteenth Annual Report of the Inspectors*, p.3.

their return to Eastern), and the cost of operating the prison from the beginning – their reports becoming more extensive over time. Whereas from the 1850s onward the administrators urged the state legislature to review their reports before passing penal legislation (as we have seen), in the 1830s and 1840s, the administrators had urged their critics around the Atlantic World to review their reports before passing judgement on the Pennsylvania System and Eastern. The administrators repeatedly emphasized, as the inspectors did in their 1835 report, that the figures and discussions in their reports allowed observers "to obtain[] a true knowledge of the Institution."[72] In the late 1840s, particularly concerned with insanity and mortality, Eastern's Physician Robert Given chided his reader, "it is only by comparison between extended tables of this kind [exhibiting the prison's health and mortality statistics], that anything like just and philosophic deductions can be drawn" about the appropriate mode of prison discipline.[73] In this sense, the model of scientific inquiry – if not always the terminology – had been the administrators' model from the start because of the importance of data or evidence to their efforts to neutralize the calumnious myths.

Over time, however, their reliance on science *per se* became more pronounced. The administrators' first references to science appeared sporadically in the 1840s, but science became a common referent from 1859 onward, particularly among Eastern's inspectors.[74] By the 1860s and 1870s, Eastern's inspectors routinely referred to the "prison science" or "penology," sometimes as a "branch of social science" or "as an element in social science."[75] This change was primarily discursive – their overall strategy of emphasizing experimentation or data collection and analysis remained unchanged.

In this later period, penal science provided a framework through which the inspectors could claim their system's superiority – largely in ways they had attempted to establish from the beginning. As the inspectors explained in their 1859 report, "In physical sciences successful

---

[72] Eastern State Penitentiary, Inspectors' Report, *Sixth Annual Report of the Inspectors of the Eastern State Penitentiary of Pennsylvania*. Philadelphia: J. W. Allen, 1835, p. 6.

[73] Physician's Report, idem, *Seventeenth Annual Report of the Inspectors*, p. 31.

[74] In the annual reports published between 1859 and 1880, only the annual report published in 1878 lacked a reference to "science." Even this report, however, contained references to "scientist," and "scientific."

[75] Eastern State Penitentiary, Inspectors' Report, *Forty-First Annual Report of the Inspectors*, p. 13, 33. This trend likely also reflects the influence of Richard Vaux as President of the Board of Inspectors, as I shall discuss in the next section.

experiment is proved by demonstration." They had offered such a demonstration, which, they believed, should be sufficient. "If the united evidence of three decades, as to the practical effects of the separate system, cannot be relied on as exemplifying its real character, then one must look in vain for higher sanction than such cumulative evidence, to attest that which is claimed to be indubitable."[76] Eastern's inspectors in this later period were such proponents of penal science and its emphasis on evidence because their evidence, they argued, favored the superiority of the Pennsylvania System when compared with the Auburn System. Their annual reports, the inspectors claimed in 1866, "prove beyond reasonable cavil, and in satisfaction of intelligent inquiry, that our system of penitentiary punishment compares favorably so far as its results are to be considered, with any system yet adopted."[77] Specifically, according to the inspectors in 1870, "the facts, statements, deductions and experience" described in the reports prove the Pennsylvania System is "as wise, as beneficial, as effective, as any now established by law."[78] No one had ever "successfully refuted" their claims that "the separate system is the safest, the best, the most scientific or philosophic system."[79] Science offered credibility to these long-made claims of their system's superiority.

Throughout these later decades, Eastern's inspectors claimed that the central reason why Eastern was criticized or overlooked was the absence of objective, scientific observers. As the inspectors explained in 1860, when "fully and impartially investigated ... the separate system of Penitentiary punishment converts, convinces and conquers." Too often, however, "sordid, sinister or selfish purposes" interfered.[80] Stated more scientifically, the inspectors explained they needed an "unprejudiced and disinterested student of penal science" to witness the Pennsylvania System's success.[81] If only observers would look at the data, the inspectors

[76] Eastern State Penitentiary, Inspectors' Report, *Thirtieth Annual Report of the Inspectors of the State Penitentiary for the Eastern District of Pennsylvania.* Philadelphia: M'Laughlin Brothers, 1859, p. 6.

[77] Eastern State Penitentiary, Inspectors' Report, *Thirty-Seventh Annual Report of the Inspectors of the State Penitentiary for the Eastern District of Pennsylvania.* Philadelphia: McLaughlin Brothers, 1866, p. 25.

[78] Eastern State Penitentiary, Inspector's Report, *Forty-First Annual Report of the Inspectors*, p. 7–8.

[79] Ibid., pp. 9–10.

[80] Eastern State Penitentiary, Inspector's Report, *Thirty-First Annual Report of the Inspectors*, p. 8.

[81] Eastern State Penitentiary, Inspector's Report, *Forty-First Annual Report of the Inspectors*, pp. 7–8.

argued, the Pennsylvania System would be vindicated. Indeed, the year before, the inspectors were dumbfounded that they did not have more converts:

It would be admitted without hesitation, in almost any known science, that a theory was either proved or disproved by the experience gained in its practical application during forty years. The investigations of so long a period would, among men capable of judging, be generally accepted as evincing the truth or falsity of the fact or principle in dispute. To disturb or deny the result thus reached would, before a competent tribunal, demand the most irrefragable evidence. To oppose successfully facts thus obtained, and the logical deductions from them, requires some other theory, and its thorough investigation as shown by experience of years, in a form similar in its minuteness and accuracy to the one with which a comparison is to be made.[82]

Evidently, they thought, common observers were neither "men capable of judging" nor part of "a competent tribunal."

This claim was a central point in the defense of the Pennsylvania System, and in their own claims to expertise: Critics of the system were biased or ignorant individuals who refused to analyze the data objectively. As the inspectors claimed in their 1860 report, the Pennsylvania System "has struggled against ignorance and prejudice, resulting from an unwillingness to investigate its principles, or a disbelief in its utility."[83] The challenges were really twofold, as they explained in 1862. On the one hand, "so much ignorance exists on the subject of convict separation"; on the other hand, "the most mercenary tests are only thus applied to systems of prison discipline," including the question, does the prison "yield for profit."[84] Making matters worse, the inspectors wrote in 1871, there were impostors "professing to be possessed of general information on penal science as applied to prison populations and systems of convict punishment, who entirely mistake the principles, and are ignorant of the practical results, which these Reports exhibit of the Pennsylvania system of Penitentiary convict discipline."[85] As Eastern's inspectors saw it, the

---

[82] Eastern State Penitentiary, Inspectors' Report, *Fortieth Annual Report of the Inspectors of the State Penitentiary for the Eastern District of Pennsylvania*. Philadelphia: M'Laughlin Brothers, 1869, p. 6.

[83] Eastern State Penitentiary, Inspector's Report, *Thirty-First Annual Report of the Inspectors*, p. 21.

[84] Eastern State Warden's Report, Inspector's Report, *Thirty-Third Annual Report of the Inspectors*, pp. 43–44.

[85] Eastern State Penitentiary, Inspector's Report, *Forty-Second Annual Report of the Inspectors*, p. 34.

deck was stacked against the Pennsylvania System because they were the only scientifically rigorous experts capable of evaluating its merits.

Eastern's inspectors longed for the day "[w]hen penal jurisprudence is elevated to the position of a science." They explained in their 1866 report that for penology to truly become a science, prisons must operate scientifically. First, prisons had to be "managed by higher interests than profit and loss." So long as prisons were judged by their ability to turn a profit – one of the strongest criticisms of the Pennsylvania System and Eastern – prison management would not be "elevated to the position of a science." Second, prisons had to be supervised by qualified individuals. Anticipating later Gilded Age and Progressive Era reform politics targeting patronage, the inspectors added that "those intrusted with their [prisons'] direction" must "have a better claim to their positions, than the temporary supremacy of political parties." Relatedly, prisons would not be managed scientifically until prison administrators had "large experience, acquired capabilities, and patient and intelligent devotion to the subject. ..." (These requirements, of course, matched the characteristics Eastern's inspectors applied to themselves.) Most important, once penology is "elevated to the position of a science ... then, and then only, will Pennsylvania find her penitentiary system approved and adopted."[86] When science ruled the day, the Pennsylvania System would receive fair assessments and recognition of its superiority.[87]

CONFRONTING OTHER PIONEERS OF PENOLOGY

Despite the inspectors' efforts, the mantle of professional penologist was bestowed in the 1870s on other men who, while bringing prestige to their states and institutions, increasingly gained recognition as individuals. In addition to embracing science as enthusiastically as Eastern's administrators, these penal reformers also created the formal structures that signified professional status. Two men in particular – Enoch C. Wines and Zebulon Brockway – stood out.

Enoch C. Wines gained recognition through his work with the New York Prison Association (NYPA). Along with his fellow NYPA member,

---

[86] Eastern State Penitentiary, Inspector's Report, *Thirty-Seventh Annual Report of the Inspectors*, p. 36.

[87] There was another, more selfish motivation. As the inspectors explained in 1859, elevating penology to a science would also "awaken Legislative mind to the conception of the importance of institutions which are more than receptacles for convicts, wherein incarceration is not the only object to be attained." Eastern State Penitentiary, Inspector's Report, *Thirtieth Annual Report of the Inspectors*, pp. 7–8.

Theodore W. Dwight, Wines toured the nation's prisons, which they later described in a widely read report published in 1867. Wines went on to found the National Prison Association in 1870, hosting increasingly frequent national and international prison congresses and publishing their various *Proceedings* and *Transactions* as repositories of penal knowledge.

Zebulon Brockway, also of New York, became a popular figure at these meetings. Brockway had established a system of confinement for salvageable (i.e., young, but not juvenile, first-time) offenders involving labor, religion, and education at Elmira Reformatory, the nation's first adult reformatory. The Elmira System became the template for prisons built in this period.[88]

Wines and Brockway became particularly popular in part because their ideas fit well with the reigning penological ideas. In the postbellum era, prisoner reformation was regaining prestige, partly in reaction to the dominance of profitable prisoner labor over penological decisions within prisons.[89] Wines and Brockway had called for and outlined a new "prison science" to achieve reformation.[90] For the second time in the nineteenth century, New York had eclipsed Pennsylvania's role in penal reform – this time for ideas that, from the administrators' perspective, were not at all new. In this context, penal discussions took on an increasingly personal dimension for Eastern's administrators.

That Wines, Brockway, and others were gaining such fame for their efforts was particularly painful for Eastern's inspectors. From their perspective, none of these "new" ideas were innovative; they had been endorsing the same factors – and (mostly) practicing what they preached – for decades. Indeed, Eastern's administrators had stayed true to the rhetoric of reformation far longer than other prisons' administrators and even some penal reformers. Recent critiques of prison labor in which the profit motive supplanted penological concerns, for example, were tropes Eastern's administrators had been reciting for decades. In 1872, the inspectors especially were devastated "that elsewhere than in Pennsylvania, … [men were] claiming the merit of bringing to the notice of thoughtful men the question of convict reform and penitentiary punishment, and the serious defects in the administration of penal

---

[88] Pisciotta, *Benevolent Repression*. See also Sullivan, *The Prison Reform Movement*.
[89] See especially Rebecca M. McLennan, *The Crisis of Imprisonment: Protest, Politics, and the Making of the American Penal State, 1776–1941*. New York: Cambridge University Press, 2008.
[90] Pisciotta, *Benevolent Repression*.

laws. ..." It was a matter of "justice to the State of Pennsylvania" –
the inspectors were careful not to claim the insult to their own work – to
recognize "the labors of some of her citizens for nearly a century."[91]

Lack of recognition was particularly egregious because Eastern's
administrators had long lamented that penal reformers, other prison
administrators, and legislatures were neglecting Eastern's example. In
their 1863 report, the inspectors expressed their "earnest hope, that
their [annual reports'] utility might be recognized by all engaged in the
important work of administering systems of prison discipline."[92] Months
after Wines and Dwight's 1867 report was published, Eastern's inspectors
sounded even more disheartened, complaining, "Public attention to [our
reports] has been so often invited, and as yet with but so little interest
excited in them." The beleaguered inspectors felt "best satisfied yearly
to increase the amount of this information, trusting that when these
Reports shall be considered by earnest men, their labors will be thereby
greatly aided in those investigations which will be regarded as of primary
importance...."[93]

More was at stake than simply Eastern's reputation, however. For some
administrators, this was personal – their professional status had become
part of their identity. By the 1870s, Richard Vaux had been a member
of Eastern's Board of Inspectors for nearly thirty years and its president
for more than twenty years. Between 1850, when he was elected secretary of the board, and his death in 1895, Vaux may have written most
of the inspectors' annual reports[94] and they clearly reflected his influence. Vaux had been one of the most avid users of scientific discourse
and, although a lawyer by training, he frequently presented himself as a
"social scientist." An 1870 issue of *The Evening Telegraph* introduced
Eastern's annual report (probably forwarded by Vaux himself) with the

[91] Eastern State Penitentiary, Inspectors' Report, *Forty-Third Annual Report of the Inspectors of the State Penitentiary for the Eastern District of Pennsylvania*. Philadelphia:
McLaughlin Brothers, 1872, p. 22.
[92] Eastern State Penitentiary, Inspector's Report, *Thirty-Fourth Annual Report of the
Inspectors*, p. 6.
[93] Eastern State Penitentiary, Inspector's Report, *Thirty-Ninth Annual Report of the Inspectors*, pp. 23–24.
[94] See Barnes, *The Evolution of Penology*, p. 240. While the president and/or secretary of
the board would write the first draft of the annual report, it was collectively revised and
then voted on by the entire board. See Eastern State Penitentiary, *Minute Books of the
Board of Inspectors and Board of Trustees of the Eastern State Penitentiary*, Volumes
1–4. Eastern State Penitentiary Collection, Record Group 15 (#15.44). Pennsylvania
State Archives, 1829–1885.

subheading, "Hon. Richard Vaux as a Social Scientist – Facts, Figures, Theories, and Results."[95] Despite having also served as the Recorder and Mayor of Philadelphia and in the U.S. House of Representatives, Vaux's work as a penologist was central to his identity.[96] It is not surprising, then, that he was furious when others in the field received more attention for similar work.

Rather than giving up, in the 1860s and 1870s, Eastern's administrators redoubled their efforts to achieve recognition for their prison and for themselves. In 1872, Inspector Richard Vaux wrote a 143-page "Brief Sketch of the Origin and History of the State Penitentiary for the Eastern District of Pennsylvania, at Philadelphia." Writing at the direction of the Board of Inspectors that he himself controlled, Vaux would send his monumental history to the International Prison Congress (organized by Wines) to be held in London a few months later. Vaux made his object perfectly clear: Eastern's long-standing use of the Pennsylvania System was underappreciated and excluded from recent debates and he would correct this injustice. He explained,

Within the past few years public meetings have been held in the United States, convened for the purpose of considering the subject of penal jurisprudence and the various plans of prison discipline for the punishment of offenders against the law. Whatever of merit these meetings may have promised, it has become a question, if the energy which marked the efforts of many of the participants therein was not more prominently exerted in discussing collateral questions, than in investigating the direct issues between the separation of convicts and their congregation, while undergoing punishment for their crimes. It may be doubted if the Pennsylvania, or the "separate" and individual-treatment system of Penitentiary discipline, has received at any of these conventions, that unbiased and calm investigation, which a liberal spirit of disinterested inquiry should have prompted.[97]

The field had moved away from the Auburn–Eastern debate, but Vaux sought to recalibrate discussions away from what he saw as "collateral questions" and restore Eastern to the spotlight it had long deserved.

---

95 *The Evening Telegraph*, "Cherry Hill: Annual Report of the Inspectors of the Eastern Penitentiary of Pennsylvania," 13:91 (1870), p. 1.

96 Vaux was not alone. As Walters has explained, for reformers (including Eastern's gentlemen reformers), "reform was more than just another job. It was an important part of oneself." Roger G. Walters, *American Reformers, 1815–1860*. New York: Hill and Wang, 1978 [1997], p. 14.

97 Vaux, *Brief Sketch*, p. iii.

Eastern's administrators had previously been receptive to similar congresses, as these congresses had been receptive to them.[98] The newer congresses – under Wines' control – were not. Prison administrators from around the world had been asked to contribute written descriptions of their prison's discipline to enable scientific comparisons to determine the best mode of incarceration. Yet, in Vaux's opinion, "[w]hatever of merit these meetings may have promised," their discussion increasingly focused on "collateral" questions rather than the important competition between separate and congregate confinement. In 1874, Vaux raised this topic repeatedly at the National Prison Congress held in St. Louis, where he served as an interim president, but with embarrassing results. Wines severely edited the essay Vaux contributed to the conference's *Transactions*, reducing Vaux's discussion of appropriate systems of prison discipline, "because [it was] not directly bearing upon the questions that engaged the attention of the Congress."[99] This shift in focus slighted Eastern, in Vaux's view, robbing it of its chance to shine when compared to other prisons. Wine's action prompted Vaux, on behalf of the inspectors, to write another essay, only half the length of his 1872 piece, as part of their annual report published in 1875.

Vaux's response was most heated, however, following the Stockholm Congress of 1878. Writing the inspectors' annual report for that year, Vaux wrote dismissively of "the gentlemen who, by some process of appointment, were called the commissioners" of the Prison Congress, referring to Wines and to some extent Dwight, who also served as an American delegate.[100] These commissioners had "no authoritative capacity"; instead, they were part of the congress "chiefly by

---

98 They praised the 1846 Prison Congress at Frankfurt-am-Main (in modern-day Germany) for endorsing the Pennsylvania System. Eastern State Penitentiary, Inspectors' Report, *Eighteenth Annual Report of the Inspectors of the Eastern State Penitentiary of Pennsylvania*. Philadelphia: Ed. Barrington and Geo. D. Haswell, 1847, p. 27. Additionally, though angry at the organizers of the 1872 London Congress, Vaux cited at length "a paper prepared by request of the Committee of the English Social Science Association, and presented to the London [Prison] Congress last July." Eastern State Penitentiary, Inspectors' Report, *Forty-Fourth Annual Report of the Inspectors of the State Penitentiary for the Eastern District of Pennsylvania*. Philadelphia: J. B. Chandler, 1873, pp. 12–13. The paper won his favor because it supported the Pennsylvania System.

99 Enoch C. Wines, ed., *Transactions of the Third National Prison Reform Congress Held at Saint Louis, Missouri*. New York: Office of the Association, 1874, p. 263.

100 Eastern State Penitentiary, *Forty-Ninth Annual Report of the Inspectors of the State Penitentiary for the Eastern District of Pennsylvania*. Philadelphia: M'Laughlin Brothers, 1879, p. 48.

complimentary appointment."[101] Not only had they taken on "the duty self-imposed," but they were unscientific in their approach – a grave sin to the professional penologist.[102] For example, the commissioners seemed to think the reason for the Congress "too apparent to need argument to prove it."[103] As Vaux explained, this approach was highly problematic: "To properly prepare such information as would be required for the direction of the thought and investigation of the members of these congresses, would have been the first duty of" its organizers.[104]

Even worse, in Vaux's view, there was no substance to the meetings; the members of the Congress dealt only superficially with penal science. As Vaux described it, "the failure to treat the subject of crime-cause, its origin, its prevention, or reformatory, or punitive systems of convict punishment, in that enlarged, enlightened, and scientific method which so pretentious an assembly gave reason to expect, is, perhaps, the most marked of all its [the Congress's] results."[105] Vaux explained, "Glittering generalities might suffice for the formal and introductory meeting, when many who have never studied the foundation principles on which the science of crime punishment rests," but this was neither the first meeting, nor was there an absence of data to review.[106] At the base of Vaux's criticism was the failure of the Congress to consult the evidence produced at Eastern: "The statistical information published during the past ten years by this Penitentiary, limited as true it is to one State Penitentiary, should have been at least considered if not mentioned by the eminent and learned scientists who met to deliberate on the subjects."[107] Vaux did not present his complaint as a matter of pride; rather, repeating a familiar charge, he argued it indicated how unqualified the organizers and participants were to discuss the topic: "If so inconsiderable [sic] a source of information was unknown to the members who met at this Congress, it might be assumed that the careful research and investigation, which give value to scientific opinion, were wanting even to render the 'formulated conclusions' worthy of the name of authority."[108] As Vaux knew, the Congress's proceedings would be taken to be authoritative and would receive high praise, despite their lack of rigor.

In closing, Vaux explained why he had been critical of the Stockholm Prison Congress. He discussed the Congress "only to emphasize the efforts made in Philadelphia during the past twenty years." Ultimately,

[101] Ibid., p. 57.   [102] Ibid., p. 48.   [103] Ibid., p. 47.   [104] Ibid., p. 48.
[105] Ibid., p. 49.   [106] Ibid., p. 49.   [107] Ibid., p. 56.   [108] Ibid., pp. 56–57.

he sought to "protect them from that relegation into obscurity, which the ignorance of their character and the results that have been attained from them can even temporarily effect." Perhaps speaking to himself more than to his addressees, Vaux instructed "[t]hose who have an earnest interest in the many most important subjects" of penal science "not to be discouraged."[109] One day, penal science would be treated as a true science. When commentators "enlist unostentatious students and thinkers, who, starting from the foundation, will seek to master all the principles" and "the material is obtained after patient labor and exhaustive investigation, then may be expected such formulated conclusions as will prove, that like all other sciences, its laws are inductive demonstrations, and that they are based upon the reason of things which gives to them the force which makes them authoritative."[110] Until then, upstart parvenus would continue to receive attention for their "[g]littering generalities," limited knowledge, and unsophisticated methods, and the penal science would remain in a primitive form. So long as Wines and his ilk remained in the spotlight, Vaux believed, Eastern's illustrious history, and its administrators with it, would remain neglected and obscure.

EXPANDING PROFESSIONALIZATION AT EASTERN

A distinct but gradual shift had occurred in the administrators' public writings of the 1860s and 1870s. Establishing their own professional status had taken the place of defending the Pennsylvania System. The annual reports from the 1860s onward focused less on the calumnious myths and increasingly on the professionalism, expertise, training, and other qualifications of everyone who worked in the prison. By the 1880s, the administrators' concern with professionalization at Eastern had reached new heights – and they had better evidence of professionalization to show off.

When Warden Townsend resigned in 1881, the inspectors elected long-time overseer Michael Cassidy to become warden. They described his extensive background in their annual report: "Mr. Cassidy had been twenty years in the service of the Inspectors, in almost every station for duty, under the administration of the penitentiary. He had been on two occasions the acting warden, and held the place of chief overseer."[111] Not

---

[109] Ibid., p. 57.   [110] Ibid., pp. 57–58.
[111] Eastern State Penitentiary, *Fifty-Second Annual Report of the Inspectors of the State Penitentiary for the Eastern District of Pennsylvania*. Philadelphia: Sherman & Co.,

since the first decade, when the inspectors described Samuel Wood's qualifications to become Eastern's first Warden, had the inspectors justified an appointment. Their discussion does not appear to have been motivated by insecurity about promoting a guard to the position of warden – indeed, John Halloway had first served as clerk before becoming warden. Instead, they repeated their reference to Cassidy's experience in more general discussions of the importance of qualified staff. For example, a few years after Cassidy's appointment, the inspectors repeated his qualifications: "The chief executive, the Warden, has been employed in every department of administration. Twenty-five years ago he first came into the Penitentiary service as a carpenter, then advanced through all the grades, was acting Warden for some months on two occasions, and unanimously elected Warden in the month of April, 1881."[112] Advancing through the ranks was the ultimate symbol of Cassidy's qualifications.

Warden Cassidy also discussed other administrators and staff members' qualifications. He noted in his annual report, "Dr. Ball, the Resident Physician, is, from his professional training, entitled to respect. The Rev. Joseph Welch, the Moral Instructor, is well adapted to his position. The statistical tables were prepared by Mr. Bussinger, the Clerk of the Institution, whose fidelity, industry, care, and integrity are fully recognized."[113] Cassidy also referred to the qualifications of official visitors to the prison.[114] It seemed, in this period, that everyone affiliated with the prison had to be scrutinized for their professional qualifications because unworthy affiliates could reflect poorly on the prison.

1882, p. 82. By his promotion, Cassidy had already served as the temporary warden many times during several wardens' brief respites away from the prison (Eastern State Penitentiary, *Warden's Daily Journal*, Volumes 1–2. Eastern State Penitentiary Collection, Record Group 15 (#15.50). Pennsylvania State Archives, 1829–1877). Indeed, after Warden Halloway died in office, Cassidy became warden *pro tempore* (1869–1870), while the prison's physician, "Dr. Klapp was nominally Warden." Vaux, *Brief Sketch*, p. 82. Teeters and Shearer, describe Cassidy as Eastern's first "'career' warden"; although they refer to his rise through the ranks, the term aptly describes the way in which Cassidy embraced prison management as his vocation. Negley K. Teeters and John D. Shearer, *The Prison at Philadelphia, Cherry Hill: The Separate System of Penal Discipline, 1829–1913*. New York: Columbia University Press, 1957, p. 90.

[112] Eastern State Penitentiary, *Fifty-Fifth Annual Report of the Inspectors of the State Penitentiary for the Eastern District of Pennsylvania*. Philadelphia: Allen, Lane & Scott's Printing House, 1885, p. 9.

[113] E.g., Eastern State Penitentiary, *Sixty-Seventh Annual Report of the Inspectors of the State Penitentiary for the Eastern District of Pennsylvania*. Philadelphia: The Chas. H. Elliot Co., 1897, p. 142.

[114] E.g., Ibid., pp. 142–143.

This new obsession with the prison's overall level of professionalization manifested in other ways. By the 1880s, the administrators adopted
more traditional markers of professional status. The inspectors requested
the warden to regularly attend the national conferences and meetings on
prison and penology.[115] They also sought to hire men with specific qualifications and established a "training school" to train prison "officers,"
now rarely called "overseers."[116]

Notably, the administrators continued to fill their annual reports with
the same arguments and claims to professional expertise that they had
initiated years before, sometimes almost verbatim.[117] Although he had
not previously written annual reports, Warden Cassidy, who ultimately
became Eastern's second-longest-serving Warden in the nineteenth century and the second warden to die in office (in 1900), joined in. In 1897,
he published a book emphasizing in its subtitle his "Experience Gained
During Thirty-Seven Years Continuous Service in the Administration of
the Eastern State Penitentiary, Pennsylvania." While Cassidy noted, "It
is unfortunate that misinformation or misconception, and positive ignorance, exists of the methods in practice here," he devoted more attention
to emphasizing the importance of specialized knowledge, training, and
the expertise that comes from long experience.[118]

As Eastern's administrators sought to demonstrate their professional
status, their prison also became more bureaucratized, both internally
and externally. Over the last decades of the nineteenth century, Eastern's
administrators maintained greater contact with the Board of Charities
and Corrections (est. 1869) and the Board of Pardons (est. 1874). Eastern
also became enmeshed in a larger state-level expansion of carceral facilities: Eastern and Western were joined by a reformatory at Huntingdon in

---

[115] E.g., Eastern State Penitentiary, Warden's Report, *Fifty-Eighth Annual Report of the Inspectors of the State Penitentiary for the Eastern District of Pennsylvania*. Philadel-phia: Allen, Lane & Scott, 1888, p. 134.

[116] Eastern State Penitentiary, Inspectors' Report, *Fiftieth Annual Report of the Inspec-tors of the State Penitentiary for the Eastern District of Pennsylvania*. Philadelphia: McLaughlin Brothers, 1880, p.87; Eastern State Penitentiary, Inspector's Report, *Fifty-Eighth Annual Report of the Inspectors*, pp. 129–130.

[117] An excellent example is a section in Vaux's last annual report; Eastern State Penitentiary, *Sixty-Seventh Annual Report of the Inspectors of the State Penitentiary for the Eastern District of Pennsylvania*. Philadelphia: The Chas. H. Elliot Co., 1894, p. 110.

[118] Michael J. Cassidy, *Warden Cassidy on Prisons and Convicts: Remarks from Obser-vations and Experience Gained During Thirty-Seven Years Continuous Service in the Administration of the Eastern State Penitentiary, Pennsylvania*. Philadelphia: Patterson & White, 1897, p. 3.

1889; once Huntingdon absorbed those younger or salvageable offenders, thus removing them from the general prison population, Eastern became a specialized institutional for serious offenders for whom reformation was not considered likely.

Internally, the size of the prison population, as well as the number of men working at the prison, increased. After 1879, Eastern regularly housed more than 1,000 prisoners. With more prisoners came more staff, including, by 1897, a consulting alienist. By 1904, the prison boasted a dentist, a pharmacist, and a half-dozen consulting medical professionals (including surgeons and an ophthalmologist).[119]

By the early 1900s, Eastern was effectively a different prison. The fully pre-bureaucratic prison managed by gentlemen reformers striving to claim professional status had been replaced by a bureaucratized prison managed by authentic professionals. These transitions had begun in the 1860s as part of an effort to defend the Pennsylvania System, accelerated in the 1880s once Eastern's administrators finally replaced defense with professionalization, and were generally complete by the 1900s.

* * *

This chapter argues that by the 1870s, the Pennsylvania System was no longer the main source of identity and status for Eastern's administrators. Their earlier claims to humanitarian excellence, derived from their efforts to protect the Pennsylvania System, had given way to claims to professional expertise. Like their claims to humanitarian excellence, these claims to professional status had also begun as a strategy for protecting the Pennsylvania System, but also for protecting their autonomy over Eastern. By claiming that their unique experience as prison administrators gave them a special expertise, the administrators could situate themselves as the party most capable of evaluating criticism and proposed policy changes. As with the other strategies aimed at neutralizing the pains of their deviance, these claims to expertise were beneficial to Eastern's administrators. In this case, however, describing themselves as professional penologists or social scientists provided a new status. Unlike other strategies, claiming professional expertise did not require locating the

---

[119] Eastern State Penitentiary, *Sixty-Eighth Annual Report of the Inspectors of the State Penitentiary for the Eastern District of Pennsylvania.* Philadelphia: The Chas. H. Elliot Co., 1898; Eastern State Penitentiary, *Seventy-Fifth Annual Report of the Inspectors of the State Penitentiary for the Eastern District of Pennsylvania.* Philadelphia, 1905.

administrators' proclaimed positive attributes in the Pennsylvania System; increasingly, their claims to professional status became decoupled from the Pennsylvania System and ultimately became ends in themselves.

Their turn to professionalization as an alternative status was well timed: as we shall see in Chapter 10, in the 1860s and 1870s, publicly defending the Pennsylvania System against decades-old criticism no longer provided a legitimate platform to elaborate on its administrators' benevolence and excellence. In this context, the Pennsylvania System itself no longer offered administrators the same advantage of difference that had kept it personally institutionalized for Eastern's administrators. Having found a new source of status, Eastern's administrators no longer needed the Pennsylvania System, which was itself beginning to crumble under the weight of rapid change.

10

Fading Away

National Obscurity, Catastrophic Overcrowding, and the Individual Treatment System

How doubled many of the cells to-day. Number of Convicts at this time 666.

Warden Edward Townsend (1870), Warden's Daily Journal[1]

It was first called the "Solitary system," then it was more correctly styled the "Separate system," and now the truer and more philosophic description as modified and improved is, the "Individual system of convict discipline."

Board of Inspectors (1875), Annual Report[2]

It may be worth while to ascertain if the public whipping of such persons would not deter, when all else failed.

Eastern's Board of Inspectors (1888), Annual Report[3]

Be it enacted, &c., That the proper authorities of the Eastern State Penitentiary are authorized, at their discretion, to have any or all of the persons

---

[1] Eastern State Penitentiary, *Warden's Daily Journal*, Volumes 1–2. Eastern State Penitentiary Collection, Record Group 15 (#15.50). Pennsylvania State Archives. 1829–1877, December 15, 1870.

[2] Eastern State Penitentiary, *Forty-Fifth Annual Report of the Inspectors of the State Penitentiary for the Eastern District of Pennsylvania*. Philadelphia: Sherman & Co., 1875, p. 23.

[3] Eastern State Penitentiary, Inspectors' Report, *Fifty-Eighth Annual Report of the Inspectors of the State Penitentiary for the Eastern District of Pennsylvania*. Philadelphia: Allen, Lane & Scott, 1888, p. 123.

confined in the said penitentiary congregated for the several purposes of worship, labor, learning, and recreation ...

Pennsylvania State Legislature (1913), "An Act Relating to the Management of Eastern State Penitentiary"[4]

THE SEPARATE SYSTEM NO MORE

During the 1860s and the 1870s, various core elements of the Pennsylvania System began to recede at Eastern, both in theory and practice, privately and publicly, and more systematically than ever before. During the previous decades, for example, an ironclad rule specified that prisoners receive visits only from official visitors – the prison's administrators and staff, PSAMPP members, members of the clergy entering in an official capacity at the request of a prisoner, members of the grand jury or government officials, and those special visitors like Charles Dickens and Alexis de Tocqueville who were allowed to meet with the prisoners by special permission. At some point between 1860 and 1870, however, Eastern's administrators began allowing prisoners to receive visits from their family members.

Two cases offer a contrast. In August 1860, for the first time, the administrators authorized an exception to the rules about visitation, giving special permission to a family member to visit a prisoner. For one week, the mother of Prisoner No. 4146, Edward Jackson, stayed by her son's deathbed. According to Warden Halloway, "In consideration of [the prisoner's] low and helpless condition ... [his mother] ha[d] been permitted to remain with him day and night by authority of [Inspectors] Messrs Powers & Sheppard."[5] When the prisoner finally died "of 'Purpura' ... His mother was with him."[6] Nearly a decade later, however, visits from family members had been routinized and allowed under far less extreme circumstances. Warden Townsend noted casually in his journal, "A number of persons came with suitable permits to visit their friends, nothing else to remark."[7] So common were these visits that no other references to family and friends visiting prisoners were made in the warden's journal in

---

[4] Pennsylvania, "No. 121: An Act Relating to the Management of Eastern State Penitentiary," in *Laws of the General Assembly of the Commonwealth of Pennsylvania.* Harrisburg: C. E. Aughinbaugh, 1913, p. 708.

[5] Eastern State Penitentiary, *Warden's Daily Journal*, August 20, 1860.

[6] Ibid., August 24, 1860.   [7] Ibid., May 24, 1870.

these years. The days of prisoners being cut off from the world had come to an end.

Notably, the administrators did not hide this violation of the Pennsylvania System as they did with their other behind-the-scenes practices – far from it. By the early 1870s they publicized this practice and even included family visitation in their redefinition of the Pennsylvania System. In their report for 1871, the inspectors explained at length,

> Some persons are still under the impression that a prisoner sentenced to the Eastern Penitentiary is forthwith cut off from all connection with his family, his friends and his kind; that his association with his fellow creatures is sundered; that he is thrust into a solitary cell, and that when its door is closed upon him, he can only regard himself as immured in a sort of tomb, being left to prey upon himself, and wholly cut off from the reach of humanity. This grotesque travesty of the real state of the case, seems to underlie much of what is said adversely to the Pennsylvania system; at least by those who speak flippantly or unadvisedly.

The inspectors then explained the history of the names given to the Pennsylvania System (see Chapter 5), emphasizing their efforts to keep prisoners apart from each other – but not apart from positive influences. They noted the range of visitors allowed to each prisoner and, although they did not include family and friends on this list, the inspectors added that "he corresponds with his family."[8] The following year, however, the inspectors fully ended the charade, stating, "The prisoners receive visits from their families, especially from their mothers, sisters, wives and children, under regulations applying to each individual case." Again, the inspectors sought to emphasize that Eastern was "not of the 'solitary,' sad, gloomy, dungeon-like character which the uninformed have so long persistently applied to it."[9] Unlike their past statements, however, their statement was no longer a matter of reframing the Pennsylvania System; instead, their statement publicly broadcast the fact that they had actually changed one of their system's long-standing rules. This change was not the only one of its kind.

* * *

---

[8] Eastern State Penitentiary, *Forty-Third Annual Report of the Inspectors of the State Penitentiary for the Eastern District of Pennsylvania*. Philadelphia: McLaughlin Brothers, 1872, p. 25.

[9] Eastern State Penitentiary, *Forty-Fourth Annual Report of the Inspectors of the State Penitentiary for the Eastern District of Pennsylvania*. Philadelphia: J.B. Chandler, 1873, p. 11.

This chapter describes the rapid decline of the Pennsylvania System at Eastern in the 1860s and 1870s. I focus on and distinguish between two dimensions of the Pennsylvania System's end – its demise both in practice and in theory. As we have seen, the Pennsylvania System never fully conformed to plan and Eastern's administrators often authorized deviations that they publicly dismissed as fictions circulated by jealous competitors. However, in the postwar period, catastrophic levels of overcrowding caused the Pennsylvania System's most central components to break down in ways that the administrators fought hard to prevent or stop. Indeed, the administrators' actions in the 1860s continue to illustrate their role as the central force responsible for retaining the Pennsylvania System at Eastern – in contrast to the inert legislature. Despite the administrators' efforts, their verbal commitment to the Pennsylvania System outlasted the System's actual physical presence at Eastern. But by the mid-1870s, something had changed in the administrators' commitment: increasingly, the administrators abandoned their attempt to save the Pennsylvania System as it had existed and instead redefined it into something else. Importantly, this shift occurred after external criticism of the Pennsylvania System had abated. Thus, when Eastern's administrators finally abandoned the Pennsylvania System, they were not acceding to the public pressure that they had withstood for nearly five decades; instead, the waning of criticism had removed the administrators from the spotlight, denying them the opportunity to defend the system, and in so doing to tout their own excellence, thereby allowing the Pennsylvania System to deinstitutionalize for Eastern's administrators.

NATIONAL OBSCURITY

While Eastern was never without its (very vocal) critics, criticism of the Pennsylvania System declined in the decades before and after the Civil War. Although the *North American Review* (*NAR*) reported in 1866, "we cannot perceive that the partisan spirit of the advocates of either system has grown milder,"[10] the Auburn–Pennsylvania debate itself was attracting little notice anymore. Indeed, as another *NAR* article from 1866 noted, attention had flagged around the country and even the *NAR*'s coverage of the debate had waned since the late 1840s.[11] Questions about

[10] "Art. III [Review of Nine Works]." *The North American Review* 103:213 (1866), pp. 383–412, p. 404.
[11] "Art. VIII [Review of Three Works]." *The North American Review* 102:210 (1866), pp. 210–235, p. 210.

whether Auburn or Pennsylvania offered a superior system were no longer a major focus in penal reform discussions.

At least three factors are responsible for this shift. First, Louis Dwight – the leading force behind the Boston Prison Discipline Society – passed away in 1854, and with him went much of the zeal sustaining the Auburn–Pennsylvania debate. To be sure, others took up the torch, including the NYPA and the administrators at Charlestown, the Auburn System's model prison. But they proceeded without the lengthy annual reports of the BPDS and Dwight's religious zeal.

Second, it had become increasingly clear to most reformers and other commentators that Auburn had won. With New Jersey's rejection of the Pennsylvania System and immediate adoption of the Auburn System in 1858, Pennsylvania became the last state in the country to employ its eponymous prison system. As new states joined the Union, they universally adopted the Auburn System. Effectively, there was no more real estate to compete over. The Pennsylvania System was manifestly – and repeatedly declared – the loser. In their national survey of prisons, Dwight and Wines (the new nemeses of Eastern's administrators') reported, "The separate system of imprisonment in the United States is confined at present to the state of Pennsylvania, and exists in vigor only in the city of Philadelphia. Wherever else the experiment has been tried in our country, it has failed."[12] Moreover, most commentators believed the calumnious myths about the Pennsylvania System. Despite the efforts of Eastern's administrators to prove otherwise, state after state cited Auburn's ability to profit and lower likelihood of causing insanity among prisoners.

Third, the old debate over prison discipline – between the Auburn and Pennsylvania Systems – was displaced in the larger field by more pressing concerns. In the lead-up to the Civil War, penal reform had become less salient as reformers increasingly shifted their attention from other issues to slavery and the impending national crisis.[13] In the years after the Civil War, as social reformers once again turned their attention to penal reform, the field moved on to new debates. For one, reformers were

---

[12] Enoch C. Wines, and Theodore W. Dwight, *Report on the Prisons and Reformatories of the United States and Canada Made to the Legislature of New York, January 1867.* Albany, NY: Van Benthuysen and Sons' Steam Printing House, 1867, p. 55.

[13] Scholars have also suggested that penal reformers lost some of their zeal because of their disappointed expectations. Roger G. Walters, *American Reformers, 1815–1860.* New York: Hill and Wang, 1978 [1997], p. 17; Matthew W. Meskell, "An American Resolution: The History of Prisons in the United States from 1777 to 1877," *Stanford Law Review* 51:4 (1999), pp. 839–865, p. 864.

increasingly aware – and intolerant – of problems in America's carceral facilities, which were once again seen as patent failures.

By the Civil War, a focus on profitable prisoner labor had completely replaced discussions of or efforts to achieve prisoner rehabilitation in prisons on the Auburn System. In practice, entrepreneurs had full control of prisons and in some cases, no trace of the Auburn System's rule of silence remained as the concern for productive labor subsumed all else.[14] After the Civil War, reformers once again saw the need to encourage prisoner reformation and the new need to divest prisons of contractors and their profit motivations.

The post–Civil War period also caused new problems for America's jails and prisons. An economic downturn combined with large numbers of demobilized and often traumatized ex-soldiers – who frequently returned home to find little support and few jobs – flooding the prisons and a perceived or actual increase in the crime rate caused record levels of overcrowding. Overcrowding both produced new problems for reformers and highlighted older problems that they had previously left unresolved. Thus, in this period, reformers renewed their attention on county prisons (jails).[15] Few of these facilities had ever been comprehensively designed to follow the Auburn System or the Pennsylvania System, but overcrowding exacerbated the consequences of their long-standing mixed populations, limited efforts at reform, and poor regulation.

Relatedly, many of the discharged ex-soldiers entering prison were young adults, introducing new concerns about the state of youthful offenders. While some juvenile facilities existed in a few states, many young first-time offenders were sent to traditional prisons. To address this population's unique needs and vulnerability, New York opened its Elmira Reformatory in 1876, the nation's first adult reformatory. Like Auburn and Eastern before it, Elmira offered its own system of confinement combining labor, religion, and education; but unlike the older facilities, the Elmira System focused on salvageable (i.e., youthful, first-time) offenders.[16] Underlying this and other efforts was a preference

---

[14] Rebecca M. McLennan, *The Crisis of Imprisonment: Protest, Politics, and the Making of the American Penal State, 1776–1941*. New York: Cambridge University Press, 2008, pp. 176; 134–135, 191.

[15] Stephen Tillotson, "The Fault is in the System: Jail Reform in the United States from 1790 to 1945." Presentation at the 72nd Annual Meeting of the American Society of Criminology, November 17, 2016.

[16] Alexander Pisciotta, *Benevolent Repression: Social Control and the American Reformatory-Prison Movement*. New York University Press, 1994.

for more rigorous approaches to punishment and, more generally, a desire to improve the old ways.

By the 1860s, the field had also become much more international, which introduced topics and systems from other countries. In particular, reformers were particularly taken with a new approach to confinement, variously called the Work System, Mark System, or Irish System, by which prisoners could, in essence, work their way to liberty instead of facing a fixed-term sentence. It was initiated by Captain Maconochie in Norfolk Island (New Zealand) and later transplanted to Ireland under Sir Walter Crofton.[17] Although the Irish System primarily affected the period of time served in prison, reformers and other commentators saw it as a kind of "modification" of or "compromise" between the Auburn and Pennsylvania Systems.[18] One commentator argued that the Irish System was "destined ultimately to supersede" both systems and was their "formidable rival."[19] Said more dramatically,

The strife is no longer between Separate and Congregate systems; Auburn and Philadelphia are insignificant now in comparison with Norfolk Island, Valencia, and Dublin; it is the Irish system which now excites to controversy the practical Anglo-Saxon, the phlegmatic Dutchman, and the philosophic German.[20]

The debate over the Auburn and Pennsylvania Systems had become irrelevant.

In this reinvigorated context, Eastern's continued reliance on the Pennsylvania System simply seemed anachronistic – a "curious anomaly" according to another article in the *North American Review* article.[21] This state of affairs was, for Eastern's administrators, worse than constant criticism. Their prison, the Pennsylvania System, and they were irrelevant within contemporary debates. In their mind, they (and their predecessors) had accomplished something incredible – something worthy of study and replication – and no one seemed to recognize it. No longer in the spotlight, Eastern's administrators felt snubbed. As we saw in Chapter 9, they shifted their efforts away from defending the Pennsylvania System toward securing professional status in the larger field – with little to show for it.

---

[17] Norval Morris, *Maconochie's Gentlemen: The Story of Norfolk Island and the Roots of Modern Prison Reform*. Oxford University Press, 2001.

[18] *North American Review*, "Art. VIII [Review of Three Works]," p. 211; *North American Review*, "Art. III [Review of Nine Works]," p. 404

[19] *North American Review*, "Art. VIII [Review of Three Works]," pp. 211, 234.

[20] Ibid., p. 210.   [21] *North American Review*, "Art. III [Review of Nine Works]," p. 391.

CATASTROPHIC OVERCROWDING

Eastern's administrators would find their experiences in their own prison no more comforting. Like prisons around the country, Eastern faced record numbers of prison admissions following the Civil War. The prospect of overcrowding was already apparent before the war: The growth of the prison's population had started to match and outstrip its physical capacity, which had not increased since the 1830s. In the early 1850s Eastern received an average of 137 prisoners each year. During the Panic of 1857, this number jumped to 227. The war years – and the need for soldiers – brought some relief, reducing the average number of incoming prisoners to 163.[22] But beginning in 1865, as the soldiers came home and the economy continued its decline, admissions climbed – from 150 in 1864 to 257 in 1865 to a high of 364 in 1866. Incoming prisoners averaged 292 each year for the next four years and 244 each year in the following four years. In 1873, however, another economic recession inundated the prison with more prisoners. Between 1875 and 1879, incoming prisoners averaged 469 a year – almost the entire number of cells, but each prisoner was expected to stay for several years at least (see Figure 10.1).

The growing intake rates quickly produced overcrowding. While Eastern had a total population of 299 at year's end in 1850, during the first recession (between 1857 and 1860) it averaged 402. During the Civil War, with fewer incoming prisoners, this number declined slightly to 376 on average, hitting an eight-year low of 325 in 1864. The next year, as the war ended, however, the prison population immediately began to increase, jumping to 418 in 1865. In 1866, for the first time in Eastern's history, with a population of 569, there were more prisoners than cells and administrators were forced to double-cell their prisoners. The inspectors declared mournfully in that year's report,

It is proper to state that there were on the 1st of January, 1867, 569 prisoners in the Penitentiary. The number of cells is 540. So that the number of prisoners in excess of cells is 29. This induces the temporary necessity of putting more than one in some cells, and after great deliberation this has been done with due regard to safety and convenience.[23]

---

[22] This figure excludes prisoners for 1865.

[23] Eastern State Penitentiary, Inspectors' Report, *Thirty-Eighth Annual Report of the Inspectors of the State Penitentiary for the Eastern District of Pennsylvania*, Inspectors' Report, Philadelphia: McLaughlin Brothers, 1867, p. 17.

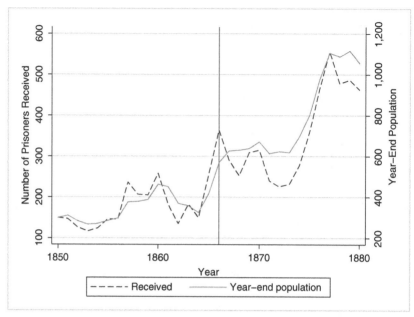

FIGURE 10.1 Approaching overcrowding: Prisoners received and total population, 1850–1879. A vertical line is drawn at 1866.

Source: Statistics collected from Eastern's Annual Reports

Recognizing "the exhausted capacity of the Penitentiary," the inspectors appended to their annual report a "Special Report" describing the dire situation in more detail. The inspectors explained that they had already done all that they could:

> By adapting our resources for temporary accommodation, five hundred and thirty-five convicts have been confined, but now we have five hundred and seventy (570) prisoners under sentence.
>
>   As a large number of convicts have been sentenced during the past two years, for the higher grades of crime, and necessarily for longer terms than heretofore, the discharges are now less than the receptions, and this added to the increase of number, requires increase of room.[24]

Never before had the prison's administrators admitted in their annual reports to double-celling their prisoners. Previously, driven by a concern to reduce their rates of insanity, the administrators had housed selected

[24] Ibid., p. 132.

prisoners together; the administrators had never publicly admitted to this clandestine practice because it was a strategic violation of the rules. In the 1860s, however, they were forced to double-cell because of overcrowding. This overcrowding, moreover, was a dire threat to the Pennsylvania System, and the administrators rarely shied away from describing the myriad threats to their prized system.

But the threat only worsened. Between 1867 and 1874, the total population averaged 641. On December 15, 1870, Warden Edward Townsend recorded in his daily log, "How doubled many of the cells to-day. Number of Convicts at this time 666."[25] With the recession of 1873, the population rose further each year – rising to 801 in 1875, 977 in 1876, and 1,106 in 1877 – and remained at around one thousand for the next five decades with only two exceptions. This rate of overcrowding was catastrophic. Since 1829, the Pennsylvania System had been lightly modified over time with marginal changes and small-scale violations in practice; these changes and violations were significant for the time, but overcrowding forced alterations of an entirely different magnitude. Ultimately, the Pennsylvania System would never recover at Eastern: By the end of the decade, it was simply impossible to house prisoners separately, each in their own cell.

Administrators' Efforts to Preserve the Pennsylvania System

Ever familiar with their prison's statistics, Eastern's administrators were unsurprised by their overcrowding crisis. During the 1850s, the administrators had cautioned the legislature of their uncomfortable proximity to overcrowding. From 1866 onward, with the advent of manifest overcrowding, however, Eastern's administrators routinely pleaded with the legislature to alleviate the growing problem.

In their 1867 special report to the legislature, the inspectors requested funds "[t]o put a second story on the first block, and increase its length, making it in all respects similar to the seventh block;" this addition would provide "accommodations for one hundred and four (104) prisoners additional." As they explained, "It will require seventeen months to complete this alteration, and when complete, the entire Penitentiary will accommodate six hundred and thirty (630) convicts."[26]

---

[25] Eastern State Penitentiary, *Warden's Daily Journal*, December 15, 1870.
[26] Eastern State Penitentiary, *Thirty-Eighth Annual Report of the Inspectors*, pp. 132–133.

When the legislature did not provide these funds that year, despite the fact that dozens of prisoners were housed two to a cell, the administrators repeated their request in their next report. In addition to requesting new cells, the administrators requested more immediate changes to the penal law, such as reducing the number of counties under Eastern's jurisdiction, thereby diverting a portion of the prisoner population to county jails or to Western.

Eastern's administrators were unified in their descriptions of the urgency of the situation. Writing to express the gravity of the situation, Warden Halloway explained in his next annual report,

We commenced the year with 569 prisoners, and ended it with 626, an increase of 57, which though considerably less than that of the former year, is more oppressive to us as we were then full to our utmost capacity without further additions.

That the time has arrived when something should be speedily done to meet this pressing necessity for greater accommodations for our convict population, can no longer be a matter of doubt. The integrity of the system, and the welfare of the community, as well as that of the prisoner, demand it.[27]

The warden went on, warning that overcrowding could have serious consequences for the health of the prison. Its "comparative freedom from the prevalence of any contagious or infectious diseases which the Penitentiary has hitherto enjoyed … cannot reasonably be expected with our present over-crowded population."[28] Physician Klapp concurred: "The number of prisoners now in the house, is more than is consistent with the design of the system, or, what is more germain [sic] to the matter in hand, with the laws of hygiene." Overcrowding thus violated the principle of separation, by requiring double-celling, while it made Eastern vulnerable to the negative outcomes they so often sought to escape. The physician made the point more dramatically: "in the sunshine of the Institution's success, [overcrowding] casts a shadow on the future."[29]

The legislature responded lethargically to the administrators' urgent requests. The legislature itself was facing a tight budget in the postwar years, which may explain their reluctance to address the situation. However, historian David Rothman has also suggested that antipathy

---

[27] Eastern State Penitentiary, Warden's Report, *Thirty-Ninth Annual Report of the Inspectors of the State Penitentiary for the Eastern District of Pennsylvania*. Philadelphia: McLaughlin Brothers, 1868, p. 93.

[28] Ibid., pp. 93–94.

[29] Eastern State Penitentiary, Physician's Report, *Thirty-Ninth Annual Report of the Inspectors*, p. 100.

toward the growing population of Irish immigrants, who represented a growing portion of prisoners, discouraged northeastern state legislatures from intervening in the overcrowded prisons. He noted, "As bad as conditions were, they seemed good enough for the Irish."[30]

Regardless of the reason, the legislature's delay caused permanent damage to the Pennsylvania System. Several months after the administrators' dire reports had been submitted to the legislature, that body finally approved funding for more cells in April 1868. However, by this time, the earlier numbers were already out of date and the funding provided was insufficient. Only 20 cells were completed by the end of 1868; added to around 550 existing cells, some uninhabitable due to their age and disrepair, these new cells were not nearly enough to either accommodate Eastern's 630 prisoners or slow the mounting tide of incoming prisoners, which continued to outstrip capacity.

In 1869, the legislature resuscitated the Commutation Law – the law that Eastern's administrators had hated so much that they previously refused to enforce it, prompting the state supreme court to scrutinize and then invalidate the law (Chapter 9). The new version of the law had removed or rewritten the offending portions that the court had previously ruled unconstitutional. When the inspectors received a copy of the bill – once again, not communicated directly from the legislature[31] – they met "to consider" the act. Nearly two weeks later, they released the first prisoners early.[32] In that year, Eastern's administrators commuted the sentence of more than 100 prisoners, as authorized by the law. The administrators continued to express their concerns with the law's legality, but without much elaboration.[33]

[30] David J. Rothman, "Perfecting the Prison: United States, 1789–1865," in *Oxford History of the Prison: The Practice of Punishment in Western Society,* ed. Norman Morris and David J. Rothman. New York: Oxford University Press, 1998, pp. 111–130, p. 126.
[31] The Board of Inspectors received a copy of the bill from Dr. Klapp, who had received it from Mr. Ruth, the Moral Instructor, who had received it from the Warden of Western State Penitentiary. See Eastern State Penitentiary, *Warden's Daily Journal,* June 2, 3, 1869.
[32] Ibid., July 10, 22, 1869.
[33] They apparently justified the law to themselves as a "recommendation," as opposed to a full usurpation on their part. However, it still troubled them: "This plan has been described as a statutory recommendation to the Executive to discharge the convict before the sentence inflicted by the judicial power expires. While it is not a pardon under the exercise of the constitutional prerogative of the Governor, it is a device which, by legislation, controls the judicial and directs Executive action. How wise such legislation may be, is no part of the province of the Inspectors to consider, much less to determine. It is now brought to the notice of the Legislature for the purpose of inviting attention to the precedent thus established." Eastern State Penitentiary, Inspectors'

Despite a lack of clear records about their decision to comply with the law *this time*, the administrators' change of heart is relatively easy to understand: It provided a means of preserving the core of the Pennsylvania System, which was facing extreme threats from overcrowding and the necessary double-celling of prisoners. By 1869, the prison population substantially exceeded capacity, reaching 630 by year's end. While the legislature authorized new cells in 1868, the construction of these would not be completed for several years and even then would be insufficient. The administrators' requests to alleviate overcrowding by altering Eastern's jurisdiction had hitherto been ignored. Early release would be the only way to reduce the prison population, even if only by a small amount. As abhorrent as it was, the Commutation Law provided a way for Eastern's administrators to preserve the Pennsylvania System.

Over the following decade, however, the Pennsylvania System continued to decline in practice as the legislature repeatedly authorized trivial forms of alleviation. In 1871, they finally altered Eastern's jurisdiction, diverting some prisoners to Western.[34] However, the alteration diverted only 27 prisoners. Warden Townsend noted charitably, "The removal of these prisoners measurably relieved our crowded condition, still we are obliged in many cases to place two convicts in one cell for want of sufficient room."[35] The legislature also authorized funding for building more cells at Eastern in 1872, 1877, and 1878. When the new blocks would be complete, the prison could house a total of 730 prisoners – still not enough for Eastern's nearly one thousand prisoners.[36]

Construction on these new cellblocks visibly illustrated the Pennsylvania System's demise. The Pennsylvania System demanded that prisoners only perform in-cell labor. While prisoners had helped to build many American prisons, including Western, for decades, Eastern's administrators had relied substantially on free labor for the main part of construction and employed only a small portion of prisoners for

---

Report, *Forty-Second Annual Report of the Inspectors of the State Penitentiary for the Eastern District of Pennsylvania*. Philadelphia: McLaughlin Brothers, 1868, p. 38.

34 Pennsylvania, "No. 275: An Act In Relation to the Allotment of Prisoners to the Eastern and Western Penitentiaries," in *Laws of the General Assembly of the State of Pennsylvania*. Harrisburg: B. Singerly, State Printer, 1871, p. 293.

35 Eastern State Penitentiary, Warden's Report, *Forty-Third Annual Report of the Inspectors*, p. 93.

36 Eastern State Penitentiary, Inspectors' Report, *Forty-Ninth Annual Report of the Inspectors of the State Penitentiary for the Eastern District of Pennsylvania*. Philadelphia: McLaughlin Brothers, 1879, p. 45.

odd jobs around the prison. Moreover, the administrators had, at least publicly, refused to acknowledge the out-of-cell work their prisoners did perform. By the 1870s, by contrast, the administrators publicly proclaimed that their prisoners were the entire construction crew. When Warden Townsend reported in 1878 that one fifty-cell block had been "completed" and another was "far advanced," he boasted that the work was performed by "but one master mechanic, the rest of the workmen being prisoners."[37] The Pennsylvania System was no more.

Indeed, the new cellblocks physically embodied the change. Straddling the front walkway and wedged in between Blocks Seven and One (near the front or southern end of the prison), the new blocks (Eight and Nine) lacked exercise yards, but they were built larger and with extra ventilation. A tenth block was added between Blocks One and Two.[38] The prison's physical plant was now just as crowded as its cells (see Figure 10.2). By 1879, Blocks Eight and Nine were complete and "fully occupied," but while they "have been some relief," the prison was "still so crowded that about three hundred (300) cells have two or more occupants."[39] The numbers and overcrowding only continued to increase over time.

Consequences

Systematically double-celling prisoners was not only a violation of the Pennsylvania System's central principle, it also created a variety of management problems. Most notably, violence at the prison increased. For the first time in the prison's history, prisoners were punished for fighting among themselves – previously, the only acts of violence were committed against prison staff or the prisoner himself (those prisoners double-celled for mental health reasons were usually closely supervised). In the late 1860s, however, prisoners "who occupied the same cell" (around the clock and generally unsupervised) turned on each other.[40] Prisoners were still expected to work and, of course, provided with tools, including

37 Eastern State Penitentiary, *Forty-Eighth Annual Report of the Inspectors of the State Penitentiary for the Eastern District of Pennsylvania.* Philadelphia: M'Laughlin Brothers' Book and Job Printing Establishment, 1878, p. 57.
38 Eastern State Penitentiary, Inspectors' Report, idem, *Forty-Ninth Annual Report of the Inspectors of the State Penitentiary for the Eastern District of Pennsylvania,* p. 43.
39 Eastern State Penitentiary, Warden's Report, *Forty-Ninth Annual Report of the Inspectors,* pp. 99–100.
40 Eastern State Penitentiary, *Warden's Daily Journal,* May 6, 1869; May 21, 1869.

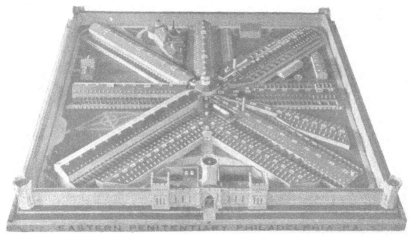

FIGURE 10.2 Model of Eastern in the late nineteenth century, c. 1895.
Cellblocks Eight, Nine, and Ten are visible at the bottom. The greenhouse and pond erected in 1843 are still visible in the upper right corner; by 1911, they had been replaced by another cellblock. *Source*: Eastern State Penitentiary, *Sixty-Sixth Annual Report of the Inspectors of the State Penitentiary for the Eastern District of Pennsylvania*. Philadelphia: Allen, Lane, & Scott, 1896. Scanned by Google. Available at books.google.com (last accessed December 1, 2018)

shoemakers' knives, leading to prisoners "fighting with Knives."[41] In one case, Warden Halloway noted, two men "assaulted each other with knives, each receiving several flesh wounds but not of a dangerous character."[42] In another case, however, the fighting proved fatal.

A shaken Warden Townsend described the "very terrible occurrence" in detail in 1872. Prisoner No. 6916, Michael Trimbue, murdered his "cellmate," Prisoner No. 6917, William R. Webb. According to Townsend, "these youths were convicted of the same crime, sentenced to the same term and came here together about one year ago." By way of explanation, Townsend recalled,

as we had a large population at the time of their reception viz 650 prisoners with only accommodation for 550, the necessity for doubling, or putting more than one in a cell was imperative, and as these boys were friends, & wished to be together, it was deemed proper under the circumstances to grant their wish. No one is aware of there even having been any difficulty or dissension between them.

He concluded, "No officer is to blame for the sad occurrence."[43] Overcrowding was responsible.

---

[41] Ibid., August 1, 1873.   [42] Ibid., June 7, 1868.   [43] Ibid., May 7, 1872.

With more prisoners and more chaos at the prison, escapes and escape attempts became more common – and more brazen. In the winter of 1866–1867, two prisoners escaped, independently, but both walked out through the front gate.[44] In the summer of 1867, Prisoners No. 5396 and 5397, who "occupied one cell," were caught "making preparations to break out making a key for their backdoor, a rope of cane about 40 ft long, &c."[45] Between the increase in violence and the growing number of escape attempts, the amount of time prisoners spent in the dark cell increased: by the late 1860s, three weeks was not uncommon, while just a few years earlier, two weeks would have been exceptional.[46]

While punishments increased, other changes illustrated a shift in the philosophical underpinnings at Eastern. In particular, the number and type of incoming prisoners, as well as the increase in violence, may have made the administrators less confident in reformation. Immediately after the war, the administrators began to pay particular attention to the young prisoners entering their prison – many of whom had been soldiers in the war. The administrators increasingly distinguished between these young, reformable criminals and old, hardened criminals. It was also in the late 1860s that the administrators began to mention a "crime class," or a group of congenital criminals, often related to one another, for whom there was no hope.[47] Soon, the administrators began recording their prisoners' family histories to identify members of the emergent crime class (although the administrators continued to maintain the prisoners' anonymity, still using their prisoner numbers instead of names). They also began enumerating the causes of each prisoner's crime, including the newly identified cause, "inherent depravity."[48] The administrators'

---

[44] Ibid., November 6, 1866; February 8, 1867.   [45] Ibid., July 22, 1867.

[46] E.g., Ibid., July 22, 1867.

[47] E.g., Eastern State Penitentiary, *Thirty-Ninth Annual Report of the Inspectors*, p.15.

[48] See especially Eastern State Penitentiary, *Fiftieth Annual Report of the Inspectors of the State Penitentiary for the Eastern District of Pennsylvania*. Philadelphia: M'Laughlin Brothers, 1880, p. 71 for a discussion of the meaning. See also references in Eastern State Penitentiary, *Thirty-Eighth Annual Report of the Inspectors*; Eastern State Penitentiary, *Thirty-Ninth Annual Report of the Inspectors*; Eastern State Penitentiary, *Fortieth Annual Report of the Inspectors of the State Penitentiary for the Eastern District of Pennsylvania*. Philadelphia: M'Laughlin Brothers, 1869; Eastern State Penitentiary, *Forty-Fifth Annual Report of the Inspectors*; Eastern State Penitentiary, *Forty-Sixth Annual Report of the Inspectors of the State Penitentiary for the Eastern District of Pennsylvania*. Philadelphia: Sherman & Co., 1876. Tables of crime causes appear beginning in Eastern State Penitentiary, *Fifty-Second Annual Report of the Inspectors of the State Penitentiary for the Eastern District of Pennsylvania*. Philadelphia: Sherman & Co., 1882.

own changing beliefs about the nature of crime and criminals reflected larger discussions in the field of penal science, anticipating a more conservative brand of penology – soon to be made famous as the field of criminology[49] – that would take shape in the final decades of the nineteenth century.[50] However, the fact that administrators were confronting record numbers of prisoners who appeared qualitatively different from previous generations undoubtedly contributed to their growing punitiveness. In 1871, for example, Warden Townsend noted privately, "there has never been so many dangerous now in our prison as there is at this time & strict vigilance is our only safe guard."[51]

Overcrowding and the Pennsylvania System's Fate

Overcrowding in 1866 should have been the Pennsylvania System's natural cause of death: The principle of separation could not be maintained for all prisoners. Nevertheless, the Pennsylvania System remained the ideal at Eastern for nearly a decade more, despite the double-celling of a large plurality of prisoners. Near the end of this period, in 1875, the inspectors offered a full history of the Pennsylvania System at Eastern (written by Vaux) in their annual report.[52] They proudly – if perhaps sadly – proclaimed of their prison, "It is the first, and now the only Penitentiary administered on the Pennsylvania System of convict discipline."[53] As the years continued, however, their references, still reciting earlier arguments, grew purposefully vague.

In 1879, the inspectors wrote, "The method of punishment should not be defeated in its operation by the utter inadequacy of prison construction." They continued vaguely and yet in a familiar fashion,

---

[49] Nicole Rafter, *Partial Justice: Women in State Prisons, 1800–1935*. Boston: Northeastern University Press, 1985.

[50] For a more well-known example of a penal reformer using the prison population to develop a theory of hereditary criminality, see Richard Louis Dugdale, *"The Jukes": A Study in Crime, Pauperism, Disease and Heredity (Seventh Edition)*. New York: Putnam's Sons, 1902 [1877]. Note that, unlike similar studies, Dugdale recognized some role of one's social context and not just heredity. By contrast, see Henry Herbert Goddard, *Feeble-mindedness*. New York: MacMillan Company, 1914.

[51] Eastern State Penitentiary, *Warden's Daily Journal*, January 28, 1871. Before 1866, wardens only rarely described prisoners as dangerous (for examples, see entries for November 7, 1838; November 23, 1844; January 23, 1855; February 28, 1855; January 28, 1856; April 5, 1864).

[52] Eastern State Penitentiary, Inspectors' Report, *Forty-Fifth Annual Report of the Inspectors*, pp. 5–59.

[53] Ibid., p. 23.

"[t]he experience of nearly half a century has thus been made operative in the material structure of a prison in which this system of prison discipline is here administered. It is only to be deeply and earnestly regretted that so few States have carefully examined this Penitentiary before they have decided on any other system."[54] By then, the annual reports contained few descriptions of the Pennsylvania System, but they routinely recycled administrators' long-standing claims about the field's indifference to it.

There were exceptions, however. When the number of prisoners who had been previously convicted entered the prison exceeded the previous year's number, Moral Instructor John Ruth explained, "This increase may be considered as indicative of the prejudicial effect of crowding. Upon the completion of the new blocks the principle of sequestration will again obtain, and our former good results may be anticipated."[55] However, with 1,584 prisoners in house, and new cellblocks that promised a total capacity of 870, there was no way prisoners could or would again be held in solitary or separate confinement.[56] Indeed, Moral Instructor Ruth was alone in referring to the "sequestration" of prisoners; while Eastern's administrators continued to endorse the Pennsylvania System, they rarely spoke in terms of solitary or separate confinement anymore. By the late 1870s the Pennsylvania System no longer existed in practice, but it no longer existed in theory either.

THE INDIVIDUAL TREATMENT SYSTEM

Before overcrowding suffocated it in practice, the Pennsylvania System was already undergoing theoretical changes. As the debate over prison discipline subsided (especially after the death of Louis Dwight in 1854), so did the need to distinguish the Pennsylvania System from pure solitary confinement. Consequently, in the 1850s and 1860s, administrators' efforts to distinguish the Pennsylvania System from a system of solitary confinement began to subside. In the continuing evolution of names for the Pennsylvania System (see Chapter 5), the administrators did not renounce "separate confinement" (initially utilized to avoid the term "solitary"), but that appellation nevertheless quietly receded into the

---

54 Eastern State Penitentiary, *Forty-Ninth Annual Report of the Inspectors*, p. 44.
55 Eastern State Penitentiary, Moral Instructor's Report, *Forty-Ninth Annual Report of the Inspectors*, p. 124.
56 Eastern State Penitentiary, Inspectors' Report, *Forty-Ninth Annual Report of the Inspectors*, p. 6.

past. In its place, administrators' references to the terms "individual" and "treatment" began to increase. In their 1858 report, for example, the inspectors referred to their "system of treatment."[57] Four years later, they referred to it as "the system of separate imprisonment of criminals, and the individual treatment of moral disease."[58] The emphasis on individual attention reappeared in 1865.[59] Finally, in their 1867 report, the emphasis on individuals became part of the "system" designation: The inspectors called it "the separate or individual system of Penitentiary discipline."[60] They explained:

the best system of punishment for crime is the *individual system*, as distinguished from *class or congregational* discipline. The idea which for so long a time has occupied the uninformed mind, that solitude and isolation were the only interpretations of the Pennsylvania plan, has been forced to yield to that truer and more perfect translation of our system which is presented under the higher signification of the individual or personal treatment of those convicted of crimes against social happiness, or the laws which create and protect it.[61]

Thus, by the late 1860s, administrators increasingly emphasized the way in which the separate confinement of prisoners allowed administrators to make "individual" assessments and customize the "treatment" to their unique needs. Rather than distinguishing the Pennsylvania System from solitary, they emphasized its difference from congregate confinement of the kind practiced under the Auburn System. This method had been implicit in the earlier discussions about the Pennsylvania System, but it increasingly took center stage in the 1860s. Indeed, references to the "Separate System," although they did not quite disappear, gradually gave way to the "Individual Treatment System" in the 1860s and 1870s.

In part, this shift in how Eastern's administrators characterized the Pennsylvania System reflected a contemporaneous shift in criminological thought. American penal reformers were increasingly taken with the idea

---

[57] Eastern State Penitentiary, Inspectors' Report, *Twenty-Ninth Annual Report of the Inspectors of the State Penitentiary for the Eastern District of Pennsylvania*. Philadelphia: F. Pierson, 1858. p. 8.

[58] Eastern State Penitentiary, Inspectors' Report, *Thirty-Third Annual Report of the Inspectors of the State Penitentiary for the Eastern District of Pennsylvania*. Philadelphia: M'Laughlin Brothers, 1862, pp. 41–42.

[59] Eastern State Penitentiary, *Thirty-Sixth Annual Report of the Inspectors of the State Penitentiary for the Eastern District of Pennsylvania*. Philadelphia: M'Laughlin Brothers, 1865, e.g., 12, 13.

[60] Eastern State Penitentiary, Inspectors' Report, *Thirty-Eighth Annual Report of the Inspectors*, p. 27.

[61] Ibid., p. 14.

of treatment.[62] For example, one of several hundred questions Wines and Dwight included in their survey of various carceral facilities, in preparation for their 1867 treatise, was, "Which class yield most easily to treatment, those who have been confined a long time or a short time?" Another part of that treatise discussed at length "[t]he object of all reformatory prison treatment" and how to achieve such goals.[63] A few years later, writing as the Secretary for the National Congress on Penitentiary and Reformatory Discipline, Wines explained, "The students of penitentiary science, the workers in the field of penitentiary discipline, in this country, have come to a substantial agreement on certain fundamental principles of criminal treatment, and are approaching such agreement in others."[64] The rise of the Elmira System in the 1870s, with its focus on a customized treatment plan for young or first-time offenders, was both a product of and popularizer of these trends. It is difficult to determine whether Eastern's administrators altered their discourse to stay current with new understandings of crime and punishment or because it reflected their own beliefs changing with the prisoner population, although it was likely a combination of both.

In addition to the impact of changing penological beliefs, however, overcrowding undoubtedly contributed to the administrators' rhetorical transition, even if overcrowding did not initiate it. With the advent of Eastern's overcrowding in 1866, administrators' references to their system as the "separate system" became increasingly inaccurate – and demonstrably so, even to outsiders. The limited cases of double-celling and out-of-cell labor that administrators had authorized previously were few enough and kept quiet so as not to damage the Pennsylvania System's reputation. The dramatic increase in the number of double-celled prisoners and the necessity of beseeching the legislature for relief made secrecy impossible. Given their embarrassing position, the administrators could not very well claim the superiority of their system if its central component was no longer practicable. As we have seen, they held out hope that, by building more cell blocks, they could return to a fully separate system. They

---

[62] Individualization was also central to the transformations of the criminal justice system in Great Britain several decades later. David Garland, *Punishment and Welfare*. Brookfield, VT: Gower, 1985.

[63] Wines, and Dwight, *Report on Prisons and Reformatories*, pp. 28, 70.

[64] Enoch C. Wines, ed., *Transactions of the National Congress on Penitentiary and Reformatory Discipline Held at Cincinnati, Ohio, October 12–18, 1870*. Albany, NY: Weed, Parsons and Company, 1871, p. 18.

even explained, in a recurring phrase from these years, that they tried to maintain the separation of prisoners "as far as it was possible."[65]

Reflecting their ongoing, if fading, optimism, the administrators retained the "separate system" designation as the still-dominant moniker into the first years of overcrowding. But their earlier references to the individual treatment system increasingly crowded out references to the separate system. Thus, in the 1868 report, they referred to it as "the individual system of Pennsylvania Penitentiary discipline"[66] and the "individual or Pennsylvania system."[67] They vacillated in the 1871 report, again referring to "the separate or individual treatment system" as well as "the separate system."[68] By the early 1870s, however, the Individual Treatment System had become the dominant appellation for the Pennsylvania System.

Overcrowding had persisted for more than five years and the legislature's too-little, too-late assistance combined with a continuing flood of new prisoners offered a bleak reality. The administrators were forced to find a way to reconcile the contradiction between their claims about the necessity and superiority of the "separate or solitary confinement" that was still central to the Pennsylvania System and the double-celling that was, increasingly, the reality at Eastern. The new Individual Treatment System was it. The clearest statement that the administrators had changed their understanding of the system came in 1873, when the inspectors explained, "the System of Penitentiary Discipline administered in this institution...is most appropriately designated as the INDIVIDUAL TREATMENT SYSTEM, because it admits of the direct personal application to each prisoner of all the influences and instrumentalities which science and experience recognize as best adapted to secure the interests of the prisoner, and of society, and dignify practical benevolence."[69] This

---

[65] For example, "The separate and individual treatment of prisoners has been adhered to as far as it was possible. Our crowded condition has made it necessary to duplicate many of the cells, and in some of the larger rooms three prisoners have been placed; these were generally invalids, and by the advice of the physician, excused from labor." Eastern State Penitentiary, Warden's Report, *Forty-Fourth Annual Report of the Inspectors*, p. 37.

[66] Eastern State Penitentiary, Inspector's Report, *Thirty-Ninth Annual Report of the Inspectors*, p. 24.

[67] Ibid., pp. 18–19.

[68] Eastern State Penitentiary, Inspector's Report, *Forty-Second Annual Report of the Inspectors*, pp. 26, 27; see also Eastern State Penitentiary, *Forty-Third Annual Report of the Inspectors*.

[69] Eastern State Penitentiary, Inspector's Report, *Forty-Fourth Annual Report of the Inspectors*, p. 11.

description of the system is strikingly different from earlier definitions, not least for its reference to science and experience, thereby incorporating in their new definition their own claims to expertise and professional status (see Chapter 9). However, the complete absence of separation and labor, two components that had long been central to their definition, were no longer included.

We can compare their description in 1873 to their definition in 1846:

The Separate system has but one essential condition; the absolute separation of the prisoners from intercourse of any kind with each other. On this may be ingrafted labour instruction, and even constant society with the officers of the prison, or with virtuous persons. In fact, these have become, in a greater or less degree, component parts of the system. In constant employment the prisoner finds peace; and in the society with which he is indulged, an innocent relaxation and a healthy influence. This is the Pennsylvania system.[70]

From around 1873 onward, administrators rarely referred to separate confinement anymore. Instead, they had introduced concepts (like individual attention) that were implicit in the system's earlier iterations but that had taken on a new role, becoming more explicit and enrobed in the new contemporary discourse.

Unlike previous name changes, this new label for the Pennsylvania System was not an effort to save it. Previously, the administrators' evolving naming practices had been strategic: In each case, the name was chosen to express the Pennsylvania System's positive qualities to explicitly challenge criticism. "Solitary confinement 'with labour' and 'instruction'" was meant to distinguish the Pennsylvania System from solitary confinement without labor, or pure solitary confinement. "Separate confinement" was meant to further clarify this distinction by emphasizing that prisoners were apart from each other but not from every living being. These name changes were attempts to insulate the Pennsylvania System from further criticism. By contrast, the Pennsylvania System's new name, and administrators' new way of describing it, represents one of the strongest ways in which we see the Pennsylvania System of 1829 fade from view in the 1870s – rather than being a reframing of the original project, the individual treatment system was an entirely different project.

Indeed, the administrators frequently emphasized that the Pennsylvania System was no longer what it was in 1829. The inspectors (especially

---

[70] Eastern State Penitentiary, Inspectors' Report, *Seventeenth Annual Report of the Inspectors of the Eastern State Penitentiary of Pennsylvania*. Philadelphia: Ed. Barrington and Geo. D. Haswell, 1846, p. 8.

Vaux) repeatedly called attention to this latest iteration, emphasizing a break with the past but never elaborating on what that entailed. Reflecting on the history of the Pennsylvania System, for example, the inspectors explained, "It was first called the 'Solitary system,' then it was more correctly styled the 'Separate system,' and now the truer and more philosophic description as modified and improved is, the 'Individual system of convict discipline.'"[71] Notably, the administrators never made explicit the central difference between the separate system and the individual treatment system – the end of solitary confinement (or rather, what they had been calling "separate confinement") – and they purposefully avoided any mention, in their theoretical discussions, of how many prisoners should be kept in each cell – a glaring omission, given their extensive discussions on other aspects of prison discipline. They certainly continued to complain about overcrowding, but their previous emphasis on one prisoner per cell disappeared.

Changes in the penal field had precipitated the transition to the Individual Treatment System, but the permanence of overcrowding accelerated the transition. The incorporation of "individual" and "treatment" had begun as the introduction of concepts that reflected changes in the field but were complementary to the original Pennsylvania System. In these early years, these terms supplemented, but did not entirely displace, the earlier emphasis on separation. By the 1870s, however, they had become a way to avoid severe contradictions between theory and practice. The new theory underlying the Pennsylvania System no longer included the separation of prisoners. Underlying all of these changes was administrators' different relationship with the Pennsylvania System: no longer the source of status – no longer personally institutionalized for Eastern's administrators – the Pennsylvania System was expendable, manipulable, and fungible.

DEAUTHORIZATION

The reimagined Pennsylvania System, now restyled the Individual Treatment System, remained a point of pride for Eastern's administrators. Though still claiming the excellence of their system, Eastern's administrators had quietly abandoned the essential features of the Pennsylvania System and increasingly embraced standard approaches to confinement.

---

[71] Eastern State Penitentiary, Inspector's Report, *Forty-Fifth Annual Report of the Inspectors*, p. 23.

The name, the "Individual Treatment System" persisted until the foundational 1829 statute was finally overridden, but by then any trace of the original Pennsylvania System was long since lost.

It is difficult to pinpoint an exact date for the demise of the Pennsylvania System. At best, we can say that the Pennsylvania System faded over the course of the 1870s, as illustrated by the combination of new visitor policies, widespread double-celling, the new cellblocks that increasingly prioritized capacity over penal philosophy, the use of prisoner labor in their construction, and the rhetorical shift in how administrators described their system. Unlike the other prisons that had briefly adopted it, multiple generations of Eastern's administrators survived the nineteenth century without formally rejecting the Pennsylvania System.

There was no sharp break with the past in how the administrators implemented the Pennsylvania System in practice or how they described it. While the chronic and insuperable level of overcrowding clearly accelerated the shift, some signs of change preceded the first instance of forced double-celling, including authorizing family visitation and the initial references to the Individual Treatment System. Moreover, as with previous name changes, it is not clear that at any point the Individual Treatment System coincided with any meaningfully changed routines at Eastern, since use of the name began before overcrowding and accelerated only after administrators tried for years to minimize its impact on their long-held routines.

Instead, the Pennsylvania System died slowly, a gradual process not traceable to a single year or act. The Pennsylvania System of 1829 had evolved in its first several decades as administrators worked out growing pains, contended with criticism, and confronted the realities of translating theory into practice. But as we have seen, during the tumult of the 1860s and 1870s irreversible changes had taken place. Certainly by 1879 there was little trace of the Pennsylvania System as it was first understood: Prisoners were crowded two to a cell, received outside visitors, and could even read newspapers; any pretension to separation, either among prisoners or between prisoners and the outside world, was over.

By the 1880s and 1890s, the Pennsylvania System was a desiccated corpse of the thing it once had been, both in what it looked like on the ground and – perhaps more strikingly – in how Eastern's administrators described it. As the prison population only continued to climb and the reigning penal science continued to reject the reformability of the crime class, Eastern's administrators became increasingly punitive in their approach, making statements that further illustrated how irrelevant the original Pennsylvania System had become. In 1888, for example, the inspectors suggested that the state should "ascertain if the public whipping of such persons [members of the crime class] would not deter, when all else failed."[72] Recall that one of the administrators' long-standing points of pride was that they, unlike the administrators at Auburn-style prisons, did not use whipping or (in their public telling) corporal punishments more generally. With the 1889 opening of the Huntingdon Reformatory, which began absorbing the more redeemable young offenders, the remaining population at Eastern consisted of a greater proportion of those prisoners who had been identified by administrators as belonging to the (irredeemable) crime class. These views contrasted sharply with administrators' earlier views that most prisoners, extracted from the bad influences within their environment and given the proper training and guidance, could be reformed into law-abiding, productive citizens. Indeed, in contrast to their oppositional orientation to field-level developments in the 1860s and early 1870s, Eastern's administrators became increasingly receptive to new developments, including the conservative tone permeating the new penology.

This shift in penological thought had profound consequences for the administrators' relationship to the Pennsylvania System, especially in its reimagined form of the Individual Treatment System, a reformative approach that clashed with the new view of criminals as unreformable. In 1894, Inspector Richard Vaux (still writing the inspectors' annual report the year before his death) noted that no system could reform a "confirmed criminal"; as though stating what he believed was obvious, Vaux explained, "The 'crime-class,' as it is known and understood, is almost beyond any human influences to change the character of most of its members."[73] When the administrators finally did publicly express reservations about the Pennsylvania System, their comments referred to its unsuitability for addressing the crime class. In their 1897 report, for example, the inspectors suggested the Pennsylvania System "may not be absolutely necessary for every convict, especially for those habitual and hardened offenders who are incapable of reform under any system."[74] The inspectors' recommendations to employ whipping and

---

[72] Eastern State Penitentiary, *Fifty-Eighth Annual Report of the Inspectors*, p.123.

[73] Eastern State Penitentiary, *Sixty-Seventh Annual Report of the Inspectors of the State Penitentiary for the Eastern District of Pennsylvania*. Philadelphia: The Chas. H. Elliot Co., 1894, p. 123.

[74] Eastern State Penitentiary, *Sixty-Seventh Annual Report of the Inspectors*, p. 8.

public statements that the Pennsylvania System was unnecessary offer a striking contrast to the nature of the annual reports written during Eastern's first five decades.

By the 1900s and 1910s Eastern was quite similar to its peer prisons in the North, although in a partial, hybridized, or strained sense. Most of Eastern's prisoners were still housed in its characteristic cells, but many had one or more cellmates. Prisoners also increasingly worked together in workshops outside their cells and exercised together in the limited space between the blocks until more new buildings were added. In 1911, construction was completed on a new tiered cellblock following the "Big House" model of prisons that characterized new prisons built at the time. Big House prisons were generally larger versions of the original Auburn State Prison, with its rectangular design and tiered cellblocks.[75] After nearly a century, an almost unrecognizable version of the Auburn System – its architecture, its congregation, its emphasis on silence, even its willingness to embrace whipping – had come to Eastern. The Pennsylvania System, by contrast, existed only in memory – and in official statutes.

Finally, in 1913, the Pennsylvania legislature officially deauthorized the Pennsylvania System. The brief statute granted administrators permission to "congregate" prisoners "for the several purposes of worship, labor, learning, and recreation."[76] The law passed with little fanfare. So unremarkable was the legislative change that Eastern's administrators made no reference to the law or to the Pennsylvania System in their annual report for that year. In truth, the new law formally authorized practices that had characterized Eastern's administration for almost half a century by the 1910s.

The Death of the Gentleman Reformer

Previous historians of the Pennsylvania System have emphasized the importance of administrators' and penal reformers' personal commitment to the Pennsylvania System, attributing its demise to the passing, in the years around 1900, of a final generation of men who truly believed in their

---

75 Many of these prisons also employed (or tried to employ) Auburn's rule of silence, factory labor by day, and solitary at night. E.g., Charles Bright, *The Powers that Punish: Prison and Politics in the Era of the "Big House," 1920–1955*. Ann Arbor: University of Michigan Press, 1996; James B. Jacobs, *Stateville: The Penitentiary in Mass Society*. University of Chicago Press, 1977.

76 Pennsylvania, "No. 121: An Act Relating to the Management of Eastern State Penitentiary," p. 708.

long-suffering system.[77] In 1895, Richard Vaux, a long-time inspector and major proponent of the Pennsylvania System, died. Warden Michael Cassidy, who had worked alongside Vaux for many decades, continued to include small references to the Individual Treatment System after Vaux's death. Cassidy had entered his office as warden after the Pennsylvania System was thoroughly decimated, but he had seen some of its better days first as an overseer hired in 1862 and serving as an assistant warden under Wardens Holloway and Townsend. Some of his earlier experience was reflected in his rhetoric as warden, but he died a few years after Vaux. Cassidy's successor, Warden D. W. Bussinger, was another member of this final generation of men who had experienced the Pennsylvania System as it had been, although his connection was the most tenuous. He had joined the prison in 1879 as the statistician and moved up the ranks to clerk before becoming warden after Cassidy's death; he was thus primarily exposed to the late-century version of the Pennsylvania System. In 1902, he made one of the last references to the restyled Pennsylvania System,

The system long in vogue in this Penitentiary is that prisoners require individual treatment; the Warden and other officials should know their prisoners and endeavor, where possible, to so direct the treatment that the prisoner may be benefited mentally and morally if he shows a desire to avail himself of the opportunity.[78]

However, Bussinger was removed from office in 1903 after "irregularities" were brought to the Board of Inspectors' attention.[79]

---

77 Barnes attributes great significance to the role of personnel changes in the Pennsylvania System's demise. For him, the death of Vaux is most important. Harry Elmer Barnes, *The Evolution of Penology in Pennsylvania*. Indianapolis: The Bobbs-Merrill Company, 1968 [1927], p. 302. Likewise, Teeters argues that a similar generational attrition in PSAMPP's ranks was responsible. PSAMPP's support for the Pennsylvania System had already declined over the last decades of the nineteenth century, as few of the Society's members who had been engaged in the intense debates earlier in the century continued as active participants. Once the last of their members who had been Pennsylvania System supporters passed away or otherwise became unable to continue participating in PSAMPP, the Society publicly acknowledged the need to abandon the Pennsylvania System at Eastern. Negley K. Teeters, *They Were in Prison: A History of the Pennsylvania Prison Society, 1787–1937*. Philadelphia: The John C. Winston Company, 1937, pp. 202–211.

78 Eastern State Penitentiary, *Seventy-Second Annual Report of the Inspectors of the State Penitentiary for the Eastern District of Pennsylvania*. Philadelphia: Allen, Lane & Scott, 1902, p. 79.

79 Eastern State Penitentiary, *Seventy-Fourth Annual Report of the Inspectors of the State Penitentiary for the Eastern District of Pennsylvania*. Philadelphia, 1904, pp. 5–6.

With the last defenders of the Pennsylvania System gone from Eastern's administration, a new group of administrators who had never known the Pennsylvania System as it really was – and who had not experienced the earlier conditions of uncertainty, embattlement, and ongoing defense that encouraged the Pennsylvania System's personal institutionalization at Eastern – was in charge. It was this group of men who finally requested legislative authorization to abandon the Pennsylvania System.

In 1905, the year after Bussinger's removal, the new warden, Joseph Byers, said what no administrator had ever before publicly admitted:

[T]he enforcement of the "separate and solitary system" demanded by existing Laws is an absolute impossibility. Either the Laws should be changed to meet present conditions and to conform to the general accepted principles of prison reform, or the State should relieve its officials of the impossible situation of enforcing Laws that cannot be enforced. On an average we have had four hundred and fifty more prisoners than cells. Two men *cannot* be put into the same cell, according to the Law of the State, the sentence being to separate and solitary confinement at hard labor. Two men *ought not* to be put in the same cell for even better reasons.[80]

Recognizing the "impossibility" of the Pennsylvania System, the inspectors reported in agreement, "The Board is of the opinion that if this Law was changed ... the public would be much benifited [sic] by the bettered condition, both morally and physically, of the convicts on their release from the Penitentiary. The reasons are obvious to anyone who has studied the conditions."[81] Notably, their recommendation was not for a simple return to the Pennsylvania System in its heyday, but rather for the new law to require "That one or not less than three convicts be confined in one cell" – either prisoners should remain in solitary or there should be three men in a cell, but never two, as this could lead to same-sex relations (a most problematic outcome in their view).[82] They

---

Bussinger was the first warden actually forced out of office; unlike Warden Scattergood, who was simply not reelected to his post, Bussinger was publicly removed from the prison.

[80] Eastern State Penitentiary, *Seventy-Fifth Annual Report of the Inspectors of the State Penitentiary for the Eastern District of Pennsylvania*. Philadelphia, 1905, p. 11.

[81] Ibid., p. 4.

[82] There was still one final reference to the Pennsylvania System. In late 1912, months before the law repealed the Pennsylvania System, Moral Instructor Welch – who had joined the prison in 1891 – remarked:

There is a continual developement [sic] in the improvement along the lines that have been inaugurated by the Board, so that we have virtually a new Institution, on the basis of the separate system as it was originally devised, so that the life and methods of today have

were apparently indifferent as to whether or not the legislature authorized
solitary confinement, so long as it resolved the legal paradox. While it
took several more years for the legislature to act on their request, Eastern's
administrators had finally requested a legislative change in the official
mode of incarceration. As we have seen, however, the Pennsylvania System
passed away long before its final supporters did.

* * *

The Pennsylvania System suffered multiple deaths between 1829 and
1913: however, even when the Pennsylvania System seemed to have died,
it lived on – a seemingly indestructible, zombie-like penality, but, like a
zombie, difficult to confuse with the creature it had once been.[83] Long
before Eastern's administrators requested the legislature to legally termi-
nate the Pennsylvania System, an earlier generation of administrators had
quietly let it die, succumbing to overcrowding, and used the new mantra
of individual treatment to hide its passing. But if we were to assume that
overcrowding was "the" reason for the administrators' decision to give
up on the Pennsylvania System, we would only be partially correct. The
administrators initially resisted the changes wrought by overcrowding;
they advocated for relief before they finally let go. These stubborn
men could have continued to chide the legislature for jeopardizing the
Pennsylvania System (as they had so often done), but by the 1870s there
was little point in doing so. The Pennsylvania System, increasingly ignored
in penological debates, no longer provided Eastern's administrators with
the advantage of difference. Instead, the administrators had found in
professionalization a new source of status. With the bonds of personal
institutionalization that connected the administrators to the Pennsylvania
System reduced to tenuous strands, they could finally let it go. It fell to a
later generation of administrators to request its formal deauthorization.

practically but little similarity or relationship to those of a few years past. Eastern State
Penitentiary, *Eighty-Third Annual Report of the Inspectors of the State Penitentiary for
the Eastern District of Pennsylvania for the Year 1912*. Philadelphia, 1913, p. 73.

No other administrator, however, seemed to share his sentiments, nor did he repeat his
remark.

[83] Zombie imagery is far from unique in punishment studies. Most recently, Page, Phelps,
and Goodman note, "penal orientations and practices are like zombies – far outliving
the actors that introduced them into the penal field and shaped their various iterations."
Joshua Page, Michelle Phelps, and Philip Goodman, "Consensus in the Penal Field?
Revisiting Breaking the Pendulum." *Law & Social Inquiry* 44:3 (2019), pp. 822–827.

Conclusion

[A] complex anachronism ... [s]ometimes called the fallacy of *nunc pro tunc*, it is the mistaken idea that the proper way to do history is to prune away the dead branches of the past, and to preserve the green buds and twigs which have grown into the dark forest of our contemporary world.

David Hackett Fischer (1970), *Historians' Fallacies*[1]

surely the faithful page of history will not fail to attract the higher admiration and warmer gratitude of posterity towards that beneficent band who, although destitute of political power and distinction, have unremittingly laboured with an philanthropy, little surpassed, on many occasions, by that of Howard, or of Jebb, to carry into execution and to perfect the plans of an humble proprietor of this once inconsiderable province – plans not only antecedent to any formed in Europe, but embracing in their far more benevolent principles, future blessings to the whole human family.

Roberts Vaux (1826), *Notices of the Original, and Successive Efforts to Improve the Discipline of the Prison at Philadelphia and to Reform the Criminal Code of Pennsylvania*[2]

THE SEARCH FOR RECOGNITION

Roberts Vaux's closing statement of his 1826 pamphlet referred to his and others' efforts to abandon the use of *ancien régime* punishments in

---

[1] David Hackett Fischer, *Historians' Fallacies: Toward a Logic of Historical Thought.* New York: Oxford University Press, 1970, p. 135.

[2] Roberts Vaux, *Notices of the Original, and Successive Efforts to Improve the Discipline of the Prison at Philadelphia and to Reform the Criminal Code of Pennsylvania.* Philadelphia: Kimber and Sharpless, 1826, p. 49.

the nascent United States and replace them with a distinctively American approach to punishment. Few questioned whether the prison, and its panoply of hidden mental and physical punishments, was in fact more humane than the old punishments. Even fewer challenged the myth that the prison was a home-grown innovation fertilized by organic American benevolence and humanity – despite its obvious debts to British and Continental developments, however much Americans transformed and reconfigured these ideas.[3] Yet statements like Vaux's – and similar statements repeated endlessly throughout Eastern's lengthy retention of the Pennsylvania System – revealed a deep insecurity about the centerpiece technology to their penal reform project.

The prison, although not as humanitarian in either theory or practice as many argued it would be, was remarkable for the time. And the men responsible for ushering it in frequently emphasized the scale of their accomplishment. As Vaux reminded his readers,

Of this shocking catalog of unjust and cruel penalties, few men, it may be supposed, would have the resolution to undertake the removal, especially when the actual condition of the prison [i.e., jail], and the mode of treating the prisoners, are considered; for it must be kept in mind, that for nearly all the [ten capital] crimes which have been enumerated, it was proposed to commute the punishment for solitary confinement and hard labour.[4]

At first blush, the intense desperation for respect, credit, and admiration embedded in these statements appears striking, especially considering the public profiles of the men involved in these efforts (Vaux's description of the men responsible as "destitute of political power and distinction" was an utter falsehood). Ultimately, however, these statements reflect an abiding need for reassurance that history would remember them positively. Why did they need this recognition?

OVERCOMING ANXIETY AND INSECURITY

Penal transformations of the kind experienced between 1776 and 1860 in the United States, particularly Pennsylvania, breed extensive uncertainty and, consequently, tremendous anxiety. There had been ideological

---

[3] For a discussion of the British influence on American developments, see See Adam J. Hirsch, *The Rise of the Penitentiary: Prisons and Punishment in Early America*. New Haven: Yale University Press, 1992. See also Ashley T. Rubin, "Early US Prison History beyond Rothman: Revisiting *The Discovery of the Asylum*," *Annual Review of Law and Social Science* 15:1 (2019), pp. 137–154.

[4] Vaux, *Notices*, p. 8.

precedents for penal incarceration and the transformation took decades to finalize, but there were many unknowns. Indeed, Vaux emphasized that "to undertake" such a difficult task required impressive "resolution" on the part of reformers – himself included – but so too did their efforts to continue on despite repeated failures. The early disasters at Auburn and Maine, and the near-disaster at Western, left a lasting impression that graphically reminded reformers, governors, legislators, and prison administrators the costs of experimenting with new punishments. This fear of failure permeated the country's penal reform efforts, but, at Eastern, constant criticism of their system only intensified that fear. The administrators' stated desire for – and explicit statements demanding – acknowledgement and accolades was one way of coping with this insecurity and uncertainty about the pragmatic and moral propriety of their work.

Adopting and maintaining a criticized, subdominant approach to punishment was its own source of anxiety, as this history of Eastern has demonstrated. But adopting and maintaining a new system of punishment of any kind was a source of anxiety experienced everywhere. Indeed, statements illustrating this anxiety were the most strident at Eastern, but they preceded Eastern and extended to other circles where the Pennsylvania System had been rejected. Undergirding the nationwide rejection of the Pennsylvania System was fear of the uncertainty prisons presented and the need to find a strategy that *seemed* to work. Few accounts of the prison's emergence and diffusion acknowledge the many fears reformers and administrators experienced about their technology at the beginning – and at subsequent periods of reform.[5] Despite adamant and apparent confidence in their new technologies – tones that previous scholars have interpreted as reflecting genuine belief or perhaps just partisanship – penal reformers, administrators, and lawmakers were deeply troubled by their work and plagued by doubts about whether they were, in fact, doing right.

5 Fear, anxiety, and insecurity have been common themes in the prison history literature, but these themes have been related to reformers' place in the world, their declining social status in the wake of the Revolution and major social change, and more generally tensions from class, race, nativity, and gender status. For example, Michael Meranze, *Laboratories of Virtue: Punishment, Revolution, and Authority in Philadelphia, 1760–1835*. Chapel Hill: University of North Carolina Press, 1996; David J. Rothman, *The Discovery of the Asylum: Social Order and Disorder in the New Republic*. New York: AldineTransaction, 2002 [1971]; Jen Manion, *Liberty's Prisoners: Carceral Culture in Early America*. Philadelphia: University of Pennsylvania Press, 2015; Mark E. Kann, *Punishment, Prisons, and Patriarchy: Liberty and Power in the Early American Republic*. New York University Press, 2005.

THE STATUS OF PRISON ADMINISTRATION

These previous accounts have also overlooked the extent to which prisons offered their administrators, reformers, and states a significant source of status. From our contemporary vantage in the era of mass incarceration, it is difficult to understand that prisons in the early and mid-nineteenth century were viewed positively and with pride. For well-to-do nineteenth-century citizens in particular, prisons were a symbol of progress, civilization, and American ingenuity (further raising the stakes if the prison should fail). As I have argued elsewhere, politicians, newsmen, and other elites in Southern states saw the prison as a means of overcoming criticism for their persistent reliance on slavery as well as capital and corporal punishment, while newly established frontier states readily adopted prisons as evidence of their own bona fides of statehood.[6] As I have argued here, however, prisons were also a significant source of status for the men who advocated for and managed these prisons. Every year, hundreds – later thousands – of people toured America's prisons. Eastern alone was visited by U.S. President James Polk, former Mexican President General Ignacio Comonfort, Edward, Prince of Wales (accompanied by a duke, a lord, and an earl), Napoleon III, the Prince de Joinville (son of former King of the French Louis Philippe), Brazilian Emperor Dom Pedro, as well as prison managers, penal reformers, politicians, and commissioners from around the country and from overseas.[7] Prison managers were interviewed or sent surveys and their signed responses were publicized in commissioners' reports or in reformers' pamphlets and annual reports, many of which were then reprinted in the local newspapers. A prison's success reflected on the managers themselves. Again, subjected to disproportionate scrutiny, Eastern's administrators offer the strongest illustration of reform's personal stakes for penal actors, even though they were not alone in blurring personal and organizational status.

Eventually, however, the status prisons offered declined relative to the status available through professionalization. Before the Civil War, systems

---

[6] Ashley T. Rubin, "A Neo-Institutional Account of Prison Diffusion," *Law & Society Review* 49:2 (2015), pp. 365–399.

[7] See Eastern State Penitentiary, *Warden's Daily Journal*, Volumes 1–2. Eastern State Penitentiary Collection, Record Group 15 (#15.50). Pennsylvania State Archives, 1829–1877 and Eastern State Penitentiary, Registers of Visitors, Volumes 1–3. Eastern State Penitentiary Collection, Record Group 15 (#15.46). Pennsylvania State Archives, 1829–1854. For more on nineteenth-century prison visitation and tourism, see Janet Miron, *Prisons, Asylums, and the Public: Institutional Visiting in the Nineteenth Century*. University of Toronto Press, 2011.

of prison discipline, not individual reformers or administrators, were the primary focus of penological thought.[8] Notably, although certain men were mentioned in connection with the creation of these systems (typically in footnotes), no single person received credit for creating the Pennsylvania System. Likewise, there is still debate over exactly who created the Auburn System because, in contrast to Philadelphia's developments, there are few primary sources on the subject of the Auburn System's creation.[9] After the Civil War, however, individual penal reformers and prison administrators (like reformer Enoch Wines and administrator Zebulon Brockway) gained attention for the systems they created or for their advocacy of specific developments. Increasingly, penal reformers and prison administrators (like Eastern's Inspector Richard Vaux and Warden Cassidy and others throughout the country) authored pamphlets reflecting on their own experience and expertise, a trend that continued into the twentieth century.[10]

BEYOND CONSCIENCE AND CONVENIENCE

Understanding how prisons offered their personnel a kind of status helps us to understand other patterns in prison administration. For decades, prison historians have revealed how the early principles that inspired new prison reforms often gave way to the practical or managerial needs of prison administration, whether custodial concerns (maintaining control over prisoners, keeping prisoners and staff safe, preventing escapes),

---

[8] The reformer Dorothea Dix was a notable exception, receiving a fair amount of personal praise; however, her efforts were focused more on mental institutions than on prisons, although she did tour the prisons and advocate on behalf of mentally ill prisoners.

[9] See, e.g., W. David Lewis, *From Newgate to Dannemora: The Rise of the Penitentiary in New York, 1796–1848*. Ithaca: Cornell University Press, 1965; Rebecca M. McLennan, *The Crisis of Imprisonment: Protest, Politics, and the Making of the American Penal State, 1776–1941*. New York: Cambridge University Press, 2008.

[10] Men like Joseph Ragen (Warden of Stateville in Illinois), Clinton Duffy (Warden of San Quentin in California), Frank Eyman (Warden of several Arizona prisons), and George Beto (Director of the Texas Department of Corrections) became famous by developing a particular mythos about themselves – several of them penned memoirs or starred in movies promoting that mythos. Mona Lynch, *Sunbelt Justice: Arizona and the Transformation of American Punishment*. Stanford, CA: Stanford University Press, 2010; Robert Perkinson, *Texas Tough: The Rise of America's Prison Empire*. New York: Metropolitan Books/Henry Holt, 2008; James B. Jacobs, *Stateville: The Penitentiary in Mass Society*. University of Chicago Press, 1977; David M. Horton and George R. Nielsen, *Walking George: The Life of George John Beto and the Rise of the Modern Texas Prison System*. Denton, Texas: University of North Texas Press, 2005; Clinton Truman Duffy, *The San Quentin Story*. Garden City, NY: Doubleday, 1950.

reducing cost, or confronting growing overcrowding. In David Rothman's phrasing, "conscience" repeatedly gave way to "convenience."[11] In other cases, we see how motivations to convert punishment into a profitable enterprise through prisoner labor can be unleashed and subsume every penal goal of incarceration.[12] Elsewhere, we see how reformers involved in prison administration present their work as benevolence, but in reality engage in repression or other misdeeds behind the scenes for their own sadistic and other unseemly motivations.[13]

Eastern's experience reveals a different source of these gaps between theory and practice. They were not simply the result of profit's domination over all decisions, the result of convenience winning over conscience, or the result of bad actors alone. Instead, a fourth motivation appears: administrators' concern for their organization itself – not its profitability, not control over its prisoners, but its reputation and longevity – without which they might lose their source of status. Eastern's administrators did violate the Pennsylvania System to maximize opportunities for profit, but, with few exceptions, not to line their own pockets; instead, their ultimate purpose was to counter intense criticism that their prison was unavoidably unprofitable and too expensive. Additionally, while penal ideology was often sacrificed by Eastern's pragmatic administrators, their goal was not simply custody and control, but rather to ensure Eastern's success, in the broadest sense.

This study demonstrates that even the most ideologically motivated prison, managed by men who theorized about punishment's purposes and eventually fancied themselves expert penologists, was first and foremost an organization. Considerations over its public reputation were controlling; its administrators were more committed to their organization's success (and to the status their positions within that organization provided) than to the original goal of reforming prisoners. Recognizing the importance of punishment's organizational context

---

[11] David J. Rothman, *Conscience and Convenience: The Asylum and Its Alternatives in Progressive America.* Hawthorne, NY: Aldine de Gruyter, 1980. See also Alexander Pisciotta, *Benevolent Repression: Social Control and the American Reformatory-Prison Movement.* New York University Press, 1994.

[12] McLennan, *The Crisis of Imprisonment*; Charles Bright, *The Powers that Punish: Prison and Politics in the Era of the "Big House," 1920–1955.* Ann Arbor: University of Michigan Press, 1996; David Oshinsky, *Worse than Slavery: Parchman Farm and the Ordeal of Jim Crow Justice.* New York: Free Press, 1997.

[13] Pisciotta, *Benevolent Repression*; Manion, *Carceral Culture.*

introduces new reasons to expect gaps between theory and practice and the subordination of penal goals.[14]

DEAD BRANCHES

While Eastern was a unique prison in a time long past, excavating its history offers other useful lessons, even for the contemporary period. Examining a failure – a model that did not take hold and in many ways was not terribly influential, except, perhaps, as a model of what *not* to do – is a relatively rare technique for case study analysis of penal history.[15] Most recent punishment studies have examined late-modern bellwethers to understand how our current situation of mass incarceration came to be. While California, Arizona, Texas, and Florida are individual states with their own unique, sometimes extreme histories, they have been profoundly influential in shaping recent national penal trends.[16] Case studies of these and other states also provide a sense of local variation – the way in which national trends are not complete. For example, states that act as bellwethers in one era can lag behind in others. During their out-of-phase periods, such states illustrate historical contingency, local culture, and individual actors' influence.[17] However, we can also learn much from case studies of history's "dead branches"[18] – the policies or practices discarded in favor of other developments – and with them, the outlier states that failed to adopt mainstream trends in favor of their own approaches.[19]

[14] See also Ashley T. Rubin, "The Birth of the Penal Organization: Why Prisons Were Born to Fail," in *The Legal Process and the Promise of Justice*, ed. Hadar Aviram, Rosann Greenspan, and Jonathan Simon. New York: Cambridge University Press, 2019, pp. 23–47.

[15] But see Michael C. Campbell, "Criminal Disenfranchisement Reform in California: A Deviant Case Study," *Punishment & Society* 9:2 (2007), pp. 177–199.

[16] Joshua Page, *The Toughest Beat: Politics, Punishment, and the Prison Officers Union in California*. New York: Oxford University Press, 2011; Jonathan Simon, *Mass Incarceration on Trial*. New York: The New Press, 2014; Hadar Aviram, *Cheap on Crime: Recession-Era Politics and the Transformation of American Punishment*. Oakland: University of California Press, 2015; Ruth Gilmore, *Golden Gulag: Prisons, Surplus, Crisis, and Resistance in Globalizing California*. University of California Press, 2007; Keramet Reiter, *23/7: Pelican Bay Prison and the Rise of Long-Term Solitary Confinement*. New Haven: Yale University Press, 2016; Lynch, *Sunbelt Justice*; Perkinson, *Texas Tough*; Heather A. Schoenfeld, *Building the Prison State: Race and the Politics of Mass Incarceration*. Chicago: University of Chicago Press, 2018.

[17] See especially Lynch, *Sunbelt Justice*; Jacobs, *Stateville*.

[18] Fischer, *Historians' Fallacies*.

[19] I thank Cal Morrill for suggesting I examine Eastern from this angle.

Far from a bellwether, and more than simple local variation, Eastern represents a particularly fruitful dead branch in this respect.

A Look at What Might Have Been and What is Not

First, dead branches like Eastern State Penitentiary and its Pennsylvania System represent the road not traveled. Thanks to its experimentation in the 1780s and 1790s, Philadelphia was the birthplace of the penitentiary, the rehabilitative ideal, and cellular incarceration – in America, at least.[20] Several decades later, Eastern offered the strongest physical manifestation of these nebulous visions, yet it immediately became a deviant prison: it was both unique and heavily criticized. Around the country, incarceration took firm hold as a strategy of punishment, but the original ideas underpinning it did not. Instead, new assumptions, techniques, and methods of confinement grew up around, and apart from, Eastern and its Pennsylvania System.

Two hundred years later, a profoundly different criminal justice system has taken shape from what those Pennsylvanians had imagined. In our contemporary context, the Pennsylvania System sharply contrasts with America's current approaches to and assumptions about crime, criminals, and punishment. To take one example, the Pennsylvania System was designed in part to maintain its prisoners' anonymity: Prisoners were known by numbers alone, and their names were not published in annual reports (unlike other states' custom of publicly naming their prisoners), practices conscientiously followed to help prisoners reenter society unscathed by the stigma attached to their criminality. Likewise, the Pennsylvania System mandated hooding prisoners in order to protect their identity – even from someone who might chance a glimpse of a prisoner's face. While these policies were not always followed or fully enforced, and they conflicted with other formal policies, the desire to help prisoners in their life after prison by keeping their incarceration secret remained a paramount value underlying Eastern's administration.

This earlier concern for prisoners' privacy is striking in an era of well-publicized mug shots, Megan's Law databases for registered sex offenders, employment and school application forms that include a box

---

[20] See Meranze, *Laboratories of Virtue*. Many writers have mistakenly called Eastern the first penitentiary, or Walnut Street the first prison; both are incorrect statements. As Hirsch has demonstrated, Massachusetts had the first state prison. Hirsch, *The Rise of the Penitentiary*. Walnut Street, however, was the first penitentiary.

that applicants with a criminal record must check, and reality television shows about police arresting suspects and about life in prison.[21] The comparison reminds us that penal policy is socially constructed and temporally contingent – by no means "the way things have always been done." Nor is contemporary practice even the natural outgrowth of previous practice, because punishment is always varied and contradictory – even when placing geographic restrictions on what we mean by "previous practice."[22] There is, thus, always a different path that leads in another direction – some other way things might have been.

In other cases, Eastern's practices may appear deceptively similar to the present context. Eastern's reliance on long-term solitary confinement has led a number of scholars to call it the "first supermax," or a progenitor to contemporary "supermaximum security prisons" that house states' ostensibly "worst" prisoners in solitary confinement and sensory deprivation.[23] Contrary to these claims, however, the motivations and actual practice behind core aspects of the Pennsylvania System again reveal substantial

---

[21] For a striking comparison, see Sarah Lageson, *Digital Punishment: Privacy, Stigma and the Harms of Data-Driven Criminal Justice*. Oxford University Press, 2020. Note that anonymity at Eastern was not recognized as part of a right to privacy, which was only recognized even for members of free society in the twentieth century, but as a practical matter to aid prisoner reentry.

[22] Roger Matthews, "The Myth of Punitiveness," *Theoretical Criminology* 9:2 (2005), pp. 175–201; Paula Maurutto and Kelly Hannah-Moffat, "Assembling Risk and the Restructuring of Penal Control," *British Journal of Criminology* 46:3 (2006), pp. 438–454; Gwen Robinson, "Late-modern Rehabilitation: The Evolution of a Penal Strategy," *Punishment & Society* 10:4 (2008), pp. 429–445; Simon Hallsworth, "The Case for a Postmodern Penality," *Theoretical Criminology* 6:2 (2002), pp. 145–163; Steven Hutchinson, "Countering Catastrophic Criminology: Reform, Punishment and the Modern Liberal Compromise," *Punishment & Society* 8:4 (2006), pp. 443–467; Ashley T. Rubin, "Penal Change as Penal Layering: A Case Study of Proto-prison Adoption and Capital Punishment Reduction, 1785–1822," *Punishment & Society* 18:4 (2016), pp. 420–441; Christopher Seeds, "Bifurcation Nation: American Penal Policy in Late Mass Incarceration," *Punishment & Society* 19:5 (2017), pp. 590–610.

[23] Daniel P. Mears and Michael D. Reisig, "The Theory and Practice of Supermax Prisons," *Punishment & Society* 8:1 (2006), pp. 33–57, p. 34; Daniel P. Mears and William D. Bales, "Supermax Incarceration and Recidivism," *Criminology* 47:4 (2009), pp. 1131–1166, p. 1132; Daniel P. Mears and William D. Bales, "Supermax Housing: Placement, Duration, and Time to Reentry." *Journal of Criminal Justice* 38:4 (2010), pp. 545–554, p. 545; Craig Haney and Mona Lynch, "Regulating Prisons of the Future: A Psychological Analysis of Supermax and Solitary Confinement," *NYU Review of Law & Social Change* 23 (1997), pp. 477–570; Peter Scharff Smith, "The Effects of Solitary Confinement on Prison Inmates: A Brief History and Review of the Literature," *Crime and Justice* 34:1 (2006), pp. 441–528; Stuart Grassian, "Psychiatric Effects of Soliary Confinement," *Washington University Journal of Law & Policy* 22 (2006), pp. 325–383.

differences with contemporary corrections.[24] While Eastern was not the uniformly humane and benevolent prison its administrators and other supporters argued it was, its commitment – both rhetorical and actual – to these values brings certain aspects of contemporary practice into sharp relief. For example, whereas solitary confinement in the Pennsylvania System was intended to reform prisoners by giving them time for reflection and separation from other prisoners who may encourage or instruct them toward further criminality, solitary confinement in today's supermax is intended to punish those who have broken prison rules or to make it impossible for the "worst" prisoners to harm (or arrange to harm) other prisoners and correctional officers. (In this sense, the supermax has much more in common with Eastern's dark cells than the Pennsylvania System.) This comparison reminds us that penal technologies – like prisons built for solitary confinement – may appear similar and may recycle components of earlier technologies but they can be used in different ways, for very different purposes, in different contexts.[25]

A History of the Present

Second, dead branches on the penal development tree give us a better sense of the forces that helped establish our current system – as well as the counterforces that failed to prevent it. If Eastern represents the road not traveled, it was not immune to pressures to adopt the more common practices. However, by examining how Eastern repelled these forces and how it did so for so long, we can begin to understand how and why other states and prisons were unable to resist. The tremendous criticism aimed at Eastern – and Pennsylvania generally – for refusing to adopt the Auburn System (the normative standard of the time), as well as other challenges associated with innovating and maintaining a unique approach, help illustrate why more states did not create alternatives to or defect from the Auburn System and why the few states that did adopt the Pennsylvania System abandoned it.

---

[24] See also Jonathan Simon, "The 'Society of Captives' in the Era of Hyper-Incarceration." *Theoretical Criminology* 4:3 (2000), pp. 285–308, p. 301.

[25] For a full history of American solitary confinement and its perennial reinvention, see Ashley T. Rubin and Keramet Reiter, "Continuity in the Face of Penal Innovation: Revisiting the History of American Solitary Confinement," *Law & Social Inquiry* 43:4 (2018), pp. 1604–1632. For a larger history across the Atlantic world, see Ian O'Donnell, *Prisoners, Solitude, and Time.* Oxford University Press, 2014, and Peter Scharff Smith, "The Effects of Solitary Confinement on Prison Inmates: A Brief History and Review of the Literature," *Crime and Justice* 34:1 (2006), pp. 441–528.

Thus, while this book is primarily a case study of a dead branch, it contributes to our knowledge of the prison's broader trajectory. This book highlights the forces that shaped the modern prison's development – forces like anxiety about innovation, pressures to conform to penal norms, and the important role of prison administrators and their organizational settings – and that continue into the present. Ultimately, understanding how Eastern became deviant helps explain why other states followed a different path – one that has led to our current penal system – and found it so difficult to diverge from that path.

Fin

Inspectors

TABLE A.1 *Inspectors, 1829–1880.*

Inspector	Tenure Began	Tenure Ended	Length	Died in Office	Politics	Law	Business	Medicine	PSAMPP Member**
Vaux, Roberts	1829	1829	<1						X
Randall, Josiah	1829	1829	<1		X				
Swift, John	1829	1831	2		X	X			
Miller, Daniel H.	1829	1831	2	X	X		X		
Coxe, Charles Sydney	1829	1835	6		X	X			X
Bradford, Thomas	1829	1851	22	X		X			X
Richards, Benjamin W.	1829	1834	6		X		X		
Bacon, John	1831	1859	28	X	X		X		X
Hood, William H.	1831	1842	11				X		X
Bevan, Matthew L.	1834	1849	15	X			X		
Patterson, Robert	1835	1847	12				X		
Vaux, Richard	1842	1895	53	X	X	X			
Porter, William A.	1847	1851	4		X	X			
Campbell, Hugh	1850	1853	3				X		
Mercer, Singleton A.	1851	1854	3				X		
Brown, Charles	1851	1853	2		X		X		
Miller, Andrew	1853	1859	6		X		X		
McKibben, Chambers	1853	1857	4		X		X		
Jones, Samuel	1854	1864	10	X				X	
Goodwin, William	1857	1859	5		X		X		
Henry, Alexander	1859	1882	24	*	X	X			X
Powers, Thomas H.	1859	1878	19	X			X		
Shephard, Furman	1859	1872	13			X			
Drexel, Anthony J.	1865	1870	5				X		
Maris, John M.	1870	1891	21				X		X
Jones, Charles Thomas	1873	1883	10						
Harrison, George L.	1879	1885	6	*					

Occupations for inspectors appointed before 1872, determined by Richard Vaux, *Brief Sketch of the Origin and History of the State Penitentiary for the Eastern District of Pennsylvania at Philadelphia.* Philadelphia: McLaughlin Brothers, Printers, 1872. Tenure determined by annual reports and Minute Books of the Board of Inspectors and Board of Trustees of the Eastern State Penitentiary. Volumes 1–4. Eastern State Penitentiary Collection, Record Group 15 (#15.44). Pennsylvania State Archives. 1829-1885.
[1] These include judge, district attorney, mayor and recorder, treasurer, state senator or representative, U.S. senator or representative.
[2] These include merchant, grocer, banker, manufacturer.
*Inspectors Henry and Harrison died either in their last year in office or the year before; unlike other inspectors who died in office, their deaths were not included in the annual reports.

Index

charity work
  by the administrators at Eastern, 77–78
  see also Board of Public Charities
children
  education, 204, 273
  see also juvenile facilities
cognitive dissonance, 226
cognitive frames, xxxix
Commissioners for the Erection of the
    Eastern Penitentiary
  appointment, xliv
  Report, 49
Commissioners on the Penal Code
  appointment, 44
  Report, 44–48
    PSAMPP response, 49
commitment
  by the administrators at Eastern, 174
  limit, 231–232
  by PSAMPP, 237
Commonwealth (The) ex rel. Johnson v.
    Halloway, see Commutation Law
Commutation Law, 270–271, 307–308
'condemnation of the condemnors', 186
confinement, *see* solitary confinement
confirmed criminals, *see* crime class
conflict
  amongst the administrators themselves,
    232–247
  between the administrators and New
    York penologists, 285–291
  between the administrators and
    PSAMPP, xl, xli, 266–271
  between the administrators and the state
    legislature,
    see also administrators (Eastern State
    Penitentiary): refusal to enforce
    Commutation Law
  see also Pennsylvania System: 'forged in
    conflict'
conformation, xxxviii
  by the administrators at Eastern
    see also Eastern State Penitentiary: as
    'a deviant prison'
confusion, *see* uncertainty
congregate system, *see* Auburn System
congresses
  reception of the administrators at
    Eastern, 288–290
Connecticut, *see* Old Newgate Prison;
    Wethersfield State Prison

conscience
  'giving way to convenience', 329–330
  see also benevolence
constraints on behavior, xxxviii
contact, *see* separation
contraband
  access by prisoners, 224–225
convenience, *see* gap between theory and
    practice
conversion costs, xxxiv
corporal punishment
  comeback, 17
  see also whipping
costs
  of Eastern State Penitentiary, xxxiii
    defended, 189–194
    see also 'sunk costs' theory
  explained by scapegoating, 160–165
  of the proto-prisons, 16
county jails, *see* jails
Coxe, Charles Sydney (Inspector
    (1829–1835))
  alliances, 233
  career, 72, 337
  conflict with Warden Wood and
    Inspector Bradford, 233–234
  investigation into Warden Wood,
    234–235, 248
  membership of PSAMPP, 73
  resignation, 232
crafts-style labor
  profitability, 164–165
creation myths
  propagated in support of Pennsylvania
    System, 174, 181–183
crime class, 311–312, 320–321
criminal code, *see* penal code
criminal justice organizations
  application of theory of personal
    institutionalization, xlv–xlvi
  see also prisons
criminal justice system
  modernization, 65–66
Crosse, James Buchanan, liv

Darrach, Dr. William (PSAMPP member
    and Physician (1837–1844))
  alliances, 236
  report on sickness among
    African-American prison
    population, 158–160

CPSIA information can be obtained
at www.ICGtesting.com
Printed in the USA
LVHW030447251022
731489LV00002B/275